Symbolism:

Modern Thought and Ancient Egypt

Symbolism

Modern Thought
and
Ancient Egypt

Michael Allswang

ISBN 978-1-09833-963-0 (print)

ISBN 978-1-09833-964-7 (eBook)

For comments, questions, orders, or permission requests,
please contact the author at: mallswang@orange.fr

Contents

Contents

Illustrations

Preface

> To understand the past—our past—is a source of vitality.
> To appreciate and understand our most distant origins is
> to live more intensely. We need the past to live better,
> with a vaster sphere of vision and comprehension. The
> past is perhaps all that remains for us after the breakdown
> of transcendence, and perhaps one of the reasons for our
> interest in the most distant past, that is, ancient Egypt.[1]

Standing behind the words in this book, like the falcon god
Horus enclosing Pharaoh in his wings, is the leitmotif of man's
consciousness. After much study, reflection, and also visits to
many ancient Egyptian monuments, I have come to the
conclusion that the development of consciousness was the
essential project of the priests of ancient Egypt, and that one of
the means they used to achieve this end was the expression of
spiritual truths by means of symbolism. The intent of this book
is by no means simply to gather facts on symbolism from other
books and present them as something "new." I am aware, in
any case, that there is nothing "new" to be said, and that this
book will only be a reformulation, arising from my own inner
and outer research and experience, of a subject that can never
be circumscribed by mere words. In this way, perhaps, such a
book could give others an insight into a subject that I have
found immensely rewarding.

---

[1] Jan Assmann, *Images et rites de la mort dans l'Égypte ancienne* (Paris: Cybèle, 2000), 28. [Our translation]

Preface

While it would be very hard not to be in sympathy with such a project as the development of consciousness, the question can be justifiably asked as to whether writing a book on such a theme goes against the premise one holds to be true: that one could never claim that consciousness could be directly raised by reading or writing books, least of all by using the catchall language of English in our analytical era as opposed, for example, to the synthetic hieroglyphic language of ancient Egypt. As Marshall McCluhan so aptly stated, "The medium is the message," and this type of writing exercise can only hinder the process of the development of consciousness on an experiential level by building up imaginary worlds and connections in the mind that hide the presence of another more real world of which we are an integral part, and which is far beyond, or perhaps underneath, thought. Nevertheless, the increased understanding, even on a conceptual plane, of man and the universe in which he is immersed can, I assume, aid anyone who seriously questions the reason for man's existence on this planet, if only by giving him a reason and motivation for attempting a search for real understanding by means other than that provided by modern day science and the books they produce; that is to say, an understanding arising from one's entire being based on inner experience and not from mere mental conceptions. The *raison d'être* for Part 1 is thus to try to put the reader in a frame of mind other than the linear, rationalist mode of our education, but to open the mind to another way of thinking based on synthesis rather than analysis. We have used examples coming from late 20th century science, holography and systems theory, because they embody concepts that can also apply to the symbolic nature of ancient civilizations.

Preface

If I choose ancient Egypt as my terrain of predilection it is because, first of all, ancient Egyptian civilization existed before the analytic thought of the Greeks came to dominate the civilized Western world, and thus provides us with another mode of experiencing in order to understand the universe in which we were born; and secondly, so much still remains of this civilization compared to others (such as Mesopotamia) from which to draw our insights. The pyramids, temples, tombs, and papyri of ancient Egypt, and the images and hieroglyphic inscriptions contained on and within them, show that this civilization was based on a profound symbolic relationship between man and the universe in which he found himself. For the ancient Egyptians, Egypt was the reflection of the cosmos on Earth in a very real sense, just as man was a reflection of the "gods" who stood for precise natural cosmic functions or laws and in no way were meant to be seen as simply anthropomorphic or zoomorphic beings of a vague higher nature invented to explain the "origin of things." To understand, then, the ancient Egyptian's use of symbolism would be to understand their conception of the universe and the role of man—our role—within it. It is thus my hope that by attempting this book, I shall be trying at the same time to further my own understanding of my role as a human being in the cosmos and, for what it may be worth, to pass whatever I may have gleaned to those who care to read this attempt.

The book is divided into two main parts, the first having to do with modern conceptions of symbolism. Included here are how symbolism is related to the cosmos and modern science, how it is used in the culture of civilizations, and how it can influence individual man by the way of religious symbols. Finally, some metaphysical principles are introduced in order to clarify further the nature of symbolism. The phrase "symbolism in ancient Egypt" seems quite straightforward as a subject, but when we break it down into its component parts—symbolism and ancient Egypt—we are left with an area of study of which seems to have no bounds. To even begin to understand the subject matter, we must first understand what is meant by "symbol," its function and how symbols are integrated into a Traditional culture such as that of ancient Egypt. Though I have read a number of authors on the subject of symbolism, my intention is not to give a survey of the literature, but to try to put forth an interpretation based upon my own experience and understanding, wherever that may lead. To this end, the intent of the first part of the book is an explanation of my understanding of the meaning and function of symbolism, which is absolutely necessary to understand symbolism in ancient Egypt, since the role of symbolism is so very far from the purely mentally-based non-Traditional culture in which we find ourselves in the West. To this end, the word "symbol" is explained in its largest sense as that by which a man can be aided in his spiritual transformation, if such is his desire. Thus, a symbol is not discussed as being limited to painted and sculptured figures, but also includes religious edifices as well as hieroglyphs and elements of myth. This part should also make perfectly clear to the reader the difference between a *sign*, which provides purely mental information, and the *symbol*, which has as its function to bring together a synthesis of meaning in such a way as to aid a person as far as possible to come to the center of himself by acting on different levels of his *being*.

After introducing the subject of symbolism, Part 2 discusses symbolism in ancient Egypt proper. The purpose here is to try to put the reader, as much as can be done with the written word, in the symbolic world of ancient Egypt. Here we discuss ancient Egyptian mind and spirituality, the pantheon of the "gods" (or *neters²*), man's nature as they saw it, the role of the pharaoh, ritual symbolism, hieroglyphs and sacred texts, as well as pyramids and temples, all the while trying to illustrate the function of symbolism as a means of organizing the Egyptian culture by the priests so as to provide a "Way" for each individual to reach, in so far as he is capable, that "inner sanctum" within himself. We also introduce mythology in general, its function in relation to symbolism, and how it is a spiritual teaching. We then go into purely Egyptian mythology and put forth our view that there are not "different" Egyptian myths but only variations on one basic leitmotif of all myth: the removal to a faraway place from man's spiritual nature and the means by which it can be brought back to its rightful home.

Interwoven in this part, the eye as a symbol is discussed, first in relation to the Mother Goddess in prehistoric cultures and then its appearances in Traditional cultures of various times and in various places. This leads up to how the eye, as one example, is used in the symbolism of ancient Egypt: in particular, as the Eye of Horus painted and carved on temples, its appearance in sacred writings such as the *Pyramid Texts*, and as an element in Egyptian mythology. Finally, we introduce the Temple of Luxor as a prime example of symbolic architecture.

---

²See page 200 for a discussion of the use of the word *neter*.

Part 1 Modern Thought

The use of symbolism in human society, its *raison d'être*, is based on two propositions: one, that there is a hierarchical order to the universe based on fundamental laws from which the universe was created and is continually maintained, and two, that there is an analogical relationship among the operation of these laws on the different levels of existence. It follows from this that everything in the universe must be connected and harmonious through the constant operation of these laws emanating from above and being manifested outwards and downwards and in all spheres of activity. We might think here of the striking of a note on a piano, where the fact of the sound produced is totally dependent on an outside force which begins the sound's movement and determines its duration and intensity, but which is then without power to alter the vibrations set in motion. These are determined by the type, length and tension of the piano string and the medium through which the sound passes. These could be seen then as the laws for that note, giving it its pitch, that is, determining its fundamental rate of vibration, and determining the inner vibrations of the piano string as well, the note's overtones. The innermost vibration is just as much dependent on the laws for the note struck as is the fundamental rate of vibration of the whole note, though many steps removed. See Figure 1.

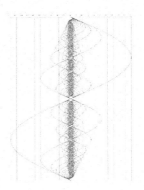

It could be surmised that, in an analogous way, the laws governing the universe are reflected in those of the solar system, which are also determinant in the structure of matter: in

Figure 1 Harmonic series caused by plucking of a string

1

atoms, molecules, cells—the stuff of which we too are made—after the first note of the universe has been struck, so to speak, by the "hand of God" (or, as it is said today, by the "Big Bang"). Yet what reaches our ears from the striking of a note is not a sequence of vibrations but a *simultaneity* of harmonic tones. And just as all the universe is eternally present from the beginning, every particular manifestation (whether the galaxy, the solar system, a human being or an atom) is more or less closer or farther away from the universal law, though completely dependent on it nonetheless through a lesser or greater hierarchy of levels existing *within* the manifestation in question.[3] It is for this reason that is said that the lower cannot be symbolized by the higher, a cause representing an effect.[4] See Figure 2.

Figure 2 Simultaneous movements of the cosmos

---

[3] These first two paragraphs were written many years ago as an introduction to an unpublished paper. It was only while finishing this chapter, I came across the book by Fritjof Capra, *The Web of Life* (London: HarperCollins, 1996), in which he discusses systems theories and the hierarchical organization of living systems.

[4] For information on the concept of symbolism, the following books provide helpful insights:

- René Alleau, *La Science des Symboles* (Paris: Payot, 1977).
- Titus Burckhardt, *Principes et méthodes de l'art sacré* (Paris: Editions Dervy, 1995).
- Ananda K. Coomaraswamy, *Coomaraswamy Selected Papers: Traditional Art and Symbolism.* Bollingen Series LXXXIX., Vol I: Roger Lipsey ed. (Princeton, N.J.: Princeton University Press, 1977).
- Mircea Eliade, *The Sacred and the Profane: The Nature of Religion* (New York: Harcourt, Brace & World, 1959).
- René Guénon, *Aperçus sur l'initiation.* 2d ed. (Paris: Les Éditions Traditionnelles, 1953).
- _____, *Le Symbolisme de la Croix* (Paris: Union Générale d'Editions, 1957).
- _____, *Symboles de la Science sacrée* (Paris: Gallimard, 1962).
- P.D. Ouspensky, *In Search of the Miraculous: Fragments of an Unknown Teaching* (New York: Harcourt, Brace & World, 1949), chapter 14.
- R. A. Schwaller de Lubicz, *Symbol and the Symbolic: Egypt, Science, and the Evolution of Consciousness* (Brookline, Mass.: Autumn Press, 1978).
- Alfred North Whitehead, *Symbolism: Its Meaning and Effect* (Barbour-Page Lectures, University of Virginia, 1927; New York: Fordham University Press, 1985).

Chapter 1 Symbolism and the Cosmos

At the beginning of the third millennium, we are now seeing that the analytic nature of the scientific method, which breaks down reality into isolated bits in order to study the part at the expense of the whole, while having its purposes, is starting to lose the backing of a growing number of scientists as a way to understand a fuller reality of the world. Relativity and quantum theory, the two basic theories by which we currently interpret the nature of the universe, are, after all, incompatible! On the one hand, Einstein demonstrated the *relative* natures of time, space and movement, while on the other, Bohr and others used *absolute* time and space in their elucidation of the nature of the atomic world. Furthermore, relativity and quantum theory have shown the impossibility of trying to understand the whole by an analysis of the parts. Relativity, for example, shows the futility of trying to fix elements in space or time by positing gravity as a function of the curvature of space-time. And quantum theory describes subatomic particles that change orbits around a nucleus without passing through the space between them, particles that simply change into each other, and those that arise from and disappear into a substratum of pure energy, which is the interchangeability of energy and matter (Einstein's E=mc2). It describes light that can be both waves and particles depending on the experiment, the impossibility of detecting both the velocity and position of an atomic particle due to the influence of the experimenter himself, and atomic particles acting in harmony even though that are at a distance beyond which the speed of light could provide information between them. The Austrian biologist Ludwig von Bertalanffy, the founder of modern systems theory, takes the point even further:

> The popular antithesis between motion and rest becomes meaningless in the theory of relativity. The antithesis of mass and energy is superseded by Einstein's

conservation law which accounts for their mutual transformation. Corpuscle and wave are both legitimate and complementary aspects of physical reality which, in certain phenomena and respects, is to be described in one way, in others in the second. The contrast between structure and process breaks down in the atom as well as in the living organism whose structure is at the same time the expression and the bearer of a continuous flow of matter and energy. Perhaps the age-old problem of body and mind is of a similar nature, these being different aspects...of one and the same reality.[5]

All these seemingly "illogical" results have led at least some scientists to return to a pre-Greek mode of thought. Tribal cultures, early civilizations, esoteric religions are all founded on the belief in a complete harmony of a universal order based on an interpenetrating hierarchy of worlds where everything has its place in both the horizontal dimension of everyday experience and the vertical dimension of states of being. A 'real' religion is thus not a simple collection of beliefs, rites, and rituals referring to spiritual matters, but is rather a sort of organism where all the parts are part of a unified whole by which man can become aware of this dual nature.[6]

These scientists, despite their 'scientism,' are perhaps searching for a whole which allows for the understanding of the parts rather studying the parts to comprehend the whole. For example, quantum theory never posits 'things' but only relations. Atomic particles cannot be understood as isolated entities but only through their relations among other particles and energies. Furthermore, there are also non-local relations where each event is influenced by the whole universe, where only probabilities can be assumed from the dynamics of the whole system:

[5] Ludwig von Bertalanffy, *General System Theory: Foundations Development, Applications*, Rev. Ed. (New York: George Braziller, 1969), 247-48.

[6] Frithjof Schuon, *The Transcendent Unity of Religions,* Revised ed. (Wheaton, The Theosophical Publishing House, 1993), 108.

> Whereas in classical mechanics the properties and behavior of the parts determine those of the whole, the situation is reversed in quantum mechanics: *it is the whole that determines the behavior of the parts.*[7] [Our italics]

This conception, that "the whole determines the behavior of the parts" is a return to the metaphysics of the East where, in no wise can the lower influence the higher, but where ever more subtler influences or energies of a higher order can and do influence lower forms of energies in an ordered hierarchy of interrelated levels down to the physical world that we know only too well. This leads to David Bohm's concept of "unbroken wholeness"[8] where the analysis only of the parts is inherently flawed, since the larger systems in which they exist, even up to the universe as a whole, influence the parts' behavior.

As a means for trying to understand the world of symbolism, we might look to two models modern scientific thought has developed: holography and systems theory. By looking at these models developed from a modern scientific point of view, and however far they are from what René Guénon would call "traditional science," we hope they could help develop in ourselves, if nothing else, at least the beginning of feeling for what might have been an ancient worldview based on an interconnected dynamic universe—and so be able to more easily intuit how symbolism functions in such a civilization.

Holography

The holography model arose from a theory of Dennis Gabor in the 1940's to store images by means of light diffracted from an object. He developed a mathematical scheme by which these

---

[7] Fritjof Capra, *The Turning Point* (London: HarperCollins, 1983), 70-6.

[8] David Bohm and B. Hiley, "On the Intuitive Understanding of Non-locality as Implied by Quantum Theory" (preprint, Birkbeck College, University of London, 1974). Quoted in Gary Zukav, *The Dancing Wu Li Masters: An Overview of the New Physics* (New York: William Morrow and Company, 1979), 315.

images could be reconstructed, which he called "holograms" (from the Greek "*holos*" or whole and "*gramma*" or message, hence "whole message"). The physical realization of a hologram was made possible by the invention in the 1960's of the laser, which emits a beam of light having coherent light waves, that is, they all have the same frequency rather than the mixed frequencies of ordinary light. Now any wave phenomenon, such as light or ripples in a pond, create interference patterns when the waves meet. For example, if you drop two pebbles in a pond, the concentric waves created will interact with each other such that crests meeting crests or troughs meeting troughs will produce a larger wave, while crest meeting a trough will cancel each other out. The result of all these meetings creates, at any moment, an interference pattern.

The same effect is created by interfering light waves, and the interference pattern of light diffracted from an object and captured on film is called a hologram. This is achieved by firing a laser beam through a partially silvered mirror called a "beam splitter" so that one beam (the object beam) is diffused on the object, then diffracted onto a film, and the other (the reference beam) is sent by mirrors to be diffused directly on the film. The two colliding beams create an interference pattern which is recorded as a hologram on the holographic plate. What is interesting here is that each point of diffused light is spread over the entire surface of the film making it blurred. Looking at the film, one only sees a seemingly meaningless swirl of abstract concentric circles, but which contain within it an order representing the "holographed" object. To realize this order within, one only has to shine another laser beam through the film to create a three-dimensional image of the object in space that allows you to actually walk around it as if it was a real object. See Figure 3.

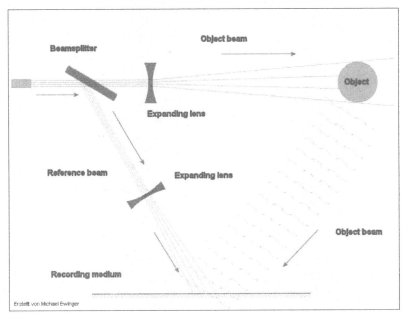

Figure 3 A holographic setup

Another interesting facet of a hologram is that if you cut the film of a hologram in pieces, each piece will still give you an image of the whole object, though the smaller the piece of film, the less distinct the image. That is to say, the whole image is found in each part or each part contains the whole. The discovery of the hologram has resulted in the use of the holographic model in many different domains. Apart from the field of Bohm's holomovement discussed previously to explain the cosmos, it has also been used to explain the functioning of the brain in the work of Karl Pribram.

Looking at the universe using the hologram as a metaphor, we might say that just as every part of a hologram contains all the information of the whole image, so we might say that every cosmic particle contains all the information of the whole of the cosmos. Bohm's theory supports this idea by supposing an immense sea of energy connecting everything that we experience as the 'material world' with the whole universe; that is, everything is connected to everything else by a substratum of finer energy, just as every point in a hologram is connected to the whole image by a diffused interference pattern of light. While this seems very elegant as a description of reality, what evidence is there to support it? By assuming subatomic particles are not separate entities, but an extension of a fundamental energy connecting everything in the universe, the holographic model answers the question of how particles can act simultaneously in a synchronized manner at a distance where even the speed of light would not be enough to provide the information necessary for them to act together (a puzzle arising out of quantum mechanics).

In a hierarchical universe, where the same basic laws obtain at each level, we should be able, on the plane of human existence, to observe other examples of this model. And we can if we note the fact that just as every point in a hologram contains the whole image, every cell in our bodies contains in its genetic material (DNA) the code for creating an entire human being. Stanislov Grof says:

> Although each somatic cell is a trivial part of the entire body, it has through the genetic code access to all the information about the body. It is conceivable that in a similar way all the information about the universe could be retrieved from any of its parts.[9]

Another example of the holographic model in the body is the nature of the functioning of our brains, at least as it has been theorized in the holographic model of Karl Pribram, an American neurophysiologist who found in holography a means of explaining how memories are stored in the brain. Pribram and others have shown that when parts of the brain are removed from animals, learned tasks are not forgotten, which can only mean that the memory is dispersed in some manner throughout the brain. From this fact, Pribram used the holographic model to suggest that memories are not encoded in the neurons but rather

---

[9] Stanislav Grof, *Beyond the Brain: Birth, Death and Transcendence in Psychotherapy* (Albany: State University of New York, 1985), 80.

in the interference patterns of the nerve impulses that crisscross the brain. This model also explains the immense amount of information that the brain stores, since memory does not depend on location, and how every bit of information is immediately linked to every other bit of information through the interference patterns, just as is the case with a hologram.

One observer puts the theories of Bohm and Pribram together to provide the following insight:

> [I]f the concreteness of the world is but a secondary reality and what is 'there' is actually a holographic blur of frequencies, and if the brain is also a hologram and only selects some of the frequencies out of this blur and mathematically transforms them into sensory perceptions, what becomes of objective reality?
>
> Put quite simply, it ceases to exist. As the religions of the East have long upheld, the material world is maya, an illusion, and although we may think we are physical beings moving through a physical world, this too is an illusion.
>
> We are really 'receivers' floating through a kaleidoscopic sea of frequency, and what we extract from this sea and transmogrify into physical reality is but one channel from many extracted out of the superhologram.[10]

To reiterate the reason for the above discussion, the holographic model was presented in order to emphasize how each symbol in a symbolic world must be understood not only in its limited aspect of a particular meaning as a structuralist approach would perhaps have it, but as an integral part of a whole metaphysic that is diffused into the symbol. We will see that it is only by perceiving the symbol in a particular way that this metaphysic can be brought forth and experienced—illuminated, as it were— by the symbol.

---

[10] Lia Wolf-Gentry, "*The Universe as a Hologram*," Internet article, March 1997.

Systems Theory

In the same vein as the holographic model, there is a modern systems view of the universe that has emerged from the scientific realm that also reflects the ancient metaphysical concept of hierarchy; that is to say, that the universe can be understood only as a continuing interaction of its parts creating through self-organization a hierarchy of relative wholes making up the one great whole of the universe. Lee Smolin, in his work *The Life of the Cosmos*, reminds us of the limits of the Newtonian reductionist viewpoint. In fact, it is impossible to depict reality by describing a part of the world without reference to the whole of it. To describe even where something is or when something happened requires that the rest of the world be implicated. Making a theory of the whole universe is then quite another matter, for given that there is nothing outside the universe, there is no reference point by which events can be described, but only other events within it. The order and structure that we see in the universe thus arises from a "process of self-organization, by means of which the world has evolved over time to become intricately structured."[11]

One aspect of this view is called the "bootstrap" theory put forward by Geoffrey Chew beginning in 1968. While it was conceived in relation to subatomic particles, its underlying philosophy is profoundly at odds with the reductionist view of the universe. In Fritjof Capra's words, "bootstrap" theory sees the universe under a radically different light than that of classical physics:

> According to this view, if the properties of any one particle are determined by the interactions with all the others, while that particle itself participates equally in the determination of the properties of those others, then the laws of physics are a kind of system in which the

[11] Lee Smolin, *The Life of the Cosmos* (Oxford: Oxford University Press, 1997) 13-18.

influence of any one particle on the others feeds back to effect its own properties. The laws of physics then cannot be postulated a priori, one must find a self-consistent set of properties and interactions such that each particle in the system both contributes and is determined by the network of interactions.[12]

If we exchange the word "particle" for "symbol" in the above citation, we have a beautiful statement of the symbolic nature of, for example, ancient Egyptian civilization. While Grof calls this viewpoint the "dawning of a new paradigm," it is in fact a return to a worldview prevalent throughout the ancient world.

From this conception of the universe wherein reality is in the relation of its parts and not in the parts themselves, that is, reality is conceived of as being a process rather than a static structure, comes other lines of thought subsumed under the name "systems theory" and which now encompasses such concepts as "complexity," "self-organization," "emergent properties," "dissipative structures," "autopoietic networks," and so on. Of course, whole tomes have been written on these subjects and, at the risk of not doing justice to the proponents of these theories, we can only provide here a cursory introduction, our aim being to sensitize the reader to another way of reading the world, a way that is closer to ancient thought processes, but arising out of the modern scientific mentality.

Systems theory is based on certain fundamental concepts that are quite at odds with the Newtonian view of the world.[13] Rather than looking at the parts of a system as isolated entities or analyzing the interaction of parts of a system one at a time and noticing the effects of mutual interaction on each, systems theory looks at different things in their mutual interactions *as a*

---

[12] Ibid., 64.

[13] Much of this section is based on the work of Capra, *The Web of Life*.

whole, and how this whole is affected by various influences. As Smolin puts it:

> The basic understanding that life on this planet constitutes an interconnected system must be considered to be one of the great discoveries of science....[T]here can be little doubt that it is necessary to understand life on this planet as an interconnected system to have any sense of what life is and why it is here.[14]

He goes on to point out that looking at evolution in terms of one species at a time is fruitless, since species evolve together, such as predators and prey where the extinction of one species could lead to the extinction of another for whom the first was its food. And to look at life on earth without considering the movement of the planet in the solar system which effects climate, can only give a very partial picture. From this systems viewpoint, Darwin's natural selection is only a part of the theory of how life evolves on earth. However, this way of understanding goes very much against the grain of our minds.

That which is seen as common among different entities of a system is viewed in terms of *organization* rather than by virtue of a common substrate (such as atoms and molecules) making up the parts. A system is not viewed as being in isolation, but as a subsystem of a larger system, which in turn is also a subsystem of a still larger system, and so on, thus creating a highly complex hierarchical order, which in fact is not made up of "parts" but rather of "pattern[s] in an inseparable web of relationships."[15] In this way, each system acts as one whole among others for the level above, retaining a certain amount of freedom at its own level and encompassing lower-level systems within it. Each level in the hierarchy, each "whole," is seen as having properties beyond its "parts" which come into being at that level and are

---

[14] Smolin, *The Life of the Cosmos*, 146.

[15] Capra, *The Web of Life*, 37.

thus called "emergent properties" that produce ever-higher levels of complexity.

Stuart Kauffman, one of the leaders in the science of complexity, has this to say:

> How do we use the information gleaned about the parts to build up a theory of the whole? The deep difficulty here lies in the fact that the complex whole may exhibit properties that are not readily explained by understanding the parts. The complex whole, in a completely nonmystical sense, can often exhibit collective properties, 'emergent' features that are lawful in their own right.[16]...Life, in this view, is not to be located in its parts, but in the collective emergent properties of the whole they create.[17]

Because each system is enclosed and influenced by the systems above in the hierarchy, any system must therefore "tend" towards the *raison d'être* or "purpose" of the systems above it. With this point in mind and the fact that the universe is a hierarchy of systems from subatomic particles to clusters of galaxies, if we only "knew" the purpose of the highest-level system beyond which no more systems exists, we would understand the reason for ourselves as systems in this universal hierarchy, the ultimate reason for own existence. Given that everything depends on everything else, however, to "know" any one thing completely would mean to "know" everything else as well, which is quite impossible. Thus, systems thinking leads to the conclusion that science can never reach ultimate Truth, but only approximate and relative truth defined in hypotheses and theories.

The great question here is, of course, what does "know" in this context really mean? Can we "know" higher systems, higher

---

[16] Stuart Kauffman, *At Home in the Universe: The Search for the Laws of Self-Organization and Complexity* (New York: Oxford University Press, 1995), vii-viii.

[17] Ibid., 24.

energies by our normal thought processes through analysis as classical science would have it, or is there another "knowing" based on direct experience, direct knowledge, as partakers of inner practices of all ages would have it, practices that are necessarily universal in space as well as in time, since man's essential nature is always the same wherever and whenever he exists.

The beginning of modern systems theory can be said to have begun with the work of Ludwig von Bertalanffy in the 1930s. He saw living systems as not obeying the second law of thermodynamics, which says that all closed physical systems evolve towards ever-increasing disorder or entropy because some mechanical energy is always dissipated into heat which cannot all be recovered. In this way, "the entire world-machine is running down and will eventually grind to a halt."[18]

Bertalanffy saw, however, as did others of his time, that living systems, rather than progressing towards disorder, evolve on the contrary from disorder to order, to ever-increasing complexity. He observed that the reason for this seeming contradiction was that living systems were not "closed" but "open" because "they need to feed on a continual flux of matter and energy from their environment to stay alive."[19] In contrast to closed systems, which tend towards thermal equilibrium, open systems "maintain themselves far from equilibrium in [a] steady state characterized by continual flow and change,"[20] and do so by the processes of metabolism and self-regulation. In other words, living systems were *self-organizing*.

Another offshoot of this general trend towards systems thinking was "cybernetics" a term coined by Norbert Wiener in 1948 to

---

[18] Capra, *The Web of Life*, 48.

[19] Ibid.

[20] Ibid.

mean "the science of control and communication in the animal and the machine."[21] The main contribution to systems theory from cybernetics was the concept of feedback loops resulting in self-regulation of processes and in "patterns of organization." The concept of feedback mechanisms has led to theories whereby the atmosphere and biosphere of the earth are maintained in balance allowing for the generation and maintenance of life due to feedback mechanisms arising from plant and animal emissions of gases.[22] Theories were also developed to explain the maintenance of stars (regulating the force between the nuclear reactions and the pressure of the gases) and even of galaxies (regulating the relationship between the creation of stars from gas and dust in the interstellar medium and the ejection of the same from explosions of dying stars).[23] The point is that the object of study is not the discrete entities making up a biological or mechanical system but the flow of information in the process of self-regulation within the system— which is a radically different way of observing the world.

From this beginning, Ilya Prigogine in the 1960s developed his theory of dissipative structures in open systems far from thermal equilibrium:

> According to Prigogine's theory, dissipative structures not only maintain themselves in a stable state far from equilibrium, but may even evolve. When the flow of energy and matter through them increases, they may go through new instabilities and transform themselves into new structures of increased complexity.[24]

This increasing order and complexity comes about not through the nature of the components of a system, which can be quite

---

[21] Ibid, 51.

[22] J. E. Lovelock, *Gaia: A New Look at Life on Earth* (Oxford: Oxford University Press, 1987), 64-83.

[23] Smolin, *The Life of the Cosmos*, 130-131.

[24] Ibid., 89.

simple, but rather the *number* of the components all acting in simultaneous movement, such as the number of molecules in a cell or neurons in a brain. The nature of this complexity can be understood when we consider the "three-body problem," that is to say, that that we cannot even mathematically understand the nature of the mutual influence of just *three* celestial bodies moving in space. The complexity is thus found in the *organization* of the components and the innumerable possibilities by which the components can interact.[25] Systems composed of myriad components spontaneously form themselves, it seems, into patterns of organization, or a *whole*, that has its own "emergent properties" beyond those of the components making it up.[26]

As the number of interactions, the complexity, of a system increases, it eventually reaches what Prigogine calls a "bifurcation point,"[27] a point at which either chaos ensues or a "phase transition" to a new order, a new level, happens, where properties arise forming a new whole supported by the myriad interactions of the level from which it emerged.

This network or "pattern of organization" is limited by a boundary but still open to the flow of energy and certain types of matter that allows it to maintain itself. We can here think of a brain, made up of untold numbers of neurons having an outer membrane through which it receives nourishment and information. The neurons themselves, cells made up of countless proteins and other molecules, are separate in structure yet open to all the other neurons to which they are connected. Francisco Varela, *et. al.*, in *The Embodied Mind*, says:

---

[25] M. Mitchell Waldrop, *Complexity: The Emerging Science at the Edge of Order and Chaos* (New York: Simon & Schuster, 1992), 86.

[26] Francisco Varela, et. al., *The Embodied Mind: Cognitive Science and Human Experience* (Cambridge, Mass.: The MIT Press, 1993), 88.

[27] Ilya Prigogine, *The End of Certainty: Time, Chaos, and the New Laws of Nature* (New York: The Free Press, 1997), 68-70.

> The brain is thus a highly cooperative system: the dense interconnections among its components entail that eventually everything going on will be a function of what all the components are doing. This kind of cooperativeness holds both locally and globally: it functions within subsystems of the brain and at the level of the connections among those subsystems....These subsections are made up of complex networks of cells, but they also relate to each other in a network fashion. As a result the entire system acquires an internal coherence in intricate patterns, even if we cannot say exactly how this occurs.[28]

Or we can consider the biosphere and atmosphere as a whole, the infinite diversity of living forms, bounded by the earth's ozone layer and magnetic and gravitational fields, far from thermodynamic equilibrium, constantly fed by energy from the sun and dissipating heat into space. The complex pattern of organization within such systems, up to even galaxies and perhaps even the universe itself,[29] are not controlled by any particular entity: the pattern spontaneously arises from the interactions among the components themselves and the influence of larger systems of which they are apart and the smaller systems of which they are composed.[30] Furthermore, the complexity does not allow for any one element to take control, since it could never know all the interactions taking place within the system. Only by mutual interaction with other elements in constant adaptation with each other does change arise and in unpredictable ways.[31]

Another theory of self-organization was developed by the Chileans Humberto Maturana and Francisco Varela in the 1970s. They called it "autopoiesis," meaning "self-making" or

---

[28] Varela, *The Embodied Mind*, 94.

[29] Smolin, *The Life of the Cosmos*, 159-60, 172.

[30] Ibid., 170-71.

[31] Ibid., 147.

"the pattern of organization of living systems."[32] To be "self-making" the autopoietic nature of living systems demands that each component of the system transforms or creates other components in the same system. Thus, while the structure may change over time, its organizational pattern remains the same. Parts of cells, for example, continually die and are recreated by other parts of the cell, while the organization of the *whole* cell continues as it is over time. Changes in a system's structure may also occur over time that are the result of its adaptation to a changing environment. Thus, while a living system's behavior depends on its structure, this structure can change over time by continual interactions with its environment. Evolution, according to the autopoietic theory, does not arise through random mutation of genes and natural selection, but by a mutual influence between living systems and their environment. Which came first: bees or flowers? Can they exist without each other? Or is there a mutual influence where the structure of the flower is influenced by the bee and the structure of the bee influenced by the flower? A mutual evolution. From this point of view, the universe is an interconnected web of nested hierarchies from subatomic particles to clusters of galaxies, (with human beings somewhere in the middle) all of which interact in one grand mutually influencing "web of life."

Is there some ultimate purpose to all this change and movement? Is there a purpose to man in this scheme of things? From third-millennium science arises the same ultimate questions that ancient cultures tried in their manner to answer in their myths. The modern science of cognition, of "knowing," as defined by Maturana and Varela, brings to light the concept of "mind" as the process of life itself. Mind is not something we can delimit as a particular "thing," since it is a continual interaction among all the mutual influences impinging on each other in the

---

[32] Capra, *The Web of Life*, 189. The following explanation of Maturana and Varela's theory owes much to Capra's description of it.

universe, processes which allow existing organizational patterns to exist over time through self-generating hierarchical structures. Given this framework, "knowing" then means that...

> sensory and motor processes, perception and action, are fundamentally inseparable in lived cognition. Indeed, the two are not merely contingently linked in individuals; they have also evolved together....[P]erception is not simply embedded within and constrained by the surrounding world; it also contributes to the enactment of this surrounding world...[T]he organism both initiates and is shaped by the environment"[33]

In more simple terms, "knowing" is not simply a mental process, but the total interaction that takes place between a living organism and its surrounding environment; or, as Maturana and Varela put it, "To live is to know."[34] The means by which an organism interacts with its environment is what the theory calls "structural coupling,"[35] that is, an organism is "coupled" to its environment by continually interacting with it through its physical structure, thus producing structural changes in itself while keeping the pattern of overall organization intact. In other words, how an organism interacts with the world depends on its physical structure. Any organism will respond to only those stimuli with which it can be "coupled." Thus, all members of the same species will "know" the world in essentially the same way. For example, a bat, which is blind, may not respond to light waves but will react (change its structure) in response to certain sound frequencies. Any particular organism thus creates its own world depending on how its structure enables it to respond to only those stimuli among the myriads in which it is bathed. As Capra puts it:

---

[33] Varela, *The Embodied Mind*, 173.

[34] Humberto R. Maturana and Francisco J. Varela, *The Tree of Knowledge: The Biological Roots of Human Understanding*. Rev. ed. (Boston: Shambhala, 1998), 174.

[35] Capra, *The Web of Life*, 213-4.

> Cognition, then, is not a representation of an independently existing world, but rather a continual bringing forth of a world through the process of living.[36] The interactions of a living system with its environment are cognitive interactions, and the process of living itself is a process of cognition. ...In this new view, cognition involves the entire process of life—including perception, emotion, and behavior—and does not necessarily require a brain and a nervous system.[37]

A human being arriving at a certain level of complexity, can couple structurally not only with the external world but with his inner world as well, thus producing a world of language, thought and consciousness, which is but a by-product of the cognitive process, not the process itself. Understanding a symbol intellectually is not the same as experiencing it with one's whole being. As always, "the map is not the territory."

From a modern theory of cognitive science, we approach the global hierarchical view that Traditional civilizations had of the cosmos, and which is needed to even begin to understand the meaning of even one symbol in an ancient civilization.

William Brian Arthur, a member of the Santa Fe Institute where much of "third-millennium science" developed, makes this connection between complexity and ancient Chinese Taoism:

> [T]he complex approach...is total Taoist. In Taoism there is no inherent order. 'The world started with one, and the one became two, and the two became many, and the many led to myriad things.' The universe in Taoism is perceived as vast, amorphous, and ever-changing. You can never nail it down. The elements always stay the same, yet they're always rearranging themselves.[38]

---

[36] This echoes von Bertalanffy's statement: "Man is not a passive receiver of stimuli coming from an external world, but in a very concrete sense *creates* his universe. From *General System Theory*, 194.

[37] Capra, *The Web of Life*, 260.

[38] Waldrop, *Complexity*, 330.

It seems to us that what is missing from the systems theorists' analyses however "relational" they may be, is the possibility of an understanding arising from a different type of knowledge than that resulting from perception and thought.[39]

What seems impossible to imagine to those arising from a strictly scientific background is the possibility for one to have a different understanding of the world arising from a deeper or higher level of being *even though their theories are based on hierarchical premises.* Does one who has realized spiritual liberation view the world in the same way as one who has not? Is it possible that such a liberated soul understands and acts by virtue of finer energies within himself corresponding to the same that fill the universe? Do spiritual practices allow for these energies, corresponding to a different dimension, to become active within oneself to provide a different knowledge that cannot be described in words? Is there "nothing in fact that needs to be transcended, but rather something that needs to be realized."?[40] And "that truth, being sacred in its essence, belongs to a dimension that transcends thinking as cogitation and which therefore requires…the intervention of a supra-rational factor of grace or, at least, of inspiration,…a transpersonal agency."[41] Is there, in fact, knowledge beyond that which can be measured but only related through symbols? And is it this knowledge which the ancient Egyptians and others left us in their writing, art, statues, and monuments? We can only leave the question open.

---

[39] Smolin, *The Life of the Cosmos,* 199.

[40] Perry, *On Awakening and Remembering: To Know Is To Be* (Louisville, KY: Fons Vitae, 2000), 34.

[41] Ibid., 37.

Chapter 2 Symbolism and Civilization

Trying to understand the symbolism of ancient Egypt is fraught with uncertainty, since we do not have the advantage of living in the civilization in which the symbols came to be. And though much has been left in the sands of the Egyptian desert, much as been lost by which the keys to the symbols can be read. Even if we plunge into a study of all the existing remains of Egyptian civilization, it would still be like learning a new language as an adult; that is to say, the resonances of words (which are also symbols!) do not go deep enough to touch the emotional forces associated with words as they are learned in childhood. For this reason, the intuitive understanding of Egyptian symbols can only be that much harder to achieve. And this even more so because the Egyptians never "explained" their symbols, never addressed the thinking function per se, so that "knowing" the symbols by analysis, reason, and speculation is impossible. Understanding the symbols having to do with Egyptian religion can only mean a sort of intuitive knowing arising from one's own embodied experience. The purpose of these symbols can be understood from these quotes of René Guénon:

> [B]y virtue of the correspondence that exists among all levels of reality, truths of a lower order can be considered as a symbol of those of a higher order and therefore serve as a 'support' in order to arrive analogically at the knowledge of the latter.[42]…Another consequence of the law of correspondence is the numerous meanings included in every symbol: anything, in fact, can be considered as representing not only metaphysical principles, but also the realities of all levels higher than its own.[43]

---

[42] René Guénon, *La Crise du monde moderne,* 3rd ed. (Paris: Gallimard, 1956), 86.

[43] René Guénon, *Le symbolisme de la croix,* 3rd ed. (Paris: Union Générale d'Editions, 1956), 52.

Therefore, it is important not to believe that one has found the one meaning behind any symbol, for the symbol embodies a law that can be found at all levels of existence. The word "symbol" itself comes from the Greek *symbolon*, which was one half of a piece of pottery that when matched with the other half provided a means of identification of the two parties holding the pieces, or more abstractly, that the part represents the whole. The "discovery" recently that the three pyramids of Giza may represent the three stars in the belt of the constellation of Orion may be quite true at the cosmological level, but one should not assume because of this that one has found *the* meaning of the pyramids. What, for example, does Orion represent for the Egyptians? What laws or principles does it embody? What is its relation to other constellations in the sky? What meaning is there in the fact that the belt is at the level of Orion's waist? Does this have a relation to the fact that the pyramids were constructed both above and below the level of the Earth? These and a multitude of other questions could arise that show the constant interdependence of symbols on both the vertical levels leading to ever more principial knowledge and on the horizontal level showing the interdependence of all things at any particular level. As Coomaraswamy says in terms of the art of the Middle Ages:

> If the mediaeval artist's constructions corresponded to a certain way of thinking, it is certain that we cannot understand them except to the extent that we can identify ourselves with this way of thinking.[44]

Now, if we assume that the Egyptian civilization was based on a spiritual project, it is still quite possible for us to understand, paradoxically as it may seem, the deeper meaning of the symbols rather than the cultural or historical meanings that might be attached to them. Since the essence of man's nature, what constitutes the species *homo sapiens*, is the structure of the

---

[44] Coomaraswamy, Ananda K. *Christian and Oriental Philosophy of Art* (New York: Dover, 1956), 29.

organism rather than the patina of the particular culture in which a person happened to be born, a person's spiritual development involving the development of his essence can only take place on the same basis and incorporate similar inner experiences whatever the epoch, whether ancient Egypt of 6000 years ago or today.

Figure 4 Ancient Egyptian statue

In Egyptian art, proportion was of the utmost importance while the subject itself had almost none other than being a symbol for something else, and this was because their viewpoint was directed not toward a variable present but rather toward that which was the same for all eternity. The *raison d'être* of their statues was not to immortalize a living person but to act as the material support for the spiritual being of the defunct, the *ka*, which was imbued within it. Aesthetics for itself played no part in Egyptian art but was a means of integrating the spiritual realm into the human.[45] See Figure 4.

Whereas we may never know the social and historical allusions that could help us decipher the symbols because we can no longer live in the civilization which gave rise to them, perhaps from our own inner experiences we can nonetheless come to understand their spiritual meaning. Again, whereas we are apt to suppose that the religious significance of Christianity stands or falls with the actual

---

[45] Erwin Panofsky, *Meaning in the Visual Arts*, Ch. 2: "The History of the Theory of Human Proportions as a Reflection of the History of Styles" (Chicago: The University of Chicago Press, 1982), 61-2, 98, 105.

historicity of Jesus, we find an Indian commentator (Nilakantha) saying of the Krsna Lila, believed historical by most Hindus, that the narration is not the real point, that this is not an historical event, but is based upon eternal truths, on the actual relation of the soul to God, and that the events take place, not in the outer world, but in the heart of man:[46]

> The real traditional mind, whatever form it assumes, is always and everywhere basically the same. The various forms, which are especially adapted to such and such mental conditions, to such and such circumstances of time and place, are but expressions of one and the same truth. But one must be able to situate oneself at the level of pure spirituality to discover the fundamental unity behind this apparent multiplicity.[47]

However, this meaning is by no means a one-to-one relationship, like a flag representing a nation. The meaning of any Egyptian symbol is contained in the entire culture of the civilization, a sort of "bootstrap" theory of Traditional civilizations. That is to say, in order to understand Egyptian symbols, one would have to know the myth from which they might be extracted, the meaning of the *neters* ('gods') representing metaphysical cosmic principles, the basic nature and function of the animals, plants and body parts used in them, the purpose of various paraphernalia utilized in rites and ceremonies, the clothes and ornaments worn by various functionaries in the society as well as those worn by the *neters*, and so on. Like a hologram, the whole is contained in each part so that by starting from any particular symbol one could be lead from association to association through the whole gamut of Egyptian symbolism.

Given the above, it is obvious that any one symbol cannot be "explained" or "translated" or "known" in itself, but only as an

---

[46] Ananda K. Coomaraswamy, *The Transformation of Nature in Art* (New York: Dover Publications, 1956), 159.

[47] Guénon, *La Crise du monde moderne*, 51.

25

integral part of a connection of elements creating a whole having a purpose beyond the meaning of any of its parts. Whitehead puts it very well in terms of dogma, of which symbols are the expression:

> You cannot convey a dogma by merely translating the words; you must also understand the system of thought to which it is relevant...You cannot claim absolute finality for a dogma without claiming a commensurate finality for the sphere of thought within which it arose.[48]

To understand Egyptian symbolism, we must then understand the basic project of the civilization, the "whole" in which each symbol contributes to its realization. Therefore, given the religious texts, temples and pyramids, pantheon of gods and all the other remains of the ancient Egyptian civilization, one would have to be blind not to assume that ancient Egyptian civilization had a profoundly religious basis and that the entire society was geared to realizing the spiritual development of its people. In the materialist world in which we live today, this may seem very far from what we consider the 'normal' or 'natural' life in human society, but one only has to project oneself into the Middle Ages of our own Christian civilization to get a feeling for what such a society might have been: to imagine the mentality of the people filling the cathedrals, worshiping the saints, following the religious processions taking place to celebrate the round of religious holy days (now called holidays!), where the words of the priest carried real weight. Of course, just as in our day and in all times, medieval society as well as the Egyptian, was filled as well with crime, evil and all the social problems of any large community of people. But the point we are making here is that the general mentality of the people in both the Middle Ages and ancient Egypt, the *weltanschauung* by which people made sense of the world in which they lived was a religious one, however

---

[48] Whitehead, Alfred North, *Religion in the Making: Lowell Lectures, 1926* (New York: Fordham University Press, 1996), 129-30.

that might be interpreted according to one's place in society: to venerate and serve God (or the gods) "who created all," to "do good" so as to achieve peace in the afterlife, or transform oneself spiritually to achieve in this life liberation from worldly fetters.

The Beginning of Civilization[49]

The history of civilization is based on one fundamental overarching fact: the mind of man was attuned, in times immemorial, to the finer energies that form both the transcendent nature and the substrata of the universe, but at a certain moment in man's history, a "fall" took place that caused the mind to split off from this energy and so was no longer immersed in what might be called the "cosmic flux." Before this break, which created a hiatus between these two modes of knowing or consciousness, man lived, so to speak, in "Paradise": through the direct experience of an illuminated mind he did not feel himself in any way separate from the world around him, but, like a bird flying in a flock, he continuously moved and navigated effortlessly through his life in constant identity with himself, with his kind, and with nature, which were all one intertwined matrix of Being. In such a world, the mind experiences everything intrinsically: beings and things in the microcosm are apprehended as materialized loci of energy, just as stars are formed from nebulae in the macrocosm. Rather than, after the fall, mind-stuff being the consequence of simple sense perceptions filtered through the apparatus of thought, and in so doing, losing their dynamic nature, the mind was continually irrigated by energies coursing through the world underlying everything existing. The essential was this higher mind existing behind and above the different personalities and roles of the lower self. Since this real world is one of fullness of Being, man

---

[49] This section is greatly influenced by the work of the Frenchman Pierre Gordon, especially *The Original Revelation* (Châteauneuf de Mazenc, France: Arma Artis, 2004). [Translated into English by Michael Allswang]

can only live up to his potential, be normal, when he is attuned to this world in a concordant state of consciousness. Due to his degeneration after the fall, however, man no longer really existed "since his mind does not directly connect with *what is*,"[50] his state of consciousness being nourished only by sense impressions. And it is just this remembrance of another way of knowing, of experiencing oneself in a luminous world outside of human time and space, that was the impetus for the creation of civilization, a notion which we will develop further on.

Even today, tribes isolated in jungles and forests…

> …conceive the world not as being made up of dense matter, but as a world of energies, a living world, full of mysterious forces with which they must live in harmony. In their minds, events are produced not by contact of matter in space, but by the influence of one inner energy on another inner energy. And their basic concern is not, as has been believed for so long, to feed themselves and to fight, but to be related to what they believe to be the real world and to make this world favorable to themselves.[51]

Their whole world revolves around the rites and ceremonies created to put the participants in contact with this higher world of finer energies. The most revered among the people in these societies are not those who have the most riches or those who are the bravest warriors, but those who have contact with the "other world," the shaman, the sorcerer and the witch doctor (which later became "priests" in high civilizations). We can only surmise that the earliest societies, before the great civilizations of Mesopotamia and Egypt, had the same fundamental basis, though being much closer to the original immersion in Being, their mental level could only have been much higher in this respect than what exists today as the degenerate remains of what

---

[50] Gordon, *The Original Revelation*, 8-9.

[51] Ibid., 31.

once was a search for a lost world of purity. In those earliest times, magic (based on supernatural powers) and religion were one and the same, along with all symbols, rites, ceremonies, and myths: everything had as its goal to help man return to the "lost land."

And it is just this that was the original impetus to the creation of civilization: the desire to return to the world of light that in man had become but a spark ensconced in the depths of his being, and which moved him, and moves him still, to find a way out of the shadows. All human endeavor, whether philosophy, history, art or literature, thus has as its ultimate source of inspiration in the decline of man from this initial higher state and his intuition that as he is something is missing within him, which is none other than that dynamic illumination that man had lost contact with in primordial times.

The Fall

However, for whatever reason, like an infant just beginning to realize his separateness from his mother and the world around him, man began to see himself as a unique creature, as not being immanently connected to everything in his environment through the particle of universal Being within him that sustained his existence. It was this "original sin," when man ceased to be completely transparent and open, ceased to play his role in the universe as a channel for universal energies, when he began to apprehend the universe only on a physical level through his senses that the motive behind, and the *raison d'être* of, civilization was born. For when man fell from his divine immersion in Being, there remained in the depths of his own being the remembrance of the immortal energy coursing through his body.

> Attached to Being by his constitutive principle, man longs to again experience Being and cannot be satisfied with surface impressions, which is all his intellect has to feed on in the present age....Thrown thus into an opaque

> cosmos, he ineluctably tries to find again these worlds of
> light and to weave a path towards them in the midst of
> the darkness in which he struggles.[52]

The problem was that after the fall, man's mind, rather than being a channel for universal Being, became, on the contrary, a barrier preventing the flow of finer energies in himself because of his belief in the most reduced part of that mind: the reception of sense impressions and their interpretation by rational thought. Nothing changed in the world, nothing changed in the cosmos, it was only man's mind that became crimped and distorted so that what once was pure and natural "participation" *within* beings and things in an *essential* union became separate and blocked. Rather than the "world of light" that he once knew, man, after tasting the apple, descended into what Plato called a cavern of shadows, able only to see the world "through a glass darkly":

> Created free, he lives in chains; formed attached to
> Being, he lives apart from it; instead of living within the
> essence of the world, he is nourished on sensations; far
> from uniting with the existence of things, he clings to
> their reflections. The cosmos, where everything is ablaze,
> has for him become opaque and impenetrable. His own
> making of human space and time envelops him in a shell,
> cutting him off from both God and creatures, from Being
> and beings.[53]

Man, as the synthesis and reflection of the universe, always had everything within him to become free from the bondage of his warped nature that over time has found itself ever farther from its participation in its rightful home within Being. Rather than naturally swimming within the radiant cosmic energies everywhere within and around him, his manner of knowing, of understanding, changed dramatically after the fall and so he was forced to strive to find a passage through the darkness of brute

---

[52]Ibid., 5.

[53]Ibid., 18-19.

matter to an opening where he could breathe free once again in the light of the cosmos. Man's actions were once conditioned not by his own thoughts, instinctive emotions and repetitive habits; rather they were motivated by a receptivity to higher energies that allowed him to live on a level where action was instantaneous because every option was seen at once and only the most harmonious in terms of himself and his environment was immediately embarked upon. There was no obstruction to action because man's mind was directly connected to Being and its unlimited energy. "Choice" was thus not dependent on individual volition but was guided by a higher level of "seeing." Without this ability to live a higher life, man can only live in his animal nature of ignorance and suffering, where "love becomes sex, liberty but instinctual mechanisms, and ideas get bogged down in images."[54] One only has to remember the now dim experiences of early childhood where everything was imbued with the intensity of newness to realize how our scientific "education" has destroyed our receptivity to the real world and which can be viewed as the fall for each individual arising from the general fall of humanity. What before the fall was a *vision* based on eternally present energies had become a *conception* based on a linear perception of space and time.

Another way of looking at man's fall was his splitting off from unity. No longer was human society based on the intrinsic experiencing of the unity of all human beings where even the idea of individual appropriation was inconceivable. Rather human society became divided into spiritual and secular, subdividing endlessly into smaller and smaller sects and organisms, each rivaling and fighting each other for supremacy until each individual became a world unto itself unable to unite with even another human being. As man moved further and further away from his home in Being, he became more and more

---

[54] Ibid., 22.

unable to feel united with another and saw everything through his own limited self. Because the channel of love was blocked (for what is love but the overflow of cosmic energy from one being to another), he lived in his own cocoon, and ended up living only for himself, whatever justifications spewed from his mouth.

Man's devolution can also be seen as a decline of understanding from the knowledge of Being to a sense-based and purely empirical knowledge so that science, too, became a separate field of endeavor, split off from its principle in Being so as to study finer and finer aspects of nature—but to what end? Man forgot his *raison d'être* on earth: to find his way back to his origin in Being and so increase the harmony of the cosmos through himself as a channel of energies instead of a dam hindering the cosmic flux.

Art

Before the "fall," there was no need for "art." Man, incarnating Being, did not feel any need to create works as his life was totally satisfying. It was only after the fall, that "art" arose, that is, the need to create works by the first priests as messages to show man the way back to his initial Self. The beauty of these images and sculptures can only be a by-product of the *message* given to the artisan by the priest, works never created for their own sake or the glory of the artisan who made them. To look at the art of ancient Egypt, Mesopotamia, or any other Traditional civilization as simply artistic objects without delving into their significance in terms of their role in the rites, myths, and religion of that civilization, is truly to study the most superficial aspect of these works and, in sum, a waste of time. We can provide a myriad suppositions as to the meaning of prehistoric cave art of 15,000-40,000 years ago, or the beautifully carved animals on the pillars of Göbekli Tepe in what is now Turkey, around 12,000 years ago, but we will never know their real significance for lack of knowledge of their culture.

In the last centuries what we now call art has become totally subjective outpourings of individuals having no meaning beyond the psychological motivations of their makers. Nevertheless, man will continue to create and create he will—if not out of knowledge and understanding of what is needed for humanity to return to its rightful place in the cosmos—out of a desire coming from he knows not where to escape from a prison of the limited world in which he finds himself, to push back the boundaries of his mind and the limited place for his 'soul.'

The First Priesthood

This great event, this "fall from grace," ignited among those who still had remembrance of the former state, ways to return to it. Those 'priests' who understood this need devised a society to reach this goal and provide the means to transmit the knowledge of it to future generations. Difficult as it is now to understand that it was a priestly caste, that is, men of high knowledge, that formed the first civilizations when all we see around us as leaders are men with no real understanding, even sociopaths and liars, whose sole aim is power and money for their own sake, and who act not from sacred principles but from outworn ideologies, petty intrigues, and sentimental emotions.

What we now call "myth" is in fact the symbolic story of ancient man and the primordial Tradition developed by ancient priests:

> Such is the basis, as well, of all human traditions. Under the names Pure Land, Jade Mountain, Mount Meru, Albordj, Holy Island, Heart of the World, the Pole, the quintessence, pure gold, Agarttha, the Philosopher's Stone, and so on, one finds everywhere what Christianity calls, from the parables in the Gospels, the lost treasure, the misplaced jewel, the buried realm that men should bring out of the darkness. This truly primordial notion gives the key to man, history, religion, magic, art and science, to all the greatness and all the misery of man.[55]

---

[55] Ibid., 18.

This, then, is the fundamental duality that has been behind all men's strivings since the beginning of civilization: man lost and apart from the real world of pure Being in which he was once immersed and man struggling to return to this paradise that he once knew. All Tradition, all myth has to do with one or the other of these two fundamental realities—*man lost* and *man returning*—and which has engendered all religion, history, art, literature, and poetry. Of course, in our day, the degradation has reached such a point that even the recounting of the most trivial of events becomes "literature" and the most subjective sentimental emotion becomes "art," but still, it could be said that these works in themselves become symbols of our times, not for what they say, but for what they do not say. It seems that these last generations in the world have cut completely with this primordial duality. Living on an untethered boat, with no sail or motor, going nowhere, but always believing that the latest technological advancement will provide the answer to the search for fulfillment, the great majority of humankind live floating in a sea of unmeaning, totally cut off from their spiritual home or any idea that it even exists.

All civilizations, up to modern times, were, in fact, developed to provide man with a support in his quest to return to the higher world from which he was ejected. Without keeping this notion in mind, a study of ancient symbolism will in no way bear fruit. For symbolism as practiced in Traditional societies had as its goal the transformation of man's being, his way of knowing, his means of experiencing the world, to free him from the carapace that blocked the essential energies of the universe from mingling with those within his own being. In short, symbols and myths were created by "those who knew" to allow mankind to return to the "Golden Age" that was once his normal state. Rites, symbols, and myths were created not as simple mental reminders, but as transforming agents that, if received in the right way, could open channels to the inexhaustible reservoir of energy that makes up the universe. It should also be kept in mind that rites, symbols and myths taken out of their context may have a certain minimal effect by reminding man of his real purpose in the cosmos, but it is only when they are integrated into a whole matrix of other symbolic agents, that is, into a civilization, that they have real transforming power. Mircea Eliade tells us:

> A religious symbol not only reveals a pattern of reality or a dimension of existence, it brings at the same time a meaning to human existence... A religious symbol translates a human situation into cosmological terms, and vice versa; to be more precise, it reveals the unity between human existence and the structure of the Cosmos.... It follows that the man who understands a symbol not only 'opens himself' to the objective world, but at the same time succeeds in emerging from his personal situation and reaching a comprehension of the universal. Thanks to the symbol, the individual experience is 'awoken' and transmitted into a spiritual act.[56]

What is necessary to understand in order to follow our discussion of symbolism and civilization is that the mentality of man, *from a certain point of view,* has been in a state of continual decline from the beginning of man as a separate species until our present day. That is to say that the mind of man, in the beginning, was of a different nature than man in our time and that he lived then in a state of awareness that today only the very few ever achieve. Of course, most observers today would say the opposite, given the standard of living many millions have arrived at, the technological advances, and the longevity people enjoy compared even to a century ago. And *from another point of view,* this is quite true: man has advanced his knowledge of the material plane and has made vast advances in understanding nature and natural processes—but at the terrible cost of no longer directly experiencing the world of

---

[56]Mircea Eliade, *Myths, Rites, Symbols: A Mircea Eliade Reader.* 2 vols. (New York: Harper & Row, 1975), 350-51.

Being he once knew in primordial times. This study takes, then, as its guiding thread, not the material advancement man has achieved, but man's level of consciousness throughout time as exemplified by the civilizations whose remains have come down to us in the form of a Tradition that is carried on by certain individuals of great understanding.

There are two basic types of civilization in which to observe these symbolic agents: that of tribal man, that is, men living within relatively small tribes more or less isolated from other cultures, and that of the great ancient civilizations of Egypt, Mesopotamia, India, China, Persia, Pre-Columbian America, and the European Middle Ages.

Tribal Man

To begin to understand what the mentality of original man would have been, one can look at the tribes that still exist in the isolated regions of the world. The religious rites and ceremonies of these tribes are often of a complexity and symbolism that bespeak a high understanding of the cosmos and spiritual truths. The most revered persons of these tribes are the men, and sometimes women, who through spiritual disciplines find a way to reach another way of perceiving the world based on connections with a finer and higher energy. Out of the many tens of thousands of years of human existence, it is only since the time of the ancient Greeks that mankind began to see the materiality of the world as the only reality, to which in our day has spread to the entire planet, leaving only small groups of seekers scattered here and there who still believe in another higher world that can be attained in this life.

One of the means tribal man uses to bring man to a higher level of being is through rites of initiation. Through these rites, the novices are stripped of their ego formed from societal norms and made to experience another world, another consciousness, of which they previously had no inkling.

In tribal society, the individual is totally subsumed by the group due to the tremendous emotional attachment to group beliefs arising through initiation rites and continually reinforced through rituals and ceremonies:

> In primitive societies...the nature and order of the world, or certain specially important features of this order, are a mystery, in the sense of a received doctrine, revealed in many cases at the critical moment of adolescence, when the mind is most plastic and impressionable. The rites of initiation are of a terrifying character, often including protracted torture. They are well calculated to affect their object, which is to enforce these socially important representations with the strongest emotional color and power. They are not to be pale intellectual opinions, at the option of the individual to take or leave upon his own estimate of their probability; they are to be objects if indefensible faith, charged with awful and tremendous feelings, fraught with associations of the most terrific experiences.[57]

These initiation rites are thus meant to produce a loss of personality and even consciousness due to the severity of the rituals made on both the body and mind of the initiates. The rites are meant in fact to create a 'new being' following upon the death of the old that had taken place during the rites.[58] The initiates are taught the secret spiritual lore and rituals of the tribe and sometimes even given a new name. In this way, the things and beings of this new world become "sacred," for their entire previous life has been "sacrificed" to arrive at this point (the roots of the two words being the same). What is common everywhere is the assumption that there are cosmic energies of a higher order that can transform man from within. But to have access to these energies, a man or woman must die to his or her

---

[57] Ibid., 46.

[58] Lévy-Bruhl, *How Natives Think* (Salem, NH: Ayer, 1984), 352-53.

previous life of imagination and ignorance and so be open to the light within of which he or she was previously totally unaware.[59]

What must be emphasized here is that in contradistinction to modern civilized man, tribal man is in no way 'individual' in his attitude or thoughts, which are totally subsumed by the group. All beliefs and practices are, and can only be, those of all members of the group:

> We may be certain that, the further we go back into the prehistoric past of any race of mankind, the less the individual will count, and the more his social group, however it may be defined, will be the unitary factor.[60]

Even our modern pretension to individuality can also be put into question: we are not born into a *tabula rasa* but a society and language having ready-made concepts, categories, and ways of thinking that we are obliged to follow (for lack of any alternative) as we grow up and mature.[61]

The Hopi language, for example, does not have tenses, rather time is related to distance; the farther away an event is geographically, the more it is in the past. This fact colors the nature of how a Hopi experiences and conceives the world. Cornford in fact puts the whole purpose of our book in question:

> Translation from one language to another is impossible, from an ancient to a modern language grotesquely impossible, because of these profound differences of collective representation, which no 'translation' will ever transfer.[62]

---

[59] Gordon, *The Original Revelation*, 35-6.

[60] Cornford, F.M., *From Religion to Philosophy: A Study in the Origins of Western Speculation.* (Princeton, NJ: Princeton University Press, 1991), 48-58. [First published in 1912 by E. Arnold, London]

[61] Ibid., 45.

[62] Ibid.

Traditional vs. Modern Civilization

It was the ancient Greeks who began to look at the parts in and for themselves at the expense of the whole, who began to individualize man as an independent element, falsely raising him out of nature so to speak, as if the philosophers themselves were not part of the world they was analyzing. It was this mentality that the West followed, and has been following, up to our day. We saw through our previous discussion of quantum physics the dead end to which this has led. Perhaps, we are in fact, as Fritjof Capra says in the title of his book at "the turning point," an era where science is beginning to look for the Whole once again:

> At the beginning of the century, when physicists extended the range of their investigations into the realms of atomic and subatomic phenomena, they suddenly became aware of the limitations of their classical ideas and had to radically revise many of their basic concepts about reality.[63]

René Guénon goes far beyond even this attitude for—however "revolutionary" the scientific ideas of Capra may be—Guénon would consider them to be a positive blip on a curve heading straight downward. For him, the modern systems approach, however closer to reality it may be compared to the reductionist approach, is still impregnated with scientism, with what can be measured, relegated uniquely to the physical level of existence, and not based on any metaphysical principle whatsoever:

> The profane sciences, of which the modern world is so proud, are really only the degenerate residue of ancient traditional sciences. Moreover, quantity itself, to which modern science endeavors to reduce everything, is, so to speak, from the point of view by which it is envisaged, only the 'residue' of an existence emptied of everything that constituted its essence.[64]

---

[63] Capra, *The Turning Point*, 33.

[64] Guénon, *Le règne de la quantité*, 13.

The metaphysic of the ancient Traditions exists now in text and practice ready to be studied and experienced, but even if Western scientists take the above words to heart, we fear it may still be many hundreds of years before a return to this hoary knowledge—albeit with a new language—becomes general, and this only if a cataclysm does not arrive first because of man's ego-centered relationship to the world. The problem with contemporary man is his inability to go beyond the study of the parts thus blinding him to the Whole. It is for this reason that modern man cannot understand how the symbolic expression of Traditional societies can be compatible with the science of our time, for he excludes *a priori* everything that cannot be measured and thus limits his experience to only the physical plane.[65]

Schuon compares the superficiality of modern mentality to the deeper mind of Traditional man:

> [E]verything is touched on and nothing is assimilated; ideas no longer bite into the intelligence, which slides over concepts without taking time to really to grasp them. The modern mind moves 'on the surface,' all the time playing with mental images, while not knowing their possibilities and role; whereas the traditional mind proceeds in depth, whence come doctrines, which may seem dogmatist, but are fully sufficient and effectual for those who know what a doctrine is. Twentieth century man has lost the sense of repose and contemplation; living on husks, he no longer knows what fruit is like.[66]

To understand more fully what might have been the mentality of man in a Traditional culture, we are now going to look more closely at the work of perhaps the greatest exponent of this symbolic language, René Guénon (1886-1951), whom we have previously cited, a Frenchman born in Blois, France as a

---

[65] Frithjof Schuon, *Stations of Wisdom* (Bloomington: World Wisdom Books, 1995), ix.

[66] Ibid., xi

40

Catholic, who spent many years in Paris publishing numerous articles and books, and who finished his life as a Moslem Sufi in Cairo.[67] As a young man, he frequented many different sects, cults and temples, from Gnostics to freemasons, but gradually came to know true masters of the Hindu, Taoist and Islamic traditions from whom he received initiatory knowledge. Through his fine discrimination and metaphysical bent, he was able to separate the wheat from the chaff and produced a work of unparalleled acuity in terms of Traditional thought, cosmology, metaphysics and symbolism all the while providing a devastating critique of modern Western civilization.

According to Guénon, a civilization by definition must be based on metaphysical principles, principles which can only be expressed in symbolic mode. We have already briefly discussed the mentality of tribal cultures, but we need to understand the nature of a high Traditional civilization and its symbolic mode of expression, such as that which existed in the Christian Middle Ages, in ancient Egypt, India, China, Mesopotamia, Persia and others. Just as words over time lose their original sense, so civilizations as embodied in the mentality of their people lose the meaning on which they were founded. To help us understand the symbolism of ancient civilizations and the principles behind them, a comparison between our own civilization with those of ancient traditions can only be of great help. This is why the work of René Guénon can be so useful, since not only does he present Traditional symbols from their deepest spiritual and metaphysical level, he also provides an analysis of modern civilization in terms of how far it has traveled from its original foundation based on Universal Law.[68]

---

[67] Paul Chacornac, *La Vie Simple de René Guénon* (Paris: Les Éditions Traditionnelles, 1958), *passim*.

[68] The works of René Guénon that deal mainly with this theme are the following (with date first published):

- *Introduction générale à l'étude des doctrines hindoues* (1921)

The general tenor of Guénon's critique of Western civilization can be summarized in these opening words of *Orient et Occident*, published in 1924 when he was 38:

> Modern Western civilization appears in history as a veritable anomaly: among all those of which we have more or less complete knowledge, this civilization is the only one that has developed in a purely material way. This monstrous development, whose beginning coincides with what we have come to call the Renaissance, has been accompanied—as it fatally had to be—by a corresponding intellectual[69] regression. We do not say equivalent, for it has to do with two orders of things between which no common measure can be made. This regression has come to such a point that Western man of today does not know any longer what pure spirituality could be, or even suspect that such a thing could exist, from which arises their disdain, not only for Eastern civilizations, but even for the European Middle Ages, whose mentality escapes them no less completely. How to make understood the interest a totally speculative knowledge might have to people for whom intelligence is only a means to act on matter and turn it to practical ends, and for whom science, in the restricted sense that they have of it, is worthy in so far as it is, above all, susceptible to produce industrial applications?[70]

This limited view which modern man has of beings and things, the culture-centric attitude which assumes that "progress" can be measured by the amount of the gross national product, is not, of course, universal. As Spengler says:

- *Orient et Occident* (1924)
- *La Crise du monde moderne* (1927)
- *Autorité spirituelle et pouvoir temporel* (1929)
- *La Métaphysique orientale* (1939)
- *Le règne de la quantité et les signes des temps* (1945)

[69] Guénon reserves the word "intellect" and its derivatives for that which relates to knowing by direct perception, a "knowledge of the heart," rather than the individual's reasoning faculty to which we often apply this same word. For this reason, we sometimes translate this word as "spiritual," depending on the case.

[70] René Guénon, *Orient et Occident*, 3rd ed. (Paris: Les Éditions Véga, 1964), 19-20. [This and the following citations of Guénon are our translations.]

We men of the Western Culture are, with our historical sense, an exception and not a rule. World-history is our world picture and not all mankind's.[71]

Guénon's critique of the Western world, which we are going to further develop by contrasting it with his conception of a Traditional civilization, will enable us to see how difficult it is for us, living today in the West, to even begin to understand the mentality of those living in the East, let alone ancient peoples. But Kipling, it seems, was wrong, for East and West *have* met and the East, once based on Tradition and spiritual principles, is in the process of succumbing to the naked materialism of the West. While all this may be true, it is probably just as true that this process is happening by law. According to the ancient traditions, all civilizations, once born from Universal Principles, pass through periods of growth, maturity, decline and death.

The project of every being in Traditional civilization is to become one with the whole, to be integrated and impregnated at once with the universe. This type of being is far from the analytical thought of modern Western man that originated in ancient Greece; so far away, in fact, that to understand Traditional man, to understand, for example, the symbolism of ancient Egypt, it would take, it seems, a conversion of the likes of St. Paul on the road to Damascus. Humanity does not necessarily evolve in one direction and a people that seems 'backward' or 'archaic' from a modern material point of view may in fact be evolving towards a completely different aim.

Another difficulty for Western man to understand the nature of ancient symbolism would be, it seems, his total concern for practical material benefits, which can only lead to a spiritual emptiness, misplaced morality, and sentimentality. Guénon, as usual, says it best:

---

[71] Oswald Spengler, *The Decline of the West,* abridged ed. (Oxford: Oxford University Press, 1961), 12.

> [T]his degradation of intelligence...leads to its identification with the most restricted and inferior of all its uses: action on matter for purely practical ends. This so-called 'intellectual progress' is thus indeed no more than 'material progress' itself.... In truth, most of Western humanity does not conceive intelligence in any other way. It is reduced for them, not even to reason in the Cartesian sense, but to the tiniest part of that reason, to its most elementary operations, to what always remains in strict relation with the perceptible world, which they have made the unique and exclusive field of their activity.[72]

This citation, which seems to us to cut to the very heart of modern Western mentality, is completed by the following, which describe the shifting sands on which modern Western civilization is based:

> Be that as it may, what the West calls its civilization, others call barbarity, because it lacks precisely what is essential: that is, a principle of a higher order.[73]... Pure intellect being suppressed, each particular and contingent domain is considered independent so that, trampling on each other, all is mixed up and confused in an inextricable chaos. Natural relations are inversed: that which should be subordinate affirms itself as autonomous and all hierarchy is abolished in the name of a chimerical equality, both in the mental as well as the social order. And, since equality is, in spite of all, impossible in fact, false hierarchies are created in which anything at all is put at the top: science, industry, morality, politics or finance, for lack of having the only thing that could, and normally should, be supreme, that is to say once more, lack of real principles.[74]

In contrast to this description of the spiritual bankruptcy of the modern world, Guénon describes Traditional civilization as

---

[72] Confirming Guénon's viewpoint 76 years later, one only has to look at the frenzy for "new technologies": computers, mobile phones, interactive television, Internet communication, and so on, that is proliferating in our day.

[73] Guénon, *Orient et Occident*, 37

[74] Ibid., 148-49.

based on metaphysical principles that are necessarily the same wherever they are found. They are always the same because these principles are not relative to any particular culture but reflect truths that are universal in both space and time:

> By reason of the universality of its principles...all traditional doctrines are in essence identical. There is and can only be one metaphysics, whatever the diverse ways by which it is expressed, in so far as it is expressible at all using the language at one's disposal, which, besides, always only has a symbolic role. And if this is so, it is simply because the truth is one, and also because, being in itself absolutely independent of our conceptions, it imposes itself in the same way on all those who understand it.[75]

According to Guénon, the result of this lack of principles and of higher goals in Western civilization, which is now spreading over the globe, is a society in constant change, with people totally infatuated with the latest fashion in clothes, technology, economics or even ideas. Because there is no higher purpose to the society as a whole, the last thing is taken as the ultimate reality by which their 'happiness' will be attained—*without any reference to a higher principle.* Because of this lack of principles, there is this frenetic pace to achieve, to be the first, to act for action's sake without any interior goal in mind. In the scientific realm, this leads for the most part to research for the sake of research, to finding one's niche in the academic world rather than to find real answers to important questions. Even psychology, Guénon says, supposedly turned towards man's interior, stops at what is most superficial and exterior of the profound nature of man's being. And taking the place of true intellect is a moralism based on pure sentimentalism, easily seen in the proliferation of various Christian sects totally lacking any

---

[75] Ibid., 193.

45

doctrine whatsoever, and which appeal only to a person's emotions. As Whitehead says:

> Thus religion is solitariness; and if you are never solitary, you are never religious. Collective enthusiasms, revivals, institutions, churches, rituals, bibles, codes of behaviour, are the trappings of religion, its passing forms. They may be useful, or harmful; they may be authoritatively ordained, or merely temporary expedients. But the end of religion is beyond all this.[76]

The result of such a civilization is the total inability of people to understand the essential nature of metaphysical doctrines:

> The far-eastern theory of 'non-action,' the Hindu theory of 'deliverance,' are things inaccessible to that ordinary Western mentality for which it is inconceivable that one could dream of liberating oneself from action, and even more so that one could effectively arrive at such a thing. Furthermore, action is commonly looked at only under its most external forms, those which correspond strictly to physical movement. From this arises the need for speed, this feverish movement, which is so particular to contemporary life, to act for the pleasure of acting, which can only be called agitation.... Nothing would be easier than to show how this is incompatible with all that is reflection and concentration, thus with the essential means of all true knowledge.[77]

Apart from the materialism and sentimentalism of modern Western civilization, Guénon also faults the modern conception of science as another proof of the degradation of the West in relation to Traditional cultures such as that of ancient Egypt. In fact, we could even say that science has become the real 'religion' of our time in the sense that final judgment on the nature of the world, of the cosmos, is given to scientists and not to the churches, temples and synagogues, which have been relegated to moral judgments, good works, and easing of

---

[76] Whitehead, *Religion in the Making*, 15.

[77] Guénon, *Orient et Occident*, 85-6.

consciences. Some may say that this is all for the better, since belief is based on fact found through the scientific method. The problem, however, is that the scientific method is only concerned with what can be measured, and anything or any phenomena that cannot be measured is, for the mainstream culture, considered as non-existent. Even psychology is only considered a science in so far as one sticks to measuring brain waves or monitoring neuro-transmitting chemicals. Furthermore, this Western science is not based on any higher-order principles, any sense of hierarchy and order in the universe. Nature is simply divided up according to what meets the eye (microscope and telescope included): astrophysics, molecular biology, geology, chemistry, etc., and each subject is studied without any relation to a higher or lower order of existence, or in other words there is no knowledge of a hierarchical ordering of the world and the influences flowing between them. All this is in contradistinction to Traditional civilizations where knowledge flows from a higher metaphysic and where a study of the natural world has a necessary, if limited, place as a search for symbols of a superior order, as a support for reaching the known ultimate goal of the society and each individual within it: the attainment of transcendence.

In Traditional society, it is the priest who has the knowledge, not the 'scientist'; or, even better, the priest is the scientist, for in Traditional society, there is really only one science, the science of transformation, of the spiritual elevation of man. All activity in such a society is geared to this end, and without understanding this essential point it would be impossible to even begin to decipher the symbolism of ancient cultures.

Guénon's blast at Western science is not at science per se, but at its claim to encompass the whole gamut of knowledge without considering the possibility that there are also unseen 'facts' that partake of another order of existence, cannot be assimilated to the scientific method and which concern the realm of Being.

These unseen 'facts,' while not measurable, are presented in a metaphysical doctrine by the founding priests of any civilization. The Bible is not a 'book of wisdom' or a collection of edifying stories; neither is it a set of moral injunctions; or at least its ultimate meaning is not any of these, but rather a metaphysical treatise on man's possible spiritual evolution. A metaphysical doctrine is based on inner experience of a spiritual nature and thus concerns itself with what is beyond the rational mind used by science. While "meta-physical" may mean that its domain is beyond the perception of the five senses, this does not mean that man cannot enter into and experience a reality not based on the senses and thought.[78] It is this possibility that modern science denies, at least implicitly, and it is this denial that Guénon rails against.

What are the basic points that Guénon finds fault with in modern science, which he labels a "superstition"?[79] Above all, it is its analytic rather than synthetic nature leading to an ever greater fragmentation of knowledge into smaller and smaller parts and losing itself in the enumeration of innumerable facts. This analytic and reductionist nature of modern science has been the basis of modern thinking for only 300 years out of the 6000 man has been writing down his thoughts, not to mention the unknown tens of thousands of years of preceding oral traditions.

It would be good at this point to point out the many thousands of years that *homo sapiens* have existed to show how extremely limited in time the modern conception of the world has existed. The latest estimates, based on fossil and DNA evidence, shows that modern man, *homo sapiens,* appeared in Africa around 200,000 years ago and his first known symbolic manifestations took place 80,000 years ago with African rock carvings.

---

[78] Thought, in the Hindu tradition, is considered simply as another sense on the same level as the "five senses."

[79] Guénon, *Orient et Occident,* 41.

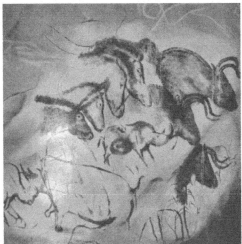

Beginning around 40,000 years ago, *homo sapiens* spread over Europe and began the cave paintings of animals and geometric drawings that we can see at Lascaux, Chauvet, Altamira and many other places. See Figure 5.

Figure 5 Prehistoric art in the Chauvet cavern in France

We must assume that any human who could paint with such dexterity must be able to have a certain conception of the world he lived in, and which was carried on orally from generation to generation by the society in which he existed, just as our modern conception is carried on by the civilization in which we are born into.

In 1994 a prehistoric site was discovered at Göbekli Tepe in southeastern Turkey that was dated around 11,000 years ago, around 6,000 years before Stonehenge in England and the Great Pyramid in Egypt. The site is made up of circles of huge T-shaped pillars reaching as high as 16 feet and weighing up to 10 tons, with at least one ring reaching 65 feet across. It is estimated that there are at least 16 more rings to be unearthed. On the pillars in relief are intricately carved animals such as foxes, lions, scorpions, bulls, and many others. Whether these reliefs were a form of symbolism is impossible to say, since no other kind of inscriptions, against which they could be compared, have yet been found at this site or any other of that epoch. Now the reason we are bringing up this site is that no remains of people living in permanent settlements at the site were found, thus providing evidence that the site was essentially ritual in character, perhaps one of humanity's first temples. See Figure 6. Also, from the excavations made so far of thousands of bones of wild animals, the people who lived at Göbekli Tepe did not have domesticated animals nor farmed agricultural products. These discoveries go against the common view of

prehistorians that breeding and agriculture were necessary for settled communities to arise with the organization and resources to develop a hierarchical social structure allowing temples like Göbekli Tepe to be constructed. If in fact religion preceded breeding and agriculture, it cannot be said that religion was a social invention used to unify a people as many would attest, but rather was based on man's desire to return to, or attain to, a state of higher consciousness.

Figure 6 Monument at Göbekli Tepe

The civilization that created Göbekli Tepe and those before were based on a hunter-gatherer culture that eventually gave way to the Neolithic sedentary farming and breeding culture, so that…

> …one goes from a horizontal world where man considers himself a species among many others, to a vertical world. In the world of hunters-gatherers man situates himself at the same level as the animals he is chasing. Then having become a farmer and breeder, he feels as though he is separated from the rest of nature, at the summit of the animal hierarchy, and inscribes himself in another hierarchy dominated by the gods.[80]

---

[80] Lemercier, Olivier, quoted in Jean-François Mandoty "Comment l'homme a changé de nature*", Les Cahiers de Science & Vie*, No. 124 Aug.-Sep. 2011 ("Aux origines du sacré et des dieux "), 50. [Our translation]

This separation from nature was the preparation for the modern rationalistic outlook that began with the early Greek philosophers only around 2600 years ago, before which, according to what we know from their remains, civilization was based on a divine, mythological and hierarchical basis. Before modern science arose with the Renaissance, medieval thinking was enveloped by that of the Church, which saw nature as a symbol and reflection of 'God.' The understanding of Natural Laws was undertaken not to *use* the laws of nature to ameliorate man's lot, but to see more fully how they fulfilled 'God's purpose.' In essence, the world was not to be analyzed, but simply lived in by the grace of an all-powerful and unknowable God. From the Renaissance precursors—Copernicus (1473-1543), Kepler (1571-1630), Galileo (1564-1642) and Bacon (1561-1626)—arose the thought of René Descartes (1596-1650) whose two main assertions were to create the intellectual uterus for the modern age: one, that ultimate Truth could be known not through Pope and priests but only through reason and science, a science based on mathematical laws from which the knowledge of all nature could be deduced through analysis; and two, that mind and matter were totally distinct and in no way could the one influence the other, which led to his view of the universe as pure machinery that could be completely known through a study of the arrangement and interactions of its parts.

While this view led to the scientific discoveries of the modern age, it refuted the Eastern idea, held for thousands of years, of an interpenetrating dynamically and organically interrelated hierarchy of increasingly subtle worlds in which Descartes' physical world existed as the lowest and most inferior.

The man who nailed shut the analytic scientific method as the basis for the West's worldview was Sir Isaac Newton (1642-1727). As did Descartes, Newton used experimentation and analysis as his means of uncovering the riddles of nature. For Newton, matter was made of homogeneous indivisible particles existing in absolute space and time, neither of which had any influence on the particles moving within them. From this, Newton developed his universal theory of gravity, which had governed Western scientific thought until Einstein. According to Newton, the whole universe was created by God: the particles, the forces between them and the laws of motion. From then on, the universe ran as a great machine of cause and effect with God no longer needed to interfere in its functioning. With this as his basis, Newton developed his laws of universal gravitation, which seemed, for all intents and purposes, to perfectly describe the movement of celestial bodies and other natural phenomena. Descartes' vision of a mechanical world seemed confirmed:

> This picture of a perfect world-machine implied an external creator; a monarchical god who ruled the world from above by imposing his divine law on it. The physical phenomena themselves were not thought to be divine in any sense, and when science made it more and more difficult to believe in such a god, the divine disappeared completely from the scientific world view, leaving behind the spiritual vacuum that has become characteristic of the mainstream of our culture.[81]

The result of such a mentality is summed up by Schuon:

> When a man is deprived of the divine 'existenciation' or when he believes himself so to be, he must find something to take its place, on pain of collapsing into his own nothingness, and he does so by substituting for 'existence' precisely this kind of 'dedication' to action. In other words, his imagination and his feelings capitulate to the ideal of the machine; for the machine has no value except by virtue of what it produces, and so man exists only by virtue of what he does, and not what he is; but a man defined by action is no longer man, he is a beaver or an ant.[82]

---

[81] Capra, *The Turning Point*, 52-3.

[82] Schuon, *Light on the Ancient Worlds,* 2d ed. (Bloomington: World Wisdom Books, 1984), 40.

Even though Einstein's relativity and the quantum mechanics of Heisenberg, Bohr and others has disrupted this mechanistic view from the beginning of the 20th century, these theories, while satisfying physicists as being closer to reality, have not as yet fundamentally challenged the worldview of man in the West, no doubt because of their extreme abstraction which leaves man unable to visualize in his mind what these theories propose. Stuttering attempts at other models of reality, those of holography and systems theory discussed above, also undermine the "world as machine" viewpoint, but these are a far cry from becoming paradigms in the near future.

We might say that most people are very happy with "bread and circuses," the material results and distractions which Western science has wrought, and it is only a small minority in the modern world who intuit that there is something dreadfully wrong with life in the West, and increasingly over the whole globe, and that a supreme effort must be made to counter this downward tendency, at least on an individual level:

> [Since] the nature of the world—society—is to fall, to disintegrate, and to degenerate,…it requires on the part of man an incessant effort to overturn this downward pull and to rise, or at least not to fall, for which he needs to enroll all of his modalities of being from the intellectual to the existential"[83]…[B]eing born entails suffering for he must struggle to reverse the downward tendency of the cosmogonic projection, the inertia and ceaseless pulling and tugging of which relentlessly seeks to drag him down and away from the happiness of his celestial origin.[84]

Guénon, apart from his criticism of the above mechanistic and fact-laden viewpoint of modern science, goes on to argue the lack of any theory based on universal truths and which is thus continually superseded by the next theory always accompanied

---

[83] Perry, *On Awakening and Remembering*, 84.

[84] Ibid., 146-7.

by a touting of a false idea of "progress" towards a vague conception of some illusive "truth." The result of all this is that men are cut off from any higher principial order, and that, in sum, they cannot see the forest for the trees. To this he contrasts Traditional science, based on metaphysical principles that are never lost sight of, and to which any science is only a secondary manifestation:

> The ancient conception, which has always been that of the East, holds any science as valid less than what it is in itself than what it is in so far as it expresses in its own way, and represents in the scheme of things, a reflection of the immutable higher order in which all that possesses some reality must necessarily participate. And, as the nature of this truth incarnates itself, in a way, within the idea of tradition, all science thus appears as an extension of the traditional doctrine itself, as one of its secondary and contingent applications.[85]

According to Guénon, rather than the continual 'progress' of the world that the material results of science would have us believe is the case, we are in fact very far into the last of the four ages, the Hindu Kali-Yuga or its equivalent in the West, the "Age of Iron." That is to say, we are near the end of a cycle and the beginning of another, and the fact that we are at the end of the last age means that we are at the farthest point from the spiritual principles of the beginning and, in general, totally immersed in the material, physical world. As Guénon says, "This fall could be characterized as a progressive materialization, for the expression of the principle is pure spirituality."[86] Even philosophy, taken today by many as the highest endeavor of the human mind, is, according to Guénon, at the service of the degeneration of the society and the scientism which has become its basis. Ever more rational and 'scientific,' it has completely lost sight of true knowledge based on pure spirituality,

---

[85] Ibid., 54-5.

[86] Guénon, *La Crise du monde moderne*, 17.

something which Shakespeare echoed when he wrote: "There are more things in Heaven and earth, Horatio, than are dreamt of in your philosophy."

Another point which Guénon puts forward against modern civilization that is totally against the grain of modern-day thought, and no doubt brings down a rain of insults and abuse whenever it is heard, is his belief that all knowledge is not for everyone. In the nature of the Biblical saying not to "throw pearls before swine" or the Koran's "but none understands them save those who know," he advances the belief that the hierarchical nature of the cosmos is necessarily reflected in the hierarchical nature of human society and thus, rather than the modern viewpoint that falsifies nature by promoting the idea that all knowledge should be given to everyone equally, which means lowering its meaning so that it can be taken in by the largest number, knowledge should be preserved at its most superior and purest level and handed down only to those capable of receiving it in its unadulterated form.

The preservation of spiritual knowledge was undoubtedly one aspect of the caste system in India, where metaphysical knowledge was only taught within the Brahman caste of priests. Now the caste system, according to Guénon, is "nothing but the difference in nature existing among human individuals, and which establishes a hierarchy among them."[87] In the European Middle Ages, for example, the clergy, the nobility, the third estate and the serfs corresponded to the four Hindu castes Brahmana (priests), Kshatriya (administrative, military), Vaishya (economic), and Shudra (worker). This hierarchical nature of society is in fact the case in any Traditional culture, where it is always assumed that there are "those who know" and those who do not. In ancient Egypt, there was the "House of

---

[87] René Guénon, *Autorité spirituelle et Pouvoir Temporel,* 3rd ed. (Paris: Les Editions Véga, 1964), 16-7.

Life," a school attached to the main temples that, as far as we know, handed down knowledge of the highest order. Guénon makes the point that because of the "scientism" reigning in the modern age, any knowledge that is not so-called "scientific" is immediately discredited and not even considered as worthy of being taught, even to an elite, if such a thing would even be possible in our democratic age. It is for this reason, according to Guénon, that metaphysical thought is almost never studied in the West in its pure form, that is, as a means of approaching spiritual transformation, but only as a means of fulfilling the requirements of such and such university degree.

What would it mean in the West for metaphysical thought to be taught and an "intellectual elite" be constituted as Guénon defines it, which is not to be confused with the Western notion of the same term? Here, Guénon assures us that such a teaching is not a question of universities or other such organizations as they presently exist in the West.

In our ultimate goal of understanding the symbolism of ancient civilizations, we must understand what "learning" means in a Traditional high civilization. For this reason, we continue with what Guénon would consider necessary to create an "intellectual elite" in the West:

> The first difficulty is to reach those who are qualified, and who could in no way even suspect their own possibilities. A second difficulty would then be to make a selection and to eliminate those who believe themselves qualified without them effectively being so. But we should say that no doubt this elimination would take place almost by itself. All these questions would not present themselves where an organized traditional teaching exists, where each can receive according to the level his own capacity and up to the precise degree that he is capable of reaching....[88]

---

[88] Guénon, *Orient et Occident*, 171-73.

Thus, to understand the symbols of such a Traditional civilization as ancient Egypt, symbols which represent the metaphysical basis of the civilization itself, is no easy matter. It is not a question, as one would normally do in the West, to "go to school" or "take a course." In a Traditional society, understanding of metaphysical truths, reading the symbols of the culture at their most profound level, thus depends on individual aptitude and not on "organized education."

Which gives us pause as to our goal of trying to understand ancient symbolism. But nevertheless, Guénon does provide a means for approaching a study of symbolism; no doubt the one he used in his many studies of various Traditional symbols[89]:

> [O]ne must start from the highest, that is, from principles and then gradually descend to the various orders of applications always rigorously observing the hierarchical dependence existing between them.[90]

It seems then that in order to really understand the metaphysical principles behind the symbols of ancient civilizations, much more is needed than simply filling our minds with the viewpoints of the innumerable others who have taken up such a task and provided us with dictionaries and encyclopedias of symbolism. What is needed is rather for us to attain a degree of contemplation that allows for metaphysical knowledge to be *directly* experienced in ourselves at the highest level of purity we are capable of. Only then can we even begin to conceive what the spiritual aim of Egyptian civilization might have been. It is only this direct experience of metaphysical truths that can allow us to understand real spirituality. Modern man as he is does not even suspect that this possibility exists, believing as he does that only his reasoning mind can provide him with knowledge.

---

[89] For example: *Le Roi du monde* (1927), *Le symbolisme de la croix* (1931), *La Grande Triade* (1946), *Symboles fondamentaux de la science sacrée* (1962).

[90] Guénon, *La Crise du monde moderne*, 52.

The content of any symbolism taken in its deepest meaning can always be taken in a hierarchical sense so that any 'thing' can be taken as a symbol of something higher leading up to ultimate principles:

> In this way, from level to level, all things link up and correspond to contribute to a universal and total harmony; for harmony...is nothing but a reflection of the principial unity within the multiplicity of the manifested world—and it is this correspondence which is the real basis of symbolism. This is why the laws of a lower domain can always be taken as symbols of the realities of a higher order, where they have their deepest meaning and which is at the same time their principle and their aim.[91]

This is also why we can never say that such-and-such a thing *only* represents such-and-such another thing without referring to the level of existence on which the correspondence is based, for both things could represent a principle higher than both and on which each is based at its own level of existence. Which is to say that all things manifested in this world, while being real and actual at their level of existence, are at the same time symbols of a higher law or principle by which they acquire their essential meaning. Therefore, when we study the symbolism of a Traditional culture like that of ancient Egypt, where this principle was not only known but implemented by the priests in terms of created representations, architecture, and the organization of society, we have a means of understanding the signification of many things in the culture through a study of metaphysical principles and their application within the culture. We must therefore assume that what we are studying was created with a higher knowledge possessed by a caste of priests.

The pharaoh, for example, should never be considered as simply the "head of state" or "king of the Egyptians" as we are wont to

---

[91] Guénon, *Autorité spirituelle et Pouvoir temporel*, 22. [Our italics]

say, for he represented much more than that. As the bearer of both spiritual authority and temporal power, he incarnated within himself the unity of the 'center' harmonizing the two natures of the world and from which all spiritual and temporal authority flows at different levels of existence: from the spiritual arises knowledge; from the temporal arises action, but action based on the knowledge of the spiritual is incarnated in his being. By acting spontaneously according to principles, pharaoh thus creates order in the land, for "all action that does not arise from knowledge lacks a principle and is no more than vain agitation...."[92] To carry this symbolism further, we could say with Guénon that the function of the Pope or the "Pontiff" (from the Latin meaning "bridge") represents the link between Heaven and Earth for all men of the Church in the same way as did the function of the pharaoh for the Egyptians. The symbolism of the Sphinx also represents these two *hierarchical* principles united in one spontaneous being, which can be interpreted as spiritual and earthly, immovable and moving, knowledge and action, wisdom and force, and so on, depending on the level and perspective on which it is being considered.[93] See Figure 7.

While in Part 2 we will discuss more thoroughly the function and symbolism of the pharaoh, we wish here to simply show the type of thought necessary to understand Traditional symbolism in all its ramifications.

Now certain symbols have to do with rites[94] that take place through the direction of the priests, and since a symbol is a sort of frozen ritual gesture, it is important to understand on what the rite itself is based—which Guénon succinctly provides in these words:

---

[92] Guénon, *Autorité spirituelle et Pouvoir temporel*, 44.

[93] Ibid., 51.

[94] From the Sanskrit *Rita*, "order."

[T]he rite is, etymologically, that which is accomplished conforming to 'order,' and which consequently imitates or reproduces at its level the very process of manifestation; and that is why, in a strictly traditional civilization, any act whatever assumes an essentially ritual character.[95]

Figure 7 The Sphinx of Giza

In other words, a rite is accomplished, at the level of man, as a microcosm of a cosmic manifestation, itself based on metaphysical principles. That is why, on studying certain ancient symbols, it behooves us to always keep in mind not only the level of the rite to which it may refer, but its correspondence at the level of the macrocosm, that is, the manifestation of the same law at the cosmic level, and the metaphysical principle behind this chain of manifestation where the lower is always the symbol of the higher.

Another aspect of Egyptian symbolism that is so important is geometry and its use in the architecture of the temples and pyramids of ancient Egypt, a point largely elucidated by R. A. Schwaller de Lubicz in his monumental tome, *The Temple of Man,* of which we will have more to say later. Here is what Guénon has to say on the subject:

---

[95] Guénon, *Le règne de la quantité et les signes des temps*, 43.

> [G]eometry is nothing else than the very science of measurement, but it goes without saying that it is a question here of a geometry understood above all in its symbolic and initiatic sense, and of which profane geometry is no longer but a simple degenerate vestige, deprived of the profound meaning that it had at the origin and which has been entirely lost for modern mathematicians. It is on this that are essentially based all the conceptions assimilating divine activity as the producer and arranger of worlds by way of 'geometry,' and consequently by way of 'architecture' also, which is inseparable from it.[96]

Again, when studying the symbolism of geometry in temples and sacred monuments of ancient Traditional high civilizations—symbols in themselves of metaphysical principles—and the forms by which these principles took shape in architecture, all has to do, according to Guénon, with the qualitative symbolism of number and direction so important in Traditional civilizations, rather than the actual quantitative measurements which so interest modern archaeologists, both academic and "new age." The pyramid, for example, is composed of triangular sides ascending from a square base meeting at a point. Now the square represents the number four, the triangle the number three and the point one. Understanding the pyramid then, would be a question not of measuring all the possible lines and angles, nor of digging inside and around it looking for clues, but rather of finding a way to comprehend the metaphysical principles behind the numbers four, three and one as represented by the triangles ascending from the

Figure 8 The Great Pyramid of Giza

---

[96] Ibid., 45-6.

square to arrive at a point. It is this type of understanding that we need to pursue. See Figure 8.

Another important point to keep in mind when looking at symbols in ancient Traditional civilizations is to never consider them as 'art' in the modern conception of the term. Art as we know it did not exist in these cultures. There was no such idea of 'creating beauty' or "art for art's sake." Beauty was always a by-product of that which was created for the purpose of supporting metaphysical principles, and whose content was controlled by the priests. As Coomaraswamy reminds us: "Works of art are reminders; in other words, supports of contemplation."[97] Or even more deeply, we might say that Beauty *is* Truth in that the highest Truth corresponds to its reflection in man, and when this Truth is expressed in a perceptible way by an artisan according to the knowledge of the priests, a person considers it "beautiful" because it relates to what is highest and deepest in himself. The 'artist' then was really an artisan at the service of the priests who held the knowledge to be expressed in the work.

For this reason, one never sees the maker's signature of any "work of art" in a Traditional culture. On the other hand, the artisan was more than just a technician. If he was a painter or a sculptor, it was because his nature led him to be a painter or a sculptor and not otherwise: "In the traditional conception…each person should normally fulfill the function to which he is destined by his very nature."[98] Furthermore, since the craft or 'art' corresponded to the nature of the artisan, it could be the basis for an initiatory work leading to the transformation of the artisan himself:

> We cannot too much emphasize that contemplation is not a passion but an act: and that where modern psychology

---

[97] Coomaraswamy, *Christian and Oriental Philosophy of Art*, 10.
[98] Guénon, *Le Règne de la quantité et les signes des temps*, 83.

sees in 'inspiration' the uprush of an instinctive and subconscious will, the orthodox philosophy sees an elevation of the artist's being to superconscious and supraindividual levels.[99]

Again, this is not "art for art's sake" or even more appropriately in our time, art to be sold. Rather it was a means to express Truths of a higher order all the while providing a support for the artisan to attain the Truths he was endeavoring to express:

> [I]f initiatic knowledge was born for him from his trade, the latter in its turn will become the field of application of this knowledge, from which he can no longer be separated. There will thus be a perfect correspondence between the interior and the exterior, and the work produced will no longer be only an expression to any degree whatever and in a more or less superficial manner, but a truly adequate expression of he who will have conceived and executed it, which will constitute a "masterpiece" in the real sense of the term.[100]

Therefore, in a Traditional civilization such as ancient Egypt (as well as in tribal cultures discussed previously), all objects of daily life, apart from their functional use, were also a support for understanding higher principles. In studying objects of ancient civilizations, no matter how seemingly banal, such as a comb or a cup, we should always keep in mind this double aspect if we do not wish to simply become "list makers" of ancient objects. In Traditional societies, each object is not only made for the practical purpose it had in daily life, but also as a symbol reflecting a higher plane of existence. In this way, it acts to remind the user of the object of a level beyond the current state in which he finds himself, and in so doing helps him to rise to this same level.

---

[99] Coomaraswamy, *Christian and Oriental Philosophy of Art*, 38.
[100] Ibid., 85-6.

Also important when discussing ancient civilizations, are the notions of geography and history held then and now. If we try to look at these aspects with our modern preconceptions, we will no doubt find only absurdities, which is exactly the case for many modern archaeologists and historians of the ancient world. For example, the battle of Kadesh between the Egyptians and the Hittites was liberally depicted on Egyptian temple walls as a great Egyptian victory, though the evidence points to it being more of a stalemate. This is generally taken as "political propaganda" by some modern archaeologists and historians who look at ancient civilizations as if the individuals comprising them had the same mentality as us in the 21st century. A battle depicted on a temple should no doubt be understood rather as an interior battle "of the soul" in the same way as it is understood in the Hindu *Bhagavad Gita* or the saints

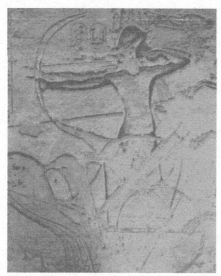

Figure 9 Ramses II at the Battle of Kadesh

on the facades of European cathedrals of the Middle Ages standing on top of defeated demons—or even on top of kings, which does not mean, of course, they defeated them in battle! See Figure 9.

In the same way, geography was not meant to explain the disposition of places as they were in the physical world, but as symbols of "place" in an interior order of the spiritual world. Thus, when the ancients spoke of a place as the "center of the world" they were not speaking of a political center, but a center of spiritual forces that is everywhere. The same holds true for the cardinal directions: when one reads in the hieroglyphs of ancient Egypt the word "West," the notion of "West" as a place of death and rebirth—however that is interpreted according to one's understanding—should be constantly kept in view; and the word should not be simply looked at as a physical direction in space.[101]

From Synthesis to Analysis: The Ancient Greek Pre-Socratics

The Traditional symbolic view of the world, prevalent everywhere in the ancient world, began to lose its hold on men's minds in the land of the Greeks during the first millennium B.C., eventually leading to the purely mental speculations of the pre-Socratic philosophers: from Thales around 630 BC through Anaximander, Xenophanes, Heraclitus, Pythagoras, Parmenides, Empedocles, Anaxagoras, Zeno and many others up to Socrates around 470 B.C. and beyond.

Our purpose here is simply to point out the different mentalities arising from a mythological, symbolic and holistic lived experience of the world as was the case, for example, in ancient Egypt, and that arising from a scientific, reasoning, and mental experience that arose in ancient Greece. As this latter perspective began with the pre-Socratic philosophers, it is at this point of rupture that the two visions can no doubt best be compared.

There is one point above all others that we would like to emphasize on this question. And that is that the pre-Socratics, perhaps for the first time, used their minds not for any practical purpose, but to pursue knowledge for its own sake. Now this enterprise, to study the world solely through mental speculation, is fraught with huge consequences, for it entails the use of the human machine in a totally one-sided manner: where the

---

[101] See René Guénon, *Le Symbolisme de la Croix* (Paris: Union Générale d'Editions, 1957).

reasoning mind reigns and emotion, sensation and instinct have no place. This may seem quite proper to the modern mentality where emotion and instinct are seen only as "getting in the way" of a "reasonable" approach to solving problems or reaching goals, but it is totally at odds with the Traditional approach on which ancient civilizations were based: the self-transformation of man into a transmitter of spiritual energies. Now this self-transformation entails the integration of all of man's parts: the mental yes, but also, and even more important, the emotional and physical, so that the entire being is attentively receptive to the energies in which he is bathed. It seems, perhaps for several reasons which we will try to elaborate, that the pre-Socratics had completely lost this Traditional religious nature and purpose of man's existence.

Before the pre-Socratics, people made sense of the world through myth, the Greeks, of course included. The pantheon of Greek gods as described in Homer's *Iliad* and *Odyssey* and Hesiod's *Theogony* was the common denominator of most all the Greek peoples. We all learned in school of Zeus, Dionysus, Aphrodite, etc., but we were never taught what was behind these stories, what they represented, for myth is not, as most modern commentators would say, simply a means to explain what is not known, an invention of the mind to make sense of how the world began or what, for example, lays behind the roar of thunder. Perhaps these myths as simple explanations of the existence of the world and natural phenomena were enough to satisfy the minds of most in the ancient world, but the origin of myth goes much deeper. In the beginning they were created as symbolic stories of an esoteric knowledge held by the priestly class, a knowledge geared not only to an understanding of the laws of the universe in itself but the reflection of these laws as found in human society and, most importantly, within man himself, who was considered in the ancient world as the microcosm of the universe, and in whom was contained all universal laws.

More precisely, as Tradition tells it, myths arose at a certain stage in the prehistoric past when man was, due to a certain degeneration of civilization, no longer able to grasp the meaning of abstract symbols such as a *mandala*, which in themselves were created—when man lost his natural connection to the transcendent—as an aid to find his way back to the ever-present center of himself where that connection is made. We would even propose, if one goes back far enough to the original meanings of the myths that have come down to us, and at the risk of going against all contemporary thought on the subject, that there are really only two mythic motifs in all civilizations: *separation* and *return*. On a macrocosmic scale, there is the separation of the original unity of the universe into first duality and then into multiplicity, and the return of the energies of these parts back to the Whole. On a microcosmic scale, there is the separation of man from his connection to the original unity of the universe which always and forever exists within himself, and his return back to this connection through spiritual practice: the return of the Prodigal Son.

According to Cornford, the breaking up of the whole into parts to be analyzed and studied, did not happen all at once and that original Greek speculation was profoundly influenced by religious concepts. Pure scientism, he asserts, did not exist among the pre-Socratic philosophers.

We propose that in the "first age" a higher state of being existed in man based on a finer energy. The change from the ancient to the modern way of experiencing the world begins long before the pre-Socratics, and which can be gleaned from the Greek myths which were part and parcel of Greek civilization. The great change in thought at that time was the relegation of the myths to stories which had lost their symbolism to men's minds and thus no longer were taken as a basis for reality: "Myth is left behind. The word *mythos*...is now redefined and devalued as the sort of story that the old poets used to tell and that old women still tell to children..." [102]. That is to say that the creation and functioning of the world no longer relied on the gods but took place as natural events.

Given the above, the whole history of modern civilization can be said to be the progressive individuation, the increasing belief by man in his own separate existence, the continual augmentation of the illusion that he is somehow "outside looking in" on the world, an existence that has become more and more based solely on man's thought divorced, alienated even, from his body and emotions, until we arrive at the ultimate absurdity of Descartes' "I think, therefore I am," which is the natural result of what began in Greece about six centuries before the Christian era and spread by Alexander the Great to the then known civilized world:

> The [Greek] philosopher sought to grasp and consider reality, to discover whatever might be permanent within it, so as to know what it truly was. But precisely in so doing he distanced himself from Being, which was manifesting itself in the presencing of all particular beings. For in his seeking, he reached out not simply to receive with openness, but also to control. Here, according to Heidegger, lies the real origin of the modern technological age. [103]

In order to understand this crucial moment in history, we must first understand how the nature of man's mind evolved as he went from a tribal way of life to large civilizations such as those of ancient Egypt, Mesopotamia, Persia, and Greece. We have seen that tribal man had a symbiotic relationship with his social group and with the surrounding nature that was integrated through totems with the tribe.

---

[102] Burkert, Walter, *Greek Religion* (Cambridge, Mass.: Harvard University Press, 1985), 310-12.

[103] William Lovitt, introduction to Martin Heidegger, *The Question Concerning Technology and Other Essays* (New York: Harper & Row, 1977), xxv.

In primitive times everything in nature was 'sacred,' including its structure, and this was so because the natural world was seen as an extension of the structure and behavior of human society. There was, in fact, no delineation between human society and the natural environment in which it existed and so the whole world was "one comprehensive system of custom and taboo."[104] Because the natural order was based on human society with its social and moral constraints, it too partook of the sacred, of what must and must not be done. A clan's totem, whatever animal or other natural element it may be, is considered identical with the clan, and the totemic rites and ceremonies concern the clan not as a collection of individuals, but the clan as an undivided whole out of which a member could not even conceive of existing. It is in this first primitive stage that there is no need of a god or anything else to represent a power outside of the group.[105]

The result of the growth in numbers of men in society, and their concomitant needs of greater organization, led to the development of the pantheons of gods that we see developed almost everywhere in ancient civilizations. What were before unknown and mysterious powers, demons, or spirits, that tribal man venerated through his rites and ceremonies, developed into various gods and goddesses that took on various forms—anthropomorphic, animal, fantastic, or other—that became fixed in images created in various media such as pictures, statues, and monuments.[106] The sorcerers, shamans, and witch doctors became the priests of organized religions.

---

[104] Cornford, *From Religion to Philosophy*, 55.

[105] Ibid., 71-78.

[106] Many examples of this process can be found in Jane Ellen Harrison, *Prolegomena to the Study of Greek Religion* (Princeton, NJ: Princeton University Press, 1991), *passim*.

Here, in fact, was the first break in man's relationship with nature, the first step towards what would become the separation of his thinking mind from the rest of his being. A man or woman was a sorcerer or shaman because he or she was in touch with certain higher energies through a state of being arrived at from knowledge provided by tribal elders or through spontaneous inner movements. The feeling of oneness that was natural in a tribal setting became, in a large civilization, a 'Teaching' developed by knowledgeable priests, and an organization to propagate this teaching. That is, a means was developed to not lose the unity man once had felt with all that surrounded him, in a word: man developed *religion*, with all its attendant rites and ceremonies, so as to, in etymological terms, keep him 'yoked' to the universe and not lose what he once had

naturally in the tribe. Some of these rites, such as the those found in the Greek mysteries of Dionysus involved ecstatic dancing and orgiastic revelry, a sort of last gasp at Oneness, in a bid to create a state that brought man out of his head into a

Figure 10 A painting of Dionysus by Gerard de Lairesse 1680

completely emotional and bodily ecstasy, or, in other words, to reach that feeling of wholeness once felt by a man with his tribe and natural surroundings. See Figure 10.

Here is how Nietzsche puts it in *The Birth of Tragedy*:

> [T]he hero is the suffering Dionysus of the Mysteries, the god experiencing in himself the agonies of individuation, of whom wonderful myths tell that as a boy he was torn

to pieces by the Titans[107] and now is worshiped in this state as Zagreus....[W]e are therefore to regard the state of individuation as the origin and primal cause of all suffering, as something objectionable in itself....But the hope of the epopts [initiates] looked toward a rebirth of Dionysus, which we must now dimly conceive as the end of individuation. It was for this coming third Dionysus that the epopts' roaring hymns of joy resounded. And it is this hope alone that casts a gleam of joy upon the features of a world torn asunder and shattered into individuals.[108]

The religion of Orpheus in Greece was no doubt of this nature:

The great step that Orpheus took was that, while he kept that old Bacchic faith that man might become a god, he altered the conception of what a god was, and he sought to obtain that godhead by wholly different means. The grace he sought was not physical intoxication but spiritual ecstasy, the means he adopted not drunkenness but abstinence and rites of purification.[109]

The sacred marriage in the mysteries conducted at Eleusis in ancient Greece surely was a witness to this,[110] and the rituals of ancient Egypt even more so.

Cornford's approach, totally social in nature, allows for a collective force beyond the individual. However, he bases this force only on a prehistoric "group consciousness" at the psychological level. We can see in our time how an individual can act in a group as he would never do alone, for example, at a political rally, where only certain actions are permitted and others prohibited by the group, if only implicitly. Cornford's whole thesis posits a "group consciousness" that proceeds over a long time to "individual consciousness." From this scenario,

---

[107] As was the Egyptian god Osiris by his brother Seth.

[108] Friedrich Nietzsche, *The Birth of Tragedy and The Case of Wagner*, tr. Walter Kaufmann (New York: Vintage, 1967), 73-4.

[109] Ibid., 476.

[110] Ibid., 548-553.

he puts forward that the notions of "soul" and "god" grew, respectively, out of the collective force of the group and its defining power. The sorcerer and the witch doctor thus arose, as those capable of still receiving this higher energy and so were endowed with a special sacred status, which eventually degraded into the priests and religious organizations of large civilizations.

We propose however that the beginning of real religion did not begin in this way but rather came about as was discussed earlier in the work of Pierre Gordon, that is to say, early man was endowed with a higher level of being, a finer energy attuned to cosmic energy. When man became gradually incapable of receiving this energy as civilization demanded more and more organization and control rather than spontaneous action based on this superior level of being, true religion began as a means to bring man back to this primordial state of which he began to feel the lack. It is our belief that the "sacred" had no need to exist in earliest times, since what became "sacred" was previously natural to man. Certain spiritual individuals carried on the real tradition showing the way to this natural superior state of being (often called "mysticism"), but underground so as not to undergo the wrath of organized religion. On this subject, Cornford has this to say:

> The doctrines of mysticism are secret, because they are not cold, abstract beliefs, or articles in a creed, which can be taught and explained by intellectual processes; such beliefs no one has ever desired to conceal, except from fear of persecution. The 'truth' which mysticism guards is a thing which can only be learnt by being experienced...; it is, fundamentally, not an intellectual, but an emotional experience—that invasive, flooding sense of oneness, of reunion and communion with the life of the world, which the mystical temperaments of all ages seem to have in common, no matter in what theological terms they may happen to construe it afterwards.[111]

---

[111]Ibid., 198-99.

We believe that Cornford is very right in this analysis except when he calls the "mystical" experience an emotional one. The "mystical" experience is not an emotional event but arises from a higher cosmic energy within the human being who is open enough to experience it. The role of one "who knows," a spiritual master, is to teach man the way to be open to this higher energy, not through emotional or ecstatic means, but by showing the path to dissolving man's inbred belief in his capacity to know everything through his mental apparatus, which completely cuts him off from the divine.

Such a profound change in mentality towards rationalism and scientism could not have happened overnight but was the fruit of a long process that entailed political, social, and religious changes, which resulted in…

> …an open society in which the values of the past become relatively unimportant and radically fresh opinions can be formed both of the community itself and of its expanding environment…. It is that kind of change that took place in Greece between the ninth and sixth centuries B.C….The growth of the polis, the independent city-state, out of earlier aristocratic structures, together with the development of foreign contacts and a monetary system, transformed the Hesiodic view of society and made the old divine and heroic archetypes seem obsolete.[112]

The tradition arising from the ancient Mycenaean civilization with its ruler that controlled all according to a strict hierarchy was no more. New relations between citizens of the *polis* were established that allowed anyone to affirm his thought as he saw fit. In this way, the secularization and rationalization of thought that occurred with the pre-Socratics was the logical outcome of

---

[112]Kirk, G. S., Raven, J.E., Schofield, M., *The Presocratic Philosophers: A Critical History with a Selection of Texts,* 2d ed. (Cambridge, U.K.: Cambridge University Press, 1999), 73-74.

a new social order.[113] In this new order, the ancient rites, symbols and idols have lost their sacred, secret, mysterious, and emotionally-charged quality. Idols are now seen as simple statues, rites as repeating "events," thus leaving what was once taken as sacred truths to be now open to discussion and interpretation.[114] Miletus, where philosophy as we know it today originated with Thales, was an important center of commerce, and was thus conducive to the arising of the scientific attitude based on a practical point of view.

The relationship that developed at that time between myth and philosophy was very complex and cannot simply be explained by a simple rationalization of mythic thought. The *raison d'être* of myths, their function as symbolic stories providing spiritual truths, lost this original function sometime in the distant past, leaving only a residue of meaning without that sacred and mysterious character that led one to search for something beyond themselves. Filling this void, the mind came to invent whatever it wanted concerning gods and the universe.

How the symbolic Greek myths lost their *raison d'être* as guides to man's spiritual development, and became simple systemized categories of gods and tales of their doings, is lost in the prehistory of ancient Greek civilization, a process that lasted over hundreds of years until the time when man interacted with the world only through his thought instead of with his entire being.[115] What was once a cultural unity of which man *qua* man was an integral part, became a collection of separate intellectual domains: religion, philosophy, literature, art, and so on.[116]

---

[113] Jean-Pierre Vernant, *Les origines de la pensée grecque* (Paris: Presses Universitaires de France, 1962), v-vii.

[114] Ibid., 116.

[115] Kirk, *The Nature of Greek Myths* (London: Penguin, 1990), 240, 300-02.

[116] Ervin Laszlo, *The Systems View of the World: A Holistic Vision for Our Time* (Cresskill, NJ: Hampton Press, 1996), 76.

Now the interests of these early philosophers was to *explain* nature: to describe the organization of the universe and all it contained: the movement of the heavenly bodies, various meteorological events, the life of animals, plants and minerals, and in the human realm, all the aspects of human existence from the biological to the social. At the same time, they were interested in the more fundamental questions of the universe such as, on a microcosmic scale, what are its basic constituents?, and, on the macrocosmic, how is it unified?[117] While both myths and philosophy try to explain nature, the thought of the philosophers was based on a radically different viewpoint, moving from the particular to the general and from the practical to the theoretical.[118] The physical world was no longer defined in terms of religious moral criteria, but rather of relations between its parts and their interactions.[119] It should be emphasized, however, that we are not interested here with the *content* of Greek philosophical speculation, but rather with the *minds* of the pre-Socratic philosophers and how they came to function as they did.

Any philosophy cannot arise from nothing. All humans are bathed in the civilization and culture in which they are born. As we noted, the first known philosophers, Thales and his followers Anaximander and Anaximenes, hailed from the Greek town Miletus in what was then Ionia on the western shores of Asia Minor (what is now Turkey) in the sixth century B.C. It is assumed by certain scholars that they must have been influenced by the astronomy of the Babylonians and by the Egyptian civilization as well, with whom they no doubt had contact.[120] It is surmised as well that Hesiod, writing a generation after

---

[117] Barnes, Jonathan, *Early Greek Philosophy* (London: Penguin Books, 1987), 13.

[118] Kirk, G.S., *The Nature of Greek Myths*, 289.

[119] Vernant, *Les origines de la pensée grecque*, iv-v. [Vernant citations are our translations.]

[120] Barnes, *Early Greek Philosophy*, 14-15.

Homer's *Iliad* and *Odyssey*, was influenced by the Hittite culture in Anatolia, and who furthermore tried to give order to the ancient Greek myths thus influencing the pre-Socratics by his attempts to synthesize and systematize the supernatural realm.[121]

Whatever the influences, the thought of the pre-Socratics was highly different from what came before. Rather than a world where every event was the result of the will of the gods, the world had its own intrinsic order that could be understood by the mind of man. The pre-Socratics did not dispense with the gods entirely: while they might have been the cause of the birth of the universe, they did not interfere in its functioning,[122] and their cosmogony was in fact based on the model of the pantheon of gods and their genealogy.[123] What in fact occurred was that the personification and anthropomorphism of nature in terms of gods and their relations gave way over time to viewing natural phenomena and their interactions as intrinsic forces in their own right without the need for divine intervention:[124]

> It was inevitable that, when the gods had become completely human persons, some skeptical mind should refuse to believe that a thunderstorm in Asia Minor was really due to the anger of a deity seated on the summit of Olympus....There is no longer a supernatural background, peopled with fragmentary or complete personalities accessible to prayer and sacrifice or amenable to magical compulsion. Intelligence is cut off from action. Thought is left confronting Nature, an impersonal world of things, indifferent to man's desires and existing in and for themselves. The detachment of self from the object is now complete.[125]

---

[121] Kirk, *The Presocratic Philosophers*, 34, 44-5.

[122] Barnes, *Early Greek Philosophy*, 16-17.

[123] Kirk, *The Nature of Greek Myths*, 296-97.

[124] Kirk, *The Presocratic Philosophers*, 72.

[125] Francis MacDonald Cornford, *Before and After Socrates* (Cambridge, UK: Cambridge University Press, 1932), 15-7.

In the same way, Newton was profoundly religious, believing wholeheartedly in the Christian tradition, but this in no way prevented him from trying to explain the functioning of the universe according to universal laws.

How is it that modern civilization has come to this impasse (called "progress"), to this loss of the symbolic understanding of the world based on metaphysical principles? Guénon gives us a clue perhaps when he explains that the West considers its foundation to be in the classical age of Greece and Rome and, in a sort of linear process believes it has been progressing ever since towards the "Good" with a long hiatus, to be sure, during the "sleep" of the Middle Ages, but which then "awoke" as the Renaissance, a rebirth, of the classical age.[126] In truth, this Western mentality was born from the ancient Greeks whose thought processes progressively deviated from those of the Traditional civilizations of Mesopotamia, Persia, India, China and Egypt. It was the Greeks, after all, who began to *analyze* the world from a purely mental perspective, who tried to understand nature by breaking it down into its separate parts rather than look at the world in the Traditional way as a whole of which all the parts, including man himself, are interrelated and have meaning only in these relations. In sum, the culture of modern civilization is, in the words of Frithjof Schuon:

> ...more and more the absence of culture: the mania of cutting oneself off from one's roots and of forgetting from where one comes.[127] ...[I]n losing a symbolist and contemplative perspective, founded both on impersonal intelligence and on the metaphysical transparency of things, man has gained the fallacious riches of the ego; the world of divine images has become a world of words.[128]

---

[126] Guénon, *Orient et Occident*, 28.

[127] Schuon, *Avoir un Centre* (Paris: Editions Maisonneuve & Larose, 1988), 32.

[128] Schuon, *Light on the Ancient Worlds*, 29.

While Nietzsche had this to say:

> [I]t is the fate of every myth to creep by degrees into the narrow limits of some alleged historical reality, and to be treated by some later generation as a unique fact with historical claims... For this is the way in which religions are wont to die out: under the stern, intelligent eyes of an orthodox dogmatism, the mythical premises of a religion are systematized as a sum total of historical events;...the feeling for myth perishes, and its place is taken by the claim of religion to historical foundations.[129]... [T]here is, to be sure, a profound illusion...the unshakable faith that thought, using the thread of logic, can penetrate the deepest abysses of being, and that thought is capable not only of knowing being but even of correcting it. This sublime metaphysical illusion accompanies science as an instinct that leads science again and again to its limits...[130]

Now symbol and myth are how ancient religions revealed their Teachings, a path to a state that was once man's birthright. How was it that the pre-Socratic philosophers in Asia minor used their minds not to continue on this road to spiritual rebirth, but to analyze the world with a goal of finding knowledge *for its own sake*.

When science was born in Greece, the distinction between levels of existence, natural and supernatural, physical and metaphysical, experience and revelation, was implicitly denied. The Ionian philosophers simply assumed that the whole universe was on a single plane of existence, the natural one, the one we experience through our senses, and thus everything in the universe, including that which was once laden with mystery, could be open to rational knowledge and scientific inquiry.[131]

What was it that brought the Greek mind to this crucial break in the history of humankind? What was it that broke the river of

---

[129] Nietzsche, *The Birth of Tragedy*, 75.

[130] Ibid., 95-6.

[131] Cornford, *Before and After Socrates*, 14-5.

man into two streams: one concerned with finding truth in spirituality by direct inner experience; the other breaking off to find truth in philosophy through intellectual analysis, and in science by experimentation with the physical world, the latter stream leading to our present Western civilization? Why there? Why then? In the previous pages, we have proposed some possible influences, but in the end, these, of course, are unanswerable questions, the answer to be found in the whole development of Greek civilization, from the Neolithic age through an era that included a prehistoric past marked by settlers invading the Peloponnesus and other nearby lands around the beginning of the second millennium B.C.,[132] followed by the Mycenaean era with its royalty, and finally leading up to the later development of the Greek city-state.

---

[132]Robert Drews, *The Coming of the Greeks: Indo-European Conquests in the Aegean and the Near East* (Princeton, NJ: Princeton University Press, 1988), 225.

Chapter 3 Symbolism and Man[133]

In order to understand how symbols can affect man, we must look now at man's nature. How is man constituted so that he can be influenced in a way that would go beyond his thought to affect his innermost being. As we saw in our discussion of the nature of the cosmos, man is a hierarchy of constituents from atomic particles to man as a whole, each level, we proposed, obeying laws of the cosmic levels higher than himself. Just as everything is eternally present for the universe, the cosmic sea, the macrocosm, so for man, the microcosm, everything within him can also be experienced in an eternal now arising from the depths of his consciousness—"As above, so below," says the Hermetic tradition. The whole point of religion, of spiritual practice, it can be said, is to arrive at this possibility, and spiritual symbolism is one of the means to this end.

Figure 11 Dance of Shiva

Quantum physics has shown that in the final analysis, there are no 'particles,' no 'smallest thing,' of which everything is made, an idea that perhaps began with Democritus and other pre-Socratic Greek philosophers. When we arrive at the interior of the atom, we find only relations, not objects, where particles can only be conceived in relation to the whole, where particles and energy turn into each other, and where the observer affects what is being observed, or more to the point, becomes a participant in a process, so that by observing a particle (that is, exposing it to

---

[133] Much of the insights expressed in this section come from the teaching of G.I. Gurdjieff.

photons) the particle's location is changed. The result of this vision of the universe is that nothing is isolated and separate but rather that everything is continuously connected and mutually influencing each other on both the horizontal and vertical directions in the magnificent and organic dance of Shiva. See Figure 11.

In the words of Ananda K. Coomaraswamy:

> One must have learned that an access to reality cannot be had by making a choice between matter and spirit considered as things unlike in all respects, but rather by seeing in things material and sensible a formal likeness to spiritual prototypes of which the senses can give no direct report. It is not a question of religion versus science, but of a reality on different levels of reference, or better, perhaps, of different orders of reality, not mutually exclusive.[134]

It would be very interesting to discuss each of the levels of which we are made up: how our organs function alone and together, the inner workings of our cells, the role of molecules and atoms, and so on, but this is much beyond the scope of this book. Suffice it is to say that influences from any one level of our being affect all the others. We cannot understand a human being by studying only one level, for example, the molecular or cellular, for the laws on any one level must be understood in relation to all the other levels and the whole of which it is a part. Otherwise, we would be left with the absurd view that the movements of the atoms in my brain determine what I am thinking. Just as the particle and wave natures of subatomic particles are on different functional levels (the wave is a "probability wave," that is, an abstraction of the activity at the particle level), as are as well the hardware and software levels in a computer (one cannot describe a computer program in terms of the movement of electrical

---

[134] Ananda K. Coomaraswamy, "A Figure of Speech or a Figure of Thought," *The Door in the Sky: Coomaraswamy on Myth and Meaning,* ed. Rama Coomaraswamy (Princeton, N.J.: Princeton University Press, 1977), 174.

impulses in the chips), so mind and body cannot be looked at as being on the same hierarchical level. As Maurice Nicoll put it in his book on the symbolism of the Bible:

> So there are different forms of truth, on different levels. But if a man thinks only from his feet he cannot understand levels. He thinks only on one level and so turns things into opposites which are not opposites.[135]

So when discussing a human being, we must be very careful to specify which level we are considering. When we eat a certain food, drink a certain substance, or take a certain drug, our atoms, cells, organs and our awareness can all be influenced simultaneously. Influences from above, higher energies, sometimes enshrined in spiritual ideas and symbols, can also influence all our levels. Reading phrases from religious texts, listening to sacred music, taking part in Traditional rites, entering holy monuments can also influence our entire being in a very real way. At this level of mind, it makes no sense to look at the "hardware" of atoms, molecules and cells: "[I]n using the laws of physics as a measuring rod of 'reality,' we are attempting the impossible task of explaining the higher in terms of the lower, the animate in terms of the inanimate."[136] This book is concerned, in fact, with how spiritual symbolism can aid us in deepening (or raising) our consciousness:

> The true foundation of symbolism is...the correspondence existing between all orders of reality, which connects all of them with each other, and consequently stretches from the natural order taken as a whole to the supernatural order itself. By virtue of this correspondence, all of nature is itself only a symbol, that is, it takes on real meaning only if we regard it as a support in order to elevate us to the understanding of supernatural or 'metaphysical' truths (in the proper

---

[135] Maurice Nicoll, *The Mark* (London: Vincent Stuart, 1954), 5.

[136] Kenneth Walker, *Diagnosis of Man,* revised ed. (Harmondsworth, U.K.: Penguin Books, 1962), 72.

etymological sense of the word), which is precisely the essential function of symbolism.[137]

Symbolism is a language and a precise form of thought; a hieratic and a metaphysical language and not a language determined by somatic or psychological categories. Its foundation is in the analogical correspondence of all orders of reality and states of being or levels of reference....[138]

It should always be kept in mind, however, that since 'the map is not the territory,' "the image whether in the mind or in the work is only a means to knowledge, [it is] not in itself knowledge.[139]

What is necessary is not to have a symbol but to be a symbol. In this spirit, all objects and all actions are not symbols in themselves but ways and means of enhancing the living symbolism of man.[140]

Having accepted the premises of symbolism, however, we are still left with the question of what we must bring to the symbol in order to activate its potential force, for given the premises of order and hierarchy, what we receive from the symbol will be in proportion to what we bring to it. If we do not abandon ourselves to what is higher, which can only be equated to stupidity, a symbol is dead to us. This stupidity is manifested by...

...an indifference to light, or a refusal, whether passive or active, to heed the call of the luminous and ascending tendency (sattva) in divine manifestation....[It] is characterized by a lack of a sense of proportions whereby the lesser or imperfect or impure is preferred to the greater, the perfect, and the pure. In a word, the stupid man prefers himself to God.[141]

---

[137] Guénon, *Aperçus sur l'initiation*, 132-33. [Our translation]

[138] Coomaraswamy, *The Door in the Sky*, 170.

[139] Guénon, *Aperçus sur l'initiation*, 132-33. [Our translation]

[140] Abraham Joshua Heschel, *Man's Quest for God: Studies in Prayer and Symbolism* (New York: Charles Scribner's Sons, 1954), 126.

[141] Perry, *On Awakening and Remembering*, 80

To understand the world directly, rather than filtered by the senses and thought, symbolism is a way by which man can expand his understanding of the world. On whatever level we *are*, this will be the level on which the symbol acts. If everything in the universe is connected through laws operating on different levels, then within everything, including ourselves, can be found a reflection of the entire universe. Reasoning thus, we must know what connects one level to another to understand how symbols can act on different levels, and what *in us* corresponds to this. What must we bring to the symbol? Schuon says:

> [A] symbol can be interpreted either 'horizontally' from the standpoint of analogy, or 'vertically' from the standpoint of identity: it is the difference between concentric circles which reflect the center and radii which attain it.[142]...In a word, art, as symbolism, is the searching—and the revelation—of the center, in ourselves as well as around us."[143]

Coomaraswamy states:

> [T]he principle involved is that true knowledge of an object is not obtained by merely empirical observation or reflex registration..., but only when the knower and known, seer and seen, meet in an act transcending distinction.[144]...Aesthetic experience...an inscrutable and uncaused spiritual activity...is thus only accessible to those competent. Competence depends 'on purity or singleness of heart and on an inner character or habit of obedience tending to aversion of attention from external phenomena; this character and habit, not to be acquired by mere learning, but either innate or cultivated, depends on an ideal sensibility and the faculty of self-identification with the forms depicted.[145]

---

[142] Schuon, *Stations of Wisdom*, 70.

[143] Schuon, *Avoir un Centre*, 37. [This and further citations from this book are our translations.]

[144] Coomaraswamy, *The Transformation of Nature in Art*, 6.

[145] Ibid., 50-1. [The internal quote is from the Hindu text of Visvanatha, *Sahitya Darpana*, III.]

In sum, spiritual symbolism is based on the notion that the mind can never grasp spiritual forces directly but only through the symbol, and that the symbol can help man achieve knowledge of the spiritual by leading him to experience eternal macrocosmic Being through the progressive unveiling of this Being within himself.

Symbolism and Consciousness

Consciousness is, in a sense, what we are; it is the level of existence on which we exist, and, as we mentioned above, the interaction between us and the symbol can only take place on this same level. It has been said that the universe can be found in a grain of sand, but for that, he who observes must be blessed with a universal consciousness. A raising of our consciousness must, it seems, go hand in hand with a deeper understanding of the symbol. Using the words of the physicist:

> [I]n intelligent perception, the brain and nervous system respond directly to an order in the universal and unknown flux that cannot be reduced to anything that could be defined in terms of knowable structures.[146]

The main point being made here is the difference between the process of thought arising from memory and the experience of apperception[147] springing from a direct connection to the universal nexus. It is thus of utmost importance as to which of these two events, thought or direct knowing, provokes the nerve impulses and chemical reactions in the organism which we experience either as "logical reasoning" or "deeper awareness." What is difficult for us to grasp is how this "deeper awareness" or new form of consciousness occurs, because we try to understand it through our process of thought, which is incapable of grasping this experience. Higher states of consciousness, while knowable, are not explainable. The mind is incapable of grasping a higher state of

---

[146]Bohm, *Wholeness*, 53

.

consciousness because this state is essentially a different type of connection between man and the totality of his environment, a higher state of being whereby microcosmic man is being directly fed by a higher cosmic level in which this new state of consciousness, a new attention and apperception, is created. Just as we can never see our own eyes directly but only as a reflection in a mirror, so we can never directly apprehend our own consciousness but only reflect on it with our reasoning apparatus. Consciousness, simply stated, is our relationship to the world; it is the expression of our being part of the universe, and, like listening to music, we cannot use our logical mind to grasp what is a direct experience, which is not at all dependent on thought.

There is the case, for example, of a woman who was operated on for a brain tumor, and to do so the blood circulation had to be completely stopped. To allow this, they cooled the body to practically 0° for a half an hour. During this time, the electroencephalogram was completely flat, yet the patient had, during this period, a "near death experience" where she found herself in a tunnel with a luminous point at the end, being called by her grandmother, and so forth; the point being here that she had an experience that did not depend on her brain which had been put in abeyance. Through what process then did she have this experience? Where is consciousness located? Or is it located in any place at all?[148]

Again, it is the essential function of a spiritual symbol to deepen our relationship to the world, to elevate our

---

[147] We use the more rarely used word "apperception," which for us seems to more clearly define how a symbol facilitates the relationship between a human being and his environment, rather than the words "perception," which is taken most often to refer to the sense of sight, or "reception," which seems too concrete. The American Heritage Dictionary defines "apperception" as 1) "Conscious perception with full awareness." and 2) "The process of understanding by which newly observed qualities of an object are related to past experience."

[148] Eléna Sender and Hervé Ratel, "La vie rêvée des morts" in *Science et Avenir* (Paris: February 2002).

state of consciousness by raising ourselves to a plane above the physical world and opening us to what is behind and beyond it.

Now being that one of the leitmotifs of this book is precisely consciousness, not consciousness theoretically but consciousness as a living reality, we must discuss in more detail what we mean by consciousness and the process of its development. For what is the purpose of discussing consciousness if it does not have the same essential meaning for the writer and the reader. After all, so many books have been written on the subject from vastly different points of view. From the modern Western scientific viewpoint, consciousness has been simply described as the results of measurements of bodily functions such as brain waves during thinking and feeling. A more traditional view describes consciousness in terms of states experienced during meditation. To use the same word "consciousness" for both begs us to at least try to clarify what we mean by this word.

In the last century, William James defined psychology as the study of consciousness. A long sterile interlude then intervened whereby behaviorists tried to decipher human comportment by observing, for example, mice running through a maze. It is true that many researchers have returned to the study of different states of consciousness, that is, hypnotic and drug-induced states, sleep, the so-called normal waking state, trance states, psychotic states and states invoked by meditation. This is undoubtedly more interesting than watching mice evading shocks or pushing levers to gain food, and yet the assumptions underlying their approach remain quite the same. From this so-called scientific 'objectivity' they measure the breathing rate, cardiac rhythm, brain waves, and so on, and gather the subjective impressions of their human subjects in various 'states of consciousness,' and from all this to draw some valid conclusions. "First, let's gather our data; from that we will make our theories" is their attitude. Now this attitude, which is at the very basis of the methodology of scientific research as we know it, this would-be "objectivity" towards phenomena both exterior and interior to man, seems to us a monstrous lie. One *chooses* what is observed, the choice being based on personal criteria, conscious or not, thus involving the researcher in his experiment despite himself. I think it would be much more fruitful for a researcher to say: "As for me, this is what I believe. I choose this theory because I like it. It is harmonious, elegant, and it corresponds to my own experience in the world. Now I am going to test it in different conditions to establish the limits of its utilization."

There is no disputing the fact that science has its place; it is rather the underlying attitude of the modern mentality which assumes that scientific research will eventually lead to a comprehensive understanding of the "whole" that is in question here. This attitude, which would have us believe that given enough time all will be made clear through science, is simply not tenable.[149] Science, it is true, can help us to understand the functioning of a limited part of the world at a particular time, but the synthesis, the understanding of the whole, comes only with the elevation of consciousness, not with its analytical study. And this is so precisely because "elevation of consciousness" means a deeper connection to the cosmos and thus entails a more comprehensive understanding of its

---

[149] It should be noted that there are scientists who have taken this position, such as Richard Feynman: "Yes! Physics has given up. We do not know how to predict what would happen in *a given circumstance*, and we believe now that it is impossible, that the only thing that can be predicted is the probability of different events. It must be recognized that this is a retrenchment in our earlier ideal of understanding nature. It may be a backward step, but no one has seen a way to avoid it." From Richard Feynman, *Six Easy Pieces: The Explained Fundamentals of Physics* (London: Penguin Books, 1998), 135.

And Jacob Bronowski says, "[N]one of our explanations can be true, that in some sense there is no ultimate truth accessible to us for the simple reason we have to make a cut in the universe in order to do experiment at all. We have to decide what is relevant and what is irrelevant. Since I hold that the universe is totally connected, that every fact has some influence on every other fact, then it follows that any cut you make at all is a convenient simplification." From Jacob Bronowski, *The Origins of Knowledge and Imagination* (New Haven: Yale University Press, 1978), 69.

multiple levels. Science, on the other hand, deals only on the level of what can be measured, only on the physical plane, and has led to many marvels that make our life safer, healthier and more comfortable. What has become a disaster for modern man, however, is that just because of this success on the practical side, the scientific method and positivism have so invaded every aspect of modern life, including our universities, that even the possibility of other levels of reality is almost universally denied, at least implicitly—and often explicitly. René Guénon says:

> [Science is] knowledge that has a certain reality, since it is valid and effective in a somewhat relative domain; but it is an irremediable limited knowledge, ignorant of the essential, a knowledge lacking first principles, as it is with everything that belongs in its own right to modern Western civilization. Science, as our contemporaries conceive it, is uniquely the study of phenomena of the perceptible world, and this study is undertaken in such a way that it cannot, we insist, be bound to any principle of a higher order.[150]

Now, it is studies such as experiments measuring brain waves that creates confusion by putting what leads us away from a deeper knowledge on the same level as what leads us towards it. We must begin with our own felt conception of man, his *raison d'être* elucidated perhaps in a spiritual doctrine, but *confirmed by our own lived inner experiences.* It is only later that the facts can then be put in their proper place in relation to this living doctrine. An inner experience that science calls "subjective" because it cannot be measured, is, for a person experiencing it, nonetheless quite "objective." In Kenneth Walker's words:

> [I]t is ridiculous to ignore the existence of consciousness merely because it provides no data which can be weighed or measured.[151]

---

[150] Guénon, *Orient et Occident,* 46.

[151] Walker, *Diagnosis of Man,* 85.

Science can analyze the wavelength of the color red, for example, or the chemical composition of salt, but it can in no way measure the act of one experiencing the view of red or the taste of salt, which does not make the experience any less real:

> Consciousness is unshareable. Your consciousness is your own, mine is my own. Since consciousness is unshareable, the whole direction of one's life should be towards experiencing everything for oneself, to be consciousness to oneself of oneself, to see for oneself and to be able to do for oneself. Only in this way is anything created in oneself, and once created it is one's own and is permanent and real.[152]

There is, in fact, if one looks carefully in the writings of the religious traditions of the world, another 'sacred' science based not on physical measurement but on the development of consciousness, which is as exact as modern science, if not more so, but based on the development of one's being and whose results can be known by direct inner experience. It is our contention that symbolism is the only means by which this science can be expressed and that the writings, images, sculptures, and monuments of ancient civilizations are a teaching of this sacred science.

Those who wish to follow a 'Way' must be quite careful, for it can be a long and arduous journey. One can be led to give up the quest by any number of justifications or one can become attached to the symbols themselves—the sin of idolatry—completely forgetting what they are meant to represent.

Now, we have already said that consciousness is the level on which we exist and interact with the cosmos; or, in other words, the level of understanding in the largest sense of the term, that is, all that we know and understand, all that we incorporate and incarnate in ourselves at any particular moment. This then leads

---

[152]Nicoll, *The Mark,* 24.

us to the idea of the degree of consciousness and the important distinction between consciousness itself, inner vision, and the contents of consciousness, what is seen from within. Light is perhaps the best analogy here. Light allows a relationship to exist between our eyes and the objects of the external world. But we cannot see light; it is rather by the means of light that we are capable of seeing a narrow spectrum of the material world. In the same way, consciousness is our awareness of our relationship to the cosmos—not through our senses nor through reasoning, where the sense perceptions are interpreted in terms of past experience—but our relationship in terms of our entire being. One can even say that the more one is only mentally related to the world, the less conscious one is, that is, the less one is aware of one's organic participation in the cosmic order. And just as we cannot see light, although through it we observe the material world, so we cannot be aware of our own consciousness even though it is our means of being aware of our interrelationship with the cosmos. Using the word "consciousness," in fact, is simply a way of conceptualizing our relationship to the world from the point of view of our own Self, whereas the reality is the relationship—not the Self-in-the-world, as if the two were separate entities, but rather the Self-is-the-world, where we are but a hierarchical congelation of increasingly subtle matter in the continuum of universal substances. The more this continuum is "understood" and "experienced," the more we are inwardly aware of the interrelationship between ourselves and the cosmos, that is, the higher our level of consciousness. This is perhaps more easily understood in Coomaraswamy's words:

> But if the liberated being...or saint in a state of grace is thus free to act without deliberation as to duty, it is because for him there no longer exists a separation of self and not-self.[153]

---

[153] Coomaraswamy, The *Transformation of Nature in Art*, 21.

We see, then, that our consciousness may have infinite levels and may be compared to the iris of the eye which allows infinite gradations of light to enter from the outside. Generally, however, we can say that as children, and for the most of us to the end of our days, our immersion in the world is based on imaginary thoughts, a totally subjective mental relationship where one's organic connection to the cosmos through diverse levels of energy is not even suspected let alone consciously experienced. The possibility does exist, however, which we may have experienced in flashes, of a more objective relationship, at least to ourselves, where our thoughts, emotions, and movements are separated from a Self which is able to observe them, still a purely mental phenomenon. We may also consider a further stage where the mind connects with, or descends into, the body as a whole, where the mental function is replaced as the initiator of action by a relationship of the body to the environment, including here under the word "body" all the mental, emotional, and physical functions. These three stages are illustrated in Figure 12.

In the state we find ourselves in at present the finer energies of the Spirit—the "Grace of God"—with which we are filled in a higher state, are blocked by the ego, the smaller self, the personality, everything that we are by way of imitation, education, socialization, everything that we are because of our destiny to be born in a particular family within a specific culture in a certain epoch. Since we believe that this is all we are or can be, our energy serves only to support this ever-present belief in this ego-ridden self:

> The whole tradition of the Philosophia Perennis, Eastern and Western, ancient and modern, makes a clear distinction of existence from essence, becoming from being. The existence of this man So-and-so, who speaks of himself as 'I,' is a succession of instants of consciousness, of which no two are the same; in other words, this man is never the same man from one moment

to the next. We know only past and future, never a now, and so there is never any moment with reference to which we can say of our self, or of any other presentation, that it 'is'; as soon as we ask what it is, it has 'become' something else; and it is only because the changes that take place in any brief period are usually small that we mistake the incessant process for an actual being.[154]

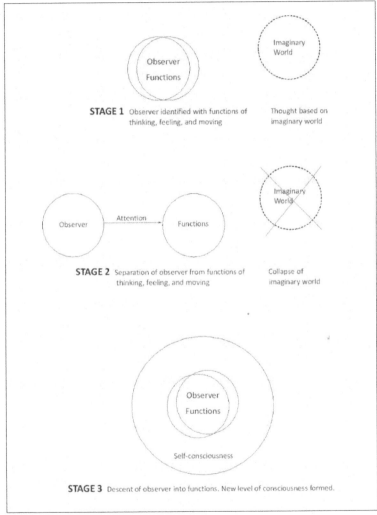

STAGE 1 Observer identified with functions of thinking, feeling, and moving — Thought based on imaginary world

STAGE 2 Separation of observer from functions of thinking, feeling, and moving — Collapse of imaginary world

STAGE 3 Descent of observer into functions. New level of consciousness formed.

Figure 12 Stages of consciousness

---

[154] Ananda K. Coomaraswamy, "The Vedanta and Western Tradition," (1939) in *Coomaraswamy Volume II, Selected Papers: Metaphysics*, Roger Lipsey ed., Bollingen Series LXXXIX. (Princeton, N.J.: Princeton University Press, 1977), 426.

Yet, inside this outer self might there not be a real Self as well, a Self not based on ordinary thought full of false ideas supported by continually stimulated emotions, but based on what we are by everything linking us to the cosmos. As discussed above, we are composed of smaller worlds, that is, cellular, molecular, atomic, and at the same time we wholly belong to vaster worlds: terrestrial, planetary, galactic, and universal. Through all these worlds our being is sewn on each level into the cosmic tissue. Our little self, our ego, is no more than a continual affirmation of a social identity, taken on for the most part unconsciously, in order not to feel its nothingness in the universal order. Man as he exists at present is a lie, a lie that is hardened every instant by the constant affirmation of a social role in conformity with the false idea that each of us has of ourselves. We affirm ourselves in an imaginary world created purely and simply from clouds of thoughts arising from emotional waves. True, we have a social role to fulfill, but to believe that this is the end-all of our existence, is to cut ourselves off from much greater inner and outer worlds of meaning and experience and to imprison ourselves in the smallest of cells, all the while believing in our power and freedom.

Every man has choices to make in life in terms of the experiences he allows himself to undergo. Should we not carefully choose those to be repeated? Yet to do so, there must be a goal by which experiences are measured. First, what do we want? Then, what are the means? One must never confuse a temporary change in one's state of consciousness with a permanent change in one's state of being. A 'mystic' experience does not make a saint, except in one's imagination. Rather, it is only when there is a *balanced* integration of mind, emotions, and body that a real change in one's state of being is possible and that can be equated with an elevation of one's consciousness on a more or less permanent basis. Science has shown that even on the automatic, physical level, what is often called "mind," is a complex interweaving among mental, emotional, and bodily states:

> The hypothalamus, the brain stem, and the limbic system intervene in body regulation and in all neural processes on which mind phenomena are based, for example, perception, learning, recall, emotion and feeling, and...reasoning and creativity. Body regulation, survival, and mind are intimately interwoven. The interweaving occurs in biological tissue and uses chemical and electrical signaling...[155]

But to go beyond this automatic interaction and allow finer energies and thus higher consciousness to appear, there is no little pill, but rather a long and difficult conscious interior work engendering much suffering, a suffering that must be accepted voluntarily for any results to be achieved. We are not talking here of that suffering which is basically a self-pitying whose "resentment at having to suffer masks a self-indulgence which, in the last analysis, prevents self-transcendence."[156] Just as the splitting of the atom releases tremendous energy, a radical splitting of mind and body can also release energies which result in various powerful but uncontrollable psychic states. But it is also true that the fusion of atoms creates inconceivably greater energy such as that taking place in the heart of that radiating equilibrium that we call the sun.

It seems clear that our only pretension to real freedom is the possibility we have of liberating ourselves from this identification we experience with our thoughts, emotions, and movements. An animal or a child does not have this possibility to separate himself from himself, to see himself think, to see himself feel, to see himself move, whereas we have this possibility but are unaware of it. Except on rare occasions when

---

[155] Antonio R. Damasio, *Descartes' Error: Emotion, Reason, and the Human Brain* (New York: Quill imprint of HarperCollins, 2000), 123.

[156] Perry, *On Awakening and Remembering*, 137.

we are moved by some unexpected occurrence, we are completely identified with our functions acting in the world. But instead of being natural, acting in accordance with our essential nature, we are under constant tension, living as we do in an imaginary world created by our largely unconsciously learned beliefs and thoughts which are themselves deformed by the modern way of life, thus putting us in conflict with our innermost predispositions.[157] It is noteworthy that, Antonio Damasio, a scientist steeped in the scientific method, has this to say about our ability to be aware of ourselves:

> The sensory images of what you perceive externally, and the related images you recall, occupy most of the scope of your mind, but not all of it. Besides those images there is also this other presence that signifies you, as observer of the things imaged, owner of the things imaged, potential actor on the things imaged. There is a presence of you in a particular relationship with some object. If there were no such presence, how would your thoughts belong to you? Who could tell that they did? The presence is quiet and subtle...In that perspective, the presence of you is the feeling of what happens when your being is modified by the acts of apprehending something. The presence never quits, from the moment of awakening to the moment sleep begins. The presence must be there or there is no you.[158]

Damasio, for all his insight, butts against the limit separating man as he is as man as he could be, for, as I see it, a new higher state of being is just that state where, by continual practice, one becomes continually aware of oneself acting in the world, at first only by constant effort but eventually as a new incarnated state of being incorporating a higher level of consciousness.

---

[157] P. D. Ouspensky, *The Psychology of Man's Possible Evolution* (New York: Random House, 1974), *passim*.

[158] Antonio Damasio, *The Feeling of What Happens: Body and Emotion in the Making of Consciousness* (New York: Harcourt, 1999), 10.

Now the way out of this state of identification, imagination, and stress in which we find ourselves is through meditation within a tradition that corresponds to our possibilities, to our own particular nature. We must carefully choose what road we are to follow for a long inner work is assuredly necessary, a work under the guidance of those who have already traveled the road we have chosen. It appears to me, at least at the beginning, that the work of meditation is above all a work on one's attention. In fact, the only freedom we have, as we are, is the freedom to *momentarily* place our attention in one place or another—and in truth *we are no more than just there where our attention is*:

> Attention is as necessary to consciousness as having images. But attention is not sufficient for consciousness and is not the same as consciousness."[159] ... "Consciousness results in enhanced wakefulness and focused attention.[160]

The problem is that our thoughts never stop turning, and our mind is almost never connected to what the body is doing:

> [U]nless a person has an operative center of consciousness which secures him from drifting through the *Samsara*, or which immunizes him from stray thoughts...his consciousness is a fertile seeding ground for an incessant stream of usually loosely connected and often disparate musings, preoccupations, or reveries that feed and multiply, parasite-like, on his vital substance.[161]

Our body begins to act, or an emotion arises, stimulated by something outside or inside us which then generates a thought reinforcing the 'reasonableness' of the act or emotion. Meanwhile, the body has continued to act by momentum while "I" am busy thinking about the justifications of my action and never really present to myself acting in the world. The first goal,

---

[159] Ibid., 18.

[160] Ibid., 182.

[161] Perry, *On Awakening and Remembering*, 196.

it appears, is to become connected, that the mind, emotions, and body work together in harmony. Now the beginning is to try to separate ourselves from our functioning, to stop believing that this active set of personalities fashioned by imitation and education is grounded in reality. As the father in Pirandello's play *Six Characters in Search of an Author* says:

> But that's the whole essence of the drama, sir, as I see it—the fact that we each think of ourselves as one person, but it's not true. We're all so many different people, sir, as many as we have the potential to be. We're one thing with one person, and something quite different with another! Meanwhile we labour under the illusion that we're the same with everybody, and that we're the same in everything we do. Well, that's not so—it's simply not true.[162]

To come to such an understanding, we must look at ourselves as though we were a stranger. It is not a question of doing more bodily activity, reading more books, or having more emotional experiences. There is nothing we have to change in our lives. We must simply be attentive to what we do, and perhaps by themselves the habits of all kinds, from simple bodily cravings to the subtlest emotional configurations, once seen as the habits they are, will cease to have the hold on us that they do. I say "simply," but it is not so simple. We have almost no control over our attention and even to begin to understand the machine that we are, it is just these habits that identify us with our inner and outer activity that must be opposed; and yet, being 'in' our habits, it is almost impossible to be aware of them. Thus, all this work is almost impossible without the aid of those who can watch over us, give us shocks when we are taken by our habitual functioning.

---

[162] Luigi Pirandello, *Six Characters in Search of an Author* (London: Nick Hern Books, 2003), 34.

Another great problem is that our personality does not want to be scrutinized at all. It does not want to be put out for display in front of the 'inner eye.' It flees the moment that the lies, the fears, the cravings, the pride, the awkwardness that make up our personality start to become apparent. It likes so much more to think of itself as intelligent, handsome, well-bred, spiritual, or any other such splendid dream:

> Sometimes we use our minds not to discover facts but to hide them. We use part of the mind as a screen to prevent another part of it from sensing what goes on elsewhere. The screening is not necessarily intentional—we are not deliberate obfuscators all of the time—but deliberate or not, the screen does hide.[163]

But if we are able to gather the courage to stay present in front of ourselves and to accept the suffering that this observation entails, the imaginary world that we have created around ourselves is slowly going to disintegrate, that is, the unconscious beliefs that continually support our make-believe world will start to become apparent. And this is not easy in the least: to see that we can be as stupid as we are intelligent, fearful as courageous, deceitful as sincere, to see ourselves as the exact opposite of the image of ourselves that we have built up in our minds. It is, moreover, equally as difficult to accept that we do not know what we are going to say, what we are going to do, from one minute to the next, to really understand that we can *do* nothing, that we are puppets controlled by everything around and within us, that we have no control, neither of ourselves nor our lives, nor of the lives of others, that everything happens and that all we can do is be witness to the turning of the wheel of life. In the words of Coomaraswamy:

> This is the only orthodox doctrine, namely, that man as he is in himself, 'this man' who does not know what is true but only what he likes to think, who does not know

---

[163] Damasio, *The Feeling of What Happens*, 28-29.

what is right but only what he wants to do, and who knows nothing of art but only what he likes, is not a free man and makes no choices, but is pulled and driven by forces that are not his own because he has not mastered them.[164]

To come to this realization of our nothingness is the beginning, but to reach the beginning is extraordinarily difficult. It has been said that if we could observe ourselves long enough, perhaps something would appear to our attention, a sensation of our own body which could act as a support for a real change of consciousness to a higher level encompassing all that takes place at the level of our functioning: our thoughts, emotions, and bodily activity. At this higher level of vision, then, we would no longer 'see' through the filters of thought deformed and limited by our emotions, by our outer personality. On the contrary, everything would be observed from 'on high,' so to speak, objectively. And it would only be from the height of this elevated vision that we could really control ourselves, for on this summit we would no longer be prisoners of our thought, emotions, and body. It would only be from there that we could truly say we were capable of acting, doing, creating in the real sense of these terms. In proportion as this new state of consciousness was being created, our ego, our personality, our 'feeling of self,' would leave the imaginary world of thought and, like a child, begin to become one with everything it does naturally. It would begin to think, to feel, to move, quite freely and in an integrated way. The psychological distinction between what one thinks one is and what one does would disappear: "Verily I say unto you, Whosoever shall not receive the kingdom of God as a little child shall in no wise enter therein," said the Christ. But now, with the turn of the spiral, there would be another level of consciousness, a higher vision surveying all one's functions and able to guide them in doing what this new master had decided.

---

[164] Coomaraswamy, *Metaphysics*, 370.

The raising of consciousness, then, is the awareness concomitant with the deepening connection between the mind and the body along with the diminution of the ego. In other words, the level of one's apperception is the result of the level of one's being in its relation with the cosmos. The wider one's connection, the deeper one's impressions and understanding beyond simple sense impressions and thought.

At this 'repairing of the human machine,' one has arrived at the 'beginning,' so to speak, at a certain interaction of mind and body allowing the reception of finer levels of cosmic energy. As the prodigal son comes back to the father, we have arrived at that state of being which our birthright as humans, above the animals, has entitled us to have. We have finally retreated from the "outer darkness" to come back to our own body, our house, to the naos of the Temple, to the center of the Cross. It is only here, from this Center, that the vertical axis of higher spiritual energies can now infuse us with its power leading to states of consciousness that, as we are, we cannot even suspect.

It is the role of spiritual symbolism to influence and aid in the progression of this voyage to the Center. We now need to see how the apperception of the symbol affects its efficacy, that is, the role of the person who is in relation with the symbol.

Symbolism and Apperception

Alfred North Whitehead proposes this definition of symbolism:

> The human mind is functioning symbolically when some components of its experience elicit consciousness, beliefs, emotions, and usages, respecting other components of its experience. The former set of components are the 'symbols,' and the latter set constitute the 'meaning' of the symbols. The organic functioning whereby there is transition from the symbol to the meaning will be called 'symbolic reference.'[165]

---

[165]Whitehead, *Symbolism*, 7-8.

He goes on to say that the "symbolic reference" is that dynamic element of the human mind that creates the synthesis between the symbol and its meaning, and that this synthesis must be based on a common element between the two. This does not guarantee, he says, that a given symbol will invariably produce a given meaning in the person perceiving the symbol, for the relation between the symbol and its experienced meaning is a complicated one depending on a number of given factors at any given time, but especially the nature of the mind of the person perceiving the symbol. In fact, it would often be impossible to distinguish between what is "symbol" and what is "meaning" given the organic relationship between the two. For example, if one enters a cathedral and finds oneself changed, is the cathedral the symbol and the new state the meaning it has produced in my experience, or is the state the symbol and the cathedral the meaning by which my state may be interpreted. In the same vein, considering language, there is no reason to assume that the word "table," spoken or written, is a symbol giving the meaning to the physical object that is a table any more than the table as a physical object is a symbol giving meaning to the word "table."

When we see a table through our eyes, we have no choice but to give meaning to what we perceive. We cannot "not know" a table upon looking at what is, though on a more basic perceptual level, it is but a grouping of colored shapes (as certain modern artists would even insist). According to Whitehead, this is the most fundamental type of symbolism, that is, the immediate inference from sense perceptions of the eye to the meaning of physical entities,[166] In support of this Jacob Bronowski says:

> [E]ven the perception of the senses is governed by mechanisms which make our knowledge of the outside world highly inferential. We do not receive impressions which are elemental. Our sense impressions are themselves constructed by the nervous system in such a

---

[166] Ibid., 2.

way that they automatically carry with them an interpretation of what they see or hear or feel.[167]

And still further, the neuroscientist Antonio Damasio says:

> [W]hen you and I look at an external object, we form comparable images in our respective brains, and we can describe the object in similar ways. That does not mean, however, that the image we see is a replica of the object. The image we see is based on changes that occurred in our organisms, in the body and in the brain, as the physical structure of that particular object interacts with the body...[T]he images we experience are brain constructions prompted by an object, rather than mirror reflections of the object. There is no picture of the object being transferred optically from the retina to the visual cortex. The optics stop at the retina....There is a set of correspondences, which has been achieved in the long history of evolution, between the physical characteristics of objects independent of us and the menu of possible responses of the organism.[168]

So even this most basic symbolism is not direct knowing; it is not pure experience but an inference—true, a subconscious, automatic, not reasoned inference, but an inference none the less. To see the truth of this, one only has to continually stare at an object for a certain time with a certain type of attention so that after a while its meaning in terms of its utility can begin to fade in importance in favor of a simple tableau of color, shape and shadow, what the cubists were doubtless trying to show us in their paintings, *which in itself is still a lower level of inference.*

A more exterior level of symbolism is language. Just as we cannot *not* know a table when we see one, we cannot *not* understand the word "table" when we hear it. Nevertheless, if we repeat a word to ourselves over and over again, its meaning fades to our mind and becomes gibberish. Why this occurs is

---

[167] Bronowski, *The Origins of Knowledge*, 43.

[168] Antonio Damasio, Looking *for Spinoza: Joy, Sorrow, and the Feeling Brain* (New York: Harcourt, 2003), 199-200.

because "meaning" is not the result of a pure one-on-one relation between a thing and what it represents, but an understanding of its relation within a particular context. It is the extent of this context as experienced by the perceiver that deepens the meaning of the symbol for him. This is why the same symbol will be experienced differently for each person perceiving or experiencing it.

An analogy and good example of what we mean by "meaning" beyond rational analysis can be found in our hearing of music.[169] When we speak of music, for example music played on a piano, we normally associate with this term that of "melody" by which we receive the idea, the meaning, that the composer put into the work, and that we receive as a feeling such as sadness, joy, exaltation—which we may or may not, however, be able to put into words. Now what we are hearing physically is actually a succession of tones that arrives at our ears from the vibrations of the air set in motion by piano keys hitting a taught string, which then stimulate our inner ear to send electrical impulses to the brain. Physically that is all that is happening. There are, in fact, tune-deaf people who cannot hear melody at all, the meaning behind the sounds, but only the tones themselves: in fact, "When we hear a melody, we hear things that have no counterpart in physical nature."[170] So, we ask, what is the fundamental difference between a monkey randomly hitting the keyboard and a pianist playing a Mozart sonata? Why do we hear melody? Whence comes the meaning?

The answer may be found, perhaps, in that we do not hear, in fact, only tones but tones as a part of a whole, of the seven-tone system which our culture has handed down to us from antiquity. Each tone, having a "dynamic quality" appropriate to itself

---

[169] Victor Zuckerkandl, *Sound and Symbol: Music and the External World* (Princeton, NJ: Princeton University Press, 1969), *passim*.

[170] Ibid., 23.

reverberates from a specific level within this tonal system. We "know" directly what is right, what is music, and not merely sound, even though we cannot say why. The meaning of music arises not from acoustics, the vibration of air hitting our eardrums, neither from within us, our feelings, that some say we apply to certain tones, but from within the tones themselves as representatives of a certain level in a hierarchy that corresponds to this same hierarchy within us and which originates and is coeval with the cosmic hierarchy present in all creation.

Above, we called the hearing of music an analogy. The reason for this is that we can equate the function of hearing music on one level with the function of consciousness on another. For just as we *hear* a melody through the dynamic quality of tones at a particular level as part of a whole, so we *receive* higher energies according to our level in the universal hierarchy of forces (which is our definition of consciousness). Due to this analogy, music itself can be a powerful spiritual symbol if it is based on the same numerical qualities as those existing in universal laws. In the words of Fabre d'Olivet paraphrasing a Hermetic treatise:

> ...music is not merely, as is imagined today, the art of combining tones or the talent for reproducing them in the way most pleasant to the ear: that is only its practical side from which result the ephemeral forms, more or less brilliant according to the time and place, the taste and whim of peoples, which make them vary in a thousand different ways. Music regarded in its speculative aspect is, as the Ancients defined it, the knowledge of the order of all things, the science of the harmonic relationships of the Universe; it rests on immovable principles which nothing can alter.[171]

From the above, we see that the human mind functioning symbolically does not and cannot separate the perception from

---

[171] Fabre d'Olivet, *Music Explained as Science and Art: and considered in its analogical relations to Religious Mysteries, Ancient Mythology and the History of the World*, tr. Jocelyn Godwin (Rochester, Vermont: Inner Traditions International, 1987), 39-40.

the meaning, which is an ingrained part of the synthetic experience of any perception taking place in, or having an impression on, the human mind. It is the nature of this synthesis that we are interested in here. While the perception and its meaning are independent of each other on the one hand, they are interdependent on the other. How they combine is dependent, Whitehead says, "on attention and on the activity of conceptual functioning, whereby physical experience and conceptual imagination are fused into knowledge." Whitehead even says that "It is a matter of pure convention as to which of our experiential activities we term mental and which physical." And this is so because any perceptual experience has an immediate concurrent mental quality of symbolic reference providing meaning. We are again in front of the old philosophical question: "If a branch falls in the forest, is there noise if no one is there to hear it?" He continues, however, by stating that "there is no conscious knowledge apart from the intervention of mentality in the form of conceptual analysis," which brings us to the purely human level of mental functioning.

Again, we come to the double nature of man, in this case in terms of his mental activity, which is of two natures: analytical (linear) and symbolic (synthetic). Analytical thinking belongs to man's mental apparatus on a single level. It is based on education, language, and a training of the mind that results in logical reasoning. Symbolic activity is the fusion of a concept with a certain lived experience. This fusion produces understanding that cuts through the levels of which man is made and may or may not be expressible in words. The depth of this understanding provoked by a symbol depends therefore on the inner and outer experiences that the person being affected by the symbol has undergone and the degree to which these experiences have assimilated into the person's total understanding. This means that the symbol has meaning in terms of context, environment, and lived relationships, for, as we have seen, nothing exists in isolation. Whitehead goes on to say:

> We enjoy the symbol, but we also penetrate to the meaning. The symbols do not create their meaning: the meaning, in the form of actual effective beings reacting upon us, exists for us in its own right. But the symbols discover this meaning for us. They discover it because, in the long course of adaptation of living organisms to their environment, nature taught their use.... The how of our present experience must conform to the what of the past in us.[172]

How we perceive and react in the present depends on all our past experience ingrained in the depths of our consciousness. Our relationships to symbols are, as Whitehead says, "precisely our reactions to them." We are not outside of a world looking at elements that are apart from us. Our brain is not making snapshots or a video of some objective world waiting for us to discover. On the contrary, what we observe arises from what we are, our state of being. This is our *experience*. There is a relationship between me and what I perceive, and it is this relationship that is the true reality. *Subject and object are one.* A symbol can refer to this experience but can never replace it, and only one who has had more or less the same experience would be able to fully understand the symbol. The beginning of modern civilization began when man began to believe that his *thought about* the world was reality and not his *experience in* the world.

Knowing the world symbolically is how we learn to function among the myriad sense perceptions we experience. We learn by imitation to use what we know to stand for what we do not know. For example, we don't really know what "red" is, but symbolically we can visualize the color in our minds and use a particular word to name it, whereas we would be quite at a loss to describe "red" to someone else. And so it is with all sensory experience. Can we describe the taste of salt, the touch of silk? Symbolism does not necessarily involve language, and in fact even before language the child acquires a sensory-motor intelligence by which perception is ordered and schematized, thus allowing the arising of mental symbols to represent the knowledge of what was previously experienced as action or perception.[173] Jean Piaget, who made a lifelong study of the intellectual development of children has shown that language can develop only after a certain sensori-motor intelligence has been acquired and which results in the assimilation of a "logic of action involving the establishment of relationships and correspondences (functions) and classification of schemes...in short, structures of ordering and assembling that constitute a substructure for the future operations of thought."[174]

That is to say, the *structure* (as opposed to the *content*) of thought is based on bodily experience and relationships unconsciously assimilated, so that language is impossible until a certain level of learning in this manner is attained, for it is only through established structures that new structures can be assimilated. In the words of Piaget:

> The organizing activity of the subject must be considered just as important as the connections inherent in the external stimuli, for the subject becomes aware of these

---

[173] The work of Jean Piaget provides much information on the acquiring of the symbolic function in children:

- Herbert Ginsburg and Sylvia Opper, *Piaget's Theory of Intellectual Development: An Introduction* (Englewood Cliffs, NJ: Prentice-Hall, 1969), 72-85.

- Jean Piaget, *The Child's Conception of the World* (Savage, MD: Littlefield Adams, 1929), 161-62.

- Jean Piaget, *The Child and Reality: Problems of Genetic Psychology* (New York: Penguin Books, 1976), 16-18, 57, 73-4, 83, 117, 153.

- Jean Piaget and Bärbel Inhelder, *The Psychology of the Child* (n.p.: Basic Books, 1969), Chap. 3, 51-91.

[174] Piaget and Inhelder, *The Psychology of the Child*, 13.

connections only to the degree that he can assimilate them by means of his existing structures.[175]

Our deepest level of knowing, then, does not start in school and is not based on thought (which itself is based on language), but rather on the intelligence of the body begun in infancy, or even earlier in the womb. Our unconscious is thus a nested collection of experiential knowledge, each level based on the previous one and enlarging on it by applying the basic structures and schemes to larger and more complex arenas of experience. In this way, once knowledge becomes assimilated, our awareness of it disappears and becomes a substructure around which another level of knowledge can be built through subconscious relationships between the larger whole and these what have become incarnated parts.

This process, if continued, can lead to the incarnation of the ego, our "sense of self," without which higher spiritual states of being could not develop. This would not mean that the ego somehow volatizes but that its functioning, through loss of fear, would no longer "require" constant control, which implies a higher level of awareness. On a lower level, the proverbial difficulty of learning to ride a bicycle and the subsequent automatic ease of it once learned comes to mind. It must be emphasized here that we are not discussing the content of knowledge, what is learned by the memory in terms of facts and concepts; but rather the increased understanding of our relationship with the environment, which is really a question of enlarging our consciousness. In other words, the increase of consciousness is equivalent to becoming progressively more aware of one's integration into larger and larger wholes, not conceptually, but by an assimilated inner experience resulting in a definite change in one's state of being. This change of being is experienced as a greater harmony in functioning of the parts of oneself (mental,

---

[175] Ibid., 5.

emotional, corporeal) as well as a greater permeability to the cosmic energies in which we are immersed due to a "letting go" of unnecessary and often unconscious tension.

Now, it is just this—the development of our being through experience—as opposed to acquiring more and more purely mental knowledge, that symbolism in its deepest sense is concerned with. Based on metaphysical principles, symbols can be applied to various domains: historical, psychological, cosmological, etc., all of which, by obeying the same fundamental laws, provide essential meaning to those prepared to receive them.

Symbols are created by man to emphasize the importance of what is being symbolized, thus bringing into the equation the intensifying of the emotions arising from the contemplation of the meaning of the symbol. Nevertheless, this reaction will simply be a reflex to the symbol unless "conscious attention" is present to provide the meaning of the symbolic reference. If "conscious attention" becomes the natural state of being, (that is, the ego has become incarnated into the subconscious and has thus given up center stage) then inner or outer action provoked by a symbol is no longer mediated by thought but is rather a direct response to the environment and thus cannot be "wrong." The same idea on a lower level of reality is provided by Piaget:

> There is intelligence before speech, but there is no thought before speech. In this respect, let us distinguish intelligence and thought. Intelligence for the child is the solution of a new problem, the coordination of the means to reach a certain goal which is not accessible in an immediate manner; whereas thought is interiorized intelligence no longer based on direct action but on a symbolism, the symbolic evocation by speech, by mental pictures, and other means, which makes it possible to represent what the sensori-motor intelligence, on the contrary, is going to grasp directly.[176]

---

[176]Piaget, *The Child and Reality*, 11.

The main point being discussed here is that mind does not depend only on thought, nor, if we believe the systems theorists[177], on any "thing" at all. Rather mind is a *process* assimilated to the process of living. Since life "consists in continually sucking orderliness from its environment,"[178] the organizing activity of life is, as the theory goes, what we call the process of mind. Now since this organizing activity does not depend only on mental activity, but also on the emotional and sensorimotor functions, the process of knowing or cognition goes far beyond simple thinking or even the need for a brain. Here again, the scientist Damasio can help:

> The inescapable and remarkable fact about these three phenomena—emotion, feeling, consciousness—is their body relatedness.... But all of these processes...depend for their execution on representations of the organism. Their shared essence is the body.[179]

A bacterium for example has no brain, yet it perceives its environment and reacts to it.[180] Also, since an imagined bodily movement results in the same pattern of electrical waves, both cortical and muscular, as the actual physical execution of the movement itself, it could be surmised that a symbol could affect a person beyond the mental down into the essential physical nature of the person being influenced.[181] Symbols, as means of knowing, can thus affect a person's entire being on a deeper level through perception and emotion than simply through thought. A symbol has power because our perception of it and its action are one. We are always fooled, however, into believing

---

[177] Capra, *The Web of Life*, 168.

[178] Erwin Schrodinger, *What Is Life?* (Cambridge, UK: Cambridge University Press, 1967), 73.

[179] Damasio, *The Feeling of What Happens*, 284.

[180] Capra, *The Web of Life*, 170.

[181] Piaget, *The Psychology of the Child*, 68.

that "I" the subject am observing "it" the object, when in fact myself and the object are one:

> It is the same elements that go to compose my mind and the world. The situation is the same for every mind and its world, in spite of the unfathomable abundance of 'cross-references' between them. The world is given to me only once, not one existing and one perceived. Subject and object are only one. The reason why our sentient, percipient and thinking ego is met nowhere within our scientific world picture can easily be indicated in seven words: because it is itself that world picture. It is identical with the whole and therefore cannot be contained in it as a part of it.... The world is given but once. Nothing is reflected. The original and the mirror-image are identical. The world extended in space and time is but our representation...Experience does not give us the slightest clue of its being anything besides that...[182]

A symbol, whether words, sounds, graphic representations, gestures, or buildings may or may not have an effect on the perceiver. The effective charge of most symbols depends on its association with a certain meaning in history, which is carried over in the civilization through its culture. A person confronted with a symbol but ignorant of its associations will not be affected in the same way as one who is steeped in the culture from which the symbol arose. Which is not to say that certain symbols may affect a perceiver at a level deeper than that conditioned by culture, especially certain musical forms, which, through their rhythm, and vibrations may produce the same effect in every person because they touch what is universal in the human species, that is, beyond the words, images and melodies belonging to any particular culture. A symbol to be evocative must contain within itself that which brings forth the connections relating to a certain aspect of existence. A thing becomes a symbol in so far as it evokes the history of the perceiver's relation to that symbol coming from his own

---

[182]Schrodinger, "Mind and Matter" in *What Is Life?*, 127, 128, 136.

experience. An evocative word in one's own language may provoke feelings and sensations because of the emotions connected with one's lifelong experience with the word and its associations. A word from a language that one does not know, would not be evocative at all. The symbol of the Eye of Horus, may produce a certain effect if I am aware of the myths surrounding it and its embedded relationships within ancient Egyptian civilization. The more profound the symbol, the less the meaning must be learned, but is natural to the human being *qua* human being. On the other hand, there is no such thing as pure perception without the perception being molded by preconceived patterns of thought based on experience. In this sense, a symbol can evoke a synthesis of perception, emotion and thought into an effective experience. Let us quote Whitehead once again:

> Thus symbolism, including the symbolic transference by which it is effected, is merely one exemplification of the fact that a unity of experience arises out of the confluence of many components.... Each component by its very nature stands in a certain potential scheme of relationships to the other components. It is the transformation of this potentiality into real unity which constitutes that actual concrete fact which is an act of experience.[183]

Now, to see deeper means to see wider, to see more connections—connections we usually do not see—between us and the symbol, and between the symbol and its environment. A thing as symbol is like a focal point from which the world we see expands in meaning; it is a support by which the relationship between our attention and the thing enables our consciousness to rise. It is an organic relationship so that to see deeper into the symbol one must be in a higher state of consciousness, yet the symbol itself is at the same time a support to this end. As an

---

[183]Whitehead, *Symbolism*, 86-87.

example of what I am trying to express, I would like to insert here a little piece I wrote about a certain experience that happened to me in Algeria some years ago:

> I remember well in Oran, sitting alone in my hotel room looking out the window, when below me, a little to the right, my eye was caught by a tile on a roof. It was a tile like any other tile, only being different in that it caught my eye. Slowly I began to see it, the jagged edge on the right, the little white droppings towards the lower half, the redness peeping through the dirt, the black surrounding the red, the shadow of a dark bird that streaked above, the play of light, of the sun and the penumbra shifting around the shape. As I looked at this tile—five, ten, fifteen minutes—this dirt-streaked tile hardly revealing the red of the earth from which it came, I began to decipher the essence of its nature.
>
> What am I saying? How can I explain? Except that I became the tile. I felt this tile as part of the roof, that it had no meaning in itself, and I drew back and became one with the roof whole, and, more quickly now, I felt that this roof had no meaning in itself apart from the walls on which it lay, the people within, the other roofs of the town of which it was but one; and the whole town of Oran became my world, the European quarter and the Arab, the palms, the gulls wheeling over the plazas; and I felt at once that the town had no meaning in itself and I knew, I knew without seeing them, that it was but a part of the desert to the south and of the sea beyond the way; and that I, too, had no meaning in myself but was a part and had my place in this one universe. And how can I describe the fire inside me, the joy that radiated like a bright, burning nova, the light that illumined my darkened soul; and I saw and I knew, and how long I stayed by my window I could not guess, but when I noticed the evening sending its obscurity across the sky, I looked once again at that dirt-encrusted tile, and with a serenity beyond measure, I knew I had discovered for once and all what Beauty meant.

I do not doubt for a moment that this experience, real though it was, was mixed with much imagination born of desire and had to do with a chance emotional state not supported by will or purpose. Yet it did give a feeling for the interconnection of all things, and of how anything can serve as a means to see more of the universal nexus in which we too are enmeshed. Aldous Huxley points to this fact when he wrote:

> [S]ome of those few who do desire spirituality and deliverance find that, for them, the most effective means to those ends are ceremonies, 'vain repetitions' and sacramental rites. It is by participating in these acts and uttering these formulas that they are most powerfully reminded of the eternal Ground of all being; it is by immersing themselves in the symbols that they can most easily come through to that which is symbolized. Every thing, event or thought is a point of intersection between creature and Creator, between a more or less distant manifestation of God and a ray, so to speak, of the unmanifest Godhead; every thing, event or thought can therefore be made the doorway through which a soul may pass out of time into eternity.[184]

And ultimately, isn't this the essential function of the symbol: the transformation of man's consciousness, of his state of being, so that he lives in a higher and deeper world, or in the words of Titus Burckhardt concerning the real function of art:

> The aim of art is to make the human environment, the world in so far as it is fashioned by man, a part of that order which most directly manifests divine Unity.[185]

Symbolic Thought

It is through the concept of levels that symbols find their justification because a symbol *adds* new values to an object or action without affecting its particular and immediate value apprehended by the senses. The symbol is a *support* by which meaning is focused and synthesized on the 'idea' beyond the

---

[184] A. Huxley, *The Perennial Philosophy*, 269.

[185] Titus Burckhardt, *Principes et méthodes*, 12. [This and further citations from this book are our translations.]

representation and so elevates man to the spiritual or objective world—and in so doing frees him from his subjective or personal situation. That is not to say that he escapes his personal situation, but that it takes on greater meaning by being seen as a necessary and integral part of a larger whole, that a manifestation *in life* is ultimately identical with its spiritual cause, or, in other words, is outside of time and exists in the 'eternal present.' This can only be understood, however, if we can see that true symbols are always concerned with the same thing, that is, creation seen in one of its multitudinous aspects, which is identical with the maintenance of the present world. Or otherwise said: "Creation is not a series of events in time, but a speculation about the principles of life and the arrangement of the cosmos."[186] Emile Mâle provides us with a beautiful description of this symbolic mode of thought in Traditional cultures where he describes the mind of Christian man in the European Middle Ages:

> Some attempt must be made to understand the medieval view of the world and of nature. What is the visible world? What is the meaning of the myriad forms of life?... Is it merely appearance or is it reality? The Middle Ages were unanimous in their reply—the world is a symbol. As the idea of his work is in the mind of the artist, so the universe was in the thought of God from the beginning....If this be so then in each being is hidden a divine thought; the world is a book written by the hand of God in which every creature is a world charged with meaning. The ignorant see the forms—the mysterious letters—understanding nothing of their meaning, but the wise pass from the visible to the invisible, and in reading nature read the thought of God. True knowledge, then, consists not in the study of things in themselves—the outward forms—but in penetrating to the inner meaning intended by God for our instruction.... All being holds in its depths the reflection of the sacrifice of Christ, the image of the Church and the virtues and vices. The material and spiritual worlds are one.... In the Middle

---

[186] R.T. Rundle Clark, *Myth and Symbol in Ancient Egypt* (London: Thames and Hudson, 1959), 82.

Ages the idea of a thing which a man framed for himself was always more real to him than the actual thing itself, and we see why these mystical centuries had no conception of what men now call science. The study of things for their own sake held no meaning for the thoughtful man.[187]

And so it is true for all Traditional art. Coomaraswamy, when writing of Buddhist art, has this to say:

The practice of an art is not traditionally, as it is for us, a secular activity, or even a matter of affective 'inspiration,' but a metaphysical rite.... No distinction can be drawn between art and contemplation. The artist is first of all required to remove himself from human to celestial levels of apperception; at this level and in a state of unification, no longer having in view anything external to himself, he sees and realizes, that is to say becomes, what he is afterwards to represent in wrought material.[188]

This same analysis has been made in terms of tribal cultures in our own century. Note, however, that tribal cultures in our day do not necessarily give a correct view of early man, and no identity between them should be assumed. Tribes living in remote areas may be of quite different stages of development, depending on the history of the tribe. It could be but a remnant of a once-flourishing civilization or one whose culture has been modified in countless ways by contact with modern civilization. Lucien Lévy-Bruhl, a French anthropologist, discussed in his writings tribal mentality in terms of what he calls the "law of participation,"[189] which is not easily defined, since it involves the direct experience of the individual member of the tribe. Perception, according to Lévy-Bruhl, is not a simple mental phenomena, but involves emotional and motor elements as well; and, in terms of tribal man, as opposed to man in our civilization,

---

[187] Emile Mâle, *The Gothic Image: Religious Art in France of the Thirteenth Century* (London: The Fontana Library, 1961), 29, 34.

[188] Coomaraswamy, *The Door in the Sky*, 160-61.

[189] Lévy Bruhl, *How Natives Think*, ch. II.

the emotional and motor elements take on a much greater force. For this reason, a tribal man, "participates" to a much greater degree in the life around him, and thus he lives more greatly what he sees, hears, and experiences in general.[190] He does not categorize and analyze as we are wont to do by filtering everything through the mind, but rather 'knows' immediately and intuitively due to the collective symbolic meanings of the tribe of which he is but a part and of which he cannot conceive of himself otherwise. As Lévy -Bruhl puts it:

> The consciousness which he has of himself is not the awareness of a person complete in himself, but of a person for whom the raison d'être, the essential conditions of existence, are found in the group of which he forms part, and without which he would not exist."[191]

Our value of "thinking for oneself" is thus an unknown concept for tribal man. Intimately connected to this feeling of group solidarity is how tribal mentality experiences the world. In the words of Lévy-Bruhl:

> We have found that his mind does more than present his object to him: it possesses it and is possessed by it. It communes with it and participates in it, not only in the ideological, but also in the physical and mystic sense of the word. The mind does not imagine it merely; it lives it.[192]

Because of this intense lived experience, man-made symbols are rare in tribal cultures in which *everything* is a symbol of a living mysterious reality in which he too participates as a member of the tribe, and which is reinforced by his institutions and rites. He has no need of concrete or mental symbols to remind him of this,

---

[190] This mentality can be compared to that of the child as expounded by Jean Piaget, who himself makes the comparison between the mentality of the child and tribal man as described by Lévy-Bruhl. See Jean Piaget, *The Child's Conception of the World.*

[191] Lucien Lévy-Bruhl, *The Notebooks on Primitive Mentality* (New York: Harper & Row, 1975), 77.

[192] Lévy-Bruhl, *How Natives Think,* 98-9, 106, 362.

to bring him back to a reality which he lives every day:

> Because religion is a response to the conditions of
> alienation in a civilization, religion is unnecessary in a
> culture of hunters and gatherers. The culture of hunters
> and gatherers is spiritually personified; every event is
> part of a story, every part is connected to the whole, every
> act is flooded with the sacred. When an entire way of life
> is sacred, the people do not have to build churches and
> sing hymns on Sundays.[193]

> For Durkheim...so far were primitive people from being
> self-conscious that they had virtually no 'personalities'
> and indeed were barely individuals at all, as we
> understand those terms. Lacking 'selves,' and
> uninterested in thinking for themselves, for them the
> prescriptions and sanctions of the 'group-mind' were
> everything....It is just this sort of profound
> epistemological difference that we moderns, whose lives
> are founded upon the idea of critical, individual thinking,
> find hardest to conceive, much less to bridge.[194]

Lévy-Bruhl expresses very well the experience of a tribal
mentality, this "participatory" mode of experiencing that we
mentioned above in terms of Piaget's description of child
development, a mode in which perception and action coexist in
the same experience. It is this direct mode of experiencing the
world which modern "civilized" man is incapable of as he is, but
which he can perhaps find again through a certain type of work
on himself. It is not that man should become *only* as a child or
have a tribal mentality, but that he arrives at a state of being in
which a higher state of attention allows his relationship with his
environment to be completely natural and spontaneous without
him being completely identified with it. As we mentioned
earlier, man must go beyond his ego, not by struggling against

---

[193]William Irwin Thompson, *The Time Falling Bodies Take to Light: Mythology,
Sexuality, and the Origins of Culture* (New York: St. Martin's Press, 1981), 103.

[194]Robert Ackerman, discussing Emile Durkheim in the forward to the book by
Cornford, *From Religion to Philosophy*, x-xi.

it; but on the contrary, by accepting it so completely that it becomes ingrained in one's being, incarnated in one's body, to such an extent that its action becomes entirely spontaneous, and due to this acceptance, and other factors, *another level of consciousness is present* to survey the functioning of this now subservient ego. It must be stressed that this spontaneity has nothing to do with "unconscious instinctiveness' or anything of the sort. Titus Burckhardt describes this difference well:

> It is important to not confuse the "non-conscious" (Wu-nien) or the "non-mental" (Wu-hsin) of dhyana Buddhism with the "subconscious" of modern psychologists, for the state of intuitive spontaneity that the method of dhyana actualizes is obviously not below the normal individual consciousness, but quite to the contrary, above it.[195]

Gregory Bateson, one of the precursors of systems theory, had an intuitive feeling for the importance of hierarchy in terms of learning and consciousness. This hierarchy he calls Learning I, Learning II and Learning III. Learning I, he says, is behavior learned by rote, stimulus-response, or reward-penalty. "Learning II" is taking a specific case of Learning I and generalizing the concept so that it may be used as a *pattern* in other contexts to create certain *unconscious* habits of perception and behavior. This could be the general state of most human beings. The next step would be to take the nature of Learning II and generalize it to a yet higher level: "Learning III." Here, the unconscious nature of Learning II would then be the result of habit rather than conscious choice. Bateson goes on to say:

> But any freedom from the bondage of habit must also denote a profound redefinition of the self. If I stop at the level of Learning II, 'I' am the aggregate of those characteristics which I call my 'character.' 'I' am my habits of acting in context and shaping and perceiving the contexts in which I act. Selfhood is a product or

---

[195] Burckhardt, *Principes et méthodes*, 194.

aggregate of Learning II. To the degree that a man achieves Learning III and learns to perceive and act in terms of the contexts of contexts, his 'self' will take on a sort of irrelevance.[196]

What then is the result? What is the experience of a man of "Learning III"? Bateson quite understood the importance of this question. In his own words: "Learning III is likely to be difficult and rare even in human beings. Expectably, it will also be difficult for scientists, who are only human, to imagine or describe this process."[197] Bateson provides three possible scenarios to those who unlock the key to unconscious habitual behavior: 1) psychosis, 2) a return to a simple stimulus-response comportment, or 3) an oceanic feeling of oneness with the entire universe.[198] While all this may be true, there is one possibility he left out, which is precisely that which we are trying to deal with in this book: the appearance of a new level of consciousness, a constant attention and inner presence in the body that can survey the workings of the ego and its mechanical functioning. Concomitant with this new state of being there seems to occur a hierarchical understanding of man and the cosmos whose expression can only take place through the use of symbol.

Following Lévy-Bruhl,[199] we can now put forward the *raison d'être* of symbols and myths and why they arose, which is intimately linked to the development of man's mental processes. First of all, we need to do away with *stages* of thought, so present in early anthropological literature, such as a progression from animism/totemism to symbolical/mythological to rational/logical, because these aspects of human thought are always present in different civilizations.

---

[196] Gregory Bateson, *Steps to an Ecology of Mind* (New York: Ballantine Books, 1972), 304.

[197] Ibid., 301.

[198] Ibid., 305-06.

[199] Lévy-Bruhl, *How Natives Think,* 362-386.

The mental processes of tribal man were based not on the individual *qua* individual, but as an individual as a member of a community. He does not need symbols and myths because...

> ...the prelogical and mystic collective mentality is still actively predominant in the social group. The feeling of symbiosis effected between the individuals of the group, or between a certain human group and one which is animal or vegetable in substance, is directly expressed by institutions and ceremonies.[200].

In other words, the mental process is not one of reasoning, analysis, or 'figuring out,' but a *direct* response to natural phenomena based on a *collective* belief in what constitutes appropriate behavior. We almost used the word "consensus" instead of belief, but this would imply that each individual arrived at the same conclusion through his own thought processes, which is not at all what we are trying to express. Tribal man acting as part of the community, is analogous to a cell acting as part of an organ. It is the organ as a whole which guides the cell to react to external stimuli to protect the integrity of the organ's structure and function. This is the sole purpose of the cell, which has no individual initiative and would die if it were extracted from its surrounding cells, from its environment within the organ. In like manner, tribal man acts in relation to his community to protect and continue the tribe constituted by its traditions, ceremonies, and way of life. There is no thought of being "independent" or "creative." For tribal man, he *is* the community and his thought is guided by the common mentality of the tribe. Now what is this common mentality? We can never really know the origin of the traditions and customs of a particular people or tribe, as these are lost in the mists of time, but we can try to understand the *process* by which these customs and traditions function through the *minds* of the tribe's members.

---

[200]Ibid., 363.

Claude Lévi-Strauss, perhaps the most well-known of French anthropologists, used the concept of "totemism" as a means of deciphering tribal man's mental processes, an exercise which we find quite convincing. Where we do *not* agree with him is in his description of Lévy-Bruhl's concept of "participation."[201] While Lévi-Strauss opposes the two concepts, we believe that they are profoundly complementary. Totemism has been identified by some anthropologists as a kinship and/or mystical relationship between a man or a clan and a natural object, most usually an animal, but also a plant or inanimate entity such as the wind, an outcropping or other particular feature of the landscape, etc., which is the "totem." This relationship, then, provides a basis for organization and ritual within the tribe, with various taboos relating to contact with the totem, marriage according to the person's relation with the totem, and so forth. While many theorists considered this a stage in the development of man's thought, Lévi-Strauss saw totemism as a classificatory scheme, a means by which tribal man made order of, and organized, the world and the society in which he lived. This makes perfect sense if one looks at the sacred monuments of high civilizations, such as Egyptian temples, Christian cathedrals, Buddhist stupas, and so on. Such monuments are meant to be a re-creation of the universe, a means of ordering, in human terms, the components of the world. For example, the lower registers of Egyptian temples often have friezes made up of marsh plants thus representing the primordial waters from which the world arose; while the domes of medieval European churches are often decorated with stars to represent the heavenly realm. And are not columns in so many cultures but stylized representations of trees in the natural world?

Tribal man, rather than create a building to represent the order of the universe, often uses nature itself: not friezes, domes, and

---

[201] Claude Lévi-Strauss, *The Savage Mind,* translated from the French by Lilian A. Clare (Chicago: University of Chicago Press, 1966), 268.

columns, but snakes, eagles, and trees. Rather than organizing society around, for example, the Church, he orders his world according to his own "church," the objects in the natural world that he finds all around him. The relation of clans and animals is therefore not one of kinship or mystical connection, but metaphor: human society as a reflection of the natural world, just as the Egyptians, on a much vaster scale, created a whole civilization as a reflection of the universe. Thus, the choice of animals to which different clans are associated depends not so much on the animal itself but its place within a system of nomenclature:

> ...the system becomes coherent when it is seen as a whole set...The terms never have any intrinsic significance. Their meaning is one of 'position'[202]...the alleged totemism is no more than a particular expression by means of a special nomenclature formed of animal and plant names (in a certain code, as we should say today), which is its sole distinctive characteristic, of correlations and oppositions which may be formalized in other ways, for example, among certain tribes of North and South America, by oppositions of the type sky/earth, war/peace, upstream/downstream, red/white, etc.[203]

If a certain animal or plant is used in relation to another, the one chosen depends on the function and characteristics of the particular species based on observation in time past and lived experience in the present. In this way a snake, which lives closest to the ground, may be opposed to the hawk, eagle, or other high-flying bird. Thus the "snake" clan may be related to the "eagle" clan as a means of naming and discriminating between them. The particular characteristics of the totem may be handed down in the myths and traditions of the tribe on the basis of pairs of opposites, and, ingrained as they are in the collective psyche,

---

[202] Ibid., 54-5.

[203] Claude Lévi-Strauss, *Totemism,* translated from the French by Rodney Needham (Harmondsworth, UK: Penguin Books, 1963), 161.

provide metaphors for social relations between people and groups in human society.

This analysis of totemism, which in reality does away with it as a concept of kinship or relationship between man and animal or other natural entities, rather describes a symbolical approach to classification of nature and society, a particular mode of thought that assigns each thing its place in the world, a place reflected symbolically in human society so that man partakes of the universal order, keeping anarchy at bay:

> The thought we call primitive is founded on this demand for order. This is equally true of all thought but it is through the properties common to all thought that we can most easily begin to understand forms of thought which seem very strange to us. A native thinker makes the penetrating comment that 'All sacred things must have their place'.... It could even be said that being in their place is what makes them sacred for if they were taken out of their place, even in thought, the entire order of the universe would be destroyed. Sacred objects therefore contribute to the maintenance of order in the universe by occupying the places allocated to them.[204]

This tribal mode of symbolical thought was also present in ancient Egypt, and still exists now in our own Western civilization. The essential difference among the three is that while tribal man uses nature, and ancient civilizations used a pantheon of 'gods,' modern civilization uses mathematical symbols and formula to organize the world in thought. It is the physicists, after all, the Einsteins, Heisenbergs, and Bohrs, who have taken over the role of ancient priests by providing the myths and symbols by which we try make sense of the world. The great difference between ancient symbolic modes of thought and modern scientific rationalism is that modern man, by cutting up and studying the parts, has lost all feeling for, conception and understanding of, the *whole*. His mind is fragmented, filled with

---

[204] Lévi-Strauss, *The Savage Mind*, 10.

myriad facts but without any sense of the relative importance of things and beings in relation to the world hierarchically above and below to what is his current focus of interest. Thus the function of the parts in terms of the whole and the hierarchical relationships between different levels of being in the universe has been completely lost, though, as we have seen, modern thought, reaching this dead end at the end of the second Christian millennium, is beginning to find its way back to a larger vision at the beginning of the third. The result of this progressive loss of the hierarchical vision of the world is expressed in these words of René Guénon:

> [H]istory clearly shows that ignorance of this hierarchical order always and everywhere leads to the same consequences: social disequilibrium, confusion of functions, domination by ever more inferior elements, and also intellectual degeneration, first by the forgetting of transcendent principles, then, from one loss to another one arrives even at the negation of all true knowledge.[205]

Tribal man, on the other hand, understands the whole because he *lives* it rather than *thinks* it. Without trying to bring back the theory of the "noble savage," there is no reason to disregard Levy-Bruhl's approach to understanding the thought of tribal man through the concept of "participation" because one accepts Lévi-Strauss's theory. The two theories do not contradict but on the contrary nurture each other. Participation is the result of group solidarity and mental coherence within the tribe. Because tribal man has a more integrated lived experience without mental reservations, this does not mean that he cannot use his intellectual faculties to make sense and order out of the world. It is just this ability to be one with his tribe that provides the perception of 'wholeness' experienced in nature, where everything has its place in an ordered world. Certain tribes have

---

[205] René Guénon, *Autorité spirituelle et Pouvoir Temporel,* 3rd ed. (Paris: Les Editions Véga, 1964), 111.

a very complex metaphysical system that is so intertwined with daily life that for them there is no separation between spiritual and daily life.[206] It is only when man becomes more individual, more withdrawn from the group mentality, where feelings become atrophied and the relation between mind and body withers, that, in sum, he becomes less whole himself, that the feeling of participation lessens, that his understanding of the whole weakens.

How the symbolic thought of ancient Egypt and other civilizations emerged can perhaps be understood because of the increasing complexity of civilization as society developed from small tribal clans to large nations encompassing vast areas. The difference between the mentality of tribal man, ancient civilizations and our own, can be seen as a gradual degradation of the integration man's being, so that instead of an integrated whole, man has become in our day a disembodied machine, or rather three separate machines: one that thinks, one that feels and one that moves, with only the slightest conscious connection between the three. Taking the individual's degree of symbiosis with the group, the thought of tribal man is totally subsumed in the clan or tribe's group consciousness, which is, contrary to "civilized" man, an integrated combination of mental, emotional and motor processes functioning as a whole. Furthermore, his symbols are taken directly from the natural world. As the organization of society became more complicated with growing numbers of people belonging to hierarchical subgroups having different functions (e.g., castes in India), civilizations developed on a larger scale, such as those that existed in Egypt, Mesopotamia, India and China. This increasing specialization led to a lessening of the participation of man in life as he became more and more attuned to his own interests over those of the group, and more head-driven to survive, since he could no longer

---

[206] For example, the Bororo people of Brazil. See Claude Lévi-Strauss, *Tristes Tropiques*, (Paris: Plon, 1955), 259-60.

simply follow a tradition that was slowly losing its perennial nature. This mentality is reflected in the more abstract nature of his symbols. Rather than using natural elements directly, we see them combined, for example, in animal/human hybrid gods or abstracted by the use of higher symbolic content, such as the pharaoh as intermediary between the realm of gods and that of man. This abstraction is reinforced by the use of geometric symbols (e.g., the *ankh* in Egypt, the swastika in India, the spiral in the Celtic tradition) to stand for basic principles, though still in relation to the Whole where man has his place in the cosmic hierarchy.

In our day, we have reached a life lived in mega-cities, at such a distance from the natural world that practically all that participates in life is our mental apparatus, with our emotions and body being but atrophied appendages of what was once an integrated whole. Starting with the Greeks, as man became more and more alienated from the group consciousness, individual man took it on himself to analyze and dissect the natural world in its own right rather than see it as a level in a cosmological hierarchy and thus symbolic of a higher realm. In our civilization, starting with the Renaissance, this attitude has reached the point that we know today: where science and knowledge are divided up into a myriad of disciplines that do not talk to each other, where men become experts in an infinitesimal part of the universal whole, completely losing sight of the relative importance of things and beings in a hierarchical and perhaps spiritual universe, where everything is put on the same level of importance through the use of mass technology such as TV, the Internet, and the smartphone, and where any form of discernment has disappeared from public discourse in order to appeal to the greatest number and reap the highest profit. This mentality is reflected in the symbolism of modern civilization based on science, an abstraction so far from experience that reality is symbolized by elements that can never be seen: atoms, electrons, quarks and the like.

A spiritual symbol, on the other hand, addresses itself to the whole man and not just his intellect, a man understands and is affected by a spiritual symbol in proportion to what he *is*, not what he knows with his mind. Thus, a symbol can only be effective in one who has already realized its meaning in himself, and from this we can say that a symbol, in its deepest meaning, relates not to knowledge of the mind, but to knowledge of *Being*, and more particularly, to a man's *own* being. As Coomaraswamy says, "The mediaeval and Asiatic artists did not observe; they were required to be what they would represent..."[207] and P. D. Ouspensky: "The transmission of the meaning of symbols to a man who has not reached an understanding of them in himself is impossible."[208]

It would seem that the world of Traditional societies, whether ancient high civilizations such as existed in Egypt, India or Mesopotamia, or tribal cultures in our own time, are symbolic in their structure and in the mode of thought of the people who comprise them. In trying to understand what this might mean, we can say perhaps that in these cultures nothing is taken, is seen, in itself existentially existing without reference to its place in the order of the universe—that is to say, its place not in terms of time and space but by virtue of its *function*, of the role the object or action performs within its particular context and the analogous functions in larger or smaller worlds. The structure of the dwellings, the layout of the village or town, the social hierarchy, the music and dance, everything is symbolic in that everything is seen to conform to the creation and structure of the cosmos itself as related in their myths and legends and by what

---

[207] Coomaraswamy, *Christian and Oriental Philosophy of Art*, 126.

[208] Ouspensky, *In Search of the Miraculous*, 280.

is observed in the natural world. William W. Quinn, in his study of the works of Guénon and Coomaraswamy, says this:

> Generally speaking, primitive culture in the Traditional view is one in which all activity, regardless of how mundane or banal it is considered in modern Western culture, is sacred, since it has a divine archetype or referent or paradigm in mythology.[209]...By virtue of the fact that every activity in Traditional society is grounded or connected in a higher metaphysical principle—a first principle—the culture can be seen as a substantive mirror image of the essential principles on which it is established and of which it is reflective.[210] ...Every aspect of Traditional culture, therefore, is integrated with the rest in such a way as to be fused into a whole, the whole being sacred and reflective of the Tradition.[211]

One observer of an African tribe shows us that for the Dogon of Mali, as much as for the medieval Christian described above, all material objects, even the most humble used in daily life, are charged with extra meaning, and are identified with a certain stage of the original creation, while at the same time containing the whole. The rim of the open end of a simple pot, for example, symbolizes the circumference of the moon before baking and that of the sun after it has been fired.[212] The Dogon also believe that the dirt floor of their houses represents the earth and the flat roof represents heaven, with the ceiling of the lower story representing the space between the two. Upon entering the house, the outside door is the male sexual organ with the vestibule representing man, the following big central room represents woman, with the door between the two being the woman's sexual organs. The storerooms on each side represent

---

[209] William W. Quinn, The *Only Tradition* (Albany, N.Y.: State University of New York Press, 1997), 178-80.

[210] Ibid, 189.

[211] Ibid, 191.

[212] Marcel Griaule, *Conversations with Ogotemmêli: An Introduction to Dogon Religious Ideas* (London: Oxford University Press, 1965), 94-5.

the woman's arms so that the central and storerooms together show the woman on her back ready for intercourse. In sum, the lower story of the house represents for the Dogon the act of creation.[213]

Are we to infer, then, that all people in Traditional societies, having this symbolic outlook, live in a higher state of consciousness? Of course not. The answer resides perhaps in the distinction between what one could call exoteric and esoteric symbolism. Exoteric symbolism, as we see it, is concerned with a certain mode of thought, a way of thinking, that immediately links and classifies objects or actions by their function, and through this function enables connections to be made between it and an analogous object or action in a larger or smaller world. In this way, the nucleus of an atom or of a cell, the heart of man, the hearth of a hut, the Holy of Holies of the Temple, the Priest-King of the nation, the sun of the solar system, can all be related in terms of the directing force of a 'center.' Nevertheless, this mode of thought is 'vertical' in its form, but 'horizontal' as to its structure within the human being, that is, it is the mental apparatus working by analogy rather than by dissection as modern Western man is want to do. Having a symbolic outlook may nevertheless prevent a man from identifying too closely with what he perceives with his senses—since the material world is not for him the ultimate reality—and thus leave him more present to himself and open to other influences.

Esoteric symbolism, on the other hand, is concerned with a different mode of *being,* not merely a different use of the mind. Otherwise said, an esoteric symbol affects the whole man and thus by-passes the reasoning apparatus. Thus, every environment in which a man lives is a symbol for that man, for it conditions, focuses, and evokes something within him. The clothes a man wears, the house in which he lives, the city, the

---

[213] Ibid., 90.

country, the planet, the cosmos itself, are symbols which affect the whole man, elevating him or causing his fall—whether he is conscious of them or not. Life itself, it may be said, is nothing but a symbol for every man living within its stream.

What are we to make then of symbols such as the *mandala* and the *yantra* discussed above, for here we have a special case? These are esoteric symbols and can only be effective within the particular religious context in which they are utilized. They are attuned to a certain mentality which has been conditioned by the cultural milieu of the religion in which they are used. To really understand the ancient Egyptian symbol of the Eye of Horus, for example, we would need to be immersed in Egyptian civilization, which is, alas, no longer possible, and so this book, or any book, can only be a very poor substitute for a real understanding of a lived experience.

An esoteric symbol is created by "one who knows" in order to elevate man to the spiritual realm, to change his state of being, to raise his consciousness; but for this to take place, for the symbol to *become* spiritual, a man must be prepared; for, as we have said, a symbol acts at the level of the man. One function of exoteric religion is, in fact, to prepare man to be elevated by the esoteric symbolism of that religion. If a man is to follow the moral injunctions of a religion (to be honest, kind to others, and so forth), it is not as an end in itself, but in order to free man from the emotional upheavals of violence and retribution, to be inwardly still and so allow the energy of the symbol to penetrate to his innermost being during the ceremonial rite in the Temple.

It must be said that esoteric symbols are not received in the same way by different persons. What a consciously created symbol is for one man, is not necessarily the same for another. A man's receptivity depends on his state of being. What for the one is meaningless or, conversely, gives simply a new way of thinking about some aspect of himself or the cosmos, for the other is a means by which he is freed from just this existence conditioned by his thought. Though, it is true, that the former can be preparatory for the latter; for to be elevated by a symbol a man would be helped, one would think, by having knowledge of his position and function in the cosmos, and so eventually be prepared to assume what he believes.

Symbolic Language

Whether we call it "the perennial philosophy," "the primordial Tradition," or "an ancient language," there exists a means of transmitting what have always been known as sacred truths that relate to man's spiritual transformation within a hierarchical cosmos. The term "perennial philosophy" was coined by the German philosopher and mathematician Gottfried Wilhelm Leibniz in the beginning of the 18th century and made popular by the book of the same name written by the Englishman Aldous Huxley in the middle of the 20th.[214] It is interesting to note that during the centuries in between the lives of these two men, the content of this "philosophy" was almost completely forgotten in the Western world. But we should first say that the "perennial philosophy" is not actually a philosophy as the word has come to be understood. Philosophy, as we know it today, began with the speculative thinking of the ancient Greeks and consists of inquiring into the nature of reality through logical reasoning rather than experiment or direct experience. In opposition to this, the "perennial philosophy" could best be described as a metaphysics in which ultimate reality consists of a spiritual energy by which all things and beings are created, maintained and infused with Being.

Here one may ask "What is Being?" But the answer cannot be given in words, but only in the lived experience of the feeling in oneself of the connection to a higher energy that is infused throughout the body, an energy of which we are usually totally

---

[214] Aldous Huxley, *The Perennial Philosophy* (New York: Harper & Row, 1970).

unaware but which is constantly present, for this energy is everywhere, including within us.

As a corollary to this metaphysics, since man is of two natures, one external acting in the world and another internal grounded in this same spiritual essence, it is his destiny, if he chooses to follow it, to become aware, in the world *and in himself*, through direct experience, of this finest of energies by a process of spiritual transformation. And furthermore, there is a definite Way by which this can be achieved, or, as we called it previously, a "sacred science" to be studied which provides the guideposts by which this Way can be followed. Schuon provides this description of the "perennial philosophy":

> [A] religion is orthodox on condition that it offers a sufficient, if not always exhaustive, idea of the absolute and the relative, and therewith an idea of their reciprocal relationships, and also a spiritual activity that is contemplative in its nature and effectual as concerns our ultimate destiny.[215]

It is precisely the metaphysical nature of the "perennial philosophy" that became completely lost in the age of science, industrialism and materialism that took over the West since Leibniz' time. It is only now, at the beginning of the third millennium, thanks in part to the technology science wrought, that more and more people have access to the traces of the "perennial philosophy" in the religions, symbols, myths, legends, fables, fairy tales, and customs of peoples of every time and place, not the least of which in ancient Egypt. As to how any specific person interprets and uses this eternal knowledge is another matter indeed. In Meister Eckhart's view as cited by Coomaraswamy:

> Thus with reference to the interpretation of scripture and myths in general, and the same holds good for any other kind of art, the material things in them, they say, must be

---

[215]Schuon, *Light on the Ancient Worlds*, 137-38.

translated to a higher plane....All the stories taken from them have another, esoteric meaning.[216]

So, let us leave the word "philosophy" behind and concentrate on "perennial," for it is just the eternal nature of this knowledge that is important and provides it with meaning. Whatever era: ancient epochs or modern times; whatever civilization: high and far-reaching having great cities and far-flung trade networks, or tribal and circumscribed in forest or bush; whatever place: Africa, Europe, Asia; whatever the means of its symbolic expression (for it is necessarily symbolic): myths, fables, fairy tales, nursery rhymes, images, monuments, music, dance, ritual—it always carries the same essential message. And this is so because the essence of the universe and the essence of man, the eternal ground of Being, are one and unchanging—which is why it is sometimes called "the primordial Tradition."[217]. Kenneth Walker put it this way:

> Most works devoted to the comparative study of religions are really studies of religious husks. Only a few deal with the grain. And the reason for this is at once obvious. It is only the husk that differs; the grain, the inner soul, of all great religions is the same. Divested of all special names, the fundamental abstractions of all the great world religions are identical, variations of the great eternal Religion, suited to different minds and different races.[218]

It is this eternal nature of the "perennial philosophy" that allows it to be expressed by symbols: just as the content of this

---

[216] Coomaraswamy, *The Transformation of Nature in Art*, 84.

[217] A term used by René Guénon. See *Introduction générale à l'Etude des Doctrines hindoues* (Paris: Les Editions Véga, 1952), 71, which was perhaps borrowed from the book by the French Taoist, Matgioi (Albert Puyou): *La Voie Métaphysique*. 3d ed. (Paris: Les Éditions Traditionnelles, 1956), Chap.1 "La Tradition Primordiale" [First published 1904-1907]. This term was used later by Huston Smith. See Huston Smith, *Forgotten Truth: The Primordial Tradition* (New York: Harper & Row, 1977), x.

[218] Walker, *Diagnosis of Man*, 178.

"philosophy" does not depend on time and place, neither does its expression. In the words of Coomaraswamy:

> The ultimate reality of metaphysics is a Supreme Identity in which the opposition of all contraries, even of being and not-being, is resolved; its 'worlds' and 'gods' are levels of reference and symbolic entities which are neither places nor individuals but states of being realizable within you.[219]

It is nonetheless true that symbols may very well be part of a symbolic language of a particular culture, but what we are saying is that the *meaning* can always be interpreted because of the unchanging message the symbolism contains, such as the "ancient language" that Maurice Nicoll talks about in his exposition of the parables of Christ in the New Testament.[220] This takes, however, a certain immersion in the symbolism in order to apply its meaning to one's own inner experiences, and, it should be emphasized, *it is from this relationship of the symbol with one's own inner life that symbolism derives its unique value*; and it does so by providing the means for understanding to arise in one who is ready, and not from any sort of one-to-one mental mapping of symbols to their meaning or creation of classificatory schemes. That is not to say that the meaning can be interpreted by *anyone*, for as Huxley says: "Knowledge is a function of being. When there is a change in the being of the knower, there is a corresponding change in the nature and amount of knowing."[221] Or, as we have already mentioned above, the understanding of the symbol takes place at the level of one's being. These words of René Guénon concerning Chinese ideographic characters are worth citing here:

---

[219] Coomaraswamy, *Metaphysics*, 6-7. [Our italics]

[220] Maurice Nicoll, *The New Man: An Interpretation of Some Parables and Miracles of Christ* (New York: Penguin Books, 1972), 7.

[221] Ibid., vii.

> All the meanings possible for these characters can be grouped around three principal ones, which correspond to the three basic degrees of knowing, of which the first is perceptible, the second rational and the third pure intellect or metaphysical. So, to limit ourselves to a very simple example, the same character could be employed analogically to mean at once sun, light and truth, only the nature of the context permitting one to recognize, for each case, which of these meanings it would be suitable to use.[222]

The etymological meaning of the word "Tradition" is to "hand over" or "hand on," which leads to the notion of transmission. A tradition is, therefore, cultural elements transmitted from generation to generation. It is our contention that a certain knowledge has been handed down from prehistoric times, at first orally, and then symbolically in any number of ways, as enumerated above. Elements of this knowledge can be found in all traditions, those dead and those still existing up to our day: Egyptian, Mesopotamian, Hindu, Persian, Chinese/Japanese, Greek, Roman, Judaism, Christianity, Islam, the many tribal cultures which are too numerous to name, and no doubt many others. It should be understood that this language is in no way "secret," "hidden," or "occult." It is simply symbolic, and it is so only because this is the only way this knowledge can be expressed *and received*. The knowledge transmitted is of a *meta*-physical nature (*meta*, beyond the physical, though in our view, only because it has not yet been experienced), knowledge that cannot be expressed in a rational discursive manner, because this knowledge has to do with *Being* and not with knowledge acquired purely on a mental plane. This idea, that knowledge can be gained through one's being and not through one's mental apparatus, is totally alien to the Western mentality, and for many will make no sense at all, ingrained as we are by our education in the scientific positivist mentality of the modern era. We can only affirm, and for others to discover

---

[222] Guénon, *Introduction générale á l'Etude des Doctrines hindoues*, 137.

for themselves, the truth of it or not, that there is a symbolic language handed down from time immemorial providing guideposts to cosmological and spiritual understanding. This symbolic language is created by those with a deep understanding of spiritual truths with the express purpose of transmitting a higher meaning beyond the literal expression of the symbol. This higher meaning cannot be understood by reasoning, but must be grasped intuitively based on one's own inner experience and faith in a 'higher' world: "To reject the notion of the superior is to reject both discernment and transcendence," says Mark Perry[223]. And he says as well: "Man must learn to think with his heart, which implies the extinction of the mind."[224] And in fact, the deepest meaning of the symbol can only be understood when one does not "think" at all, that is...

> ...when the intellect no longer intelligizes, i.e., when there is no longer any distinction of knower and known, of being and knowledge, but only knowledge as being and being as knowledge..., 'One is what he thinks' and is no longer one who thinks of anything; that is Gnosis.[225]

In this way, the higher meaning depends for its understanding on the equivalent level of being of one who receives it. It has long been known that truths of a higher nature lose their meaning when given discursively, that spiritual reality, based on the eternal, can never be effectively described in a linear time-based language. A rational "explanation" of a symbol would not provide the affective charge necessary to provoke the understanding of the symbol's higher meaning. A symbolic language, as discussed previously, goes deep into inner recesses of a person's subconscious, touching levels that would not be affected if a simple reasoned explanation were provided. Certain

---

[223] Perry, *On Awakening and Remembering*, 122
[224] Ibid., 55.
[225] Coomaraswamy, *Metaphysics*, 388-89n.

fables, stories, scriptural passages, etc., may seem paradoxical, simplistic, or even outright bizarre, simply because one is reading its literal sense instead of the higher meaning which it also contains. It is in fact just this paradoxical, too simple or bizarre literal nature of the symbol that works on the subconscious mind to raise the understanding of it to a higher level. Consider here the nature of a seemingly absurd Zen koan that a disciple is asked to ponder until he arrives at another level of understanding. A symbol, as Maurice Nicoll says, is "a *transforming* instrument in regard to meaning."[226] And this meaning can only be expressed by analogy, since direct knowing cannot be 'explained':[227]

> [M]etaphysics deals for the most part with matters which cannot be publicly proved, but can only be demonstrated, i.e., made intelligible by analogy, and which even when verified in personal experience can only be stated in terms of symbol and myth.[228]...The use of symbolisms which are contrary in their literal but unanimous in their spiritual sense very well illustrates the nature of metaphysics itself, which is not, like a 'philosophy,' systematic, but is always consistent.[229]

---

[226] Nicoll, *The New Man*, 4.

[227] Perhaps our age has come to the end of its scientific tether given these words of the neuroscientist Antonio Damasio: "*Explaining* how to make something mental or something ours in scientific terms is an entirely different matter from making that something mental and ours *directly*." Damasio, *The Feeling of What Happens*, 308.

[228] Coomaraswamy, *Metaphysics*, 8.

[229] Ibid., 324.

Chapter 4 Spiritual Symbolism

The function of a spiritual symbol works *outside of time*, for its purpose is to act on all levels of which we are made, the levels of being existing simultaneously within us, with each level obeying laws that continually act within those laws higher than itself, like a set of Russian dolls, and yet with each level influenced by all the other levels and the One Whole on which each level ultimately depends. We must thus go further into what we believe is the order reigning in the universe—and then its reflection in a human being—in order to understand how a symbol can have an effective influence on man.

Our language does not have the means of expressing this idea of a "simultaneous sequence," for language is linear and cannot be made to accommodate that which is progressively deeper or higher, yet simultaneous in time. And it is just this limitation of language that is the *raison d'être* of symbolism. We cannot try to "figure out" or "make sense" of a symbol, for what it is depends not on what we *think* but on what we *are*, on our being, our state of consciousness, and consciousness is nothing if not a question of level. A symbol responds to what is deeper or higher in us, and without keeping this constantly in mind, the concept of symbolism must rapidly lose its essential meaning. In the words of Coomaraswamy:

> It must be borne in mind that from the Indian point of view enlightenment and perfection are always virtually present, that is, not to be acquired by any means but only to be revealed, when the mirror of the soul is cleansed from dust. This is a metaphor particularly applicable in the aesthetic field; aesthetic contemplation cannot be taught; all that can be done is to break down the barriers that stand in the way of realization.[230]

---

[230] Coomaraswamy, *The Transformation of Nature in Art*, 199n.

A symbol then cuts through all the levels within us, providing a reflection of the same function in each of them. At each level, the function of the whole can never be described by simply detailing the parts, for the whole is always something more. For example, we could not understand the functioning of a computer by examining only the hardware and not the software. And by examining each of its atoms, we would never understand the function of a molecule. By examining each of its molecules, we would never understand the function of a cell. By examining each of its cells, we would never understand the function of an organ. By examining each of its organs, we would never understand the function of man, and so on. We can only understand an element in a hierarchy by knowing of what it consists and of what it is a part. Since everything is in movement as part of a larger whole, our understanding grows as a function of our ability to make connections between the different levels of our being with the dynamically interpenetrating hierarchical levels of the cosmos. Any one level only begins to take on meaning as a trinitarian relationship between itself and the level below and the level above, with the level below acting as a symbol for the one above. And even this meaning can only be partial since each level influences all the others. As Lovejoy says in his book, *The Great Chain of Being* when discussing Pascal:

> It is not merely, for Pascal, that an infinite world is too big to be exhaustively investigated by us—though that of itself, he declares, means that no single part of it can be really understood, since 'its parts all are so related and interlinked with one another that it is impossible to know the parts without knowing the whole or the whole without knowing all the parts.'[231]

We are far here from a simple reductionism that says that all events arise and are determined from the movements of atomic

---

[231] Arthur O. Lovejoy, *The Great Chain of Being: A Study of the History of an Idea* (Cambridge: Harvard University Press, 1964), 128. [The quote from Pascal is from his work *Pensées*.]

particles. The English philosopher Alfred North Whitehead developed a theory of "organic mechanism" which comes quite close to what we are trying to express:

> [M]y theory involves the entire abandonment of the notion that simple location is the primary way in which things are involved in space-time. In a certain sense, everything is everywhere at all times. For every location involves as aspect of itself in every other location. Thus every spatio-temporal standpoint mirrors the world.[232]

It should be emphasized here that it is the *experience of the connection* between the part and the whole which counts here and brings understanding, not the simple knowledge that the connection exists. In the words of a modern physicist:

> ...wholeness is what is real, and...fragmentation is the response of this whole to man's action, guided by illusory perception, which is shaped by fragmentary thought. In other words, it is just because reality is whole that man, with his fragmentary approach, will inevitably be answered with a correspondingly fragmentary response. So what is needed is for man to give attention to his habit of fragmentary thought, to be aware of it, and thus bring it to an end. Man's approach to reality may then be whole, and so the response will be whole.
>
> For this to happen, however, it is crucial that man be aware of the activity of his thought as such; i.e. as a form of insight, a way of looking, rather than as a 'true copy of reality as it is'.[233]

Or in the words of Werner Heisenberg, one of the fathers of quantum theory: "...we have to remember that what we observe is not nature in itself but nature exposed to our method of questioning."[234]

---

[232] Whitehead, *Science and the Modern World*, 91.

[233] Bohm, *Wholeness*, 7.

[234] Werner Heisenberg, *Physics and Philosophy: The Revolution in Modern Science* (New York: Harper & Row, 1962), 58.

We are now going to discuss, in a very general way, two types of symbols: graphical images and sacred monuments.

Graphical Symbols

Since we do not know in detail how symbols were used in ancient rites, such as that of Egypt, we will take the *yantra* and the *mandala* of the Hindu and Buddhist traditions, respectively, to see how an image is *made* a symbol and used just to this end within a Traditional religious context. It should first be said that it is not enough that an image or other type of symbol comes from a religious tradition; the form in which it is expressed is equally important. As Titus Burckhardt says:

> In order for art to be called "sacred," it is not enough that its subjects come from a spiritual truth, it is also necessary that its formal language witnesses the same source....[S]pirituality is, in itself, independent of forms, but this does not at all mean that it can be expressed and transmitted by any forms whatever....[A] symbol is not simply a conventional sign; it manifests its archetype by virtue of a certain ontological law....[T]he symbol is, in a way, what it expresses....Real art is beautiful because it is true.[235]

Furthermore, it is not necessary that the artist or artisan understand the deeper meanings of the symbol which he is creating as long as he follows the forms established by the Tradition, for it is the Tradition which "guarantees the spiritual validity of the forms."[236] In other words:

> The original intention of intelligible forms was not to entertain us, but literally to 're-mind' us. The chant is not for the approval of the ear, nor the picture for that of the eye..., but to effect such a transformation of our being as is the purpose of all ritual acts.[237]

---

[235] Ibid., 5-7.

[236] Ibid., 7.

[237] Coomaraswamy, *The Door in the Sky*, 134.

As an example of a spiritual form, the Hindu *yantra,* a series of concentric, interconnected triangles with four apexes turned upward and five downward, and with four "doors" on each side of a surrounding enclosure, is similar in meaning and function to the Buddhist *mandala,* a sanctuary or palace of the gods in the center with the images of the deity or deities to be emphasized and four flights of steps leading up to four gates, each on a side enclosing the palace and guarded by terrible figures. Both are representations of the cosmos seen in its complementary aspects as an enduring simultaneous hierarchy of levels of being and its manifestation as an extension in time and space. All symbols, in their deepest and highest meaning, must embody the unity of these two complementary aspects of existence.

Figure 13 A yantra

Thus, a symbol is an attempt to embody the reality of the world, what we *would* experience if we could only *be* —and therefore "see" this reality. See Figures 13 and 14.

The *yantra* is thus a visual symbol used in the Hindu tradition— in the context of a yogic way of life—as a support for meditation. It is a means of concentrating the psychic forces through the visualization of a diagram representing, on the one hand, the eternally present hierarchy of states of being and, on the other, the eternal expansion and contraction of forms in time and space. Thus, the meditator, having a metaphysical understanding of the principles on which the *yantra* is based, can, if he is sufficiently prepared, be led, by the evocative nature of the symbol, through the levels of being in himself ('overtones' of the cosmic hierarchy represented in the diagram) to the center of his *own* being. Now this center is invisible, being outside of time and space, and in the diagram, it is that which the fifth and central apex of the downward pointing triangle is meant to touch. We must not ignore the frame of the diagram with its four doors leading outwards to and inwards from the four cardinal points. Through his concentration, the meditator enters, so to speak, through the doors, coming from the subjective experience of his multitudinous thoughts and feelings into the objective reality of his innermost being where he realizes his connection with the universal processes.

Figure 14 A mandala

The *mandala* is also used in the same way as a support for concentration, as a defense against mental distractions and as an aid for the devotee to find the center of himself, represented by the central "palace," the site of the various divinities representing the fundamental nature of existence. In ritual, the *mandala* is drawn on the ground and for the devotee to enter it is equivalent to an initiation, having first undergone the ordeals represented by the 'guardians of the doors'—terrible images of consciousness who not only protect the central 'palace' against outside forces of destruction, but who "carry the struggle into the enemy's camp and hence assume the violent and terrible aspect appropriate to the forces to be combated."[238] In entering the sacred space of the *mandala,* where the gods have descended, the initiate, however, does not attain anything more than what he has already realized in himself

---

[238] Mircea Eliade, *Yoga: Immortality and Freedom* (Princeton: Princeton University Press, 1969), 221.

through his own efforts under the guidance of his master. See Figure 14.

The visualization of the *yantra* or *mandala* is meant to evoke in the meditator those higher states of being which the images themselves represent:

> In India, in particular, a symbolic image representing some 'divine attribute'...is in no way an 'idol,' for it has never been taken for other than what it really is, a support for meditation and a supplementary aid to realization."[239]

The efficacy of the symbol, however, is dependent on the preparation and understanding of the meditator. One might even say that these images become symbols in proportion to the understanding of he who observes them. The fact that everything contains the universal laws and may serve as symbols is in no way denied by the existence of images created with knowledge to expressly evoke those states necessary for transformation, which, outside of a sacred context, are left completely to chance. The ancient Egyptian hieroglyphs, for example, are a perfect example of symbolic images imbued with several levels of meaning.

Symbolic Monuments

When we speak of symbolic monuments, we do not mean, for example, commemorative monuments relating to a victory in war or a monument honoring some great individual. We are concerned here with monuments that are central to the spiritual underpinnings of a culture, that is, "Temples" which provide the connection between man and the cosmos in a Traditional civilization. Examples would be, in ancient Egypt, the Temples of Luxor and Karnak and the Great Pyramid at Giza; the Ekur, temple of the god Enlil in the Sumerian city of Nippur; the

---

[239] Guénon, *Introduction à l'étude des doctrines hindoues*, 4th ed, 201. [Our translation]

Esagila or great temple of Marduk in Babylon; the standing stones of Stonehenge in ancient Britain; the Buddhist stupa of Barabudur on the island of Java; the ancient temple of the Hebrews in Jerusalem; the Pyramid of the Sun at Teotihuacan, the ancient Mayan temple of Tikal; the Cathedrals such as those of Chartres in France, and the Kaaba in Mecca. See Figure 15.

Figure 15 Chartres cathedral, exterior and interior

In order to even begin to understand the purpose of such ancient monuments, we must first make an initial assumption as to their symbolic nature, that in fact they were built as symbols reflecting a reality beyond the visible and as a means to reach that reality for those who followed the rites that took place within their walls. We propose that in any society based on Tradition, that is to say, based on the knowledge of fundamental cosmic laws as transmitted through the priests of that Tradition, every manifestation of that society will be a reflection of those same laws, and that the monuments—for which there was almost no limit to the expense of energy and time for their building— would be the utmost expression of them. Otherwise, we must leave these often colossal structures as being only tombs, observatories, or having some other practical function, which in fact they might have had as well. René Guénon, whose whole work might be called a study in symbolism, states in support of our assumption that "every edifice constructed according to strictly Traditional formulas expresses, in the structure and disposition of its various parts, a 'cosmic' meaning...referring both the world and to man."[240] And in the words of Titus Burckhardt:

> The fundamental diagram of the temple is thus a symbol of the divine Presence in the world....[241] The analogy between the cosmos and the plan of the temple is reflected in the interior organization of the plan."[242]

A monument, as symbol, built according to laws existing everywhere in the natural world, can then be a means whereby we are led back through the chain of cause and effect in proportion as our understanding of it deepens until we finally arrive at the One Source—not through reason or analysis, but rather through intuition and synthesis based on lived experience, an accepting attentiveness to the One Reality seen in all its diversity. In Burckhardt's words:

> Otherwise said, the temple has a spirit, a soul and a body, like man and like the universe.... [E]ach phase of the architectural work is at the same time a phase of spiritual realization.[243]

> [A] strong link...exists between the meaning of the temple as the body of divine Man and its cosmological meaning, for the cosmos represents, in its most general sense, the 'body' of the revealed Divinity.[244]

If we look at these constructions as symbols, the fact that the purpose of a spiritual symbol is precisely to say something that cannot be expressed in a rational mode, the understanding of the

---

[240] René Guénon, "Le symbolisme du dôme," *Symboles de la Science sacrée* (Paris: Gallimard, 1962), 243. [Our translation]

[241] Burckhardt, *Principes et méthodes*, 34.

[242] Ibid., 38.

[243] Ibid., 51.

[244] Ibid., 71.

symbol is ultimately only possible through the spiritual transformation of the man searching to understand it. This process is aided by the influence imparted to the receptive individual within the structure by virtue of the inherent correspondence of the laws followed in the construction of the edifice with those in the individual himself, each person influenced by the spirit of the structure according to his own receptivity.

Monuments such as those mentioned above are composed of numerous elements. Not only are the form, plan, measurements, and interrelationships of the structure itself to be considered, but also their placement with regards to other nearby or distant monuments and their relation to the movement of various heavenly bodies. Then there are the sculptures, carvings, frescoes, paintings, and glasswork representing beings and things having their own symbolic significations. In fact, one function of a truly sacred monument is to create the whole of the universe in microcosm wherein every detail can be related to the whole. The symbols, then, that adorned these monuments were not created as decoration, but as an integral part of the message to be "read" by each at his own level of understanding: history, moral teaching or esoteric knowledge. It is never a question in Traditional societies of individual inspiration, subjective imagination, of "art for art's sake." Each figure, each sculpture followed a strict canon so that the symbolic meaning would not be lost. It was only from Knowledge that the construction flowed—through the master-craftsman, the masons, the sculptors, and down to the populace or slaves hauling the carts and dragging the stones.

Because of the synthetic nature of the society in which Traditional monuments were built, the construction of monuments as a translation of knowledge into symbols, to be effective, could only be carried out according to certain rites which in themselves conform to the very laws which the monument was meant to express. A symbol "is only, as it were, the fixation of ritual gesture,"[245] and the end result, that is the monument itself and all it contains, can be said to be the symbol of the laws that went into its construction. We have texts describing the rituals of the founding of ancient Egyptian temples, and the construction of the European cathedrals in the middle ages by the autonomous lodges was in itself a matter of ritual attested to by the rites of the freemasons, which have been handed down to us over the centuries (with the concomitant loss of their real significance). "We must remember that all artistic operations were originally rites, and the purpose of the rite...is to sacrifice the old and to bring into being a new and more perfect man."[246]

The starting point for many modern attempts at the decipherment of sacred buildings has been to translate the knowledge inherent in their construction into the language of number and geometry. It would seem that the success or failure of such an enterprise would depend on the degree of understanding which the researcher possessed regarding the symbolic nature of number. Through the measurement of sacred buildings and monuments, such structures have been found to follow certain definite proportions and regular geometric forms, which in turn conform in their construction or orientation to the movements of celestial bodies. For example, geometrical forms are associated with their respective numbers (as a triangle is to three), which are in turn seen as symbols of spiritual truths (as three is to the Trinity). Now the ultimate meaning for one making such studies can only depend on his motivation and understanding: the difference between simple research and search for Truth.

---

[245] René Guénon, "Rites and Symbols," *The Sword of Gnosis: Metaphysics, Cosmology, Tradition, Symbolism*, ed. Jacob Needleman (Baltimore: Penguin Books, 1974), 366.

[246] Coomaraswamy, *The Door in the Sky*, 120.

At odds with the modern scientific viewpoint, the Traditional understanding of the ancients saw the world as a living being following definite universal laws applicable on different levels of reality, including that of man, where the spiritual was as much a part of life as the material is in our own age, where every facet of existence was understood to be interconnected through higher forces. The Cosmos is the macrocosm of which we are but a small part, and the temple on earth was constructed by the ancients to reflect these universal laws inherent in the Cosmos *as a means of transforming fallen man into conformity with these same laws.* This was accomplished through the ceremonial rites that took place within the temple's precincts, rites that followed the rhythms of celestial bodies and the seasons within a space that conformed to the laws. It might even be said that, for the ancients, the entire society and life of the people was regulated through the transformation of energies in the temple by the priest-king who, through these forces, regulated the rhythms of the people in accordance with cosmic law. Coomaraswamy sums it up in this way:

> [I]t must be realized that in India, as elsewhere, not only are temples made with hands, the universe in a likeness, but man himself is likewise a microcosm and a 'holy temple' or City of God...The body, the temple, and the universe being thus analogous, it follows that whatever worship is outwardly and visibly performed can also be celebrated inwardly and invisibly, the 'gross' ritual being, in fact, no more than a tool or support of contemplation...[247]. [A]ll these constructions have as their practical function to shelter individual principles on their way from one state of being to another—to provide, in other words, a field of experience in which they can 'become what they are.'[248]

---

[247] Coomaraswamy, *The Door in the Sky*, 177.
[248] Ibid., 202.

The residence of the Emperor in ancient China was called the Ming-Tang or "Temple of Light." It was composed of eight rooms surrounding another in the center, the whole in the shape of a square. There was an opening on each side of the room,

Figure 16 One side of a Ming-Tang temple in Kaohsiung, Taiwan

making twelve in all corresponding to the twelve months of the year and the twelve signs of the zodiac. The Emperor would circumambulate around his residence, the Ming-Tang, Temple of Light, in the space of a year by giving his ordinances in front of the opening corresponding to the month it represented. At the end of the yearly cycle he returned to the central room. In this way, it has been suggested,[249] the Emperor regulated the country in conformity to cosmic law, and the temple, by its construction, was the mirror of these laws on earth. See Figure 16.

To create in such a way a building in space so that it incorporates movement in time, to reflect the laws of Heaven through a building transforming Man on Earth: was this the ultimate purpose of these ancient monuments and was Man who stood in

---

[249] René Guénon, *La Grande Triade* (Paris: Gallimard, 1957), 135-43.

the Holy of Holies in the Temple the mediating force by which Heaven and Earth may be joined?

Other Symbolisms

Since all things in the physical world can be symbolic of a higher principial world, there is no end to the different forms of symbolism we could go on to discuss: the symbolism of the elements in alchemy, of the heavens in astrology; the symbolism of number and its reflection in geometry, music and the letters of the alphabet; the symbolism of animals and plants; of colors and gestures; of pantheons of gods; and why not even a symbolism of the invisible, of odors and radiations. And, of course, the symbolism of Man himself, the microcosm. But it is not our purpose to write an encyclopedia of symbolism here, but rather to try to expose what a symbolic vision might include. The possibility of this symbolic vision means that there is a way of interpreting the world other than that of modern science: a symbolic view of the world infuses everything with meaning and brings everything to life, since all physical manifestation, including oneself, is but a symbol of a higher cause. By living the world and its manifestation as symbolic, we can only be more detached from it, for we understand reality as that which is "behind" the physical world that we experience with our senses. In short, "awareness rises proportionately with detachment from self..."[250] Man in the midst of this symbolic world is not isolated nor alienated from it, but is an integral part of this manifestation, being both influenced by it and influencing it at once.

But there is a great chasm separating the theoretical understanding of symbolism and the actual living of it. We can perhaps get a feeling for a symbolic worldview by trying to cull out of our memory those moments of mystery we lived as a child: a walk in a forest where each of the trees seemed to have

---

[250]Perry, *On Awakening and Remembering*, 65.

its own personality; the caw of a bird in flight mysteriously indicating the way; the simple viewing of the canopy of stars at night, leaving us bereft of thought. These experiences may have been naive, yet the world was alive, intense, and felt, and it was so because it seemed full of *meaning*. Whence does this meaning arise? It arises, we think, from the sense of our being implicated in, connected with, a larger world than our own, that is, our being aware of the world as a participant in an organic process rather than an outward observer petrifying what it observes.

It is the role of any spiritual symbolism to help us regain this meaning by deepening our consciousness, increasing our awareness of the relationship existing between ourselves and the cosmos and imbuing in us a feeling for the inner qualities of things and beings such as we had as children but, hopefully, with a greatly increased level of understanding acquired through our lived experience in the world.

Chapter 5 Metaphysical Principles

To understand ancient Egypt, some of the basic metaphysical principles on which a Traditional civilization is based need to be understood. We feel that it is only through such a theoretical understanding of these principles that the meaning behind Traditional symbols can at least *begin* to be understood. Of course, tomes have been written on each of these subjects, so the following is but the slightest of introductions to them.

Metaphysics

The first point to be made is that metaphysics is, as the word implies, *beyond* the physical and thus beyond what can be measured and known by modern science and by the reasoning faculty of man. It is concerned only with the universal unity that is perpetually present, that is beyond space and time, and which can only be "known" by the realization of an equivalent metaphysical state in oneself that Guénon calls "intellectual intuition." To "know" metaphysical truths is thus to become one with the principle, that is, to realize the metaphysical state in oneself and not in any way to simply "understand" it with the reasoning mind. In other words, the more one tries to define metaphysics, the further one moves away from it:

> Metaphysics, being outside and beyond any factors of a relative order, all of which belong to the individual plane, evades in this way any systemization, and likewise and for the same reason cannot be enclosed by any formula.[251]

If one realizes one's potential as a spiritual being, "to be" and "to know" become one and the same thing, for knowledge is not limited only to thought but encompasses all of one's being, and so one acts out of pure certainty. True learning does not take place through the mind, but on the contrary the mind gives way

---

[251]René Guénon, *Introduction générale à l'Etude des Doctrines hindoues*, 124.

to a recollection of what already exists in our very depths. This does not mean that one should not study texts, for one must know where one is situated and where one wishes to go, but in the end this knowledge must be integrated into oneself and forgotten, so as not to be a means of developing the ego.[252] [253]

The "Way"

Now the means to this metaphysical realization, what is often called the "Way," is often revealed in the symbolism of Traditional cultures for those able to decipher the deeper, but not "hidden," meaning. To elaborate on what we have already discussed, the very *raison d'être* of spiritual symbolism is to help the seeker find within himself the knowledge contained in the symbol, so that one might even say that the means and the end are one: the realization in oneself of unity with what is called God, Oneness, the Absolute:

> [T]he starting point of a metaphysical formulation is always essentially something intellectually evident or certain, which is communicated to those able to receive it, by symbolical or dialectical means designed to awaken in them the latent knowledge that they bear unconsciously and, it may even be said, eternally within them.[254]

Now Traditional cultures provide the means for this realization in the form of a Teaching passed on orally from master to disciple but preserved in the symbols of the civilization, the deeper meanings of which being passed on, unknowingly by most, from generation to generation in the form of images, myths, fairy tales, dances, and so on. While Egyptian, Mesopotamian, Hindu, Chinese, Christian and other symbolisms may seem very disparate at first glance, the underlying Teaching

---

[252] René Guénon, "Oriental Metaphysics" in *The Sword of Gnosis*, 46-7.
[253] Schuon, *Stations of Wisdom*, 12-15, 42.
[254] Schuon, *The Transcendent Unity of Religions*, xxx.

can only be the same, for man has one basic essential nature. Thus, the way to the metaphysical principles we are discussing can only be the same whatever the epoch and whatever the initial means used based on any particular cultural tradition. These means, some of which having to do with concentration, attention and contemplation are beyond the scope of this book. Yet we must mention these practices because certain symbols refer to them.

In terms of the "Way," Guénon mentions throughout his works the "Lesser" and "Greater Mysteries" without ever really discussing of what these mysteries consist. Rather he points to two stages on the way to liberation corresponding to each of the two mysteries. The Lesser Mysteries thus correspond to ordinary man becoming purified into what is called in the Chinese tradition the "True Man" or what is otherwise called primordial man—"primordial" because, according to Tradition, early man in his normal state *was* this True man, but that over the millennia his state has degraded, fallen to what we are today: men outside of ourselves, off balance, out of kilter and thus closed to higher and finer forces. The Greater Mysteries refer to the way to divine consciousness after having passed through the Lesser Mysteries to the center of oneself.

The "Center"

In terms of the symbolism of the cross, the Lesser Mysteries are meant to bring us from the farthest extremities of the horizontal bar where we reside to the center of the cross, the center of ourselves, where we can come in contact with the vertical pole (often symbolized as a tree), with the spiritual forces beyond the physical world, the immovable mover around which all manifestation turns as the axle of the "cosmic wheel."

Now this place, at the center of the cross, is a point without extension and symbolizes the void which reconciles and synthesizes all oppositions. In the Islamic tradition this point is called the "Divine Station," and in the Chinese tradition the "Invariable Middle," an interior "place" where one is unified with the Divine Principle. This state is characterized by complete detachment vis-à-vis all manifestation and is called by Lao-Tsu the "peace within the void" and the "great peace" in the esoterism of Islam.[255] Guénon says:

> This absolute detachment makes him master of all things, because, having gone beyond all opposition inherent in multiplicity, he can no longer be affected by anything.[256]...[W]e have seen that all human individuals...have in themselves the possibility of becoming the center in relation to their total being. It can thus be said in a way that everyone is such virtually and that the goal to which one should aspire is to make this virtuality into actual reality.[257]

Having arrived at the center, though still on the physical plane, the Greater Mysteries is the means to "climb" the vertical axis arriving at higher and higher metaphysical states of being and so become ever closer to complete liberation as Transcendent or Universal Man.

From the above, it becomes obvious that when pondering any Traditional symbol, we should always apply it appropriately to each of these two stages on the Way. The third stage, Ultimate Deliverance, is, as said by those who have reached it, inexpressible by any means.

Order and Justice

One of the basic elements of any metaphysical understanding is the idea of order or justice, which in Egypt is symbolized by the *neter* (goddess) Maat, but without any moral or sentimental implications. It is rather that "order" is taken in the sense of

---

[255] René Guénon, *Le Symbolisme de la croix*, 113-139.
[256] Ibid., 123.
[257] Ibid., 284.

everything being in its "right" place, conforming to a hierarchical order. Every being has a place in the hierarchical order of the universe and to be "just" is to conform to that place assigned to it. It is in fact only when all beings and things are in their place that harmony reigns due to the cosmic hierarchy reflected on the different levels of existence, including the social dimension of human society. In Traditional cultures, for instance, one is born into a place in society to which one should adhere. And it is just this hierarchical organization which produces an internal equilibrium, a stasis in form, which nevertheless allows for exchanges between the different levels. For example, cosmic energies from a higher level could be integrated into a man prepared to receive them or, on another level, a lower-class person with extraordinary capabilities might become a shaman of a tribe or a high priest in ancient Egypt.

In this sense, then, "according to law" means that which is in its rightful place or that which acts rightly according to its place in the hierarchical cosmic scheme of which it is a part, an essential point in the metaphysical conception of Traditional civilizations.

Macrocosm and Microcosm

Following upon the idea of order and hierarchy is another essential metaphysical principle that we have already discussed: that having to do with the "macrocosm" and the "microcosm." Suffice it is to say here that the laws directing nature at the level of the cosmos are the same laws that direct beings at all levels within the cosmos. This factor provides the rationale for symbolic thought in that any "lawful" symbol can be interpreted at any level of existence: cosmological, human, or any other as long as the appropriate correspondences are observed in the interpretation. So, for example, different gods or beings may represent the same principle but on different levels of existence: Brahma and Ishvara in the Hindu tradition, for example, or the Father and the Son in the Christian tradition. It should be noted as well that there can be no opposition between the macrocosm and the microcosm; the macrocosm always encloses the microcosm and provides the "laws" for its existence.

Direct Knowing

In the same manner, Traditional teachings do not suppose that in a normal human being there is any opposition between what Guénon calls "intellectual intuition" or what some now refer to as "direct perception" (though we prefer "direct knowing")[258]— often symbolized by the eye and having its center in the heart— and the rational, reasoning faculty of man centered in the brain, which, in the Hindu tradition, is grouped with the five senses and the five "actions" as a means of serving both sensation and action on the physical plane.

"Direct knowing" arises from beyond the human level "descending" along the central vertical axis, so that "knowledge is not possessed by the individual insofar as he is an individual, but insofar as in his innermost essence he is not distinct from his Divine Principle."[259] Thinking, on the other hand, is one of the multiple aspects of man realized on the horizontal level of manifestation. As mentioned above, each has its rightful place in the natural scheme of the cosmos, and the problem in our age is that the thinking apparatus has usurped the directing role of the "eye of the heart" to such a point that, for most, direct knowing is not even suspected as the birthright of every human being. Thus, when studying Traditional teachings and their symbols, we should keep in mind that the goal of these teachings is to bring man back to his "Center" where the eye of direct knowing can once again function through its connection to a

---

[258] We prefer the term "direct knowing," to "intellectual intuition" since the term "intellectual" is in our day often confused with reasoning and "intuition" with guesswork. We also would avoid "direct perception" since "perception" now is almost exclusively used to designate the sense of vision on the physical level.

[259] Schuon, *The Transcendent Unity of Religions*, xxx.

higher source. The connection between knowledge and this higher "vision" is expressed in these words of the Sufi mystic and metaphysician Ibn'Arabi:

> Revelation corresponds to the breadth and form of knowledge. Knowledge of Him, which thanks to Him you obtain during your struggle and discipline, you will become conscious of later during contemplation. But that which you will contemplate of Him will have the form of the knowledge that you will have previously acquired. You progress not at all if not by the transfer of knowledge into vision; and the form is one.[260]

Non-being and Being

Another metaphysical aspect is the distinction between Non-being and Being, between the non-manifested and the manifested, between the principles behind manifestation and the manifestation itself, or, in the more common terms of the Judeo-Christian tradition, between "spirit" and "body" or still yet, "essence" and "substance." This is in no way a dualist conception, for "spirit" is not only transcendent "above," but also immanent "within."[261] Thus, the human being as a manifestation among others is of two natures: one related to Non-being, the essence above, behind and within Being, experienced as "direct knowing," and another composed of body, emotions and mind, all that we sense, feel and think in our everyday existence in a corporeal world, our organic being. This latter nature too is dependent on Non-being, the non-acting principle related to higher universal states. While the "lower" receives its existence and is "powered" by the "higher," the "lower" does not affect the "higher." A person having realized and centered himself in a higher state, can be completely

---

[260] Muhyiddin Ibn'Arabi, *Voyage vers le maître de la puissance: Manuel soufi de méditation* (Monaco: Editions du Rocher, 1994), 46. [Our translation]

[261] See, for example, René Guénon, *L'homme et son devenir selon le Vêdânta*, 29-39, 51-2.

detached from, and unaffected by, his activity in the world taking place on a "lower" level, however active this may be. For those having reached this stage, the whole world can act as a monastery. Is not this what Meister Eckhart means when he says:

> To be in the right state one of two things has to happen: either he must find God and learn to have him in his works, or else things and works must be abandoned altogether. But no one in this life can be without activities, human ones, and not a few at that, so man has to learn to find his God in everything...[262]

Schuon also makes the same point:

> If every man lived in the love of God, the monastery would be everywhere...[I]t is possible to transfer monasticism, or the attitude it represents, into the world, for there can be contemplatives in any place.[263]

The "gods" then in high Traditional civilizations such those found in Hinduism and in ancient Egypt are not, as some would believe, a polytheism where each god represents a facet of nature, such as a "storm god" and the like, but are rather symbols of metaphysical principles flowing from Unity (the "Supreme God") on which the whole civilization is based. These gods may, for example, represent different degrees of the Universal order, either on the metacosmic plane or on the microcosmic level of this order as constituted in the human being. As Guénon says:

> [W]hen we speak of different degrees of individual manifestation, it should be easily understood that these degrees correspond to those of the universal manifestation by reason of the constituent analogy between the "macrocosm" and the "microcosm."[264]

---

[262] Meister Eckhart cited in Coomaraswamy, *The Transformation of Nature in Art*, 92.

[263] Schuon, *Light on the Ancient Worlds*, 121.

[264] René Guénon, *L'homme et son devenir selon le Vêdânta*, 64.

Part 2 Ancient Egypt

In the Valley of the Queens, on my first visit to Egypt, I entered the tomb of Nefertari, the principal wife of the pharaoh Ramses II. The mysterious beauty of this moment would be hard to describe. Not knowing what to expect as I accessed the first chamber, I was overwhelmed by something that profoundly touched me in a special place within. It was akin to my first trip to France, when on the way from England I stopped at Chartres and upon entering the cathedral there I was forced to just sit down, and for at least two hours simply bathed in the atmosphere of the place not wanting to move at all without knowing why.

Figure 17 The tomb of Nefertari

Unhappily, in the tombs of the Valleys of the Kings and Queens in Upper Egypt one cannot stay very long in the tombs as other tourists are waiting their turn. Nevertheless, with a bit of *baksheesh* I gave to the guide, I was able to stay another five or so minutes alone after my group had left. What affected me so was not simply the aesthetic beauty of the images and hieroglyphs chiseled and painted in bright colors on the plastered stone walls, pillars, and ceilings, all in stark contrast to a brilliant white background, but the profound feeling that a *message* was being transmitted symbolically by every image and hieroglyphic character. I just instinctively *knew* that a profound meaning radiated everywhere from the chambers of the tomb, that nothing was placed there for purely decorative effect. In fact, this one visit led me, after I returned home, to learn to read the hieroglyphs and study the ancient Egyptian civilization in depth in order to understand what this message might be. See Figure 17.

To fully comprehend the symbolism of ancient Egypt on which the civilization was based, one would need to know, it seems, the history of its development. But alas, from all the archaeological investigations that have taken place over more than 200 years in the sands of Egypt, the Egyptian civilization seems to have been almost fully formed from its beginnings, including a calendar, myths, symbols, hieroglyphs, rituals, royalty, and a social order, all with no sign of a gradual development:

> ...the certainty we now have of the existence, since the First Dynasty, of a sound metaphysics, a complete writing, and a symbolism that serves as the basis of the whole history spread out over four thousand years.[265]

---

[265] R. A. Schwaller de Lubicz, *The Temple of Man: Apet of the South at Luxor*, Vol. 2 (Rochester VT: Inner Traditions, 1998), 834.

Unless new findings prove otherwise, this can only mean that the civilization came from elsewhere, by a people having an already developed culture, for which up to now we have no evidence. We would propose, however, that this is not the stumbling block that it seems to be. The human being, as an organism, is always the same everywhere, whether in Thebes several thousand years ago or now in New York or New Delhi. Since our interest is in the development of consciousness in man, the most interior part of his being, it is not the trappings of culture and religion that are the most important and which depend on time and place, but that which is essential to man's nature, which depends solely on his interior state of being, his relation to nature, to the cosmos, and to universal energies:

> Now, it could be argued that it is possible to understand the religious experience of the ancient Egyptians only by studying the whole society within which such experience took place—its language, its literature, its history and art, its political and economic organization, and so on.... But simply to explain religious experience in terms of these conditioning factors would be to miss something essential. That 'something essential' is not reducible to ordinary social, political, historical, or cultural circumstance, but belongs rather to the nature of human consciousness and its capacity to become receptive to numinous, and thoroughly non-ordinary, levels of reality....The experiential root of Egyptian religion is not safely located in the distance of a civilization long since past, but belongs to the very structure of the human being as a religious being.[266]

As we try to understand Egyptian symbolism, we must be open to a new way of thinking, for ancient Egypt is pre-Greek, that is, pre-analytic, where every aspect of the culture, indeed every object, took on meaning in terms of its function in the cosmos, and every element of life was the symbol of a higher invisible

---

[266] Jeremy Naydler, *Shamanic Wisdom in the Pyramid Texts: The Mystical Tradition of Ancient Egypt* (Rochester VT: Inner Traditions, 2005), 9-11.

law by which the cosmos was ordered.[267] What was divine, that is, what had power, was not only transcendent, outside of nature, but also immanent within it. Their means of expressing their knowledge was thus not to explain in words, but to create a symbol that synthesized all aspects of a particular subject. To understand the symbols, the first requirement then is for the exotic nature of the Egyptian symbolism to have disappeared through constant study so that one is free to explore the real meaning behind the symbols.[268] Ancient Egyptian symbols were not what we would call "signs" denoting a particular thing that could be put in a dictionary or to stand for something else like a road sign. Rather they took their meaning from other symbols and myths, and so their combinations, while complex and sometimes seemingly absurd, were not fortuitous. It is simply for us to try to understand the relations between them depending on different *levels* of meaning,[269] which is to say, for the ancient Egyptians, the symbol, while being *concrete*, was a *synthesis* embodying a function or principle that could be understood on different levels: spiritual, cosmological, terrestrial and individual:

> [O]ne must learn to listen to the symbolic image, allowing it to enter into and pervade one's consciousness, as would a musical tone which directly resonates with the inner being, unimpeded by the surface mentality.[270]

---

[267] Some helpful books on Egyptian symbolism are the following:

- R. T. Rundle Clark, *Myth and Symbol in Ancient Egypt* (London: Thames and Hudson, 1959).
- Christian Jacq, *La sagesse égyptienne* (Paris: Éditions du Rocher, 1981).
- Isha Schwaller de Lubicz, *Her-Bak, Egyptian Initiate* (New York: Inner Traditions International, 1978).
- R.A. Schwaller de Lubicz, *Le Miracle Égyptien* (Paris: Flammarion, 1963).

[268] René Guénon, *Initiation et réalisation spirituelle* (Paris: Études Traditionnelles, 1974), 114.

[269] Clark, *Myth and Symbol*, 218.

[270] R. A. Schwaller de Lubicz, *Symbol and the Symbolic*, 11.

In this way, principles, ideas, functions, natural processes, and psychological concepts could all be evoked and understood directly in one's being without being filtered by one's mental apparatus:

> Knowledge of this intellective source of the emotional center, in connection with the cerebral intelligence, can open our eyes to an altogether different way of thinking and acting that no longer excludes direct knowing, and that needs no physical or descriptive intermediary. Here the source of intuition resides, and this faculty can he cultivated to the point of enabling the communication of thought, with no outward signs, between sufficiently prepared people.[271]

A symbol can thus reveal meanings on different levels, but also conceal meanings for those who have not been prepared to understand them in all their ramifications. And symbols were everywhere: the slightest object of daily life was conceived to project a specific meaning due its form or representation:

> For the Egyptian every so-called 'physical' fact of life had a symbolic meaning, and at the same time every symbolic act of expression had a 'material' background; both were equally true and real.[272]

For example, a simple mirror was often made in the likeness of the female *neter* Hathor, a complex *neter* often having the shape of a cow, or just cow ears, a symbol of the mother, the matrix of the world, of birth, but also a *neter* of love, music and dance, and her name meant "House of Horus," not to mention her assimilation to the ancient *neter* Neith, a creator *neter* who 'weaved' the creation of the world. Even more abstractly, Hathor, as a cow, symbolized the passive aspect of creation.

---

[271] R. A. Schwaller de Lubicz, *The Temple of Man: Apet of the South at Luxor*, Vol. 1 (Rochester VT: Inner Traditions, 1998), 7.

[272] Alexandre Piankoff, *The Wandering of the Soul*, Religious Texts and Representations, Bollingen Series XL, Vol. 6, Completed by Helen Jacquet-Gordon (Princeton, NJ: Princeton University Press, 1972), 6.

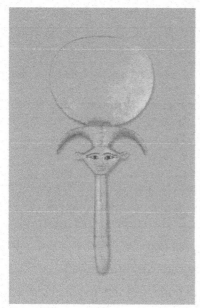

Figure 18 Mirror as Hathor symbol

Furthermore, her ears were always emphasized, calling attention to listening, a symbol of active attention, a synthesis of meanings in a simple hand-held mirror. See Figure 18.

"In the old world of Egypt everything is symbolic: each gesture of life, each religious rite, each stela, each monument, each hieroglyph—its color, its location—each representation, the form of each common object; they all obey a wisdom that situates each thing in the harmonic emplacement of its cosmic nature."[273]

From the Greeks, and up to its most extreme expression in our time, Western man has been looking at the world from 'outside,' subjectifying it through thought as a 'thing' to be analyzed and manipulated rather than being oneself an integral part of the whole. The 'rational man' starts with the facts, what he can see and measure, and tries from there to decipher their cause. The ancient Egyptians, on the other hand, started with the cause, the essence of things, to eventually arrive at their superficial effects:

> Because the principles underlying the universe are everywhere the same, analogy is a more accurate, ultimately a more 'scientific' means for arriving at an understanding of phenomena than mere measurement. This is why all sacred teachings make use of parable, analogy, myth and symbol instead of facts. Facts do not aid understanding.[274]

---

[273] R. A. Schwaller de Lubicz, *Le Miracle Égyptien*, 47. [Our translation]

[274] John Anthony West, *Serpent in the Sky: The High Wisdom of Ancient Egypt* (New York: Harper & Row, 1979), 95.

An Egyptian sage, therefore, looks at the world differently than us. He is not interested in the outward aspect of things, but rather their function within the environment in which they are embedded.[275] This environment includes the mythological past of the "First Time," where order reigned supreme and to which one should constantly try to attain. What was important was not how to change his lot over time, but how to conform to the immutable unchanging present. It is in man's interest not to promote change, as our modern thought tells us, but to 'do right' and 'be just'—not morally, but practically, that is, act according to one's place in the scheme of things—of the cosmos, of society, within himself—and so reach a level of being that was normal at the First Time. He does not divide the world up between what is material and what is abstract as we do. For him, everything is living and contains the energy of the universe. What is understood depends on one's state of consciousness: either one observes through the cerebral apparatus and sees only the outer form, or one is attuned to the cosmos through the 'intelligence of the heart,' the synthetic sense, and, through identification with the object, 'grasps' it through its energy and its function.[276] As R. A. Schwaller de Lubicz says: "I am not 'in front of' what I observe; I observe because I am that."[277] All the while thinking that one is being 'objective' through science, modern man cannot help but lie at every turn, since one's way of thinking is based on a false premise: that one can extract himself from the world which he is trying to observe, a notion that some modern quantum physicists have understood very well. In our age "one lives for the most part in illusions and cerebral constructions, and lacks contact with natural life."[278]

---

[275] R. A. Schwaller de Lubicz, *The Temple of Man*, Vol. 1, 456.

[276] Ibid., 492-93.

[277] Ibid., 505.

[278] Ibid., 375.

This type of thought must have been totally alien to the ancient Egyptians who, rather than slicing up the world in bits to study it, implicated themselves deeper within the world through rituals that were conducted to assure continuity between the human and divine levels of existence, that is, between the present and the mythological past. The Egyptologist Christian Jacq wrote:

> Egypt expresses itself essentially as a ritual civilization carrier of a fundamental truth: the constant relation between humanity and the gods is indispensable to the maintenance of harmony on earth. Such a relation can only be maintained by the celebration of rites.[279]

These rituals used symbols that evoked the functional vertical relationships operating at each level. If the sun ordered the cosmos by being at its center, so the pharaoh ordered Egypt, and the heart man—not allegorically, but in fact, the higher activating the lower, while the lower being a symbol for the higher. Thus, for the ancient Egyptian, an essential relationship existed between the sun, the pharaoh and one's own heart, a relationship which had to be kept in harmony through ritual so that one could partake of the beneficence of the 'center' flowing from the sun, through the pharaoh, to eventually irrigate the center of his own being. The goal, therefore, of rituals in any Traditional spiritual community is to "put the human being in relation…with something that goes beyond his individuality and which belongs to other states of existence."[280] Therefore, there was no distinction among "science," "religion," and "art" as we use these terms. For the Egyptians, knowledge of nature was intimately involved in the spiritual development of man, for the laws that directed natural phenomena were the same as those that man possessed. A law found in nature thus became a symbol for that same law existing within man, and its expression was the

---

[279] Jacq, *La sagesse égyptienne*, 9.

[280] René Guénon, *Aperçus sur l'Initiation* (Paris: Études Traditionnelles, 1953), 109.

sole *raison d'être* of "art":

> For Egypt, the actualization of being does not depend on belief but on knowledge. The ancient Egyptian does not believe in God; he knows him through symbols, rites and the practice of the Word inscribed in the hieroglyphs. So there does not exist a dogma, a truth revealed once and for all. There does not exist a historical representation of the divine, which is embodied at each instant for all eternity.[281]

By 3000 BC, the essential nature of Egyptian culture had been established, including the hieroglyphs, the pantheon of the *neters* (gods), and the symbols inscribed and drawn on their monuments. Until the Christianization of Egypt in the 3rd century AD, over three thousand years later, this symbolism remained essentially the same. For us, this may seem strange indeed, our cultural references being in constant flux as there is no longer any higher meaning by which civilization is ordered, and thus no lasting universal symbolism. Why the Egyptian civilization did not continue after the Greco-Roman conquest and the advent of Christianity, why it did not continue through holy books, is not only due to the destruction of its temples, the priesthood and the hieroglyphs, but because the sacred texts were never meant to be separated from the rituals in which they were a major part.[282] The sacred texts were not created to be inspirational but to have transformational power over those who took part in the sacred rituals in the tombs and temples.

Egyptian civilization was, in the words of Enel, "the basis of all Western cultures and religions, of their philosophy, their science, and their art."[283]

---

[281] Christian Jacq, preface to Max Guilmot, *Message spirituel de l'Égypte ancienne* (Paris: Éditions du Rocher, 1988), 7.

[282] Jan Assmann, *Images et rites de la mort dans l'Égypte ancienne* (Paris: Cybèle, 2000), 127.

[283] Enel (Michel Vladimirovitch Skariatine), *Le Message du Sphinx* (Paris: Arka Editions, 1998), 184. [Our translation]

Chapter 6 The Ancient Egyptian Mind

What would our minds be like if we had not spent 20-25 years or more in school and college? If we had not been forced to learn everything by rote so we could pass our tests and "be successful"? In sum, what would our minds be like if we were not trained to use only our mental capacities to learn? This training left us, and leaves us still, bereft of a whole gamut of ways to understand the world beyond our sole mental life. Might there be another way of interacting with the world that includes our emotions and our body and even higher levels of mind that allows us to enjoy a connection with universal energies? I propose that the ancient experience of the world was fundamentally different from our own. I experience myself as being separate from the world in which I live, because, like Descartes, "I think, therefore I am." The ancients, on the other hand, felt themselves as part of a nexus that included nature and society and in which they were an integral part. Because of this interconnectedness, they perceived relationships between things that supported a symbolic worldview:

> The ancients lived in a world that could be entered into and experienced in its inward depth; the moderns, oblivious of this depth dimension, are content to map in interminable detail the outer surfaces of a godless universe.[284]

When we realize that ancient Egypt began thousands of years before the pre-Socratic Greeks began to analyze the world through their ideas and theories, and before science later became the only judge of truth, it is clear that the mind of the ancient Egyptians had to be profoundly different than our own:

---

[284] Jeremy Naydler, *Temple of the Cosmos: The Ancient Egyptian Experience of the Sacred* (Rochester, VT: Inner Traditions, 1996), 23.

> We always run the risk of allowing our own mentality to
> cloud the consciousness necessary to feel and understand
> the mentality of the Ancients.[285]

In this regard, of course, we are discussing the elite: the nobles,
the priests, the initiates, and the students who came to learn in
the Temple. The mass of the population were peasants who
followed the rituals and festivals handed down through the
millennia by the elite, but without understanding their deeper
meaning.

The Egyptian prescientific view of the cosmos was based not on
scientific research but on sound, symbols and mythology that
embodied a spiritual knowledge having as its purpose, on the
macrocosmic scale, to show how the world was created and
maintained, and, on the microcosmic scale, to help in man's
transformation, the expansion of his consciousness. Their minds
were attuned to the use of symbols to provide meaning:

> Man lived quite naturally in a milieu of a 'forest of
> symbols,' since each word, each object, each element
> almost always carried several meanings in it, often
> mixing the concrete with the abstract.[286]

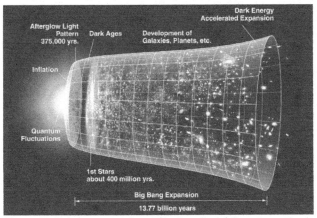

Figure 19 Creation as modern "Big Bang" and Egyptian neter Atum

---

[285] R. A. Schwaller de Lubicz, *The Temple of Man*, Vol. 1, 5.

[286] Christiane Desroches Noblecourt, *Symboles de l'Égypte* (Paris: Desclée de
Brouwer, 2004), 10. [Our translation]

If we look at Figure 19, the difference between the modern and Egyptian views of creation could not be more striking. The modern theory is a purely mental construct that is understood only through mental cogitation of the image and its explanatory texts. The Egyptian symbol is simply the *neter* Atum, the "god" of creation, the understanding of which can only come from a grounding in Egyptian myth. In such a case, the understanding of the image of Atum is immediately grasped without any need for "thinking about it."

For the ancient Egyptians, "philosophy," as we know it, did not exist: nothing was analyzed or explained. For them, we can assume that symbols and mythology were just as real in their minds as scientific proofs are for ours. Events could not be "explained" because they "lived" the events themselves and their explanation could only be conceived of as *action* and necessarily take the form of a story. Everything in nature was 'alive,' and because they were not encapsulated in their minds they were able to interiorize being, things, and events: the sun was not an 'object' but an expression of the creator *neter*[287] Re who was the active element of creation at the First Time. The sun did not follow what we would call a "law," but moved according to mythological, that is, symbolical phases: it became Kheper, upon rising (being born) in the eastern horizon; Re, moving brightly across the sky during the day; and Atum, setting in the West (dying) in the evening, thus exemplifying the Egyptian motif of death and rebirth. Re is therefore always present over time in the different centers of Egypt, whether Atum-Re in Heliopolis, Re-Horakhty in Memphis or Amon-Re in Thebes. The hieroglyphs used to write Re are a mouth and an arm, that is, speech and action. Thus, the pharaoh's words, as "son of Re"

---

[287] A *neter* is what Egyptologists normally call a "god." As the word "god" has many connotations, we use the word *neter* throughout the book, which refers to a cosmic principle or law. This is discussed in greater detail below.

and a creator *neter* himself, were the same as an act of creation: when he spoke, the deed was done. See Figure 20.

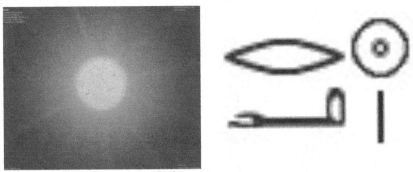

Figure 20 The sun and its hieroglyphs

The ancient Egyptians did not divide the world between the sacred and the profane, the spiritual and the physical: there was only one world in which the *neters*, or divine powers, held sway. In other words, the ancients told myths instead of presenting an analysis or conclusions.[288] Myth then is not allegory; it is the thought itself become conscious. It is not meant to be an answer to a question, but a revelation of a lived truth. For the ancient Egyptians, as for other pre-scientific civilizations, there is no difference between subjective and objective thought: what they experience with their senses is not what is *true*—because there can be no *false*—it *is* simply because it *is* in their experience of it. In the same way, a symbol and its representation are one and the same thing: in their minds there is essentially no difference between a statue of a *neter* and the *neter* itself, or the name of a person and the person himself.[289] In sum, an ancient Egyptian did not compare or analyze what he experienced with his senses. He did not think about an event; he did not ask why or how as we are want to do, but what or who was responsible for it:[290]

---

[288] H. A & Henri Frankfort, *The Intellectual Adventure of Ancient Man: An Essay on Speculative Thought in the Ancient Near East* (Chicago: The University of Chicago Press, 1977), 6-7.

[289] Ibid., 12-13.

[290] Ibid., 16.

One might say that in ancient times people lived more deeply than we do today....The essential characteristic of the ancient consciousness was that the ego was continually having its boundaries dissolved in the face of extremely powerful transpersonal forces.... Perhaps we should say that the ancient ego was not as 'strong' as it is today. The sense that an individual has today of being the source of their own thoughts, feelings, desires and intentions was not nearly so developed in ancient times as it has since become.... In the ancient world, therefore, there was not the same sense of autonomy as we have today. People felt it necessary to constantly refer to sources 'outside' themselves, if the gods [*neters*] may be so described. That is, to sources extraneous to the self-contained ego.[291]

Their idea of knowledge was radically different than our own. For them, all knowledge was spiritual knowledge, and the understanding of ancient texts and the hieroglyphs were especially important in their being able to grasp it. In their view, the world was basically static, created once and for all at the First Time as *maat*, the just order of things:

[F]or them there was no dichotomy. The gods [*neters*] were everywhere, the king was the essential priest and all acts were played out against a background of divine patterns. Gods, men, animals, plants and physical phenomena all belonged to the same great order. There were no distinct realms of being.[292]

Their understanding of the world was very much a product of their environment. Two cyclical events were of the greatest importance: 1) The Nile River, coursing through the desert, every year flooded the land with water and silt, thus providing the necessary source for life. The Nile was considered to have

---

[291] Jeremy Naydler, *The Future of the Ancient World* (Oxford, UK: Abzu Press, 1994), 7-9.

[292] Clark, *Myth and Symbol*, 26.

its source in the *Nun*, the eternal watery abyss from which life came forth and to which everything returned. See Figure 21.

Figure 21 The Nile river in flood

2) Every day the sun arose in the East at dawn and set in the West in the evening. These two cyclical events were at the basis of much of Egyptian myths and symbols. They were the natural order of things; they were permanent and thus 'right.' Death was not a final limit but rather the possibility of a new birth with new possibilities: something must die for something new to emerge. Change is thus only acceptable within a larger perpetuity, and so radical change, such as a revolution in society, was unthinkable. Like in nature, they did not hold for a strict symmetry in their constructions or their representations, though duality was very much part of their worldview as complementary opposites that created something new: death was but the precursor of life. Neither did they accept any sort of belief system, fixed rules or scheme of things that was set once and for all. A certain order was necessary, but only so far as it did not hinder continual creation and the natural development of beings and things.[293]

The desert was considered dangerous and wild, where death and chaos reigned. It was filled with dangerous beasts, evil spirits, and how the enemies of Egypt could and would enter the land. There were the Nubians to the south, the Asiatics to the east and

---

[293]Erik Hornung, *L'esprit du temps des pharaons* (Paris: Lebaud, 1996), 84-85.

the Libyans to the west. To the north was the Mediterranean Sea by which the 'sea peoples' came to invade. See Figure 22.

Figure 22 An Egyptian desert

Egypt, then, was the 'center of the world' where order reigned, and which kept disorder at bay on its frontiers and within society. All this conformed to the basic understanding of the just order of *maat* by which the pharaoh reigned. However, the chaos of *isfet* could break in at any time, which conformed to the original watery abyss, the *Nun*, that surrounded the world and continued to be a threat. The *Nun* was not structured, but an unlimited, amorphous *Non-being* from which the *Being* of the universe was created. In the *Nun* there was no time and no space. Since there was only an amorphous nothingness, there were no things, only the pure potentiality of creation, which was then made manifest by the *neter* Atum who created himself in the *Nun* through the active force of Re. The Nile divided the land into two parts: the lower, or northern Egypt of the delta, and upper, or southern Egypt of the Nile valley, a duality reflected in much of the ancient Egyptians' understanding of the world.

The concept of Creation and its continual manifestation in the world was the basis of all knowledge:

> Creation is not a series of events in time but a speculation about the principles of life and the arrangement of the cosmos.[294]

---

[294] Clark, *Myth and Symbol*, 82.

In contradistinction to our modern view, what is 'good' or 'right' is that which keeps the world in order with everything in its just place. Change was only acceptable if the underlying order was not disturbed. Sound, too, was important. In the words of Serge Sauneron:

> In Egyptian thought, speech was more than just a social tool facilitating human relations. It was the audible expression of the innermost essence of things, and it remained what it had been at the beginning of the world: the divine act that created matter. The secret of the existence of the things evoked lay in the articulation of syllables: to pronounce a word or name was not just a method of causing an image in the mind of the speaker to be evoked in that of the hearer, it was a means of acting on the object or being that was mentioned, of repeating the initial act of creation.[295]

And Isha Schwaller de Lubicz writes:

> The name given to each thing is its definition, expressed through the value of the sounds which make up its name and the signs which write it. That is why one single word can replace a description or express a theory.[296]

The ancient Egyptians saw the cosmos as having three domains: the sky, the earth, and the *Dwat*. The sky was the expanse above symbolized by the female *neter* Nut and supported by four pillars (which no doubt were also symbols). It was separated from the earth by the *neter* Shu, associated with the air. The earth was symbolized by the *neter* Geb and in which the land of Egypt existed as its center. Here we have a profound symbolism: Shu separates the divine realm Nut from the earthly realm Geb, thus creating space for creation to take place. On the microcosmic scale of man, in the same way, creation can be said to be an

---

[295] Serge Sauneron, *The Priests of Ancient Egypt* (Ithaca & London, Cornell University Press, 2000), 123-24.

[296] Isha Schwaller de Lubicz, *Her-Bak, 'Chick-Pea': The Living Face of Ancient Egypt* (Baltimore: Penguin Books, 1972), 227.

'inner space' by which spiritual energies can enter and create a 'new man' of higher consciousness:

> Shu…is consciousness itself, invisible and coextensive with the Creator, the active thought as distinct from the inert world-stuff.[297]

Figure 23 Osiris

The *Dwat,* the realm of the dead ruled by Osiris, was a vague notion associated with the night that was often implied to be underneath the earth or above in a region of the sky, a realm of regeneration but also filled with danger and terror, being the place of energies and spirits that can influence the living. The *Dwat* is thus symbolic of the interior world of man exemplified by his nightly revivifying state of sleep but prey to nightmarish dreams, and which symbolizes his underground spiritual journey of purification from darkness to light. By confronting one's own demons, accepting them instead of fleeing from them, one becomes their master, and their energy can thus be used for one's spiritual development. There is, in fact, no one road to enlightenment and the ancient Egyptian sacred texts do not provide one. Each person, therefore, has their own road to follow. To understand what was 'in the *Dwat'* was therefore to understand what the essential nature was of one's own being:

> To know this mysterious interior world was to become truly wise, because then one knew both sides of existence—the invisible along with the visible.[298]

---

[297] Clark, *Myth and Symbol*, 83.

[298] Jeremy Naydler, *Ancient Egypt and Modern Esotericism*, Rosicrucian Digest, Vol. 85, No. 1 (San Jose, CA: AMORC, 2007), 34.

It was the domain of Osiris, ruler of the dead, often called the "weary one," needing to be awakened and reborn, but also called "he who is in the egg," thus emphasizing that he is not completely dead, but is in the process of gestation to be born again. Therefore, he is always depicted as mummiform, but with his head and hands appearing outside of the enclosing cloth. See Figure 23.

The *neter* Re traveled as the sun in a 'day boat' across the sky during the day and at night entered into the body of Nut or the *Dwat* in a 'night boat' on the western horizon. Here he embraced Osiris—an important symbolic act in itself—then was reborn the next morning by Nut on the eastern horizon. By embracing Osiris, Re was invigorated with new life and able to live again. By embracing Re, Osiris was awakened from his 'weary' state to again become effective. In this act, the active and passive agencies of the universe came together to create new life. Just as the sun is reborn every day, so each Egyptian aspired to be reborn again in the afterlife, or—for initiates—to be reborn through ritual as an enlightened *akh* in this life on earth:

> The exchange between light—the sun god—and darkness—the cavern of Sokar—allows resurrection to take place at the end of the night journey, when the scarab beetle Khepri pushes the ball of the sun through the gates of the horizon as the mummiform Osiris slips back into the Duat. The renewal of creation in the depths of the earth allows the king's soul to ascend from the tomb just as it allows the sun to rise again.[299]

In sum, the *Dwat* represents the original *Nun*, the watery abyss from which creation arose, and Osiris is its personification. Through the embrace of Re, Osiris is rejuvenated, and by impregnating Isis, Osiris creates Horus, the 'True Man' incarnated in every pharaoh.

---

[299] Mark Lehner, *The Complete Pyramids* (London: Thames & Hudson, 1997), 30.

Now when we read some Egyptologists' texts, they often say things like 'the Egyptians believed the sun traveled in a boat' or 'the sky was held up by four pillars or by the god Shu,' and so on, without any attempt to analyze the symbolic nature of these images, or explain any contradictions—as if the ancient Egyptians were like little children who simply needed fairy tales to understand the world. It is as if in our day a reader of the Bible would take episodes of Christ literally, such as him 'walking on the water,' or 'raising Lazarus from the dead,' without trying to understand the deeper symbolic meanings of these events.

Figure 24 The night boat of Re

To help us understand the symbolic mind of the ancient Egyptians, let us try to decipher the image of the sun traveling across the sky in a boat, an image that was often drawn on the walls of the tombs and on funeral papyri. This image, which is of greatest importance in ancient Egyptian metaphysics, could, in fact, take an entire book to decipher using our rational mentality; nevertheless, we will shorten our explanations to the most important elements. First, the sun itself is a symbol of the creator *neter* Re who is born each morning at the eastern horizon and dies each night at the horizon in the West. This is in itself symbolic as to the cyclical nature of one aspect of eternity as seen by the ancient Egyptians: cyclical time or 'eternal return.' The sun then was not for them simply a physical object in the sky, but a spiritual power of creation as the *neter* Re. See Figure 24.

Why a boat? For the ancient Egyptians, boats were the essential means of travel. Since all towns and cities were near the Nile River, one normally took a boat to travel from one place to another. Moreover, boats have been found buried next to the pyramids of Giza, symbolizing perhaps the boat by which the pharaoh would travel to the circumpolar stars and be a "*neter* among the *neters*." So, the use of a boat would have been quite natural to the Egyptian mind and so allow the symbolism to enter their consciousness that much easier.

Every day Re traveled in two boats: the day boat and the night boat. The name of Re's night boat, *Mesektet*, is based on the root *sk* (in transliteration of the hieroglyphs), to perish, for the boat enters the realm of the *Dwat* where light is extinguished. The name of the day boat is *Mandjet*, whose root is *ᶜnd*, the dawn, when light reappears. The image of the guiding oar on the boats also carried subliminal connotations as the means of propulsion of Re's boat across the sky and traversing the netherworld. Now Re did not travel alone in the boat. Other *neters* in it show how the symbolism embraced several concepts. That is not to say that there were always the same *neters* accompanying Re. In ancient Egypt, nothing was static; no image was so iconic that it could not be expressed in different ways. There might be a basic image, such as the boat of Re, but the details could be different depending on time and place, and on the exact message that was to be transmitted—but nothing was ever depicted for purely decorative reasons. In the *Book of that which is in the Netherworld* (*The Amduat*), Re is represented as a ram-headed man having horizontal horns on which there is a disk. On the descending voyage in the day boat this figure appears within a naos, a sacred space.

In the night boat, on the ascending voyage towards his rising on the eastern horizon, he is surrounded by the coils of the Mehen serpent.

Let us take a moment to discuss the symbolism of this serpent. In *Coffin Texts* 493 and 495 it as associated with "secrets" or "mysteries":

> I am the guard of the prisoners after the secret matters (or affairs) of the Coiled One.[300]

Now R. O. Faulkner translates the Egyptian word *mḥn* (Mehen) as "The Coiled One," rather than its Egyptian name, which in no way alters the symbolism. Most Egyptologists see this serpent as protecting Re from *outside* evil, but it could just as well be that the coiled serpent also prevents what is *inside*, the enemies of Re, from escaping, holding them prisoner in its coils.[301] Spells 758-760 of the *Coffin Texts* also speak of the "roads of Mehen," the point being that the "roads of Mehen" lead to Re:

> As for him who knows the names of those paths of his, it is he who will go in to the Coiled One. As for him who knows this spell, he will never perish. He will live on what Re lives on.[302]

The serpent, then, having a forked tongue and a double penis, is a symbol for duality. Not only does it represent the negative force that causes unity to split into multiplicity, that is, the serpent Apophis, but it also represents a positive force that prevents this negative force from manifesting, that is, the serpent Mehen.

Archaeologists have found a Mehen game board from the Old Kingdom. It is in the shape of a two-dimensional coiled serpent

---

[300] R.O. Faulkner (Tr.), *The Ancient Egyptian Coffin Texts*, Vol. II (Warminster, UK: Aris & Phillips, 1994), 134-35.

[301] Peter A. Piccione, *Mehen, Mysteries, and Resurrection from the Coiled Serpent* (Journal of the American Research Center in Egypt, Vol. 27, 1990), 44.

[302] Faulkner (Tr.), *Coffin Texts*, Vol. II, 293.

with the tail at the outside and the head in the center. Different texts show that the serpent has two heads or two faces, as recounted in the *Book of the Dead*, text 172 and the *Book of Gates*, tenth division.[303] The 'game' is to advance along the serpent to arrive at the center, presumably where Re is to be found. While we do not know the rules of this game, its symbolic nature cannot be doubted:

> The Mehen game was understood as a means of transformation to rebirth through a process of journey.[304]

Another board game called *senet* is also frequently mentioned in religious literature and it too was a 'journey' to eternity. It consisted of a race between two players who moved their pieces along a path of thirty squares. To 'win the game' was thus symbolically the same as arriving at rebirth. Like attaining

success in the board game, all obstacles must be overcome to attain divine resurrection in the hereafter. See Figure 25.

in *Figure 25 The* senet *game*

As is usual ancient

Egypt, everything is suggested; nothing is explained or presented in an explicit manner. Nevertheless, from what we have just discussed, we can perhaps assume that the coiled serpent, Mehen, has more to its meaning than being a simple protection for the sun *neter* Re. The Mehen serpent may, in fact, be another symbolic means of showing the way to rebirth, the coils not only preventing distracting elements from entering into the path of ___

---

[303] Piccione, *Mehen,* 50-1.

[304] Ibid. 52.

resurrection, but also preventing energies from leaving the voyageur, energies which can be used within to raise one's consciousness. The two heads or faces of Mehen can be interpreted as the two levels which man must separate within himself: the level of life, of *doing*, and that of higher consciousness, of *being*. We can interpret, then, the "roads of Mehen" to be an esoteric knowledge of transformation and resurrection that, if known, can provide the means to overcome obstacles and "find Re," to be reborn in the light, not necessarily after a physical death, but in life itself.

In the boat there might be Isis and Nephthys, the sisters of Osiris, who were there to protect Re from the elements causing chaos or *isfet* to enter. Now if we take the metaphysical symbolism as essentially esoteric means for man to achieve higher consciousness, this would mean that Re, as the creator principle in man, needs to be safeguarded from all those elements that would prevent man from succumbing to the horizontal lower functions of mind, emotions, and body and so lose track of the vigilance needed to climb, so to speak, the vertical axis towards enlightenment.

Seth, the brother of Osiris whom he dismembered, may also be in the boat with a spear in his positive aspect of fending off Apophis, the evil serpent always ready to destroy what Re creates, the symbol of darkness as opposed to the light of Re. Thoth too may be in the boat, replacing Seth by repulsing Apophis through the power of his words.

Three other *neters*, often in the boat, are Hu, Sia, and Heka, which are personifications of the metaphysical concepts 'authoritative speech,' 'intuitive knowledge,' and 'universal energy' (often called "magic"), respectively. On a cosmic level, the Word of Re coming from intuitive understanding of the universe was necessary for the world to be created at the First Time and then recreated each day in a continuous 'eternal return.' Furthermore, for the ancient Egyptians, using speech during rituals had the power of action:

> Speaking prescribed words aloud, in a ritual context, was a process of creation, as exemplified by the very common funerary formula in which a god is asked to provide for the dead. The offerings requested are called peret em kheru, literally 'that which comes forth through the voice': the act of pronouncing the words itself was believed to call up the food, drink and other goods that were required. The written word was scarcely less powerful.[305]

But for us, Hu, Sia, and Heka are also symbols of how man creates himself as a higher being. It is only when man goes beyond his purely mental understanding that he can begin to be transformed. At a certain point of development, when man has left behind his belief in himself, in his belief that he can know only through his mind, his actions then take place immediately, at once, through the power of mind, *heka*—but not through thinking—whether manifested or not in speech. "So it is said, so it shall be done," has been interpreted as to be the power of kings, but the deeper meaning is esoteric: right action, knowing what needs to be done, appears from intuitive knowledge, the 'intelligence of the heart,' without being filtered by the rational mind. No thinking is necessary, no choice is made; on a certain level one has become so attuned to the world, so enmeshed in it, that right action takes place on its own through one's internal energy or lower *ka* being precisely in tune with that of the universal energy, the higher *ka*—thus, the word *heka*. Most Egyptologists call this action "magic," but we believe it is really a product of spiritual development and refers to a higher degree of consciousness where all that one is, all that one 'has,' is but a reflection of universal laws, and one's ego thus becomes a servant of these laws instead of believing in its own

---

[305] John H. Taylor (ed.), *Journey through the Afterlife: Ancient Egyptian Book of the Dead* (Cambridge, MA: Harvard University Press, 2010), 30.

omnipotence. Of course, one who has not been prepared, has not been stripped of the belief in is ego, can believe that his 'gut feeling' is all that is necessary, only to create chaos all around oneself.

Figure 26 Re and Osiris in one body

When the day boat reaches the western horizon at sunset, the sun descends into the *Dwat*. Here is the realm of Osiris, the "king of the dead," the "foremost of the Westerners" —the West being the necropolis where the dead lay in their coffins. Osiris was slain by Seth and dismembered, then restored by Isis enough to have a son, Horus. Horus was chosen as ruler of Egypt over Seth before the assembly of the high *neters*. When Re entered the *Dwat* he met Osiris and they embraced, the active Re and the passive Osiris, each vivifying the other. Osiris thus represents man as 'the weary one,' a man dead in life without the means to ascend to a greater level of existence. Re, the sun, representing higher levels of energy, through this embrace symbolizes the entry into man of the energies needed to progress beyond his earthly state. See Figure 26.

So, we see here the great myth of ancient Egypt: *death and rebirth*. It is this concept, manifested in different ways and in different forms throughout 3000 years that constituted Egyptian myth, which was in fact the basis of its civilization. It is not accepted by most Egyptologists that this concept of death and rebirth was not only expressed in mortuary rituals for the deceased to be reborn in the afterlife, but was also as an esoteric concept needed for man to be reborn in *this* life. However, it is our view that the mythological texts used in mortuary rituals can also be interpreted as symbolical texts expressing man's spiritual ascension while living. Erik Hornung, however, writes:

> Several writers have stressed quite correctly that no trace of mysticism can be found in ancient Egypt. The Egyptians never succumbed to the temptation to find in the transcendence of the existent release from all imperfection, dissolution of the self, or immersion in and union with the universe.[306]

That some say that no traces of "mysticism" exist in ancient Egypt is really the fault of not interpreting their texts on the level of man's ascension to a higher level of being, of consciousness, of reading the texts only in the light of man's destiny after death.

What was important for the expression of Egyptian thought was never personal but always an attempt to arrive at a *meaning* that accorded with what was created at the First Time and continued still, whether in the cosmos or in man. Time, in the myth of the death and rebirth of Osiris became the symbol of every man's death and rebirth in the afterlife—or in this life. For the Egyptians, every death was always a precursor to an event, was never a concept that needed elucidation for what was important for them was the continual creation of the First Time taking place in the present. We should never try to compare their cosmogony with ours in a logical way. Ours is based on physics and what is measurable. Theirs is based on metaphysics and what is symbolically relevant to general principles and the

---

[306] Erik Hornung, *Conceptions of God in Ancient Egypt: The One and the Many* (London: Routledge & Kegan Paul, 1983), 182.

development of consciousness. Their myths had to do with events at the beginning of time, but these events were symbols that they applied to the present world. Their myths had nothing to do with history or historical time as we know it, or, in other words, history was for them a re-enactment of myth. In fact, with each new pharaoh, their time started anew from year one because a new pharaoh represented a new creation assimilated to the First Time. Images of events, such as the common one of pharaoh slaughtering his enemies, had nothing to do with an actual occurrence. They were the symbolic means of understanding the world—not from a historical viewpoint as we would have it, but through a synthesis of meaning arising from mythical events, where each event symbolized a metaphysical principle or function that could be applied to different levels of existence from the cosmos to man's transformation into a higher being. There are, in fact, scenes of the pharaoh slaughtering peoples who no longer existed, thus affirming their symbolic intent. Such images, carved on walls at the entrance to temples, refer to the keeping of chaos or *isfet* at bay, whether in the universe, in the land of Egypt, in society, or in man.

Chapter 7 Spirituality in Ancient Egypt

Many Egyptologists use the word "religion" in reference to ancient Egypt. The etymology of the word is not completely clear; however, it could come from the Latin *ligio*, "bind, connect," thus with *re-*, we have "bind again, reconnect." This would conform to the idea that man had 'fallen' and needed to reconnect with 'God.' While this original meaning would in fact be appropriate, I think that in our day this is the wrong use of the word. "Religion" now connotes an established organization by which a person can attain to a relationship with a higher power by conforming to the tenets of that organization and following its dogma and compulsory beliefs such as in the Christian, Jewish, or Islamic "religion." It seems that ancient Egypt did not have any creed, tenets, or dogma that the people were supposed to follow. They did not need a bible to teach them because the world itself was their "religion" and the hieroglyphs the symbolic representations of the things in this world. In fact, they did not have a word for "religion," the word that comes closest is perhaps "*heka*," which refers to the dynamic energy in the cosmos and which will be discussed below. The purpose of Egyptian "religion" or "*heka*" was to realize *maat*, the right order in the universe at every level. In terms of society, *maat* did not mean equality but rather that one accepted one's place and carried out his function as one should. To understand the essence of the hieroglyphs was to understand the cosmic forces in the world, including one's inner world. R. A. Schwaller de Lubicz wrote: "Writing by images is the only way to transfer a thought directly to the intelligence of the heart,"[307] (as opposed to the reasoning faculty of the brain). Yes, there were 'priests,' but

---

[307] R. A. Schwaller de Lubicz, *Propos sur ésotérisme et symbole* (Paris: Dervy-Livres, 1977), 74. [Our translation]

they did not preach to the people, who, in any case, were not admitted to the deepest sanctuaries of the temple. In fact, there is no one word to signify what we would call 'priest.' Often, they were simply functionaries doing priestly duties in the Temple for a certain time. They did not have to have sacred knowledge, but simply had to be 'pure,' to be physically clean and without stain on their character. The priests conducted rituals over statues of the *neters*, rituals that were not performed to appease the *neter* or *neters* in question, but in a larger sense, to help them in their functioning, to keep the universe in the sway of *maat*: to keep intact the order and harmony of the universe of the First Time, where justice and truth reigns, and so keep *isfet* or chaos at bay.

Figure 27 Pharaoh offering Maat

To this end, many images in the Egyptian temples show the pharaoh handing to a *neter* a representation of *maat* as a goddess having an ostrich feather on her head. See Figure 27.

Maat is sometimes called "the daughter of Re," thus expressing the idea that *maat* existed from the time of creation and that it is the foundation of all things cosmic and terrestrial. Every ritual act was thus a repetition of a mythical act that took place at the First Time where *maat* reigned supreme. It is this that gave every ritual act authenticity and ensured, because it was just, that it would be effective in the present.[308] Maat, in a way, is more a concept than a *neter*; one never finds a temple dedicated to Maat.

Totemism in tribal societies uses nature as a way to organize the world whereas ancient Egypt used the *neters* for the same purpose. These *neters* were not meant to be worshipped but were symbols of functions in the cosmos. Like tribal man, the Egyptians could not conceive of a man apart from society— banishment was the worst of punishments—nor society apart from the natural world. Thus, both were dependent on cosmic functions or forces, that is, the *neters*. That the common people *did* worship them is no different than people worshipping saints of different religions in our day without realizing what they stand for in terms of religious symbolism.

It is often asked how the Egyptian civilization could have existed for 3000 years with basically the same belief system, the same gods, and the same hieroglyphs. It was not a question of being conservative, as many would say, but the result of a completely different way of perceiving the world and a conscious decision to keep their society in tune with the universe as they saw it. For the ancient Egyptians, there was no idea of 'progress' as our times conceive of it, no idea of a continual improvement of man's condition due to his inventiveness, which translates in our day as 'technological advancement.' For the Egyptians the standard was not an illusory future of abundance, which they would never see, but the First Time when the world was created by Atum who created himself out of the *Nun*, the primordial watery abyss, and is being created still—outside of time. The *Nun* can be compared in fact to what we call the "background radiation" that still exists from the "Big Bang," which is our mythical origin of the universe, but which we refer to as one of our latest scientific theories.

---

[308] Clark, *Myth and Symbol*, 27.

> Before there was any opposition, any yes and no, positive and negative; before there was any complementarity, high and low, light and shadow; before there was presence or absence, life or death, heaven or earth: there was but one incomprehensible Power, alone, unique, inherent in the *Nun*, the indefinable cosmic sea, the infinite source of the Universe, outside of any notion or Space and Time.[309]

The First Time was pure order, pure harmony, where everything had its place in the cosmic hierarchy. This time is *now*, nonlinear, non-temporal, an overarching time that exists always in the present moment, a time by which man judges his existence and, for those who understood, a time to which he tries to return *now* through his acts, his rituals and his speech:

> [F]or them, spirituality has to do with intuition, perception, opening of the heart, and watchfulness. So it is not seen as an intangible revelation or a set teaching, but as a succession of formulas of knowledge whose comprehension depends on the intensity and the quality of our search.[310]

> True teaching is not an accumulation of knowledge; it is an awakening of consciousness which goes through successive stages.[311]

The means by which Atum created himself *out* of the *Nun* was his awareness of the divine, of higher powers, *within* the *Nun*. By *concentrating on himself* he created himself out of the chaos, (which could very well be a direction for spiritual practice).[312] At the same time, Re was the active element by which Atum manifested himself, and so the *first* trinity was formed:

---

[309] Lucy Lamy, *Egyptian Mysteries: New Light on Ancient Knowledge* (London: Thames and Hudson, 1981), 8.

[310] Christian Jacq, *La tradition primordiale de l'Égypte ancienne selon les Textes des Pyramides* (Paris: Grasset, 1998), 8.

[311] Isha Schwaller de Lubicz, *Her-Bak, 'Chick-Pea,'* 259.

[312] Fernand Schwarz, *Égypte: Les mystères du sacré* (Paris: Éditions du Félin, 1986), 65-66.

Atum-Nun-Re. Atum, through his *mind*, created himself potentially out of the *substance Nun*, which produced *action* in the name of Re. Atum thus created order where none existed and began the creation of the world by, depending on the source, spitting or masturbating out the two *neters* Shu (light, air; active, expansion) and Tefnut (moisture, passive, limitation), thus creating the *second* trinity: Atum-Shu-Tefnut. In this way, Atum was always the *neter* of *Being* as well as *Non-being* and therefore existed as the original creation within all things.

Associated with the First Time was the concept *neheh*, a linear, cyclical time based on the continual repetition of the original creation. This time refers to the creator *neters* Atum, Amon, Re or Ptah who are not constantly reborn but always present, always immanent.[313] All renewal, all transformation thus refers to the First Time of purity. The Egyptians did not conceptualize this sense of time, but for them it was simply experienced as such: man's growth from child to old age, the changing of the seasons, the movements of the heavenly bodies, and so on.[314] The changing of the seasons was especially important because it had such an impact on their daily lives. There were three seasons of four months of thirty days. *Akhet* was the season that began the year with the inundation caused by the overflow of the Nile in July. The next season was *Peret* beginning in November, when the flood receded and crops were planted. The third season was *Shemu*, starting in March, when the harvest took place. Five days were added at the end of the year to correspond to the solar cycle. Each new beginning was not a reference to, but a symbiosis with, the original creation at the First Time. There was no idea of a progression, of progress, only renewal again and again.

---

[313] Jan Assmann, *Death and Salvation in Ancient Egypt* (Ithaca: Cornell University Press, 2005), 371-72.

[314] H. A & Henri Frankfort, *The Intellectual Adventure of Ancient Man*, 23-24.

Another concept of time held by the Egyptians was *djet*, an eternal time that referred to Osiris, the *neter* of gestation outside of *neheh* time. *Neheh* thus refers to duration, continuance, to both the past and the future, while *djet* refers only to the dynamic eternal *now* in which spiritual transformation takes place and is reserved for the immortal *neters*:[315]

> It is well known that the Egyptian notion of cyclic time permitted the bringing of the past into the present now, as with the concept of creation. I would suggest that within the same framework it would also have been possible for the religious Egyptian to bring the future into this present, so that the realities of death and movement into the netherworld with attendant rebirth could have been genuinely experienced in this life now without reference to the limitations imposed by the barriers of human time.[316]

These two concepts of eternity did not die with Egyptian civilization. They were carried on in the Greco-Roman era as can be seen in the Latin *Asclepius,* a Hermetic text of late antiquity:

> [E]ternity has no limitation within time. But time, granted that it can be limited by number or alternation or periodic return through recurrence, is eternal. Both are infinite, then; both seem eternal…. The beginnings of everything, then, are god and eternity. But because it is mobile the world does not hold first place; mobility exceeds stability in it even though, conforming to the law that keeps it ever stirring, it has a steadfastness free of motion.[317]

It is no coincidence that *djet*, refers not only to eternal time, but also to the *djet* body (see below) which is the divine body outside of time. The word *djet* is also pronounced closely to the word

---

[315] Hornung, *L'esprit du temps*, 75.

[316] Edward F. Wente, *Mysticism in Pharaonic Egypt?*, Journal of Near Eastern Studies 41, No. 3 (Chicago: University of Chicago, 1982), 178.

[317] Brian Copenhaver (Tr.), *Hermetica: The Greek Corpus Hermeticum and the Latin Asclepius* (Cambridge UK: Cambridge University Press, 1995), 86.

djed as in "*djed* pillar," which is raised in ritual ceremonies and is considered the backbone of Osiris—he who endures—the place of spiritual currents of energy. (Homonyms were considered by the ancient Egyptians as having symbolic resonances.)

Neters or "Gods"

What we call "gods" in ancient Egypt are, as noted above, not some sort of mythical or spiritual being to be worshipped and placated, but *principles or functions* by which the universe was created in the mythical First Time and continuously maintained. In short, they symbolize an agency by which a cosmic cause produces a terrestrial effect.[318] In ancient Egypt they were called *neters*. A *neter*, then, was not a circumscribed individual "god," but rather a particular expression of the *Neter-Neteru* (the Principle of Principles, Cause of Causes, or God of Gods), clearly denoting a supreme principle or deity, which is unnameable.[319] According to Schwaller de Lubicz:

> They are real powers that act when one knows how to invite them to, not by formulas of 'black magic' or other terms of sorcery, but by knowing cosmic laws.[320]

Standing, as they do, for principles or functions, they are not defined once and for all by their forms, their names, or their representations. All of these can change depending on the context in which they are found. The sun *neter* Re, for example, can be Kheper in the morning, Re itself at midday, or Atum in the evening. The heavenly cow, Hathor, can be assimilated to Isis or Nut, or other 'mother' *neters*, depending on the myth that is the most pertinent for the message to be imparted. Another

[318] Lamy, *Egyptian Mysteries*, 12.

[319] R. A. Schwaller de Lubicz, *Le roi de la théocratie pharaonique* (Paris: Flammarion, 1961), 245.

[320] R. A. Schwaller de Lubicz, *The Temple of Man*, Vol. 1, 427.

example is the *neter* Thoth, who can be symbolized by the moon, a baboon, or an ibis bird, again depending on the particular myth in which Thoth plays a part. Thus, no image or statue of a *neter* gives a complete picture of its essential nature: its functions can change depending on the mythical context in which it is being incorporated, as well as the other *neters* with which it is interacting.

Schwaller de Lubicz also says that there are three categories of *neters*: the metaphysical *neters*, such as the creator *neters* Atum, Re, Ptah, and Amon; the cosmic *neters*, such as Osiris, Seth, Isis, Nephthys and Horus, by whom the cosmos rests in harmony through celestial influences; and the natural or terrestrial *neters*, such as Hapy for the Nile and Selket for childbirth.[321]

The metaphysical *neters* are those having to do with creation before their influence results in the cosmic manifestations of the universe. In the Heliopolitan creation myth (from the ancient city of Heliopolis), the *neter* Atum was the original creator *neter* who engendered himself in the *Nun*, the primordial watery abyss. To engender himself, Atum differentiated himself from the primeval ooze in which he was enmeshed. We see here the symbolic reference to the beginning of higher consciousness in man, where one begins to see something within himself that is separate from his automatic manifestations, the "ooze" in which he is entrapped:

> The reason for being of life is to become conscious of oneself. The goal of life is cosmic consciousness, the consciousness of the All, beyond short-lived, mortal contingencies.[322]

Since he was not born of a mother, Atum was sometimes represented without a navel. Being androgynous, Atum created his children: the male Shu, *neter* of air, and the female Tefnut,

[321] Ibid., 246.
[322] R. A. Schwaller de Lubicz, *Le Miracle Égyptien*, 267.

Figure 28 Nut and Geb separated by Shu

that of moisture. In their turn, Shu and Tefnut engendered the children Nut, female *neter* of the sky, and Geb, male *neter* of the earth. Being totally attached to each other, Shu separated them allowing the air and moisture to circulate between the sky and the earth. See Figure 28.

Geb and Nut then engendered four children: Osiris and Isis, the positive aspects of the world, and Seth, and Nephthys, the negative aspects.

Geb, as son of *neters* and father of men was considered as the link between the two. Altogether, the above nine *neters* became known as the Ennead, the nine. Nine is thus a sacred number, for all manifestation flows from the Ennead. Horus, son of Osiris and Isis, is not a part of the Ennead, but is the result: the quintessence of all the *neters* of the Ennead, the perfect being, ancestor of all pharaohs, who each in turn become the True Man to which all humanity aspires to emulate. With Horus the cosmogony is complete, and the cyclical nature of the cosmos begins. From the 'nine' of the Ennead, we arrive at 'ten' with Horus, or a return to 'one,' but on a different level. Horus, therefore, is the earthly embodiment of the heavenly cycles, and

199

who thus symbolically ensures the orderly unfoldment of the world processes incarnated in each pharaoh.

Another ancient creation myth arose in Hermopolis. Here the original unorganized chaos contained eight couples, four male frogs and their consorts, four female snakes:

- Nun, the primordial waters and his consort Naunet
- Heh, primordial formlessness and his consort Hauhet
- Kuk, primordial darkness and his consort Kauket
- Amon, "the hidden" and his consort Amaunet

Figure 30 The Bennu bird

Figure 29 A lotus plant

These eight *neters* became known as the Ogdoad, the eight. The Ogdoad thus represented emptiness or Non-being from which the world of Being was created. From this Non-being, a mysterious force caused the Primordial Mound to appear, arising out of the waters, and on which the Ogdoad placed the primordial egg from which the world was born. Another myth had a lotus plant arise from the original ooze, a plant from which a beautiful child arose as the first creator. The lotus plant is a symbol of creation at the First Time: it has its roots in the mud, its stems in the water from which flowers bloom, while its leaves spread out on the water capturing the air and the sunlight—thus encompassing the four primal elements of earth, water, air, and fire. See Figure 29.

One other myth had the Bennu bird, the first life, land on the *benben* stone. It was the call of the Bennu bird that ripped through the eternal silence to mark the beginning of time. See Figure 30.

Still another myth had Thoth, the master of Hermopolis and the Ogdoad, let fall the creative Word from his beak in his form of an ibis. He was then responsible for organizing the world and establishing the rules of its functioning.

In the mythology of Memphis, the creator *neter* was Ptah, who was formed of the Ogdoad and who created the primordial egg from which the sun and thus life was born.[323] Ptah was immanently involved in the creation of the material universe and as such became the *neter* of metalworkers, sculptors, and architects. Creating an object was thus attributed not to the artisan but to Ptah and the object produced was thus assimilated to creation at the First Time. Ptah is a creator *neter*, but on a level lower than that of Atum and so he is not completely free: his actions are contingent on other *neters* which thus circumscribe his field of action. For this reason, he is always portrayed enclosed in swaddling clothes with only his head, hands, and feet protruding. See Figure 31.

Figure 31 Ptah

Figure 32 Amon-Re

In Thebes, the Creator *neter* was Amon-Re, the principle behind the sun, the creator of heaven and earth. Amon, the "hidden,"

---

[323] Stéphane Rossini and Ruth Schumann-Antelme, *Neter: Dieux d'Égypte* (Lavaur: Éditions Trismégiste, 1992), 156.

who, while being invisible, gives life to everything, while Re was the active force behind all manifestation. See Figure 32.

The question then arises: how can there be such different creation myths, each of which recounting the original creation of the cosmos? First, we cannot project our logic onto the Egyptian mind, which was completely different than our own. The Egyptians did not see contradictions where we might see them. If different *neters* had seemingly similar functions, if different myths provided diverse stories of how a certain event came about, they were not contradictory but complementary. For example, different cosmogonies arising at different places can also be seen to be different phases of the act of creation but always referring to the original act. In fact, the different cosmogonies were simply different ways of saying the same thing. What Wilkinson calls "core mythic elements"[324] remain in different times and places; it is simply their representation that changes. In terms of creation *neters* we might consider this meaning of "creation":

> The principal aim of tradition in regard to the forms and laws of the cosmos is to connect all things with their first and divine cause and thus show man their true meaning, the sense of his own existence being likewise revealed to him thereby.[325]

For the Egyptians, this message could be symbolized in any number of ways. Above all, they used concrete examples in nature to teach abstract notions, while we start with theories concocted in our minds and then try to find concrete examples to prove them. The Egyptians, for example, symbolized the action of creation by the *neter* Atum who creates himself in the *Nun*, the watery abyss, or the appearance of a mound arising

---

[324] Richard H. Wilkinson, *The Complete Gods and Goddesses of Ancient Egypt* (London: Thames & Hudson, 2003), 19.

[325] Leo Schaya, *The Universal Meaning of the Kabbalah* (Baltimore: Penguin Books, 1973), 61.

from within it, or both. The lotus flower, mentioned above, which closes at night and sinks in the water and returns and blooms in the morning, was also a creation symbol mimicking the sun, which sinks below the horizon in the evening and arises again at dawn. The one thing that they all share is that the original creator created himself out of nothing or Non-being, had neither father nor mother, and arose before the world was divided into male and female elements. The natural world provided an untold number of possibilities to symbolize abstract metaphysical notions by which the world was created and is continually maintained. The same meaning could therefore be symbolized by different beings or things. To simply look at an image and associate it with a specific *neter* by memory without at least trying to understand the symbolism of the image would be a very puerile exercise. Whatever the symbol of a *neter*, the underlying meaning is there to be read for those who have made the effort to understand. *The means to this understanding is not to try to define the function which the neter represents but to search within oneself for that which corresponds to the function in question.* In this vein, it could be said that ancient Egyptian civilization was based on *real* knowledge, that is to say, a knowledge that arises by man's identification with universal laws with his whole being and not by attempts at their analysis through his sole cerebral mentation. For this to be, however, man must have an aim:

It is the spiritual aim of all human life to attain a state of consciousness that is independent of bodily circumstance. He who recognizes the divine meaning of life knows that knowledge has but one aim, which is to achieve the successive stages that liberate him from the perishable. For things only die in their body:

Figure 34 Isis

Figure 33 Horus

the spirit, the divine Word, returns to its source and dies not.[326]

The cosmological *neters* were mythological, symbolizing the celestial influences of the heavens. For example, Horus was originally the *neter* of the sky protecting the earth, which means that it is only when the sky is in harmony with the cosmos can there be harmony on earth. Isis, the mother of Horus, is associated with the star Sirius, which reappears on the horizon after 70 days of invisibility, just when the Nile floods and is the sign for the arrival of the new year. See Figures 33 and 34.

From these examples it can be seen that it is through the agency of the cosmological *neters* that the movements of the heavenly spheres create simultaneous effects on earth, but only in so far as they are connected to their divine cause.[327] Isis is Sirius, and so, through her mastery of *heka*, divine power, she brings forth the flood, whether water on land, or cosmic energy in the body of man, which thus leads to the Isis Mysteries of late antiquity.

The symbolic representation of a *neter* could be a human being, an animal, a human being with an animal head, an animal with a human head, or a natural object such as the sun, moon, or a stone. While applying rules to anything in ancient Egypt is hazardous, it can be said that a man with an animal head represents a *neter*, that is, a principle or function. Animals for the Egyptians had powers and functions which man did not and were thus considered sacred. Any animal could have multiple meanings and should never be considered as representing only one function such as the lion only equals force.

In various contexts, a *neter* can be represented in one way or another. The creator *neters* were represented as human in their

---

[326] Isha Schwaller de Lubicz, *Her-Bak, Egyptian Initiate*, 35.
[327] Ibid., 332.

role as creators of the cosmos to exemplify perhaps man's latent possibility of ascendance to this highest level of being.[328]

Figure 35 The neter Sobek in two forms

The *neter* Sobek could be represented as a crocodile or a man with a crocodile head. As a crocodile, without human features, it appears on the terrestrial level as rapacious, 'The Great Criminal,' which needed to be subdued, while as a man with a crocodile head he would be seen as the protector of the pharaoh and even a demiurge with his own cult.[329] See Figure 35.

A *neter* could also have different forms: for example, the *neter* Thoth could be represented by a baboon or an ibis, or a man with the head of one or the other. The *neter* Hathor, spouse of Horus of Edfu or of Re, can be represented by different female *neters* symbolizing particular functions: Isis as magician, for example; the feline *neters* Sekhmet and Bastet, as violent or calm protectoresses, respectively; or the cobra *neter* Wadjet and vulture *neter* Nekhbet, mistresses of the two lands of Egypt. Some *neters* were represented by the fusion of different beings, human or animal: a hippopotamus may have a lion's head, or a scarab may have an eagle's wings. See Figure 36.

---

[328]West, *Serpent in the Sky*, 145.

[329]Ibid., 170.

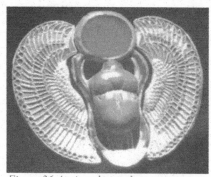

Figure 36 A winged scarab

The image chosen would signify the meaning the *neter* was to have, in the same way a determinative hieroglyph at the end of words provided the context and thus the sense of a word that could have multiple meanings. Also, the ornamentation of the *neters* was highly symbolic using specific headdresses, clothes, scepters, cult objects, as well as colors. The size of the body and its position, especially the arms and legs, all had symbolic meaning as well. It should be said, too, that even the word "*neter*" could be represented in different ways depending on the period: a seated figure with a beard, a falcon on a perch or not, a pole with a flag at the top, or a star;[330] again, the same meaning represented in different ways. Furthermore, one *neter* could be combined with another, such as Amon-Re in the New Kingdom. It could have been that a local *neter* was associated with a more influential one to provide the local *neter* with more import: perhaps metaphysically, perhaps culturally. The two associated *neters* could, in fact, combine their cosmological meanings to produce another meaning, as Hornung has proposed.

Through all these means, the symbolic representation of a *neter* could be understood at once without any explanation being necessary. It is up to us not to not try to conceptualize the *neters*, to define or classify them, but to understand their function in the cosmos and in ourselves. Concerning *neters*, we could do no more than to quote Erik Hornung:

> The nature and appearance of Egyptian gods [*neters*] are inimical to any closed, final, or univalent definition. We see them develop in history, and we see them leading a constantly changing life of their own. What a god is

---

[330] Wilkinson, *The Complete Gods*, 26-27.

cannot be defined. Whatever statement we make about him, it does not exclude a mass of other statements. Seen in another way, every god contains within himself all the information about a particular content, which took form in him and entered human consciousness in that form. For the Egyptians the gods are powers that explain the world but do not themselves need any elucidation because they convey information in a language which can be understood directly—that of myth. Every myth exhibits and interprets no more than a part of reality, but the totality of the gods and their relationships with one another exhibits and interprets the entire reality of the world.[331]

As it is said in the Leyden Papyrus 1, 350:

> Three gods are all the gods: Amun, Re, Ptah, who have no equal. 'He whose name is hidden' is Amun, whose countenance is Re and whose body is Ptah.

Heka or "Magic"

Figure 37 Hieroglyphs for Heka

Another concept that is essential to the understanding of ancient Egyptian spiritual thought and practice is that of *heka*. Now *heka* is most always translated as "magic" by Egyptologists, but we find that somewhat misleading. In our time the word "magic" suggests tricks that are done which seem impossible, or a certain force or power, totally out of the ordinary, that allows miraculous events to take place. I would assert, however, that what Egyptologists call "magic" is none other than the bringing into play the *one* energy of the universe that infuses the entire cosmos and, in its essence, is not "out of the ordinary," but rather the basic guiding force upon which the universe depends. If it is in fact "out of the ordinary," it is only because one does not have the means of being in touch with it. As John Anthony West says: "What is 'magic' to us to Egypt

---

[331] Hornung, *Conceptions of God*, 258.

was science, and in a sense even technology."[332] The two basic hieroglyphs which spell *heka* in ancient Egyptian are a wick (H) and two arms elevated (*kA*), perhaps symbolizing the reaching for that energy coming from 'above.' See Figure 37.

Now *kA* (in transliteration) or *ka* (in translation) is a symbol for this vital energy of the universe we just mentioned. So, the wick (H) followed by the raised arms *(kA), heka,* could very well mean "that which arouses the vital energy of the universe." Call it "magic" if you will. Another interpretation could be that one is looking at the arms from above so that the symbol represents an embrace, thus symbolizing the transmission of energy from one being to another, just as Re and Osiris embraced in the *Dwat* (see above). Perhaps both are possible and complementary in the ancient Egyptian way of seeing things.

So what we would call superstition or "magic," for example the cutting up of a snake in a hieroglyphic text on the walls of a tomb in order to prevent it from harming the deceased in the afterlife, would be for the ancient Egyptians a calling forth of vital forces to keep the order and harmony of *maat* in the universe, whether in the this world or the next. If ritual was followed in the carving of the hieroglyphs, perhaps accompanied by a recitation by a priest, the action would necessarily be effective due to the power of the spoken as well as the written word:

> Magic is omnipresent in the temples through the practice of rituals, even through the meaning of the architecture and sculpture, but also because of a surprising reality: the images carved on the walls are animated, living. They become alive when the ritual words are pronounced.[333]

In fact, for the ancient Egyptians it was absolutely essential to follow rituals exactly as they have been handed down, for they

---

[332] West, *Serpent in the Sky*, 101.

[333] Christian Jacq, *Le Monde magique de l'Égypte ancienne* (Paris: Éditions du Rocher, 1983), 63. [Our translation]

always refer back to the First Time, at the beginning of creation when the cosmic energy created the world from Atum, the self-created one. It is this same energy, *heka*, that is tapped through ritual to be used to create right conditions (*maat*) or prevent disorderly ones (*isfet*), chaos, which surrounds the created world, ready to break in and disrupt the world of *maat*. It is for this reason that rituals take place throughout the year, by the pharaoh, or his representative priests, who, through *heka*, keep *isfet* at bay by reinforcing *maat*:

> The sacralization of life is the most fragile thing there is. As soon as men lack attention to the divine presence, they profane the treasures that are within their reach.[334]

The principle of *heka* is anthropomorphized in a *neter* of the same name, a primordial *neter* representing the creative power of the First Time. See Figure 38.

He is found always accompanying the creator *neters* for it is the force of *heka* that created, and continues to act, in the world.[335] One sees Heka, for example,

Figure 38 Heka neter

in the boats of Re as he sails through the sky and the netherworld. This is so because Heka was at the origin of everything, even before the creation *neters* that created the cosmic *neters* symbolizing cosmic functions.

For the rituals to have the right effect, it is important that the priests be steeped in the knowledge of the energies of the cosmos through long training. When they themselves are in touch with the sensation of *heka* in their bodies, they are then able to contact cosmic *heka*, for it is one and the same universal energy. By a

---

[334] Jacq, *La sagesse égyptienne*, 85.

[335] Hornung, *L'esprit du temps*, 51.

certain inner process, the pharaoh or priest can thus allow *heka* to act in the world to restore harmony, *maat*, where it is lacking. This primal energy (perhaps it is 'light') is beyond measurement or any sort of technique to approach it. It is rather up to the pharaoh or priest to find the way to be open to it. Being *one* energy, whether in the unmanifested or the manifested world, the spiritual or the material, each can influence the other, which is the basic underpinning of Egyptian spirituality. By using ritual to connect the present world to that of the First Time, a connection is made between the primordial energy of *heka* and the material world of the present:

> Egyptian "magic" is an energy that works automatically and instantly and requires no particular medium for its transmission. When the god's creative word has been pronounced, "magic" ensures that it becomes reality.[336]

---

[336] Hornung, *Conceptions of God*, 208.

Chapter 8 Myth

The function of myth is to provide man with an understanding of spiritual truths that could no longer be understood by symbols alone. The whole spiritual evolution of man could be undoubtedly read, for certain ancient Egyptians, in the symbolism of the pyramid or of the eye, just as it can be read, for enlightened Christians, in the symbolism of the cross. These symbols, when 'read' with understanding, show man's journey to higher consciousness, but these symbols are meant to be understood by man's higher intellectual functions, which over time became atrophied according to cyclical law. Understanding was then provided by 'those who knew' through myths that made the symbols more accessible by touching man's emotions, but whose goal was the same: to show man the way from inner darkness to enlightenment:

> By no means...should the word of the myth be understood in its ordinary sense, as a childlike or fantastic, somewhat absurd poetic form. The myth is...only a means by which to explain something; it is a consciously composed lore of master ideas which may not be placed within reach of just anyone at any time....It conceals clear statements and coherent systems reserved for initiates, who alone have access to the 'deep knowledge.' The myths present themselves in layers, like the shells of a seed, and one of their reasons for being is precisely to cover and conceal from the profane a precious seed which appears to belong rightly to a universal, valid body of knowledge.[337]

Just as there is one "hero with a thousand faces," there is perhaps but one myth with "ten thousand" variations. If one looks deep enough into Egyptian mythology, it could be said that there is,

---

[337] Laird Scranton, *The Science of the Dogon: the African Mystery Tradition* (Rochester, VT: Inner Traditions, 2006). 41. Quoted from Marcel Griaule and Germaine Dieterlen, *The Pale Fox* (Continuum Foundation, 1986), 61.

in truth, only *one* Egyptian myth (and perhaps even only one universal myth) that has been cut up and given piecemeal or been provided with an infinite number of variations—or even distorted over time by those who no longer knew the myth's essential meaning. Again, this primordial myth is nothing less than man's journey from sleep to awakening, from death to rebirth, from death in life to a living higher consciousness. The myths of ancient Egypt are much more than stories invented to justify a political order based on divine kingship which many scholars propose. And this is so because the pharaoh himself is a symbol of man's possibility of obtaining a state through which a spiritual *inner* kingdom becomes possible. The pharaoh is the "True Man," just as are Buddha and Christ, and the Myth is the teaching showing the way to his realization. As the True Man, he is in perfect harmony with the order of the cosmos. As such, the pharaoh is often eulogized in the texts by the words "may he be vivifying, vigorous, and healthy." R. T. Rundle Clark, in his well-known book on Egyptian symbols and myths, says:

> For the Egyptians, mythology was not a collection of texts but a language. This is fundamental. It explains why the doings of the gods could be altered, be expanded and even reappear with other protagonists without apparent inconsistency. But myths do not have to be consistent. They belong to a way of thinking in which consistency in the logical sense is irrelevant. The myth was a way, and before the emergence of lay philosophy with the Greeks, the only way, to express ideas about the cosmos or the needs of the human soul. This is why Egyptian mythology is so simple, so absurd and sometimes so profound. It is dream, metaphysics and poetry, all at once.[338] ... Mythology was not the same thing as the telling of tales. It was the explanation of the universe by a believer in the Egyptian religion... a religious language.[339]

---

[338] Clark, *Myth and Symbol*, 263.
[339] Ibid., 267.

Figure 39 The Ogdoad

Just as there may be only one myth, in ancient Egypt there is, it could be said, only one god, Atum (in the Heliopolitan tradition) who created the manifest universe, where each manifestation was based on principles that formed a part of Atum himself. In sum, ancient Egypt was monotheistic. In the Memphite tradition it would be Ptah, and in the Hermopolitan tradition, the Ogdoad or eight primordial gods and goddesses. See Figure 39.

Whatever the tradition, after the creation of the world, what are called "gods" (*neters*) are actually representations of functional powers in the created cosmos (which are equivalent to our scientific equations representing physical laws)—or else metaphysical states of being. When we talk about "Tradition," we are not simply talking about how things were at a certain time in an historical sense. Tradition (with a capital T) has a much deeper meaning: a Traditional civilization, such as ancient Egypt, is based on spiritual truths, truths that are embedded in every aspect of the culture so that every person, no matter what their position in society, is constantly reminded of the reason for his or her existence. These reminders are given by symbols, myths, rites, and festivals by which, for those who seek, can discover deeper and deeper meanings of life and in living.

If, on a lower level, Egyptian mythology, is interpreted as showing how the universe was formed, leading up to the pharaonic monarchy based on the principle of divine kingship, this perhaps was the exoteric meaning destined to justify the pharaoh's authority. But myths are above all metaphysical statements on the structure of the present universe, the *macrocosm*, and of man, the *microcosm*, as well as every temple, town or region in which the structure of the universe was reflected. For this reason, myths also had an esoteric *raison d'être* destined for the high priests and those who could benefit from real knowledge. The symbols and myths of ancient Egypt were thus designed to describe, for those who could understand, not only the origin of consciousness, but also the means to its development. In the civilization of ancient Egypt, the monuments, symbols, rituals, and images created a perceivable universe that reflected a higher world that ordered the cosmos and provided man the means to reach this higher world. A specific animal, for example, was used as a symbol by utilizing its essential function in nature. Thus, to change any aspect of the rituals and symbols that did not reflect a change in the natural world, would be to put the community in disharmony with the cosmos and invite disaster, thus preventing man from achieving the goal of civilization: the elevation of man's consciousness, which otherwise means maintaining the cosmic equilibrium by returning energy to its source. Thus, if we wish to study the symbolism of ancient Egypt through symbols and myth, we must constantly keep in mind its essential purpose: to aid man in his climb to "the abode of the gods." As Barry Kemp says:

> [T]he Egyptian universe…concentrated on the essences of existence, free from the demeaning vagaries (and gross unfairness) of a god whose approval had to be sought.[340]

The haunting beauty of the symbols portrayed in the royal tombs across the Nile from Luxor astonishes us not because they incarnate a beauty through simple representation of things and

---

[340] Barry J. Kemp, *Ancient Egypt: Anatomy of a Civilization*. 2nd ed. (London: Routledge, 2006), 7.

beings, but rather because one feels intuitively that their beauty results from a meaning which cries out to be understood. It is from this intuition that this book is being written, all the while knowing that to cull one symbol from the mass, as we do with the eye (see below), is, in a way, to falsify the search for the ultimate meaning of Egyptian civilization. The *neters*, animals, plants, body parts, royal paraphernalia, monuments, buildings, and more are all part of one symbolic landscape encompassing a world having meaning beyond what is perceivable and utilitarian. Any one symbol thus takes its meaning from the other symbols and myths which provide the context in which it is used. Given this complex interrelationship between all the Egyptian *neters*, myths, and symbols, it would be an impossible task to write any definitive work about Egyptian symbolism. What the Egyptians taught was a universe where the *neters*, the cosmos, the earth, the temple, the tombs, the rituals and man were intimately related in a profound nesting of interrelated functions and energies in one encompassing whole where everything had its place for eternity:

> The mythology had therefore to serve two purposes. It was to give the steps whereby the universe was arranged, leading up to the final triumph of Horus and coming of the pharaonic monarchy. The other purpose—only gradually understood—was to provide a series of symbols to describe the origin and development of consciousness.[341]

Most Egyptologists, however important their work, do not concern themselves with these levels of being, as this is something that cannot be measured in the scientific domain in which they place themselves. Since it is impossible in our day to really comprehend and assimilate the totality of Egyptian civilization, as this would entail actually living within it and being privy to the secrets of the Temple, we accept our

---

[341] Ibid., 32.

piecemeal approach as a simple study that we hope will give ourselves, and any who care to read it, a further insight into the purpose of ancient Egyptian myth and symbolism and how it might be applicable to our own situation. On the same note, Heinrich Schäfer says in his work *Principles of Egyptian Art*:

> [I]t is completely impossible for us to transport ourselves into the mind of a strange people. Such an awareness of the limitations of insight or perceptiveness should never stop us from pressing forward as far as we can.[342]

And Charles S. Singleton says on his allegorical interpretation of Dante's *Divine Comedy*:

> [F]or all we may do, we shall not transform ourselves into 'readers of Dante's time.' And the truth of this must be granted. Indeed, there will always be a considerable difference between having, as by natural inheritance, a certain familiarity with a body of doctrine, and having this by a deliberate effort made to recover it and reinstate it in our minds. Yet, granting the discouraging difference, what else can we do?[343]

The Eye

Why do we take the eye as a symbol to be discussed? We could actually take any Egyptian symbol as an example, for as we have already pointed out, in a Traditional civilization everything is related, every symbol contains, like in a hologram, the meaning of the whole, at least for those having been immersed in the entire symbolism reflecting the civilization in question. If we choose the eye as an example of the symbolism of ancient Egypt, it is for two reasons: 1) The eye as a symbol appeals to us, because an eye obviously has to do with *seeing*. Now seeing in esoteric traditions often has to do with "the eye of the heart" or "the third eye," which "sees all" and is thus equivalent to being

---

[342] Heinrich Schäfer, *Principles of Egyptian Art* (Oxford: Griffith Institute, 2002), 7.

[343] Charles S. Singleton, *Dante Studies 2: Journey to Beatrice* (Cambridge: Harvard University Press, 1958), 8.

in the eternal present, a state of higher consciousness: "The presentation of the eye signifies the achievement of full consciousness but at a different level from what had existed before...," says R. T. Rundle Clark.[344] In fact, the verb "to do," "to make," is written in hieroglyphs with an eye, so to see on a higher level is to "create" a new reality. To approach the symbolism of the eye would then be to approach what is the most essential in the Egyptian spiritual tradition. 2) In reading translations of ancient Egyptian religious writings such as the Old Kingdom *Pyramid Texts* inscribed in hieroglyphs on the walls of certain pyramids of the pharaohs of the 5th and 6th dynasties, the Middle Kingdom *Coffin Texts* painted on and in coffins of the ancient Egyptian nobility, and the New Kingdom *Book of the Dead* written on papyrus scrolls and placed with mummies in their tombs, we find the eye, by far, as the most prevalent of all symbols, and which must have thus been of utmost importance to the ancient Egyptian priests. Here are some examples from the ancient *Pyramid Texts*:

> O King, I also have come to you, I fill you with the ointment which went forth from the Eye of Horus, I fill you with it. It will raise up your bones, it will reassemble your members for you, it will gather together your flesh for you; it will let your bad sweat drop to the ground.
>
> *Pyramid Texts, Utterance 637*[345]

> O Osiris the King, stand up! Horus comes and claims you from the gods, for Horus has loved you, he has provided you with his Eye, Horus has attached his Eye to you; Horus has split open your eye for you that you may see with it.
>
> *Pyramid Texts, Utterance 364*

---

[344] Clark, *Myth and Symbol*, 179.

[345] All quotes from the *Pyramid Texts* are taken from R. O. Faulkner, *The Ancient Egyptian Pyramid Texts* (Warminster, UK: Aris & Phillips, 1969).

Atum summons me to the sky, and I take the Eye of
Horus to him. I am the son of Khnum, and there is no evil
which I have done. Long may this word be in your sight,
O Re; hear it, O Bull of the Ennead! Open up my road,
make my seat spacious at the head of the gods, that I may
take the Eye of Horus to him and that I may cause to be
reknit for him that which went forth from his head. I will
cause him to see with both his intact eyes, by means of
which he will make his foes pass away.

Pyramid Texts, Utterance 524

The Eye in Egyptian Mythology

In many prehistoric traditions, we find that the eye is directly
connected with the primordial Mother Goddess. Now all the
high Egyptian goddesses are representations of the original
Mother Goddess, assimilated to the eye, which is why Hathor,
Isis, and Nut can be interchangeable and not mutually exclusive.
There have been found—in Britain, the Near East, and
elsewhere—ancient figurines of the Mother Goddess having an
eye in the place of the vulva or the navel, and even the whole
body covered with eyes. Now the Mother Goddess, as one might
expect, represents in many mythologies the matrix from which
creation is formed, the primordial soup from which evolved the
universe. It can also represent the stars of the night sky, the eyes
of the Supreme Being, which observes from above. Taken in the
context of man, these eyes see from a higher plane and thus
represent the higher consciousness of which man is capable.

In Egypt, however, we find that the primordial chaos, the
undifferentiated waters, is represented by the *neter* Nun, which
is male. Why this difference? It is our contention that the role of
the eye in the Egyptian myth of creation and in its prolongation
in the struggles of Horus and Seth, when understood, can shed
much light on this question, and on the importance of the eye as
an Egyptian symbol in general.

In studying these symbols and myths we must keep in mind that they are not linear explanations of how things happened, and were not created, in our view, to satisfy the desire to know the beginnings of things, but are rather a means to understand the functioning and maintenance of the present world at every level and especially that of man. A myth is a teaching, a teaching that can enable man to rise out of his chaotic condition of sleep and reach a higher level of consciousness, but evidently for that one must be prepared. This *Pyramid Text* shows the "dead" king being restored by Horus:

> Horus has given you his Eye that you may see with it. Horus has set for you your foe under you that he may lift you up; do not let go of him. You shall come to your (former) conditions, for the gods have knit together your face for you. Horus has split open your eye for you that you may see with it in its name of 'Opener of Roads'...

> *Pyramid Texts, Utterance 369*

The eye arises in various contexts in Egyptian mythology. The most ancient perhaps is that of the right and left eyes of the ancient falcon sky *neter* Horus who protected the earth with his wings. In this myth, his eyes represented the sun and moon, respectively. This may represent man's two natures: the sun as the all-enduring spiritual essence of man whose eye is "all-seeing," and the moon as the sun's reflection, whose eye is based on man's physical nature, his knowledge arising only from his sense impressions.

The Christian symbol of the cross also provides us with man's two natures: natural man is symbolized by the horizontal beam and transcendent man by the vertical.[346] When we are in a state of nature we are at the end of the horizontal beam, asleep to our higher possibilities. It is only when we realize our predicament and are instilled with a desire to find a "Way" to our spiritual

---

[346]See René Guénon, *The Symbolism of the Cross, passim.*

selves through a purification of our state, that we start moving along the beam to the center of the cross (also to where the transept and nave meet in the cathedral). It is here at the center where man becomes what his birthright calls for, that is a "True Man": Jesus Christ, Mohammad, Atman, Buddha—and, for our purposes, the pharaoh, a man on earth but now open to spiritual energies coming from on high and transforming his being, allowing him to be detached from his thoughts, emotions, and tensions, allowing him to "see" and to "be" in truth.

In Dante's *The Divine Comedy* we find the same two natures:

> So when the soul by the ear or the eye receives
> What grapples it and strongly cling it round,
> Time goes, and naught of it the man perceives.
> For 'tis one power that listens to the sound
> And another that which keeps the soul entire;
> This one is still at large, and that one bound.[347]

The two natures of man are in other Egyptian symbols and myths: the natures of Horus and of Seth; but also pharaoh's white and red crowns of Upper and Lower Egypt; also the Two Ladies or *Nebty* name, a titular name of pharaoh, comprising Nekhbet, the vulture *neter* of Upper Egypt and Wadjet, the cobra *neter* of Lower Egypt; and the *sema tawy*, having a vertical axis of lungs and trachea bound by the papyrus plant of the North and the lotus plant of the South. It is often carved on the base of pharaoh's throne, symbolizing him as uniting the terrestrial and the divine. As the eternal Horus, pharaoh affirms man's function in the cosmos by the action of his breathing, uniting in himself spirit and body through the heart, seat of intuitive knowledge and feeling.[348] See Figure 40.

---

[347] Dante Alighieri, *The Portable Dante*, "The Divine Comedy" (New York: Penguin Books), 204.

[348] R.A. Schwaller de Lubicz, *Le roi de la théocratie pharaonique*, 198.

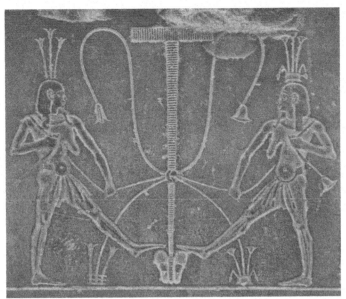

Figure 40 The sema tawy *or principle of union of two elements*

Later we find certain goddesses, such as Tefnut, Hathor, and Isis, each called the "Eye of Re," Re being the high sun *neter*, the spiritual metaphysical principle, the demiurge, the creative Word, by which the world is created, and the "Eye of Re" being its manifestation on earth as the sun. The above-mentioned goddesses thus represent, as the Eye of Re, the power of Re's spiritual forces embodied in the sun, sometimes terrible, sometimes healing.

Here, for purposes of economy, we will deal with the eye symbolism in two central myths: the myth of creation and that of Horus and Seth.

The Eye in the Myth of Creation

Different creation myths were present in different places and at different times in Egyptian history, and the one that was prevalent no doubt depended on the theology of the reigning Temple of the time, and even the same myth has different versions depending on the text we use as a reference. In whatever manner the different myths explained the creation of the world, they were in fact saying the same thing in different ways.[349] Nevertheless, there was one creation myth where the Eye was essential, that arising from the Temple at Heliopolis in the Old Kingdom.

This myth begins with the assertion that in the beginning there was only *Nun*, the primordial waters, the nonmanifest, an abyss without form, space, or light. From this abyss arose the male *neter* Atum, "the Complete One," sometimes assimilated to the primeval mound in the midst of the waters from which all things arose. Now Atum arose from the abyss on his own, that is, he is *self-created*, just as man can only become enlightened through his own inner efforts. Atum then created Shu and Tefnut, male and female, by masturbating or spitting (depending on the reference). They stayed with Atum as part of himself in the abyss, three as one, the high Trinity. Shu is the active male principle: light and air, vital breath, luminous radiation, the principle of life. Tefnut, as his consort, is the female principle: humidity, virtual energy, world order (assimilated to the goddess Maat). After a time, Shu and Tefnut become separated from Atum and become lost in the vastness of the abyss, what we might call the "fall" on the macrocosmic level. To find them, Atum, sends out his one and only eye (the original Unity) to seek them in the chaos and bring them back. To bring back Shu and Tefnut is to give them real existence by their being reattached to their creator and not lost in the primeval chaos. This also brings back *order* to the universe, and it is only the eye, the unifying eye, that can do this. On the microcosmic level of man, in the same way, it is this inner 'eye,' an active attention, that can bring order within by being detached from the chaos of one's thoughts and emotions.

When the Eye returns with Shu and Tefnut, that is, the universal order necessary for creation, Atum cries tears of joy which become mankind (which is a play on words between "tears" and

---

[349] Clark, *Myth and Symbol*, 75.

"mankind"), thus showing the relation between the cosmic macrocosm and man the microcosm. The eye, however, upon its return sees that it was replaced by another and brighter eye. The original eye becomes enraged at this, and to pacify it, Atum places it on its brow as protectress, the all-seeing cobra or Uraeus, the Eye of Re that is placed on the brow of pharaoh, symbol of his power to "see" and to act. Pharaoh, then, is man and *neter* in one being.

Now we can perhaps say that the original female principle was represented in the Egyptian cosmogony not by the female goddess Tefnut, as is so often suggested, but by the eye of Atum, which, in Egyptian hieroglyphics, is female. The eye, of course, represents "seeing"—not seeing as we know it as sense impressions—but seeing arising from spirit assimilated in the body, rather a *detachment* from the senses, a higher state of consciousness. Atum, we remember, is the "Complete One," undivided, having existence without differentiation between spirit and matter, matter infused with spirit. If Atum (male) is spiritualized essence, then his eye (female) is the consciousness realized by his total being.

Now, when Atum created the *neters* Shu and Tefnut, and thus the Trinity before manifestation took place, the organization of the cosmos began—which is reflected at every level of creation, including that of man. "As above, so below," so that man too can be ordered within. The myth, in fact, is a teaching to this end:

> I am the soul of Shu the self-created god, I have come into being from the flesh of the self-created god. I am the soul of Shu, the god invisible of shape, I have come into being from the flesh of the self-created god, I am merged in the god, I have become he. I am he who calmed the sky for himself, I am he who reduced the Two Lands to order for himself.
>
> *Coffin Texts, Spell 751*

Man has lost this perception that perhaps he had eons ago. The Shu and Tefnut within him are mingled in the chaos of his being. There is no space of Shu, no detachment. There are no fine energies of Tefnut, no higher consciousness. All is wasted through the search after pleasure, useless suffering, and lack of wisdom. In the myth, we note, it is the eye that brings Shu and Tefnut back to Atum. This eye is not passive; for it actively searches out Shu and Tefnut. This eye is "active attention," for some a seeming contradiction in terms. This spell from the Book of the Dead might give us a clue as to its meaning:

> I am he in whom is the Sacred Eye, and nothing shall come into being against me, no evil cutting off and no uproar, and there shall be no danger to me....
>
> I am he who fashioned with his Eye, and I will not die again. My striking power is in your bellies...

Book of the Dead, Spell 42

Mankind is created from Atum's tears of joy upon the bringing back of Shu and Tefnut by the Eye, of that which has been lost. This is not mankind as we know it, but man as he could be: whole, united, in harmony with the cosmos through his attachment to the Source, able to create the detachment of Shu and the energies of Tefnut through an attentive eye:

> Thus said Atum: Tefenet is my living daughter, and she shall be with her brother Shu; 'Living One' is his name, 'Righteousness' is her name. I live with my two children, I live with my two fledglings, for I am in the midst of them, both of them follow after my body, and I lie down and live with my daughter Maat; one within me and one behind me, I stand up because of them both, their arms being about me. It is my son who will live, whom I begot in my name. He knows how to nourish him who is in the egg in the womb for me, namely the human beings who came forth from my eye which I sent out while I was alone with Nu[n] in lassitude.

Coffin Texts, Spell 80

Now the eye upon its return becomes enraged that another eye, even brighter, has taken its place. In one interpretation, this brighter eye is assimilated to the sun, while in a later version of the myth it is the *akh* or spiritual being of light in man. Can it be that the act of searching itself, the original eye, was the creator of the new eye unbeknownst to itself? By searching out and bringing back Shu and Tefnut and making Atum whole, a new eye, a new perception, a new spiritual state was being created. Just as old stones from ruined temples are used in the creating of new spiritual edifices, so the old eye, now surpassed, still has its place as the foundation on which a new spiritual state can be built. As the Uraeus placed on the forehead of Atum, it protects his being from undesirable intrusions that could upset the new equilibrium, the new higher state of consciousness:

> Take the Eye of Horus and be pleased with it, put the Eye of Horus on your brow. 0 Horus who is N, take the Eye of Horus, for it belongs to you, it belongs to your body, put it on yourself, provide yourself with it, for it will provide you as a god; lift up what is on you, which is on the brow of Horus.

Coffin Texts, Spell 845

The Eye in the Myth of Horus and Seth

Here again the "one myth" is retold on a different level. As with the Myth of Creation, what was once whole has been broken, scattered, gone far away. A search is necessary to find the pieces and make whole again that which has been ripped apart.

This continuation of the basic Egyptian myth has various versions, but the general outlines are as follows: Shu and Tefnut engender the couple Nut and Geb. Nut is female and represents the sky. Geb is male and represents the Earth. Nut and Geb in their turn generate the gods Osiris and Seth and the goddesses Isis and Nephthys. Isis is the sister/wife of Osiris and Nephthys the sister/wife of Seth. This completes what is known as the Heliopolitan Ennead, or nine *neters*.

Eventually Osiris, as first born, became the ruler of Egypt keeping the chaotic waters of *Nun* at bay and providing the country with all that was necessary for civilization to flourish: writing, agriculture, animal husbandry, music, and more—in essence order and plenty. But Seth, representing disorder and chaos, jealous of Osiris, attacks and kills him by cutting him up and scattering his parts throughout Egypt. Seth then rules over Egypt with his consort and sister Nephthys. Another version of the myth has Seth trapping Osiris in a coffin and throwing it into the Nile which then ends up in Byblos on the Levantine coast where a tree grows around it. We can see here the symbolism of the soul trapped in a material body.[350] Now the killing of Osiris by Seth is symbolically necessary: life cannot be resuscitated if it first does not die. In esoteric terms, the "old man" must die for the "new man" to be born.

Just as Atum's eye searched after Shu and Tefnut, so Isis, not content to mourn, searches, with the help of Nephthys, for the parts of Osiris, finds them all and restores Osiris—except for his organ of regeneration which they could not find as it was eaten by a fish. One version says there were 14 parts, perhaps equivalent to the number of days of the waning and waxing of the moon.[351] Another version has it as 42 parts, the number of nomes (districts) in Egypt, thus equating Osiris and kingship with the whole of Egypt. Nevertheless, through her magical powers, Isis makes Osiris whole again and arouses him enough to impregnate her. This results in the birth of Horus, whom Isis raises secretly in the marshes for fear of Seth.

When Horus grows old enough, he attacks Seth to avenge his father, Osiris, who now lives helpless and weak in the netherworld. During one of their battles, Seth tears out the left

---

[350] S. Mayassis, *Mystères et Initiation de l'Égypte ancienne: Compléments à la religion égyptienne* (Milano: Archè, 1988), 36.

[351] S. H. Hooke, *Middle Eastern Mythology*, (Harmondsworth, England: Penguin Books, 1963), 69.

eye of Horus and flings it away into the abyss, while Horus rips out the testicles of Seth, thus alluding to the adversarial connection between the higher creation of the Eye, of man's quest for illumination, and the lower generation of sexual reproduction, cause of turbulence and violence.

The search and mending leitmotif of the myth continues as Thoth (or sometimes Shu or Onuris, "he who brought back the distant one"), *neter* of wisdom as well as messenger of the *neters*, goes after the eye, which was lying in bits in the darkness of the primeval waters (or other sources say in Nubia), and brings it back restored. Horus then offers the eye (that is, wholeness) to Osiris in the netherworld, reviving him. After these battles lasting many years, Horus was eventually established on the throne by the high *neters* as the rightful king of Egypt and the precursor of the pharaohs to come. Nevertheless, Seth, still necessary for creation as the negative principle in opposition to the positive principle Osiris, was given power over the desert lands. From that time on, every pharaoh is known as the *neter* Horus. Other versions in Egyptian and Greek sources can be found for various episodes of the myth.[352]

The respective roles of Horus and Seth in the myth are essential to our understanding of the meaning of the eye. What does each of them represent? If we follow the thesis that this myth is a continuation of the creation myth, then we should be able to assimilate Horus to what is transcendent in man, that is, what makes man complete, whole, spiritualized and utterly conscious—that is, arising from Atum who created himself *by himself*, who *possesses the eye*. Seth, associated with the desert

---

[352]For various versions of the myth see the following sources:

- R.T. Rundle Clark, *Myth and Symbol in Ancient Egypt*.
- E.A. Wallis Budge, *The Egyptian Book of the Dead* (The Papyrus of Ani).
- Plutarch (Trans. F.C. Babbitt) in Loeb Classical Library, Vol. V, *Plutarch Moralia*.

and wild animals, then represents what is "natural" in man, he who deprived Horus of his "sight," that is, non-transcendent man—perhaps great on the level of the earth and even necessary, but without measure to man who has become "whole" and who can "see." Many comparisons can be made of these two representations of man's possibilities: Enkidu and Gilgamesh in ancient Mesopotamia, Cain and Abel in the Old Testament, John the Baptist and Christ in the New.

The major act in the mythological struggle between Horus and Seth is Seth gouging out the Eye of Horus while Horus tears out the testicles of Seth. Now, the Eye of Horus or *Wadjet* was used in ancient Egypt as the hieroglyph used to represent the *hekat,* a unit of volume for measuring grain, the different parts of the Eye being made up of the signs for various fractions (1/2, 1/4, 1/8, 1/I6, 1/32, 1/64). See Figure 41.

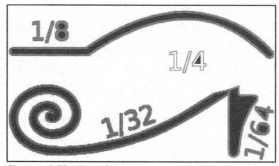

Figure 41 The Eye of Horus

These fractions, when added up, however, equal only 63/64.

The relationship between the testicles of Seth and the Eye of Horus is perhaps restated here as the lost sexual member of Osiris and the missing part of the Eye. Just as our lower nature can prevent us from "seeing," so our higher nature can be realized by the transformation of lower energies to spiritualize our being:

> Horus fell because of his Eye, Seth suffered because of
> his testicles.
>
> *Pyramid Texts, Utterance 386*

The curing of the Eye, making it "whole," "complete," or "intact" is accomplished by Thoth, who has various functions in

Egyptian mythology, sometimes represented as an ibis, sometimes as a baboon. On a cosmological level he represents the moon, with the myth referring to its waning and waxing through the number 14, half of the days of each month. Just as the moon reflects the light of the sun, so Thoth is the scribe of Re, putting in words the action of the sun *neter*. He is the messenger of the *neters* bringing their commands to man. He is the *neter* of wisdom, master of writing and time who inscribes the justice and order of the goddess Maat into the functioning cosmos. Furthermore, it is he who notes the results of the weighing of men's hearts before Osiris upon entering the netherworld after death. There is perhaps one word here to which all these functions can be assimilated, a quality that can cure the damaged Eye, bring back the lioness Sekhmet from her destructive rage against mankind in Nubia "far away," and even find Shu and Tefnut in the vastness of the abyss. This word is *discrimination*. Thoth is that wisdom which knows how to "render ... unto Caesar the things which are Caesar's; and unto God the things that are God's." To cure the Eye is, in sum, to use the wisdom of Thoth to bring the energy of Tefnut to man through the detachment of Shu, thus actualizing the perception of the eye as higher consciousness:

> The phoenix of Re was that whereby Atum came into being in chaos, in the Abyss, in the darkness and in gloom. I am Shu, father of the gods, and Atum once sent his sole eye seeking me and my sister Tefenet. I made light of the darkness for it, and it found me as an immortal. It was I who again begot the Chaos-gods in chaos, in the Abyss, in darkness and in gloom. I indeed am Shu who begot the gods

Coffin Texts, Spell 76

The final step in the drama is Horus offering the Eye to Osiris, the torpid one, in deep distress in the netherworld. Osiris is at once the king of the dead in the netherworld, in the *Dwat*, where the dead can be purified and made whole through the Eye of

Horus. All the "dead" in ancient Egypt, it should be noted, are assimilated to Osiris, waiting to be resurrected through the power of the restored Eye:

> Your son Horus has smitten him, he has wrested his Eye from him and has given it to you; you have a soul by means of it, you have power by means of it at the head of the spirits. Horus has caused you lay hold of your foes, and there is none of them who shall escape from you.
>
> *Pyramid Texts, Utterance 356*

We see that in these ancient sacred texts the offerings to the *neters* of food, drink, oil, and other items for the deceased are often assimilated to the Eye of Horus. For example:

> O Osiris the King, I bring to you the Eye of Horus, which he has taken to your brow: first quality Libyan oil.
>
> *Pyramid Texts, Utterance 78*

> O Osiris the King, take the Eye of Horus whereof I make offering to you: 2 bowls of figs.
>
> *Pyramid Texts, Utterance 193*

An offering is, of course, a type of sacrifice, and to assimilate bread, beer, oil, cloth and other offerings to the Eye of Horus is, on one level, to sacrifice their worldly value in order to make the deceased whole again in the afterlife, to make him 'complete.' What is actually sacrificed, however, is the attachment to, and desire for, these worldly goods in favor of the spiritual energies represented by the Eye of Horus, the giving of *oneself* in exchange for the vivifying effect of the offering. These energies, in consequence of this sacrifice, can come to the fore and spread their "perfume" or "ointment," *the flux of the Eye of Horus,* over the "deceased":

> O King, I have come and I bring to you the Eye of Horus. May you provide your face with it, that it may cleanse you, its perfume being on you. The perfume of the Eye of Horus is on this King, it removes your efflux and protects you from the sweat of the band of Seth. O Osiris

the King, may the intact Eye of Horus belong to you, the Eye of Horus being intact, intact.

Pyramid Texts, Utterance 29

In the words of R. T. Rundle Clark:

> The presentation of the Eye signifies the achievement of full consciousness but at a different level from what had existed before—Osiris is not revived in his original form as an earthly king. The triumph…enables the god to send out his soul; that is, to assume another and higher form of life and to escape from the trammels of material things as well as to be associated with the power which sets them moving. He is the prototype of the liberation of the human soul from the helplessness of death as well as the symbol for the liberation of the soul from its psychic hindrances in this life. On some of the tombs which contain funerary texts we are told: 'This will be useful for a man here on earth as well as when he has died.'[353]

Figure 42 Pharaoh with crook, flail, and was scepter

In this way, Osiris, through the attentive Eye of Horus, becomes reborn, which in a symbolic way shows man how he too can be reborn through a new capacity of attention, of seeing, thus establishing order in the chaos of his being—to be restored in

---

[353] Clark, *Myth and Symbol*, 179-80.

fact to wholeness. It could also be said that by offering the Eye of Horus the disruption of order caused by the death of Osiris, and by extension all the deceased, is avoided through the offerings made at the mortuary ritual that allow order to be restored in the cosmos.[354]

It is said that the "the eye is the symbol of Egypt par excellence" And this is so because the priests of ancient Egypt understood that higher vision is creation, that higher vision destroys the illusions of man, his belief in his own power of action, a belief stemming from his capacity to think, to feel strong emotions, which only blind him to higher powers arising not within him but emanating from universal energies. It is only when these illusions have been seen for what they are, and so lose their mastery, that man can be open to these higher energies and allow them to enter and transform him. So it has been said that the three scepters of pharaoh represented this higher mastery: the flail or whip, mastery over the body; the shepherd's crook, mastery over the emotions; and the *was* scepter, mastery over thought.[355] See Figure 42.

The Eye of Horus was torn out by Seth, the fall of man, but was made whole by Thoth, man's resurrection. In the same way, the body of Osiris was made whole by the gathering together of his body parts by Isis. She then resuscitated Osiris who impregnated her to create a new life in her son Horus. The Eye of Re created the universe in purity and order; the Eye of Horus brings beings and things back from chaos to this original creation of the First Time. This is the one message of ancient Egypt transmitted by its symbols and myths, and, in sum, it is the message of every true 'religion.'

---

[354] Hornung, *L'esprit du temps*, 142.

[355] Julien Behaeghel, *Osiris: le dieu ressuscité* (Paris: Berg International, 1995), 158.

[355] Paul Brunton, *A Search in Secret Egypt* (York Beach, Maine: Samuel Weiser, 1984), 163.

Chapter 9 The Nature of Man

It would be difficult to even begin to discuss ancient Egyptian symbolism without understanding the underlying *raison d'être* of the civilization, which, as we see it, was to provide the context, the environment, and the means to achieve the creation of a "new man," a man of higher consciousness, that is to say a person infused with cosmic forces in all his being. While there are no ancient extant texts that absolutely confirm this proposition, by reading between the lines of the elements of the civilization that have come down to us, it seems to us to be the only possible conclusion. Most Egyptologists claim that all the rites, rituals, monuments, and so on, were established to provide this possibility only after death, in the afterlife. But we would say that this is the exoteric meaning, while the esoteric meaning has to do with transformation in this present life for those who are able to read the symbols that have been provided throughout the civilization.

The ancient Egyptians left many texts concerning the makeup of man, not only his physical makeup, but his immaterial self as well. These different elements are usually passed over in Egyptological texts with cursory definitions, such as the *ka* equals "vital force" or the *ba* equals "soul," usually without any explanation how these entities fit into the whole of man's being and their relation to the cosmos. There is no reason that we cannot try to understand more deeply these different aspects of man as the Egyptians saw them, without assuming we have found any ultimate answer to the question. A man of ancient Egypt and a man of today may live in completely different societies, view the world subjectively in a totally different way, and have different psychologies, but nevertheless their objective organic makeup is very much the same. For this reason, we can try to deepen our understanding based on our own knowledge and experience and see how it fits in with the nomenclature of Egyptian symbolism.

It is by no means easy to pin down what the Egyptians meant by certain terms as it was not their want to explain or define anything. In one context, a term may mean one thing; in another, maybe related context, it may mean something else. It is in fact impossible to isolate the different elements of man, as no element was looked at on its own, but each had meaning only in relation to the others and to larger wholes: True Man, myth, and the cosmos. It is only in trying to understand in this way that we can begin to see how the Egyptian terms for the different elements of man's nature can be associated with our modern-day conceptions. When one reads the different texts of Egyptologists concerning the makeup of man, there is a bewildering mishmash of different definitions and conceptions that gives us hints at meaning but no clear formulations. Some use five elements to define the Egyptian conception of man's makeup, others use six, and still others seven, eight, nine, or more.

The elements that we have found dealing with man's makeup are in the list below (the terms in italics are the transliterations of the hieroglyphs, followed by an English rendering of them in parentheses). After each Egyptian word, we give a concise explanation, which are by no means a definition but rather an introduction to what we will try to explain in more detail in the following text:

- *Ha.w* (*hau*) Members of the body altogether, body
- *X.t* (*khet*) Chest or belly of a person
- *jb* (*ab*) Heart as seat of thought and emotions
- *HA.ty* (*hati*) Heart as physical organ
- *c.t* (*at*) Any part of the body
- *jwf* (*iuf*) Flesh
- *qs.w* (*qesu*) Bones
- *rDw* (*redju*) Fluids, humors

- *m.wt* (*metu*) Vessels, ducts
- *XA.t* (*khat*) Corpse
- *bA* (*ba*) Individual psyche or personality
- *Sw.yt* (*shut*) Shadow
- *rn* (*ren*) Name
- *kA* (*ka*) Vital force or energy
- *D.t* (*djet*) Divine body
- *saH* (*sah*) State of a glorified dead person
- *Ax* (*akh*) Transfigured spirit, radiant being, body of light
- *sxm* (*sekhem*) Power
- *xpr* (*kheper*) To come to be, to be transformed

Since all these elements are related, to take them separately would be to falsify our comprehension, so we will discuss them in a way that hopefully provides a means of understanding the essential nature of the ancient Egyptian conception of man. In our discussion, we will use the English rendering of the names.

We will center on the notions of 'states of being' and 'transformation' of one state to another, which we feel are the main preoccupations of the ancient Egyptian priesthood. The basic division that the ancient Egyptians made was between man as he was born and man who is transformed into a divine being. Now whether this could only happen after death of the body or through initiation rituals in this life is a matter that Egyptologists do not agree on. We would say that the Egyptian temple rituals were not simply analogical but were anagogical, that they had a transformative power to change man's state of being, and that the Mortuary ritual was a symbol of man's transformation into an *akh*, a radiant being possible to attain in this life:

> The physical body of such a man has been 'doubled' before his death by the formation of a glorious body, so that death becomes liberation rather than annihilation.[356]

---

[356]Isha Schwaller de Lubicz, *Her-Bak, Egyptian Initiate*, 384.

As our discussion develops, these two possibilities of transformation, in life or after death, should be kept in mind.[357]

Man, as he was born, was constituted in a body *hau* which is the plural form of *Ha*, a member or part of the body, thus denoting, as a collective noun, a gathering together of members, of flesh and bone elements, that is, a living body as opposed to the corruptible corpse *khat*, the incorruptible mummified body *sah*, and the radiant or divine body *djet*.[358] We see here, then, that the Egyptians, through their different conceptions of "body," meant them to be symbols for different states of being of an individual.

It is thus the *hau* body that is to be embalmed into a *khat* body and deposited in the tomb while, at the same time, the mortuary rituals create the divine *djet* body which rises to the sky to be with Re or with the *neters* that make up the immortal circumpolar stars. Now the religious texts say that this is to be accomplished on the embalming table by combining, assembling, tying together, and firming up the elements of the *hau* body, that is, the *iuf* and *qesu*, the "flesh and bones," and the *metu*, vessels and ducts.[359] It is through the *redju* that is, the divine fluids or humors circulating throughout the body that this is to be accomplished. The symbolism, referring to myth, is clear: the inundation of the Nile was considered to be the humors of Osiris, that is, the source of life, and it is these humors that must impregnate the *hau* body in order to bring together all the disparate parts into a unity in order that the body may live again. In this way, all the internal organs, known collectively as *ab*,

---

[357] This discussion was greatly influenced by a doctoral thesis written for the University of Montpellier, France by Anaïs Martin in 2013: *Le Corps en Égypte ancienne: Enquête lexicale et anthropologique*. This thesis was based on the Pyramid and Coffin Texts, the most authoritative religious texts of ancient Egypt dating from the Old and Middle Kingdoms, respectively.

[358] Ibid., 62.

[359] Ibid., 66.

'heart,' are nourished and allowed to be reconnected so that movement of the body can again take place.[360]

For the Egyptians, *ab*, or 'heart,' is not the physical organ, which is *hati*, but the seat of thought and emotions, memory and will, consciousness and desire, the immaterial center of one's being[361]—as we would say: "She has heart." or "His heart is in the right place." And it was said in Egypt "It is the tongue that repeats what the heart has thought.":

> Transcription by thought, of knowledge gained by the heart, is another thing. Consciousness of this order is putting of something perceived in relation with what corresponds with it in ourselves. In contrast with such reality thoughts that derive from an association of ideas external to your true being are excrement...Thought should translate what consciousness has written in your whole body.[362]

The *neter* signifying knowledge is Sia, whose domain is in the heart *ab* thus justifying the phrase "the intelligence of the heart" as opposed to mere mental knowledge. In fact, the physical heart was the only organ that was left in the body during embalmment and so remained available to the deceased.[363] As the directing force of one's actions, it is the *ab* that is placed on the balance in opposition to the ostrich feather symbolizing *maat*, the just order, during the judgment after death. *Ab* seems to be a more abstract notion than the term *khet*, which generally refers to the chest or belly and the emotional states that can be felt there. Another concept is *at*, a generic term meaning any part of the body,[364] and thus all the *ats* together comprise the *hau*. The *khet* and *at* are sometimes also translated as "body," though care

---

[360] Ibid.

[361] Jacq, *Le monde magique*, 15.

[362] Isha Schwaller de Lubicz, *Her-Bak, Egyptian Initiate*, 102-03.

[363] Hornung, *L'esprit du temps*, 191.

[364] Martin, *Corps*, 24.

should be taken in these cases as to their meaning in the context in which they are used.

Here we might pause and think how this symbolism of the *redju*, or the flowing of a current in the body might, in fact, refer not only to the Mortuary ritual but to the transformation of a living person imbued with a cosmic force or energy throughout the body during an Initiation ritual. The ancient Egyptians were never clear on this point, but that does not prevent us from posing the question.

The *khat* body is the body that has been embalmed, has gone through the Mortuary ritual, and been laid to rest in its tomb. Due to the rituals, the body is imperishable, will never decay, and so belongs to the divine domain. Since the deceased has been judged innocent before Osiris during the burial rites, he has the right to not only be interred and returned to a state of well-being and effectiveness in the afterlife, but also to attain a new body, *djet* (see below), one who has the state of an *akh*, a radiant being, one of the blessed dead. The heart, being the only organ that is left in the mummy, is necessary for the *khat* body to be truly effective.

It seems that there is a strict relationship among the *khat* body, the *ab* heart, and the *ba*.[365] Now the *ba* has been given numerous definitions and meanings in the Egyptological literature, and there does not seem to be any consensus as to what it is. We can say, however, that the *ba* is the whole person, but non-physical, that is liberated upon death and is necessary, along with the *khat* and the *ab*, for the deceased to become an *akh*, a divine being:

> If I am an akh, if I have gathered myself together, then my *ba* is with me, my *jb* [*ab*] is in my chest, and my *khat* is in the earth.[366]

---

[365] Ibid., 85

[366] Ibid., 85 [Our translation of *Coffin Texts* IV, 57d-g from the French.]

To become an *akh*, a transfigured spirit, it is necessary, therefore, that the mummified body be in the tomb, the deceased having had all the necessary rites, thus allowing for the *ab* heart to be animated and the *ba* to be released. For this to take place, ritual texts or "formulas for transformation into light," *sakhu*, must be recited during the Mortuary ritual.[367] The process is also called *sakhu*, which in this context means "making one into an *akh*."

> The Akh is a kind of 'body of light' or higher power of being which manifests itself after the transformations following death, or after a high initiation as well, since certain persons are granted the title of *Akhu* or *Mahakeru* ('justified') while alive.[368]

Now the word *akh* is the root of the word for "horizon," *Akhet*, where the brilliance of the sun comes forth every day in the East, signifying that creation continues according to *neheh*, or eternity seen as eternal return or cyclical time. *Akh* is also the root of the word *Akhet*, the season of the flood, without which creation of the plant world could not take place each year. The hieroglyph for an *akh* is the crested ibis, the crest no doubt symbolizing radiance. Nevertheless, an *akh* is not depicted as such, being an immaterial, transfigured spirit. The word also means "effective" or "useful," which emphasizes the higher nature of an *akh* and its role in benefitting humanity. To become an *akh* implies that one is reborn and the *akh* is continuously reborn through self-regeneration in the same way that Atum created himself out of the chaotic *Nun* at the First Time. Everything, in fact, refers to that First Time of creation. The hieroglyphs for being born is transliterated as *ms*, with the first of two characters being three skins tied together. According to Christian Jacq, this refers to a...

---

[367] Christian Jacq, *La mystère des hiéroglyphes* (Lausanne: Éditions Favre, 2010), 85-6.

[368] Schwarz, *Égypte: Les mystères du sacré*, 162.

...triple release from three envelopes corresponding to the sky, the intermediate world and the earth. And the real birth is being conscious of these three worlds.[369]

To be conscious of a world means that one is no longer under its laws, that one has become free of them, that one experiences the world from a higher level of consciousness:

In terms of human consciousness, what has now been achieved is the radiance of spirit characteristic of the akh. The human being has become a shining one. The ba has been divinized through having been brought into union with the source of its existence—the self-creating, self-renewing spirit. The realm of Osiris has been effectively transcended, and now the primary experience is that of being merged with the cosmic light that emanates from Ra.[370]

At the same time as the deceased attains the state of *akh*, he acquires the divine body *djet*. This body is in a state of

Figure 43 The ba

continuous creation for it is not fortuitous that its homonym is also *djet*, another meaning of eternity, where beings and things take part in the universal nature of the cosmos arising from the original creation, which is present still, outside of time. To become an *akh*, an individual must pass a test by giving the secret names of the door he must pass through or the parts of a boat that he must take to cross over the Nile to the other side, symbols for the reconstitution of

---

[369] Ibid., 89.

[370] Naydler, *Temple of the Cosmos*, 280.

Osiris.[371] Whether these tests refer to the dead or to living initiates is never explained in the Egyptian texts.

The *ba* is represented by a bird with a man's head, thus implying its mobility. See Figure 43. It only arises after the death of the body and the conclusion of the Mortuary rituals. According to the texts, the *ba* can leave the deceased's body and flit about on earth or in the heavens but needs to come back to the body at night to generate the body and be regenerated itself. For this reason, the body must be embalmed so it will not decay, as the *ba* cannot be regenerated by a decaying body.[372] While the *ba* is immaterial, it is not a pure spirit like the *akh*; it depends on the mummified body, the *khat* for its existence and needs sustenance like the *ka* (see below). While the *ba* is immaterial, it is still personal to the deceased person, representing his psyche or personality. The *ba* was perhaps based on the dream state of an individual, who, while sleeping (a sort of 'death'), can dream of any sort of situation in any time and in any place. Flying, for example, is a common theme in dreams. A *ba* could also eat and drink, engage in sex, and assume any sort of form—all of which may take place in dreams. One observer had this to say about dreams:

> ...primitive peoples do not discriminate between dreams and reality. Dreams are real to them, and so if their dead appear to them in dreams, they believe them to be living still.... What to later generations changes to belief is to them knowledge.[373]

Also, in near-death experiences, it is not uncommon for the person to see himself from above, just as vignettes in ancient Egyptian texts often show the *ba* perched above the tomb on a

---

[371] Jacq, *La mystère des hiéroglyphes*, 85-6.

[372] Lehner, *The Complete Pyramids*, 23.

[373] Paul Carus, "The Conception of the Soul and the Belief in Resurrection among the Egyptians," *The Monist*, Vol. 15, No. 3, July 1905 (Oxford: Oxford University Press, 1905), 409-10.

tree. Perhaps man had greater possibilities of other states of being in ancient Egypt—other than those possible in the scientific, rationalist society of today.

Also, the *bas* of the *neters* were their manifestations in nature. A *ba* of Shu, the *neter* of air, is wind, for example.[374] The most telling symbolism on this score is that of Re whose *ba* is the sun disk that traverses the sky during the day and at night descends into the netherworld, the *Dwat*, and unites with Osiris, the ruler of the dead, each being regenerated by the other. The sun is then able to rise the next day at the horizon. In the same way, the *ba* of the deceased, his subtle body, having flitted about in the world during the day, comes back to the body at night to be regenerated. Also, a living person goes to bed at night to be regenerated and to dream. On the macrocosmic level, then, the *ba* lies between the *ka*, universal energy outside of time, and physical manifestation. It is the intermediary realm of Osiris, in limbo, where one dies to be reborn and is subject to cyclic time, *neheh*, symbolized by the ram with horizontal horns, that is, on the horizontal plane[375]:

> The state of consciousness referred to by the word ba arose as a concomitant of a different kind of experience of oneself—an experience involving separation from the body and normal sense-based awareness. The term ba denotes a mode of consciousness freed from physical constraints, but nevertheless bound up with psychic conditions, many of which might be derived from attachments to the physical world.[376]

Associated with the *ba* is the *shut*, meaning shadow, usually depicted as a small man colored all in black and whose hieroglyph is a fan-like object that intercepts light. Like the *ba*, it can move freely in the world and come back to the body in the

[374] Lehner, *The Complete Pyramids*, 23.
[375] Isha Schwaller de Lubicz, *Her-Bak, Egyptian Initiate*, 178.
[376] Naydler, *Temple of the Cosmos*, 214.

tomb at night providing it with new vital energy. Unlike the *ba*, however, it does not rise to the heavens, but stays attached to the earth and the corporeal body.[377] Since the shadow never leaves the body when in the world, it could be conceived as a doppelganger of the human being, an inner nature of lower instinctive and emotional appetites that one cannot usually escape. When a man dies and has not made a connection with his *ka* in life, rather than becoming an *akh*, a transfigured being, he becomes merely a *shut*, a 'shadow' of what he could have become. Thus, a person can only separate from his shadow when he comes fully into the light as an *akh*. We can make an association of the shadow with the allegory of the shadows in the cave as recounted in Plato's *Republic*. Here, a group of people have been chained to a wall their whole life and only see the shadows of people and things that come in front of a fire behind them. For them, reality *is* the shadows, for they have no inkling of the fire behind them causing the shadows to appear. It is only when they break their chains and see the sun, which corresponds to the fire, that they can see reality. For the Egyptians, then, the shadow might stand for that nature of man that lives only by the senses and not by the real nature of the world based on the sun's immaterial power of which he has no inkling.

Another aspect of the individual is *ren*, name. A person's name, given at birth, was considered to be essential for existence. The *ren* gave a person his identity and so represented the whole person along with the body and the shadow on the physical plane.[378] By the simple act of writing a name on a statue, it identified the statue with the person it represented in such a way that the statue could be considered as the person himself. When a deceased person came out of favor with the court or the priests,

---

[377] Hornung, *L'esprit du temps*, 193.

[378] Ibid., 191, 193.

his name was often hacked off the walls of monuments, which assured his "second death."

As mentioned above, another Egyptian word for body is *djet*, the divine body, which is the last in a sequence of transformations of the body. From the physical body in life, the *hau*, to the embalmed body in the tomb, the *khat*, then comes the divine body *djet* which only exists in the divine sphere of cosmic functions *Neter-Neteru* and not in that of the earth. It is no doubt not fortuitous that a homonym of *djet*, the body, is *djet*, one of the words for eternity, the only difference in writing between the two *djets* is the addition of the determinative hieroglyph for land in the one for eternity—that is, while everything changes *on* the land, the land *in itself* remains as it is. As previously discussed, this term for eternity means that which is eternal outside of time and is complementary to the other term for eternity, *neheh*, which means eternal return or cyclical time. The divine body *djet* is thus not individual to the deceased but refers to the eternal body of Atum, the primordial *neter* that created himself out of the *Nun*, the original chaotic, watery abyss. In this way, every new *djet* body, which includes every deceased person who has become an *akh*, a radiant being, is a prolongation of the original creator and to which he is identical in nature.[379] The *Pyramid Texts* say:

> Re-Atum, your son comes to you. Unas comes to you. Raise him up to you! Enfold him in your embrace! He is the son of your divine body [*djet*] for eternity [*djet*].[380]

As the *djet* body is essentially an abstract or spiritual entity, it cannot be described physically. While the *ba* is also an abstract or spiritual entity and indescribable, it acts on the level of the

---

[379] Martin, *Corps*, 33.

[380] *Pyramid Texts*, No. 217, 160a-c [Our translation based on various English translations of the hieroglyphs]

earth and uses the spiritual power *heka*, while the *djet* acts on the level of the cosmos using the spiritual power *Akhu*.[381]

An individual is not born with a *djet* body but can only attain it when he becomes an *akh*.[382] Now all this seems to pertain to the afterlife after the mummification and the Mortuary ritual have taken place, but we propose that this attainment of a new body in the afterlife is actually a symbolic reference to man's capability, through spiritual practice, of achieving a new body in *this* life, that is, a subtle body composed of finer energies existing within his physical body. Various religions and spiritual masters have taught this notion, including Hinduism, Buddhism, Sufism, Kabbalah, Theosophism, and Gurdjieff. In them, the different bodies are associated with different levels of consciousness.

Another component of the *djet* body is the *ka*. We have here another Egyptian concept that has been the subject of various definitions and explanations. It has been established, nevertheless, that a person is born with a *ka*, which is often called a "double" of the individual. Its hieroglyph is two arms raised upwards as if to receive something from above, or as if projecting force upwards. While the *ba* is depicted as a bird with the head of a man, the *ka* is never depicted in such a way, since it is pure energy. The *ka* was formed when Atum, after emerging from the *Nun*, and standing on the primordial mound, imparted his energy to the first *neters* he created out of himself, Shu and Tefnut.[383] The *ba* is personal to an individual, while the *ka* is impersonal, a parcel of the universal energy within man, but also in everything else: plants, animals, water, and even in stones. The *ka* has nothing to do with the physical nature of man. When

---

[381] Martin, *Corps*, 36, 38.

[382] Ibid., 41.

[383] Henri Frankfort, *Kingship and the Gods: A Study of Ancient Near Eastern Religion as the Integration of Society and Nature* (Chicago: University of Chicago Press, 1978), 66.

man sees himself as the center of the world around which everything turns, a complete egotist, he is then totally unconscious of his belonging to higher realms in which *ka* reigns:

> This Me, that seems to be the true individual, is in fact nothing but a reflection of Ka and the individual's Kas. It is this that deludes a man as to the importance of his thoughts, which likewise are nothing but a play of ephemeral forces and relative values. Thought is 'the other' in relation to the intelligence of the heart...Every true value appertains to the Ka.[384]

As mentioned above, some Egyptologists see the two arms as being observed from above, symbolizing an embrace whereby the life force protects man's being or transmits it to another as well as animating it with its force.[385] In fact, most descriptions of the *ka* by Egyptologists describe it as a "vital" or "life force," that is, the energy of the cosmos that imbues everything with life, so that the *ka* of an individual is his particular allotment of universal energy that came to him through the *ka* of the pharaoh who has a special connection with the *neters*, the universal forces. The 'royal *ka*' of the pharaoh does not belong to him as an individual but belongs to the kingship and transfers from pharaoh to pharaoh over time and also refers back to Horus, the original ruler of Egypt. According to the Egyptologist Henri Frankfort:

> Re is the king's Ka...The god is the Ka of the king. But the subjects say: My Ka belongs to the king; my Ka derives from the king; the king makes my Ka; the king is my Ka.[386]

It was believed that the *ka* was nourished by the energy found in the food and drink that was provided to the deceased on the

---

[384] Isha Schwaller de Lubicz, *Her-Bak, Egyptian Initiate*, 192.

[385] Lehner, *The Complete Pyramids*, 23.

[386] Frankfort, *Kingship and the Gods*, 77-78.

offering table before the tomb. A homonym of *ka* means "bull," which, along with the two arms, is composed of the hieroglyphs for a phallus and a bull. The symbolism is clear: on the plane of the earth the bull is known for its strength and its procreative power, just as is the creative power of the *ka* on the macrocosmic level. The *ka* of an individual is received from his father and transferred in his turn to his children. It is, in this way, a social force allowing a man's energy to be transferred to a new generation on the one hand, and, on the other hand, it refers back to his ancestors from generation to generation to the original creation at the First Time. In this way, the *ka* is shown to have existed at the beginning of creation and will exist forever as universal energy:

> Ka then is the carrier of all powers of manifestation and activator of cosmic functions....the realizing principle of continuous creation....It is thanks to Ka that things are named....All aspects of Ka are found in man, but not all are in his control. The higher qualities of Ka, fed by the subtle fires of the marrow, are only incorporate in man when he has consciousness of them and mastery.[387]

A person dies when his *ka* leaves him, but a "new man" is born having a *djet* body when his *ba* has been released and rejoins the *ka*. In so doing the person becomes an *akh*, an immaterial radiant spirit. It was said that when a person dies "he goes to his *ka*," meaning that the individual's personal allotment of universal energy, his *ka*, leaves the body and reintegrates into the universal *ka* of the cosmos. We can extrapolate from this to say that to be an *akh* is to be united with the universal *ka*. An interesting passage in the *Pyramid Texts* referring to the *djet* body is this:

> He [the deceased] does not sleep at night and pass the day ignorant of his [*djet*] body during the two times of the scarab.[388]

---

[387] Isha Schwaller de Lubicz, *Her-Bak, Egyptian Initiate*, 177.

[388] Ibid., 56. [Our translation from the French. See also *Pyramid Texts*, 688 2083c]

"To not sleep at night" means not to be unconscious, and "the two times of the scarab" means night and day, which signifies that man must be attentive to his divine body at all times, otherwise he is essentially unconscious. This passage not only provides insight into the symbolic nature of ancient Egyptian texts but could reveal a notion of ancient Egyptian spiritual practice as well.

The transformation of man from the body in which he was born, the *hau* body, to the *khat* body mummified in the tomb, and the divine *djet* body in the heavens depends on the Mortuary ritual, which is based on the myth of Osiris. Just as Osiris was dismembered by his brother Seth, so death appears when the conduits *metu* (ducts and vessels) are ruptured, thus preventing the vital currents and fluids from accomplishing their task of uniting all the elements of the body.[389] Just as Osiris was dismembered into 14 parts, the number of days of the waning of the moon, so the Mortuary ritual was enacted to make the body whole again through mummification, just as the moon became full again in its waxing. By enveloping the deceased in bands of cloth made of linen, their vegetable origin provided the power of regeneration as all plant life depended on the yearly flood of the Nile, the humors of Osiris. Since life depends on the interaction of all the body's parts, when this is prevented death appears and the *ka* leaves the body. It is thus the goal of the Mortuary ritual to reunite in the afterlife all the parts of man that had been separated by death:

> The ba, the ka, the corpse, the heart, and the shadow, all separated by death, had now to be reunited.[390]

For the Egyptians, a ritual is not a commemoration of a person or an act but has effective power to enact transformation. We must remember that the ancient Egyptian mind did not demand

---

[389] Ibid., 109

[390] Assmann, *Death and Salvation*, 102.

scientific proof to enable something to be true. Science as we know it did not exist. There was no 'scientific method,' no 'trial and error'—and there was no hard line between speech and action. Ritual incantations were not recited to make people feel good, but to enable actual change to take place. An ancient Egyptian maxim states "a man lives when his name is pronounced."[391] Again, the change of states of the body may not refer solely to the afterlife, but also to the changes of state in a living man undergoing initiation rites in the temple. For this to take place, however, a man must have *sekhem*, power. We would interpret this as 'power of attention' or 'power of remaining still' so that he is not dispersed in mind, emotion, or body, but that all his parts are unified and balanced on this horizontal level:

> For man to take the path of evolution, his will must train
> the heart hati by the force sekhem and 'undo the knots'
> he has tied during his existence through the relations he
> has had with his fellow men.[392]

It is only then that he would be able to be unified on the vertical level as well, allowing the cosmic rays of Re to infuse his body with spiritual food, or, like the Nile, a spiritual flood, thus creating an *akh*, a spiritual being having a divine body, *djet*.

There is one word listed above that we have not yet mentioned: *kheper*, which has to do with 'transformation.' The hieroglyphs for *kheper* are a scarab beetle followed by a mouth. Its main meanings are to come into existence, to be born, to exist, to be, to be transformed. This word is a perfect example of how the ancient Egyptians used the natural world as symbols for abstract and metaphysical concepts. The scarab or dung beetle fashions animal dung into a ball and then pushes it, *using the sun as a guide*, to a hiding place where it is buried. Later, the female lays

---

[391] Ibid., 116.

[392] Enel (Michel Vladimirovitch Skariatine), *Les Origines de la Genèse et l'enseignement des temples de l'ancienne Égypte* (Cairo: Institut Français d'archéologie Orientale, 1935), 203.

her eggs in it so that when the larvae hatch, they have food to eat. After one month, the larva, having nourished itself on the dung ball, leaves its mummy-like cocoon to become a new scarab dung beetle. It seems to an observer, however, that the larvae come into existence *on their own* in spontaneous generation within the dung ball, just as Atum created himself from the chaotic *Nun* at the First Time. This process of generation is made into a cosmological concept whereby the sun *neter* Re is described as the *neter* Khepri when the sun rises at dawn, as the *neter* Re during its transit in the day boat across the sky during the day, and as the *neter* Atum when it goes below the western horizon at sunset to travel in the night boat through the netherworld or *Dwat*.

The *neter* Khepri is depicted as a man having a scarab beetle for a head, and represents that which comes to be, to be born, the *neter* of transformation.

As the sun descends below the horizon as Atum (or Re-Atum) into the netherworld, like the scarab hiding his ball in the earth, Khepri is regenerated the next morning in the East, just as the new scarab comes into existence from the dung ball. A common mortuary image in ancient Egypt is a scarab beetle pushing the sun, just as an actual scarab beetle pushes the dung ball in the direction of the sun, thus symbolizing the transformation of a terrestrial being into a being of light. Again, this can be taken as transformation after death or the result of rituals in life where one's state of being is transformed into higher consciousness.

Whatever the interpretation, the symbol of the scarab beetle combines the worlds of terrestrial nature, cosmic manifestation and myth into one inseparable intertwined symbol that when contemplated is received as a whole without the necessity of any rational explanation. See Figures 44 and 45.

Figure 44 Khepri as Pharaoh   *Figure 45 Khepri as Re pushing the sun*

Chapter 10 Pharaoh

In most books on Egyptology the words "pharaoh" and "king" are used interchangeably, a fact which we find not helpful to our understanding of the highest role in the Egyptian hierarchy. We cannot help but associate the word "king" with all the kings we have been taught: the kings of France, of England, of Spain and so on, and how they ruled in the cultures of which they were a major part. Notwithstanding the notion of the "divine right of kings," the kings of the Western world were not assimilated with God or the celestial realm apart from the fact that sometimes their mandate came from above and were thus not beholden to any secular power. While they could be advised and counseled, they ruled by fiat on their own terms, but they did not have spiritual authority; this belonged to the Church.

The pharaoh, on the other hand, had both temporal *and* spiritual authority since there was no distinction between the two:

> Nothing would have bent more alien to the Egyptian point of view than the possibility of separating church and state. For the Egyptians, religion was never a private matter to which individual choice could accord greater or lesser importance: as in the distant era of the prehistoric tribes, it was the very structure of social and national life, whose leadership was in the hands of the sovereign.[393]

The temple not only performed the necessary rituals for the *neters*, but also had a large economic role in providing food from their landed estates, products from their workshops, and so on. In ancient Egypt, there was nothing resembling a "Church" (there was not even a word for "religion"), unless one considered the entire society as a "Church"; that is, the entire Egyptian culture was built on metaphysical principles based not on moral imperatives but on cosmic laws, with pharaoh as the sole source

---

[393] Sauneron, *Priests*, 168.

of authority. Without this authority, the society could not function, and the people accepted this willingly for "it established for each subject his function and place in the world."[394] The pharaoh was, in fact, a symbol: he represented the ultimate level of being to which man could attain on this earth. Schwaller de Lubicz says this about the "king":

Figure 46 Pharaoh

> The royal principle on which Ancient Egypt relied has nothing in common with our concept of King. It is never a question of a man in our country like Louis, Charles, François, for example. The reigning King is a symbol, a pretext to give substance, in the mythic, mystical—and hermetical—sense, to the embodiment of a ray of original Light.[395]

This notion of kingship is supported by two names for pharaoh in Ancient Egypt: (1) *n(y)-sw.t* (in transliteration from the hieroglyphs) and which is usually translated as "king," and (2) *Hm (in transliteration)*, which means "person" but is usually, translated as "majesty" when referring to a particular pharaoh. The first refers to the king as Horus and his power arising from the time of creation. The second refers to the reigning pharaoh as a person in which this power is embodied.[396] See Figure 46.

When the pharaoh died, he ascended to the sky and became assimilated to Re, his 'father,'[397] the *neter* symbolized by the sun,

---

[394] Frankfort, *Kingship and the Gods*, 53.

[395] Schwaller de Lubicz, R.A., *Le roi de la théocratie pharaonique*, 295.

[396] Wilkinson, *The Complete Gods*, 56.

[397] James Henry Breasted, *Development of Religion and Thought in Ancient Egypt* (New York: Harper & Row, 1959), 123.

a being of light.[398] From other texts, he became one of the circumpolar stars that never set, thus assuring his immortality. He also became assimilated to Osiris, ruler of the netherworld. Here are three seemingly contradictory possibilities, but for the Egyptians were complementary notions each having meaning in its own context.

While on earth, he was Horus, the 'son of Re,' his representative on earth by which cosmic powers flowed into the world. As such, he was the only real priest, all the priests of the temples being his surrogates. He was in effect the ultimate intermediary between the duality of heaven and earth as well as that between the "two lands" of Egypt, the northern Nile delta and the southern Nile valley.[399] We could even say that the function of pharaoh was to reconcile all dualities symbolized by the mythic struggle between Horus and Seth and so resurrect the original First Time of complete harmony. The most important function, the reconciliation of the duality between the divine and terrestrial natures of man, could only be accomplished through the pharaoh. The pharaoh thus symbolizes the True Man, the integrated being that every person could become so that the divine nature hidden within him can find the channels by which man's terrestrial body is infused into a being of higher consciousness.

According to the myth of Osiris, the rulership of Egypt in the beginning was held by a succession of *neters* until it was given to Osiris, who, after his death and resurrection, became ruler of the netherworld. Osiris' son was Horus, who was awarded the rulership of Egypt by the high *neters* to put an end to the struggle for power between Horus and Seth.

---

[398] Jacq, *La tradition primordiale*, 11.
[399] Clark, *Myth and Symbol*, 30.

Every pharaoh from then on 'became Horus'[400] and, as such, pharaoh's responsibility was to realize *maat*, that is, maintain right order and justice in the world just as it was created at the First Time, whether by ensuring that the necessary rituals took place as they should or by protecting the land from incursion and chaos. The most important royal offering seen on temple and tomb reliefs is, in fact, the pharaoh offering a representation of the *neter* Maat to a divinity. Two *neters* aided him in this task: Sia, "perception" and Hu "utterance." Through Sia, he observed and understood; through Hu, his word became action and reality.[401] To ensure the functioning and maintenance of the cosmos and its reflection in the land of Egypt, pharaoh created temples for the *neters* who were incorporated into statues placed in the holy of holies of these edifices. It must be said that the temples were not places of worship, as we would assume from our experience in the age we are living in, but rather engines to keep the cosmos functioning as it should: above all, the daily rising and setting sun and the yearly Nile flood.[402] It was to this end that all the rituals in the temple took place. When the pharaoh died and was buried with the appropriate rituals, he would provide the energy for the Horus lineage to continue in the body of the new pharaoh to come.[403] Thus, the pharaoh was actually neither a *neter* nor a man, but rather, in the Egyptian view of things, the incarnation of the Horus lineage, an energy propagated from the First Time. In the words of H. A. and Henri Frankfort:

---

[400] Janice Kamrin, *The Cosmos of Khnumhotep II at Beni Hasan* (London: Routledge, 2011), 8.

[401] Assmann, *Death and Salvation*, 4.

[402] Jan Assmann, *The Search for God in Ancient Egypt*, Ithaca (Cornell University Press, 2001), 159.

[403] Stéphane Rossini and Ruth Schumann-Antelme, *Becoming Osiris: The Ancient Egyptian Death Experience* (Rochester VT: Inner Traditions, 1998), 58.

But the Egyptian did not distinguish between symbolism and participation; if he said that the king was Horus, he did not mean that the king was playing the part of Horus, he meant that the king was Horus, that the god was effectively present in the king's body during the particular activity in question.[404]

In theory, the Egyptian "king" was not part of a human dynasty that carried on from father to son. There was no "royal blood," since each pharaoh was a direct manifestation of the sun *neter* Re and incarnated the role of Horus, the early ruler of Egypt.[405]

---

[404] H. A & Henri Frankfort, *The Intellectual Adventure of Ancient Man*, 64.

[405] Stephen Quirke, *The Cult of Ra: Sun-Worship in Ancient Egypt* (New York: Thames & Hudson, 2001), 7.

Chapter 11 Ritual Symbolism

Rituals of a religious or spiritual nature can be basically of two types: 1) Religious, in the sense of propitiating gods, helping gods in ordering the universe, or introducing a person into a religious organization or cult. 2) Initiatory, in the sense of initiating a person into a new state of being where the ritual is not only symbolic but transformative.

It should be emphasized that the rituals of ancient Egypt were not meant to appease the *neters* or to ask them for favors, but to help them in maintaining the original order of the First Time. In ancient Egypt, the priest did not address a *neter* as a human but took on the role of another *neter* to address him using the "divine words," the hieroglyphs. In this way, he abandoned his own personality and so acted in the divine realm to make his words effective.[406] The priests used 'secret symbols' during the rites, which are secret only to those who have not been initiated into their sacred meanings. As recounted by Iamblichus (245 AD-325 AD) in his work *On the Egyptian Mysteries*, these rituals had power not only over the dead, but also over the initiates who attended them. The offerings and the recitations, for those who were prepared, thus had a transformative power over the dead as well as the living to enable them to live again in the afterlife (or in this life) as an *akh*, a transfigured spirit. "*Akh*" is related to the word "*Akhet*" or the Eastern horizon where the sun, and light, is born every day.[407] It is also related to the *neter* Hor*akh*ty or Horus of the Horizon. As the horizon exists between light and darkness, the day and the *Dwat* (or netherworld), it is the place where the dead are transformed into an *akh* in order to live

---

[406]Wente, *Mysticism*, 178.

[407]Werner Forman & Stephen Quirke, *Hieroglyphs and the Afterlife in Ancient Egypt* (Norman: University of Oklahoma Press, 1996), 7-8.

rejuvenated in the afterlife, just as the sun is reborn at the horizon creating light and life every day. We could say, in fact, that the *raison d'être* of the spirituality of ancient Egypt was to restore man from his fallen state to his previous divine state symbolized by his becoming one of the immortal circumpolar stars. From there we could expand on a symbolism which encompasses all the theology and cosmology of ancient Egypt and whose fundamental message is death and rebirth within the established order created at the First Time.

> Life in the hereafter was not a repose from the tribulations of this world but a long series of adventurous journeyings through which the dead soul, justified and regenerated, attained to a place in the retinue of the gods—the personifications of the cosmic forces—and eventually took part in the unceasing and eternal round of activity which permitted the universe a continued existence.[408]

Here again, we see how all the symbols and myths of ancient Egypt are related.

An Initiation Ritual at Abydos?

If there is evidence for initiatory rituals in ancient Egypt, then Egyptian symbolism can be experienced on the level of man's living consciousness and not only in terms of his physical death and rebirth in the *Dwat*.

It has been suggested by various authors that initiation into sacred mysteries did take place in ancient Egypt. This is impossible to prove however, since the Egyptians did not document in our manner how such ceremonies might have taken place or for what purpose, and perhaps the initiates were sworn to secrecy and the nature of the rituals never revealed. Most classical Egyptologists, however, do not accept that ritual initiations of a 'mystical' nature existed in ancient Egypt, since

---

[408] Piankoff, *The Wandering of the Soul*, xvii.

there has been no definite proof from the texts. Nevertheless, the interpretation of texts used in the Mortuary rituals or inscribed on pyramid and temple walls, or on papyri, can be taken as texts referring to both death and rebirth in the *afterlife* or death and rebirth in *this life*, the former being a symbol for the latter.

Initiation has a special meaning when referring to sacred ceremonies, and is different than what we now call 'religion':

> Religion takes an individual into consideration only in his individual human state...whereas the goal of initiation is to go beyond the possibilities of this state.[409] The goal of rites is [therefore] to always put the human being in relation...with something that goes beyond his individuality and which belongs to other states of existence.[410]

One aspect of this is that the initiate, through specific rites, has experiences that are not filtered by his mental apparatus, but are received directly by his entire being. Such rituals are performed by various tribal groups to bring children into the world of the adult community. These experiences profoundly affect their view of the world and their place in it, so that what they believed before becomes, if not meaningless, at least secondary to a new spiritual awakening. In other words, a person dies to one life, to the "old man," and is reborn "into a new life, or, rather, the return to an old one, that is, to that 'paradise' from which man fell, to that divine communion from which he, by his own acts, has been excluded."[411] It is from this idea that certain authors have taken texts that most Egyptologists would call "funerary" or "mortuary," recited over the deceased in the tomb, which they might very well be, but on another level to also be "initiatory"

---

[409] Guénon, *Aperçus sur l'Initiation*, 27. [Our translation]

[410] Ibid., 109. [Our translation]

[411] Lewis Spence, *The Mysteries of Egypt: Secret Rites and Traditions* (Mineola, NY: Dover, 2005), 275.

for those undergoing a ceremony in the temple. To buttress this point, it is said in the *Book of Amduat* (also called *That Which Is in the Underworld* or *The Book of the Secret Chamber*), a 'book' written on the walls of some pharaohs' tombs in the New Kingdom:

> This is drawn according to this design in the hidden place of the netherworld. The one who draws these representations is the likeness of the great god himself. *It is useful for him upon earth.*[412] [Our italics]

Other similar passages can be found in the same 'book,' thus giving evidence that ceremonies over the dead may be useful for the living as well.[413]

The Belgian Egyptologist Max Guilmot has proposed that initiatory rituals took place in the ancient town of Abydos,[414] the site of the necropolis of the first kings of Egypt beginning in 3200 BC, a place associated with the *neter* Osiris and considered as perhaps the most sacred place in all of ancient Egypt throughout its existence. In fact, all through Egyptian history many came to deposit a stele to be erected near Osiris' burial place and so attain eternal life through this proximity. Guilmot has this to say concerning initiatory rituals:

> Ritual was introduced to change the quality of the novice's soul, to raise one's consciousness to a superhuman level, and to make an eternal being out of each soul personality [by] death and resurrection so that one may symbolically experience a superhuman state and eternal life.[415]

---

[412] Wente, *Mysticism*, 163.

[413] See Wente, *Mysticism*, for a collection of texts from the funerary literature supporting this thesis.

[414] Max Guilmot, *Les initiés et les rites initiatiques en Égypte ancienne* (Paris: Éditions Robert Laffont, 1977) and *The Initiatory Process in Ancient Egypt*, Rosicrucian Digest, Vol. 85, No. 1 (San Jose, CA: AMORC, 2007). This section is based on these works.

[415] Guilmot, *The Initiatory Process*, 18.

At Abydos, in an area called "Peker," was found what was supposed to be, from 2000 BC, the burial place of the head of Osiris, the *neter* of death and resurrection, whose body was torn apart by his brother Seth. To the north of Peker was built the temple of Osiris, but nothing of this is now visible except for the outline of the temple's foundation. As the place of Osiris, Abydos became a place of pilgrimage, for it was believed that by taking part in rituals at Abydos they would be able to unite with Osiris in the *Dwat*, and so be judged fit to ascend into the sky to become a circumpolar star, that is, become immortal. What does remain in Abydos is the great temple of Seti I of the 19th dynasty, built around 1300 BC, it still being in a marvelous state of preservation. Also still standing is the Osireion, a structure built underground behind the temple in the same era. The latter is very dilapidated, but the basic structure is quite visible.

The Osireion is a structure like no other in ancient Egypt. It consists of a long dark corridor, whose walls support images like those in the tombs of the pharaohs, which leads to a large room filled with water. This room was no doubt covered by huge flat stones, now disappeared, as ten large pillars attest. A rectangular platform rises out of the water in the center of the room, no doubt symbolizing creation in the First Time. Two staircases lead to the platform which could have been used for Initiation rituals. See Figure 47.

It is Guilmot's assumption that the Osireion was built by Seti I as an imitation of the original temple of Osiris at Abydos. Of course, this can only be an assumption for there are no documents attesting to this fact. Guilmot refers, however, to certain documents such as Plate 10 of the *Papyrus of Ani*, a *Book of the Dead*, which shows pictures of the burial place of Osiris having the same characteristics as the Osireion. Guilmot then assumes that initiatory rituals were performed in the Osireion using citations from the ancient *Pyramid Texts*, *Coffin Texts*, and

Book of the Dead to prove his point. For example, from the *Coffin Texts*:

> I am a servant in the temple of Osiris!...
> Open to me!
> I am a (human) who knows
> Its magical formula,
> I was initiated into these (secret things),
> And did not repeat (them)
> to the uninitiated.[416]

Figure 47 The Osireion at Abydos

From extant texts, Guilmot assumes the ritual proceeds as follows: a preparation, where the postulant is led by Anubis (perhaps a priest with an Anubis mask) to the door of the temple (or down the corridor in the Osireion) and must answer various questions posed by the guardians of the temple to enter into the sanctuary. Then come three phases: 1) *Justification*, where the postulant is led into the Hall of Maat (Hall of Judgment) and must justify his character before Osiris by correctly answering

---

[416]Ibid., p.21.

questions and proclaiming his innocence as given in Chapter 125 of the *Book of the Dead*. Only if he is found to be without fault according to what Thoth records as his heart is weighed against a feather of Maat, that is, he is not burdened by earthly passions, may he then continue. 2) *Regeneration*, where he becomes spiritually cleansed by the ritual of entering and leaving a body of water, that is, symbolically dying and being reborn. 3) *Illumination*, where the initiate waits to be illuminated through the ritual of the apparition of Osiris. Guilmot, from the Leyden Papyrus (100 AD), sees the same three phases of this ritual at Busiris and at Karnak.[417] He summarizes:

> 'To contemplate the Mystery' is to participate in it, and it is also to resuscitate as Osiris. It is to become an Osiris. It is a crucial moment and the flashing zenith of a human life! An initiate is born. Holiness infuses the person. To Holiness, the human is bound.[418]

If, in fact, there were Initiation rituals, these were reserved for an elite, those who had been prepared for the moment through learning by experience and by studying the hieroglyphs and sacred texts. The purpose of these rituals would have been, as described by S. Mayassis, an initiation:

> This revelation thus resulted from the explanation of these symbolic ceremonies, gave the key to man's origin, his destiny, the development of the soul in terrestrial life as well as after death, a fundamental and worrying question for the Egyptians and for all men from the beginning of the world. It confided the secret of creation, of cosmogony and of theogony dissimulated in the symbolism of the myths....and the action of this transcendent operation is transmitted to the candidate in order to transfigure him into a new and better individual [and to] contribute to his acquisition of "Knowledge[419]

---

[417] Guilmot, *Les initiés*, 174.

[418] Guilmot, *The Initiatory Process*, 27.

[419] S. Mayassis, *Mystères et Initiation*, 15-16.

The Mysteries of Osiris

The Mysteries of Osiris took place during the Festival of Khoiak, the fourth and last month of the season *Akhet*, when the inundation of the land by the Nile began to recede, allowing the land, fertile with black silt ready for planting, to appear out of the waters. This ritual thus refers to the First Time when the primeval mound appeared out of the waters of the *Nun*. Evidence exists that the mysteries took place in the Middle Kingdom, particularly at Abydos, where it continued through the Ptolemaic era in all major towns.[420] At Abydos, the Festival of Osiris that took place each year was publicly defined by the procession in which effigies, or "corn mummies" (see below) of the *neter* Osiris were transported from his temple to what was considered his tomb at Peker, the necropolis of Abydos where the first dynasty kings were buried.[421] The rituals of creating

Figure 48 The neter
Ptah-Sokar-Osiris

the corn mummies (the actual Mysteries of Osiris) during the festival would have taken place in the temple during a period before the procession began. The procession itself consisted of divine boats being pulled on a sledge in which were placed the corn mummies of Osiris and of the *neter* Sokar, an ancient falcon *neter* of Memphis who became assimilated to the *neters* Ptah and Osiris to become the funeral deity Ptah-Sokar-Osiris. See Figure 48.

---

[420] Sylvie Cauville, *Le Temple de Dendera: Guide archéologique,* 2nd ed. (IFAO, 1995), 2-6.

[421] Katherine J. Eaton, "The Festival of Osiris and Sokar in the Month of Khoiak," *Studien zur Altägyptischen Kultur* (Hamburg: Helmut Buske Verlag, 2006), 35, 75-101.

Also in the boats were a bed and the 'divine members,' a set of disembodied limbs symbolizing the body parts of Osiris scattered over Egypt by his brother Seth after dismembering him.[422] The procession allowed the public, who came from all over the country, to witness this ritual of the 'rebirth' or 'resurrection' of Osiris by the power of the sun, that is, the reconstitution of his body and his rebirth in the netherworld where he is embraced by Re.[423] This was the main symbolism of the festival, and the people, in homage, set up stelae and statues in offering chapels along the way of the procession.[424]

The most extant documented place of the Mysteries was in the Osiris chapels on the roof of the temple of Hathor at Dendera in Upper Egypt, a temple continuously built and rebuilt from the Old Kingdom through the Roman era. Our discussion of the Mysteries is greatly indebted to the work of Sylvie Cauville, a contemporary French Egyptologist who documented in depth the two late era Temples of Edfu and Dendera.[425]

While the form of the ritual changed over time and place, the general symbolism remained the same. Basically, the purpose of the Mysteries of Osiris was to protect the corpse of Osiris and to prepare for his resurrection in the netherworld.[426] At Dendera, the preparation for the festival took place from the 12th to the 25th of Khoiak, the time taken to prepare the effigies or corn mummies of Osiris, the *neter* Sokar, and the relic (a body part of

[422]Eaton, "The Festival of Osiris and Sokar," 80.

[423]Sabine Pizzarotti, "Rituels et fêtes dans le temple: les 'Mystères d'Osiris' du mois de Khoiak," *Égypte Afrique & Orient*, No. 67, Sep.-Nov. 2012, 31-40 (Avignon : Centre d'égyptologie, 2012), 32.

[424]Eaton, "The Festival of Osiris and Sokar," 76.

[425]Sylvie Cauville, *Dendera : Les chapelles osiriennes*, 3 vols. (Cairo: IFAO, 1997).

_____*Le Temple de Dendera: Guide archéologique*, 2nd ed. (Cairo: IFAO, 1995).

_____*L'Offrande aux dieux dans le temple* égyptien (Leuven: Peeters, 2011)

[426]Cauville, *Le Temple de Dendera*, 68.

Osiris). The corn mummies were made of sand, barley and other elements formed in the shapes of Osiris, Sokar, and the relic using molds. Once formed, they were then watered until the barley germinated:

> The annual sprouting of vegetation from the soil is the most striking manifestation of the forces of rebirth and growth immanent in the earth; and Osiris is viewed as reappearing in the grain in the earliest texts we possess, as well as those of all succeeding periods.[427]

Barley, like the egg, is, in fact, a great symbol of transmutation from the human to the divine state of being. Just as the barley grows from a seed in the mysterious darkness of earth, and a chick from within an enveloping egg, so the deceased becomes a divine being from his gestation within the mummy. In the same symbolic way, the living becomes liberated from the obscurity of his unconsciousness through the recitation of formulas during the Mysteries.

The place of the Mysteries in the Temple of Hathor at Dendera was in the six chapels on the roof, which the ancient Egyptians called the House of Gold.[428] They represent the first temple of Sokar in Memphis where the effigies were symbolically made to prepare Osiris for eternal life, then buried for a year until the next festival of Osiris when the effigy is unearthed and a new one is created. We know the form of the ritual because it is written on the walls of the chapels, each indicating what takes place within it along with other texts such as the *Book of the Dead*.[429] See Figure 49.

Many rites and ceremonies took place during the festival, but to discuss them all and their corresponding symbolism would require a book in itself:

---

[427] Frankfort, *Kingship and the Gods*, 185.

[428] Pizzarotti, *Rituels et fêtes*, 32.

[429] Cauville, *Le Temple de Dendera*, 68, 80.

Every act was symbolic in character, and represented some ancient belief or tradition. The paste, the mixture of wheat and water, the egg, the naked goddess Shentit, i.e., Isis in her chamber, the placing of the paste on her bed, the kneading of the paste into the moulds, etc., represented the great processes of Nature which are set in motion when human beings are begotten and conceived, as well as the inscrutable powers which preside over growth and development.[430]

Figure 49 Door to chapels on roof of Hathor temple at Dendera

Basically, in chapels 1 to 3, the fabrication of the effigies took place, while in chapels 4-6 various ceremonies consecrated the effigies themselves. All this sacred ritual was conducted by priests in secret, the public only seeing the procession that took place after leaving the temple on the 26th of Khoiak, the festival of Sokar-Osiris. If there were initiates to the secrets of Osiris during the ceremonies in the chapels, we do not know,

---

[430]E.A. Wallis Budge, *Osiris and the Egyptian Resurrection*, Vol. 2 (New York: Dover Publications, 1973), 9.

since there are as yet no texts found to corroborate this thesis. The end of the ritual took place from the 27th to the 30th of Khoiak. On the 28th a ceremony took place that put the resurrection of Osiris-Sokar in relation with the rising sun and the original mound arising out of the abyssal waters.[431] On the 30th, the effigies of the last year were buried in the graveyard while the rite of erecting a *djed* pillar, the 'spinal column' of Osiris, took place, thus symbolizing the attendant verticality of the resurrection of Osiris in the netherworld through the agency of divine energy flowing down channels along the spine.[432]

We can thus see that the great "mystery" of the ritual is the death and rebirth of life, symbolized by the Osiris effigy in which the barley grains are buried in the earth to sprout at the appropriate time. For the ancient Egyptians, we can assume that the story of Osiris is not just a legend, a cute story to be told, but had a profound meaning corresponding to their cyclical view of the world. It has been shown, for example, that the ritual corresponded to the turning of the cosmos by the zodiac carved in the ceiling of chapel two and the number of days of the ritual corresponding to the waxing of the moon[433].

On a wall in chapel two, the *Wadjet* eye (Eye of Horus) represents the moon, first waning, then, accompanied by fourteen *neters* ascending a staircase, corresponding to the waxing of the moon until its plenitude.[434] This corresponds as well to the fourteen dismembered parts of Osiris that were gathered together by Isis to make him whole. Just as Osiris was dismembered by Seth and made whole by Isis, so one must have

---

[431] Pizzarotti, *Rituels et fêtes*, 39.

[432] Ibid.

[433] Sylvie Cauville, *Le Zodiaque d'Osiris* (Leuven: Peeters, 1997), 76.

[434] Cauville, *Le Temple de Dendera*, 37.

one's egoistic self torn apart by Initiatory rituals and restored as a servant to higher forces:

> Thy limbs are rejoined, thou art protected, thou hast no defect; thy limbs are rejoined, and not a member of thine is wanting.[435]

Moreover, the procession of the priests through the chapels corresponds to solar and lunar circuits.[436]

The nature of their thought processes was the only way they could create a ritual, that is, to follow the patterns of their thought in which everything was related and corresponded on different levels of meaning. Furthermore, we can only imagine that for each individual the Osiris mysteries had a profound resonance in their own life and death, whether, for initiates, a transformative death and rebirth in an initiatory ceremony or, for everyone else, a physical death and rebirth in the afterlife. On the last day of the mysteries the high point of the Festival of Sokar-Osiris was held. Here it was recited that the resurrection of Osiris took place in the afterlife, that all his enemies were defeated and that he had triumphed over death.

Other Osiris festivals took place in Egypt as well. For one, there was the Feast of the Sheaf at the beginning of the harvest season, when a sheaf of wheat was cut by the pharaoh representing the death and rebirth of Osiris. For another, there was the Feast of Lamps, when, according to Herodotus, thousands of oil lamps were lit, especially in Sais but all over Egypt as well, representing again the death and resurrection of Osiris.

The Mortuary Ritual

In the Old Kingdom, the mortuary temple for the pharaoh was placed next to the entrance to the pyramid where the pharaoh

---

[435] Budge, *Osiris and the Egyptian Resurrection*, Vol. 2, 47.

[436] Cauville, *Dendera: Les chapelles osiriennes*, 213.

was entombed. In the New Kingdom at Thebes, the mortuary temple was called the "mansion of millions of years" and was placed at the edge of the desert separate from the Valley of the Kings where the pharaohs were buried. In this way the rituals for the dead pharaoh were carried out separately in the mortuary temple, while the pharaoh in his rock-cut tomb was in the mysterious *Dwat* on his way to becoming an *akh*, or enlightened spirit in the presence of Osiris. The mourning period lasted for 70 days, beginning with the death of the individual, which corresponded to how long the star Sirius remained out of sight until it reappeared before dawn, a moment which coincided with the beginning of the annual Nile inundation[437]—another example of how an event on the individual level was symbolically connected to a cosmic manifestation. In this way, the rebirth of the deceased in the afterlife, called "becoming Osiris," is connected to the rebirth of vegetation due to the flooding of the land, the flood waters being known as the "excretions of Osiris." The funeral for the deceased was done in public, which not only allowed the family and community to mourn the deceased, it gave those who attended the opportunity to help the passing of he who died in his body to attain the afterlife. In fact, physical death for the Egyptians was not final, but a waystation to another realm of existence.[438] The aspirations of the Egyptians after death were synthesized in a common formula by which they wished to be "a transfigured *akh* in the sky with Re, powerful on earth with Geb, and vindicated in the realm of the dead with Osiris."

Archaeologists have shown that in the Prehistoric Period (6000 BC-3150 BC) the deceased, in the earlier graves, were buried in simple graves with a pot, but without being treated or positioned in any particular way. Later, in the Predynastic period, more

---

[437] Schumann and Rossini, *Becoming Osiris*, 8.

[438] Joshua J. Mark, *Ancient Egyptian Mortuary Rituals*, Ancient History Encyclopedia, www.ancient.eu, March 2017.

objects were added to the grave and the deceased was placed in a fetal position facing either east (rebirth, the rising sun) or west (the land of the dead). Late research has shown that some mummification began around 3500 BC and eventually became part of the established mortuary ritual in the Old Kingdom.

In the Early Dynastic Period (3150 BC – 2613 BC) tombs were built over the graves and developed, for those who could afford it, into the rectangular *mastaba* (Arabic for "bench"), built of mud-brick with an underground burial chamber and a tomb chapel above for receiving offerings. Also, for the wealthy, much more elaborate grave goods were added and in greater quantity. This developed into the step pyramid of the pharaoh Djoser of the 3rd dynasty at Saqqara, where increasingly smaller *mastabas* were added on top of each other. This pyramid was part of a complete temple complex whose basic plan continued in the fourth dynasty where a real pyramid form with flat sides was built at Giza. In the different periods that followed after the Old Kingdom, different types of tombs and customs developed over time and place, but the essential rituals remained more or less the same, at least for those who were able to have them.

The walls of *mastabas* destined for the royalty and nobility were decorated, beginning in the Third Dynasty, with texts and some images mainly focused on the false door, which was a niche carved and decorated to appear as a real door, though there was no actual opening. Its purpose was to allow the *ka* of the deceased to go through this 'door' and receive offerings.[439] The false door was thus the symbol of a passageway between the world of the dead and the living world above, which the deceased would pass through to receive offerings given for his benefit in the netherworld. See Figure 50.

---

[439]Kamrin, *Khnumhotep II*, 41.

In the Old and Middle Kingdoms these texts and scenes on the walls and ceilings became more elaborate as time passed, until, in the New Kingdom rock-cut tombs of the pharaohs in the Valley of the Kings, entire mythological 'books' of the afterlife were inscribed and painted. How to interpret scenes in the *mastabas* depends on the point of view one takes. It should be

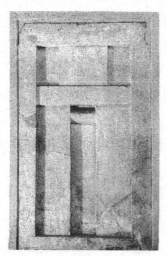

said that since the tombs were to be walled off, the scenes would never be seen by anyone, which should help us to interpret them. Some Egyptologists see scenes of daily life as representations of the activities the deceased enjoyed during his life and wanted to see magically continued after his death, or they simply represented a sort of biography of his life as a memorial— but a memorial for who, since the tomb would be walled up?

Figure 50 False door of a tomb

As for everything in ancient Egypt, we need to look at the symbolic aspect of tomb drawings and inscriptions. While some scenes may seem to be scenes of daily life, a more apt interpretation might be showing the proper rituals for the funeral of the deceased and his perpetual cult so as to ensure his effective transformation into an *akh*, an enlightened being. Many scenes show hunting and fishing activities, which, rather than indicating simple pastimes, may have deep symbolic meanings on various levels.[440]

Hunting took place usually in the marshes or the desert, places outside the orderly world of Egypt. Hunting or fishing in these places can thus be seen as being equivalent to preventing the chaotic forces of *isfet* from encroaching upon *maat* or the just

---

[440]Ibid., 86-89, 98, 104, 110, 114, 121.

order, and so allowing the sun to arise every day on the Eastern horizon. For example, the hunting of a wild bull can be interpreted on several levels. The bull, or *ka*, in ancient Egyptian, was also the name for the vital force of man in conjunction with the same cosmic force, so to lasso the bull, was to activate that force in man. Or, on a lesser level, it could be a depiction of a Traditional ritual relating to the power of the pharaoh, or it could even signify the simple catching of animals to be sacrificed as offerings to the *neters* during the burial ceremony. And likewise, the spearing of the hippopotamus can be viewed as the victory of Horus over Seth, of *maat* over *isfet*. By the middle New Kingdom, the desert-living oryx was considered to be an embodiment of Seth and the enemy of the Eye of Horus. To capture the oryx was thus equivalent to saving Horus in his role as eternal ruler of Egypt incarnated in each succeeding pharaoh. A more esoteric meaning could be to tame the chaotic forces in man so they can be used in his spiritual development. The hunting of the oryx, the jackal, the lion, and other animals of the desert can thus be seen as helping the sun *neter* in its role of creation, either by destroying its enemies—or by taming them. Also, the desert jackal, in the form of the *neter* Anubis, is the embalmer of the dead as well as that which pulls the sun boat through the heavens.

Other frequent scenes on temple walls are those of catching birds with throwsticks and clapnets, and fish with spears. See Figure 51.

Now birds and fish are volatile creatures that represent disorder. Showing the catching of them is thus a way of signifying the necessity of creating order out of chaos and continually protecting it, which pertains also to man in his spiritual quest. Fish and bird can also be interpreted

Figure 51 Birds in a clapnet

otherwise: man is both 'fish' in his human form surrounded by his environment keeping him prisoner on earth, and 'bird' is his possibility of flying up to spiritual heights.[441]

In the *Book of the Dead*, it is written in Spell 3: "May N live after death like Re every day,"[442] where "N" is the deceased. The whole Mortuary ritual, then, was to assure the deceased a continued existence in the afterlife, and, like Re, as the sun, be continually reborn every day. In the mind of the Egyptians this was equivalent to 'becoming Osiris,' which brings us back to the myth of this *neter*, for it was Horus who entered the *Dwat* and restored life to Osiris through his eye. The Mortuary ritual was in fact a reproduction of this myth and, if carried out in accordance with tradition, would result in the resurrection of the deceased in the afterlife through the power of *heka*. We see, once again, how everything in the Egyptian ritual landscape is based on fundamental symbolic myths, and how the Mortuary ritual can be interpreted not only as a creation of life after death, but as a symbolic resurrection of the 'living dead' into higher beings in this life.

The Mortuary ritual consisted of various sub-rituals of which the main ones will be discussed here: the Embalming ritual and the Opening of the Mouth ritual. We are indebted to the book of Stéphane Rossini and Ruth Schumann-Antelme, *Becoming Osiris: The Ancient Egyptian Death Experience*, for details on these rituals.

The Embalming Ritual

In the symbolic world of the Egyptians, every object, every event, was a symbol of a higher level of meaning: just as the Embalming ritual excreted the bodily fluids of the deceased, so the waters of the Nile were considered the excretions of Osiris,

---

[441]Hornung, *L'esprit du temps*, 182.

[442]Ibid., 36.

as previously mentioned.[443] The reason for mummification can be described in this way:

> The ritual aim of mummification was to transform the earthly body into a divine form which would endure forever. In the process the products of corruption were to be removed and replaced with oils, resins, natron and incense – all substances which had connotations of purity and divinity, making the body wholly divine. The intellectual counterpart to this procedure was the identification of all parts of the body with those of gods and goddesses.[444]...The mummy, surrounded by protective powers, rested in the tomb, which, in symbolic terms, was located in the Duat or Netherworld. The deceased in spirit form—as a ba or akh—left the mummy to join the gods Osiris and Ra, and to become one with them.[445]

Before the embalming took place, the body was purified with water and then perfumed. The embalming itself took place in the 'tent of purification,' which, in the New Kingdom, was erected in front of the tomb on the west bank of the Nile. To reach the tomb, the deceased was taken across the Nile in a boat, thus crossing over to the 'other shore.' The symbolic nature of this trip is shown by one caption of an image naming the boat *neshmet*, the name of the sacred boat of Osiris used in the mysteries at Abydos.[446] The *neter* Anubis was the mythic "first embalmer" and so it was he who was in charge of the Embalming ritual in the person of the priest leading the ceremonies and was called "Anubis, Superior of the Mysteries."[447] See Figure 52.

---

[443] Rossini and Schumann, *Becoming Osiris*, 8-9.

[444] Taylor, *Journey through the Afterlife*, 162.

[445] Ibid., 239.

[446] Assmann, *Death and Salvation*, 304.

[447] Rossini and Schumann, *Becoming Osiris*, 8-9.

The ritual was not just a physical event, but also a spiritual one; as each act of the embalming took place, a recitation took place corresponding to it. In fact, each hour of the ritual had its own deity and recitation:

> Typical of these spells are invocations to the presiding deities to encourage them to the utmost watchfulness and attentiveness. It was of the utmost importance that Seth, the murderer of Osiris, not penetrate into the embalming chamber. The situation was all the more dangerous in that the enemy was able to transform himself and could appear in a tiny, scarcely visible form, such as that of a flea.[448]

A single thought, therefore, could disrupt the vigilance needed for transformation. It would be unthinkable in fact not to have recitations, for it was the power of the word that made the physical acts effective on the spiritual plane. Since the priests play the role of those *neters* implicated in the ritual, the recitation was actually words spoken by the *neters*, words which gave divine meaning to the earthly act taking place. In fact, "All the parts of his body were ritually attached to particular gods and sanctuaries of Egypt, the way the scattered limbs of Osiris were before his reconstitution by Anubis...."[449] Just as Anubis was the *neter* of embalming, so he was the *neter* of the scale in the judgment before Osiris: just as the body was cleansed of all impurity, so the 'heart' of the deceased was declared pure of all imperfection.

The recitations were based on the theme of bringing together what had been torn apart in direct reference to the myth of Osiris, which is to say that the deceased was "re-membered": each limb and organ was given back to the deceased through a ritual which necessarily included a recitation by the lector priest.

---

[448] Assmann, *Death and Salvation*, 262.

[449] Rossini and Schumann, *Becoming Osiris*, 11.

Figure 52 Anubis performing the Embalming ritual

The body was again purified with water and all body hair was removed. The interior organs were then removed (including the brain) but the heart was put back in, since it was considered the seat of intelligence and emotion, and was needed so that the transfigured spirit could recollect 'what he had forgotten.' To have full control of the body in the afterlife was considered of utmost importance. The liver, stomach, lungs, and intestines were bathed in palm wine and coated with hot resin, then placed in four 'canopic' jars to be placed in the tomb with the coffin. In the Old Kingdom, the lids were plain, in the middle kingdom they had human heads, and in the New Kingdom, after the 18th Dynasty, the lids had figures of the 'four sons of Horus,' known as 'friends of the King,' were basically protectors of the deceased, and they symbolized as well the four cardinal directions:

- **Imsety**: head of a man, protected by the goddess Isis, represented the South, the Canopic jar contained the liver.
- **Hapy**: head of a baboon, protected by the goddess Nephthys, represented the North, the Canopic jar contained the lungs.

- **Duamutef**: head of a jackal, protected by the goddess Neith, represented the East, the Canopic jar contained the stomach.
- **Qebehsenuef**: head of a falcon, protected by the goddess Selket, represented the West, the Canopic jar contained the intestines.

It would be an interesting exercise to try to understand how the organ in each Canopic jar corresponded to the head of each of the Sons of Horus, the cardinal direction, and the protecting goddess. Since nothing was done fortuitously in ancient Egypt, the connections are no doubt real, but unfortunately beyond our ken. See Figure 53.

Figure 53 The canopic jars

Using natron salt, the body was completely dried up, and then made more realistic by stuffing the body with various substances such as flax, sawdust, aromatics, and astringents. The body was then perfumed and anointed with sacred oils meant to provide suppleness as well as the rectitude of the goddess Maat. It was then that the bandaging could begin by binding the various body parts in cloth, thus identifying the deceased with Osiris, who is always depicted in mummified form. The bandaging was done in an extremely rigorous way and in a definite order, with each step accompanied by recitations. During this process various amulets were placed within the cloths in particular places for reasons of protection in the afterlife; for example, a scarab amulet was placed over the heart. Through the embalming process, therefore, the deceased became identified with Osiris, the *neter* of the dead in the *Dwat*. In Egyptian mythology, Re, the sun, descended during the night into the *Dwat* where he embraced Osiris, thus providing him with his animating force and allowing him to continue his existence. In the same way, by becoming an Osiris, the deceased descended into the *Dwat* in order to awaken, to become an *akh*, an immortal transfigured spirit through the Opening of the Mouth (see below) and other rituals. When the mummy is placed in the sarcophagus, *shabtys*, or miniature statuettes, are also placed in it. These are not, as some Egyptologists would have it, to replace the deceased in the afterlife when there was work to be done to ease his sojourn there. Rather, as we see it, they are to ensure that the deceased *will be able* to participate in this work, such as fishing, hunting, harvesting, and so on.

Descending into the *Dwat* is symbolized by the mummy being placed in the sarcophagus. The lid then symbolizes Nut, the sky, and when it is placed over the sarcophagus, which symbolizes Geb, the earth, then Nut becomes symbolically impregnated by Geb, and so the deceased is given new life.[450] Here again, a ritual on earth has its meaning in cosmic mythology. We can extrapolate this meaning on a living individual as well: by descending into the depths of one's being, one's personal *Dwat*, one can perhaps come in touch with cosmic or spiritual forces.

The Tekenu

One ritual that exemplified the notion of rebirth was the *tekenu*, which was dragged on a sledge to the tomb as part of the

---

[450] Clark, *Myth and Symbol*, 50.

procession that went from the embalming chapel. A typical procession might have consisted of the priests, the family, friends, a sledge containing the coffin, another the canopic jars, and a third the *tekenu*. The *tekenu* was depicted on tomb walls sometimes as a human in a sort of sack with only hand and feet showing or just the head, usually lying down on a sledge being pulled by oxen and men. See Figure 54.

Figure 54 The tekenu being pulled on a sledge

Sometimes, however, it is just depicted as an amorphous sack, which led some scholars to believe that it consisted of all the remains of the deceased that were not in the coffin of the mummy or the canopic jars, and in this way provided the entire body to be resurrected.[451] However, this interpretation does not give the transformative symbolism that the notion of a person emerging from a hide or skin does, apart from the fact that many depictions of the *tekenu* show in fact a human being within a covering.

---

[451] Assmann, *Death and Salvation*, 300-01.

In the procession there might also be bearers of grave goods, sacred dancers, and mourners, depending on the wealth of the deceased. The *tekenu* was, as far as can be known, a *sem* priest who, taking the part of the human embryo, was covered by a hide, skin, or shroud, from which he came out of at the tomb, as would a newly born infant from the womb or the placenta, thus symbolizing the deceased being born into a new life.[452]

This mortuary ritual of the *tekenu* took place from the Old Kingdom through the Late Period and was depicted in many tombs of nobles. It has been documented that this ritual was carried over from ritual acts that took place at Buto and Sais from Predynastic times,[453] and some observers equate this ritual with shamanistic rites within early hunting cultures.[454] The ritual of 'Passing through the Skin' was also part of a processional pilgrimage to Abydos[455] as well as the pharaoh taking the place of the priest during the *Heb-Sed* Festival where he was to be reinvigorated with new life by 'passing through the skin' (see below).

The Opening of the Mouth Ritual

The Opening of the Mouth ritual was standard practice from the Old Kingdom through Roman times. It originally was performed to provide statues with the ability to enshrine the *ka*, or vital force, of the person represented by the statue and so be able to receive offerings. In earlier periods it took place in a chapel or other sacred place, but in the New Kingdom it took place on the mummy at the entrance to the tomb. It was led by the *sem* priest

[452] Alexandre Moret, *Mystères Égyptiens* (Paris: Armand Colin, 1923), 50-51.

[453] Katerina Paraskeva, *The Enigmatic "Tekenu": An Iconographic Analysis of "Tekenu" in tombs from the Old Kingdom to the Late Period* (Leiden: University of Leiden, Master's Thesis, 2012), 12.

[454] Fernand Schwarz, "Les origines archaïques de la résurrection et l'énigme du Tekenou," *Pharaon Magazine*, No. 10 (Laneuveville-devant-Nancy, France, Aug.-Oct., 2012), 47.

[455] Paraskeva, *The Enigmatic "Tekenu,"* 12.

Figure 55 Opening of the Mouth ritual

who was accompanied by a lector priest and other helpers. This ritual was extremely elaborate with about 75 different acts of which we will only discuss a few in order to point out the symbolic nature of the ritual. If it was done on a statue, the ritual was not effective until the name of the person whom the statue represented was written on the statue.[456] The result of the ritual was to reanimate the individual and sustain his *ka*—the ultimate goal being his divinization—by allowing him to eat, see, hear, breathe, and utilize the offerings provided at the ceremony, but also those offered at the tomb later by the family and others. The mortuary offerings were accompanied by recitations of the mortuary priest, and it was the sound of the priest's invocation that caused the *ba* of the deceased to come out to receive the offering. It should be remembered that for the ancient Egyptians, the *sound* of the recitations was as important as its content, for sound directly affected man through the sense of hearing, while the content needed to be filtered by the mind.

---

[456] Cyril Aldred, *Egyptian Art in the Days of the Pharaohs 3100-320 BC* (London: Thames and Hudson, 1980), 42.

The ritual was not just made up of symbolic gestures by which one could use one's reason to understand, but was seen by the ancient Egyptians as actually transformative: the deceased in fact became reanimated, albeit on another plane of existence.

The main act of the ritual was the raising of a freshly severed haunch of a bull to the face of the mummy, or an adze, a type of wood chisel that had a form like the haunch. See Figure 55.

Now the hieroglyph for a bull was the same as for the *ka*, which can be easily understood since the bull represents great force and the *ka* the animating force of the universe. But that is not all: the constellation Ursa Major, the Big Dipper, also had the same shape. So, what we have is a man-made object, the adze, symbolizing a form in nature, the haunch of a bull, which in turn symbolized the constellation Ursa Major. This constellation, at the time of the ancient Egyptians, was circumpolar, that is, it circled the pole star of the time and never set below the horizon, which meant it was immortal and a place where transfigured beings dwell. In this way, the use of the adze for the ritual of Opening of the Mouth aided in transforming the deceased into an *akh*, an immortal transfigured spirit. During the ceremony, of course, none of this was explained; it was simply understood through the experience of the symbolic ritual. We can compare this to the communion ritual of the Christian mass: one simply eats a wafer and drinks some wine, but the uniting of oneself with Jesus Christ is symbolically understood, as far as one's understanding permits.

The Daily Ritual

The elements of the Daily ritual detailed below are taken from various authors,[457] however, the interpretation of the ritual is our

---

[457] Elaine Sullivan, 2008, "Daily Ritual", on *Digital Karnak*, Los Angeles: http://dlib.etc.ucla.edu/projects/Karnak, and Emily Teeter, Religion and Ritual in Ancient Egypt (Cambridge, UK: Cambridge University Press, 2011), 46-53.

own. The Daily ritual is known to have been practiced in the Old Kingdom and was performed in all the temples of Egypt throughout Egyptian civilization. It is known from the *Pyramid Texts* and other ancient records. The daily ritual was performed in the temple in front of, and on the statue of, the *neter* to which the temple was dedicated. It was performed at dawn and repeated in abbreviated form in the afternoon and evening "at mealtime." It is not for nothing that the ritual was performed more completely at the time of the rising sun for this was the time of 'awakening,' when the power of Re, the principle behind the sun god, set in motion the act of creation on earth as it was at the First Time and which continued forever. The purpose of the ritual was not, we believe, as one author writes, to secure "the continuing beneficence of the divinities," or "the desire to satisfy and placate the god through the protection, nourishment, and service of his or her cult statue." Rather, the *raison d'être* of the Daily ritual was for man and Egypt to be *in harmony* with the *neter*, so as to reinforce the act of creation in which the *neter* participated. A *neter*, of course, was a cosmic function necessary for the continual act of creation to be effective and for harmony and order to be maintained in the cosmos symbolized by the *neter* Maat.

The statue of the *neter* was kept in the naos of the temple, the most sacred place in the sanctuary. It was believed that the statue contained the *ka* of the *neter*, what might be called its "life force."[458] One author says that by "providing the god's *ka* with the benefit of numerous offerings, the Egyptians hoped to receive patronage and approval from the god in return."[459] Again, for the reasons cited above, we do not agree with this statement, though it is the belief of many Egyptologists. While it was a high

[458] Sullivan, *Digital Karnak*, 1.
[459] Ibid.

priest of the temple who performed the ritual, he was doing so only as a representative of the pharaoh, for it was only he who could intercede with the *neters* since he was considered a *neter* himself. It is for this reason that the pharaoh was depicted on temple walls performing the ritual. The pharaoh, as intercessor and as the representative of all of Egypt was not hoping for any return for Egyptians but rather was providing the *neter* with the energy of Egypt to reinforce the *neter*'s function in the act of creation and so maintain cosmic order:

> It must be understood that in their temples, the priests were not just looking after an idol afflicted with human needs and appetites. Rather, they believed they were preserving, infused in a statue, a part of the divine omnipotence that was visible in the very life and motion of the universe. Each important moment in the course of the sun required a specific ceremony devoted to the earthly receptacle of this radiant deity. There is surely no lack of poetry or grandeur in this transposition of the essential phases of the motion of the universe into the very layout of the temple and the structure of the rituals.[460]

Since the pharaoh was the ultimate model, the True Man, it was for each Egyptian to live as did the pharaoh, according to *maat,* in harmony with himself, society, and the cosmos so that the pharaoh's intercession on behalf of all of Egypt would be effective. Thus, the statue was not in any sense being "worshipped," but was symbolically standing in for the *neter*, that is, a cosmic function which the statue embodied. We see here, then, that the ultimate reason for the ritual was for maintaining harmony and order at all levels of existence through a symbolic purification, awakening, and nourishment of the *neter* represented by the statue.

There may be some who see a resemblance, in various Catholic countries, to the dressing up of statues of the Virgin Mary who

---

[460] Sauneron, *Priests*, 91.

are then transported through the streets on holy days to be seen by the populace. But it would be wrong to equate the two rituals. In the Catholic ritual, the statues are *worshipped*, that is, they are shown reverence, not for the statue but for the personage that the statue represents, and to which one has an emotional attachment. For the elite in ancient Egypt, the ritual was not a question of emotions or sentiment (though for the populace it might be so), but a belief that the symbolic actions of the ritual had a transformative effect on the world by enhancing the force of the cosmic function that the *neter* represented.

As to the ritual acts themselves, there were about 36 different rituals that took place during the ceremony.[461] We know these rituals from their depiction and texts on the walls of temples, such as those at Karnak and Medinet Habu at Luxor. In one example, the statue of the *neter* is situated in a naos or shrine about 20 inches high in which a smaller wooden shrine held the statue of the *neter* made of gold and silver, which was about a foot high. The naos was in the holiest place in the temple, a small room in the back, normally surrounded on either side by rooms dedicated to other *neters* and the pharaoh.

Before the ritual began, the chief priest was first purified with water, incense, and natron so he would be befitting to stand in the pharaoh's stead. The ritual then began when the priests arrived at the sanctuary and performed various rituals in front of the shrine, such as burning incense and uttering recitations. The chief priest then broke the seal on the door and drew back the bolt, symbolizing the removal of the fingers of Seth from the eye of Horus, seeing once again how all the symbols of Egypt are connected by their myths.[462] In fact, "each step of the ritual was highly symbolic, referred to mythic events, and was

---

[461]Ibid., 2.

[462]Budge, *Osiris and the Egyptian Resurrection*, Vol. 1, 63.

accompanied by a set liturgy."[463] He then enjoined the *neter* to awake by chanting "Awake in peace! May your awakening be peaceful!"[464] Here again we see, as in the Osiris myth, the emphasis on awakening from sleep, so pertinent to spiritual awakening. Pure white sand was then thrown on the floor symbolizing the first mound of creation, and, after the appropriate recitations, the statue was brought out and placed on the sand. After the statue was cleaned and anointed with oils, its clothing and ornaments were changed, each element having a symbolic meaning. During each ritual act, recitations were performed, such as those corresponding to the adoration of the *neter*, the kissing of the floor before the *neter*, the offering of incense and ointments, the offering of food and drink, the robing of the statue, and the performing of various acts of purification.

Figure 56 Giving offerings of food and drink

One of the food offerings may have been a burnt offering of meat, whether of beef, lamb, or goat. Burnt offerings were often provided to gods in many ancient civilizations. The meaning of this sacrifice (a word having the same root as "sacred"), was not that one sacrificed a belonging to placate the god, but rather that one sacrificed what the offering symbolized, that is, one's animal nature that was purified in the burning of the meat, allowing

---

[463] Teeter, *Religion and Ritual*, 47.

[464] Ibid., 48.

one's divine nature, the sacred, to come forth during the ceremony and partake of the spiritual blessing. See Figure 56.

The end of the ritual took place when the priest put the statue back in its shrine, performed the ultimate purification rituals, closed the door, then bolted and resealed it. Finally, the chief priest took a sort of broom and backed out of the sanctuary, sweeping as he went, perhaps so as not to allow evil to approach the *neter* by following in his footprints.

Festivals

Festivals in ancient Egypt were a time when the distinction between the world of the living and the world of the dead became blurred. Processions took place in which statues of the *neters* were taken out of the temple and presented to the people and offerings were made at the tombs of the dead. On an even deeper level, the purpose of all the festivals that marked the Egyptian year were to associate the populace with the mythical world that gave meaning to their lives. Festivals, like everything in ancient Egypt, were meant to provide people with *meaning* of the sacred, and not simply to give sensual enjoyment.

The Opet Festival

The Opet Festival, or the Beautiful Feast of the Opet, as it is sometimes called, was a major annual festival that took place in the southern Egyptian city of Thebes (now called Luxor). It was no doubt the most important festival of the year, for its purpose was to reconfirm the kingship of the pharaoh.

Evidence of the Opet Festival only starts to appear with the reign of Hatshepsut, the woman pharaoh who reined in the 18th dynasty of the New Kingdom, from 1479 to 1457 BC. Whether there were earlier precedents, we simply do not know, however we do know that the festival lasted even up to Roman times. The main evidence for the festival comes from depictions and texts of the festival on the walls of the temples of Karnak and Luxor.

The festival began in the temple of Karnak on the east bank of the Nile with ritual ceremonies in honor of the statue of the *neter* Amon-Re to whom the temple was dedicated. The construction of this temple complex, the largest in Ancient Egypt, began in the Middle Kingdom and was added to by succeeding pharaohs up into the Ptolemaic period. See Figure 57.

Figure 57 Karnak temple complex

After the initial ceremonies were over, a procession began with the statue, placed in a boat, leaving the main temple carried on the shoulders of priests. Here we see again how the symbolism refers to myth, for the sun crosses the sky and the netherworld also in a boat, thus providing depth of meaning to the participants and onlookers.

The *neter* Amon was first attested to in the Old Kingdom by being mentioned in the *Pyramid Texts* of the Vth dynasty as part of the Ogdoad (eight *neters*) of the city of Hermopolis. Amon was called the "Hidden One." This means that by being "hidden" he is not manifest, but symbolizes the nonmanifest, the unformed, the unseen, the unknowable, from which the other gods, beings, and things are created—while he himself was self-created. According to Christian Jacq: "...existing before all things, he extracted from primordial chaos the unformed forces that were there in an abstract state."[465] Thus Amon is transcendent, but also immanent, continually infusing his force into the world, such as that of the everlasting cycle of the rising and setting sun as Amon-Re. By the 11th dynasty in the Middle Kingdom, Amon had become the chief *neter* of Thebes and eventually became the most important deity of whole country and was known as "king of the gods." Re, the sun *neter*, who was greatly honored in various regions, became assimilated to Amon and the *neter* Amon-Re was formed. However, "Amon-Re is not the synthesis of Amon and Re but a new form that exists along with the two older gods."[466] See Figure 58.

In ancient Egypt, it should thus be noted, *neters* were not supplanted so much as being merged with other *neters* who, by design or by history, had become the main focus of Egyptian theology. For example, both Ptah and Amon were considered as being the First Cause,[467] but both continued to exist, without any apparent inconsistency, a far cry from our modern mentality. As Amon-Min, the *neter* was also associated with the ithyphallic *neter* Min, a *neter* of fertility, who was also known as Kamutef, meaning "the bull of his mother," that is, he created himself from his own mother, symbolizing in this way continuous creation or immortality.[468]

Figure 58
Amon-Re
The fact that Amon-Re of Thebes grew in importance was perhaps because it was the pharaohs of Thebes who

---

[465] Jacq, *La sagesse égyptienne*, 82. [Our translation]

[466] Hornung, *Conceptions of God*, 97.

[467] Frankfort, *Kingship and the Gods*, 160.

[468] Ibid., 180.

succeeded in chasing the foreign Hyksos out of the country, who had previously controlled the northern regions of Egypt. Or it could also be for theological reasons that the priests elevated Amon-Re to the top rung of the deities. Having become the chief *neter* of Thebes, Amon-Re had as his wife Mut, meaning "mother," and their son was Khonsu, associated with the moon, the three together known as the "Theban Triad." Because three sources of energy are necessary for creation to take place, major cult centers had triads of *neters*, normally father, mother, and child: in Memphis it was Ptah, Sekhmet, and Nefertum, and at Abydos it was Osiris, Isis, and Horus

The Opet Festival always took place during the inundation season, when the Nile overflowed its banks and provided the rich silt needed for seeds to germinate and grow the crops needed for nourishing the population. It lasted at first for eleven days, but in later times it went on for 24 or even 27 days. It is not for nothing that it corresponded to the overflowing of the Nile, which was considered as an outflow of the primordial *Nun*, the original watery abyss from which creation arose. Thus, the Nile represented to the Egyptian mind the concept of rejuvenation, of rebirth, for the ultimate meaning of the festival was to renew the force of the pharaoh and as well as the generating force of Amon that needed to be infused with new energy to aid in the maintenance of the land of Egypt and even the entire cosmos. In this era the pharaoh was identified with the 'royal *ka*.' Now the *ka* is one of the constituents of the human being that we dealt with above, but basically, the *ka* arrived with a person at his birth and was considered to be the life force that kept the person alive in this world. The ka, however, was not only personal, but belonged to the higher *ka* that filled the cosmos. So, when the body died, the *ka* did not disappear, but went on to join the higher *ka*. In the same vein, the royal *ka* was the *ka* of all the pharaohs of Egypt from the beginnings lost in history up to the present time and was thus not personal to any particular pharaoh.

It was the purpose of the rituals that took place during the festival to transfer the power of Amon to the royal *ka* so that the present pharaoh would be rejuvenated, reborn and his right to rule confirmed by a re-coronation.[469] This question of being reborn, so essential to Egyptian thought and practice, was also essential to the *Heb-Sed* Festival that we discuss in the following section.

Going back now to the procession, the statue of Amon-Re was carried out of the main temple precinct, along with the royal boat of the pharaoh, and followed a path to the Temple of Khonsu where his statue joined the procession and then to the Temple of Mut to pick up her statue, both being carried in their boats. From there, the procession proceeded to the Luxor temple, either by land, through the colonnade of sphinxes, stopping at shrines along the way, or by boat along the Nile. In either case, the people followed the procession in joy and gaiety.

Arriving at the Luxor temple, the procession continued through the different courtyards; then the boats of Mut and Khonsu were placed in separate rooms, thus allowing only the boats of the pharaoh and Amon-Re to reach the most holy part of the temple in the back. There, the pharaoh, Amon-Re of Karnak, and Amon of Luxor, who, it was believed, had great powers of regeneration, met in various rituals. Upon leaving the temple, the pharaoh was now imbued with the new forces of the royal *ka* and so reconfirmed in his divine kingship, while Amon-Re of Karnak and Amon of Luxor also had their forces regenerated. The procession of the boats then returned by boat to Karnak where the statues were returned to their temples.

The Heb-Sed Festival

The *Heb-Sed* Festival or jubilee (*heb* = festival, *sed* = tail), also known as the Feast of the Tail, is known to have taken place

---

[469] John Watson, "The Beautiful Feast of the Opet – Part I: An Introduction," www.touregypt.net/featurestories/opetfestival1.htm, 1.

since very early times in ancient Egyptian history and included a repetition of the coronation ceremonies.[470] The festival primarily concerns the rejuvenation of the pharaoh after 30 years of reign and every three or four years after that. During the festival, the pharaoh went through various tests to prove that he was still able to rule,[471] such as running a course which in itself had symbolic meanings, such as the small scroll he held in his hand, signifying ownership and which affirms his rulership over the land of Egypt.[472] Certain observers believe that these 'tests' were also initiatory rites that the pharaoh underwent for him to be 'reborn' again in this life.[473]

The various rites that took place during the festival give us more insight into the symbolism of ancient Egyptian civilization and its emphasis on the resurrection of life. The patron of this festival was the creator *neter* Tatenen, who was assimilated to the first mound or the *benben* stone that appeared out of the waters at the First Time.[474] This "First Land" was also known as the Isle of Flame where Re first arose in his scintillating radiance. Another creation story tells of an incredible, luminous bird, the Bennu bird, which lands on the *benben* stone bringing light to the world. Again, here we have different motifs providing essentially the same meaning. Some of the rites were meant to reproduce the death and resurrection of Osiris through the ritual observances of Isis, Anubis, Thoth, and Horus on the body of the pharaoh, who, in effect, *becomes* Osiris in the ancient Egyptian way of thinking.[475] Time, for the Egyptians, was not linear as we would assume, but eternal and cyclical. "Becoming

---

[470] Mayassis, *Mystères et Initiation*, 224.

[471] Noblecourt, *Symboles*, 98-9.

[472] Richard H. Wilkinson, *Symbol and Magic in Egyptian Art* (London: Thames and Hudson, 1994), 171.

[473] Moret, *Mystères Égyptiens*, 97-8.

[474] Schwarz, Égypte: *Les mystères du sacré*, 52.

[475] Mayassis, *Mystères et Initiation*, 68.

Osiris" meant that as Osiris had died and been reborn, so the pharaoh could also, because in both cases this refers to the First Time when creation occurred out of the watery abyss and the first mound appeared. Creation for the Egyptians did not only happen some particular time long ago as did the myth of our 'Big Bang,' but rather the First Time was happening still and always will be happening, however difficult this may be for us to imagine.

Why is the festival called "the Feast of the Tail"? According to Enel[476], after the *Heb-Sed* festival, the pharaoh received a token of his initiation in the form of the tail of a bull or a cow that he wore on his belt. He assumes that it was a token of initiation because images of *neters* also wear this tail. Since the tail is an extension of the spinal column towards the earth, it represents the renewal of life animated by the *ka* which feeds all beings.[477]

The most telling rite of the festival is the one of the pharaoh "Passing through the Skin." But before we try to understand what this may mean, we must have an idea of what a rite actually is. For this, we rely on the work of René Guénon, who says: "Rites are symbols 'put into action', and every ritual act is an 'activated' symbol."[478] He goes on to say that a rite, in its Traditional formulation,

> has as its goal to put the human being in relation…with something that goes beyond his individuality and which belongs to other states of existence."[479] And furthermore, an "initiatory teaching…is but a preparation of the individual to acquire real initiatory knowledge through the effect of his own personal work.....From virtual

[476] Enel (Michel Vladimirovitch Skariatine), *Le Mystère de la Vie et de la Mort: d'après l'enseignement des temples de l'ancienne Égypte* (Paris: Arka Éditions, 2002), 376-77.

[477] R. A. Schwaller de Lubicz, *Le roi de la théocratie pharaonique*, 318 and Isha Schwaller de Lubicz, *Her-Bak, Égyptian Initiate*, 355-56.

[478] Guénon, *Aperçus sur l'Initiation*, 109.

[479] Ibid., 119.

initiation to effective initiation…implies the renouncing of the mental faculty, that is, all discursive faculties which from now on have become powerless.[480] [Our translations].

As to the ritual of Passing through the Skin, according to one observer "these rites were applied to the living as well as to the dead. Those who underwent them while living were the initiates of the Mysteries."[481] Nevertheless, actual proof of this is lacking.

The ritual of Passing through the Skin takes place when the pharaoh curls up like a fetus inside an animal skin in the guise of Osiris being resurrected after death. According to one myth it was Anubis, the jackal *neter* of the embalming ceremony, who gave his own skin to envelop the parts of Osiris that were gathered by Isis after his brother Seth tore him apart and scattered them. It was thus, the myth says, that Osiris was reconstituted through the magic of Anubis[482] and mounts to heaven on a *shedshed*, or the vehicle by which the 'soul' is transported to the afterlife. Whether the animal skin represents the womb, the canine *neters* Anubis or Wepwawet, or mummy wrappings, or more likely all three, the symbolism is one and the same: the great project of Egyptian civilization: *the death and rebirth of life*.

Another ritual during the *Heb-Sed* festival was the "dance" the pharaoh performed called the "dedication of the field."[483] This was not actually a dance, as some interpretations of images would have it, but rather a striding across a temple courtyard by the pharaoh. It is assumed that the courtyard represents the land of Egypt, since the pharaoh went to each of the four directions of space, first wearing the red crown of Lower Egypt, then the

---

[480] Ibid., 208, 213.

[481] Spence, *The Mysteries of Egypt*, 221.

[482] Enel, *Le Mystère de la Vie et de la Mort*, 236.

[483] See Frankfort, *Kingship and the Gods*, 85-87.

white crown of Upper Egypt. By doing so, he dedicated the land to the *neters*. In his hand, he carries a document, a sort of "will" that gives him ownership, the right to rule over the land, that has been handed down from the *neters* to pharaoh after pharaoh.

As for the coronation itself, "The coronation dais on which the throne was placed is always portrayed as stepped, and symbolized both the primordial mound that emerged from the ocean of *Nun* at the beginning of creation and a stairway linking earth and heaven."[484] Since Atum-Re was the first to appear on the primordial mound, the pharaoh thus became the manifestation of the sun *neter* on earth and the *Heb-Sed* Festival the means by which the celestial and terrestrial realms were joined.

---

[484]Naydler, *Shamanic Wisdom*, 87.

Chapter 12 Writing and Speech

By studying one symbol, the Eye, we had to discuss much of Egyptian mythology to even begin to understand its meaning. Now we will see how the Egyptians used their written language and speech to convey the meaning found in their symbolism. Perhaps only one to five percent of ancient Egyptians could read and write the hieroglyphs. When we discuss this topic, we are thus discussing the world of an elite group of priests, scribes, nobles, initiates, and the entourage of the pharaoh.

Hieroglyphs

The ancient Egyptians believed that the hieroglyphs were invented by the neters and were named *medu neter*, the "divine words."[485] They were thought to be at the origin of their civilization. The basis of much of ancient Egyptian imagery is the hieroglyphs writ large. Reliefs and tomb paintings, for instance, are often made up of large hieroglyphic signs, maybe embellished or distorted, but which can still be 'read':

> Individual hieroglyphic signs were thus often the models for parts of or even whole works of art and complex compositions, and the interaction between writing and pictorial representation was an ever present reality.... Thus, it was not coincidental that the Egyptians used the same word to refer to both their hieroglyphic writing and the drawing of their artworks, and it was often the scribe who accomplished—or at least designed—both.... On the primary level the signs are used quite clearly in essentially their normal written forms, and in this kind of primary association artworks may contain or even be wholly composed of hieroglyphs.[486]

---

[485] Wilkinson, *Symbol and* Magic, 149.

[486] Richard H. Wilkinson, *Reading Egyptian Art: A Hieroglyphic Guide to Ancient Egyptian Painting and Sculpture* (London: Thames and Hudson, 1992), 10.

Figure 59 Some Egyptian hieroglyphs

Any object could be used as a hieroglyph, whether a man or a woman, an animal, a plant, a tool, a geographic element, buildings, household furnishings, sacred emblems, etc.

Plotinus wrote: "Each hieroglyph constituted a type of science or wisdom and was represented in a synthetic manner without any discursive conception or analysis."[487] And R. A. Schwaller de Lubicz said: "Every natural thing in the universe is a hieroglyph of divine science,"[488] while his wife Isha added: "Go straight to the natural fact that a symbol exhibits. Then, having closely examined it in all its aspects, you will discern the universal law which the natural fact itself symbolizes."[489] In sum, one should never interpret a hieroglyph only by its phonetic component. See Figure 59.

 In practice, there were no more than around 500 in use before the Ptolemaic Period around 300 BC,[490] when, during this later period, thousands came to be used. It was not everyone who could read and write hieroglyphs. Those who were taught in the House of Life attached to a temple were an elite caste of scribes, officials and priests, who, depending on their aptitude, could also be taught the deeper meaning of the symbolic characters. On a linguistic level, some characters are primarily phonetic used like our alphabet, others phonetic complements that allow

[487] Quoted in Jacq, *La sagesse égyptienne*, 12. [Our translation]

[488] R. A. Schwaller de Lubicz, *Propos sur ésotérisme et symbole*, 22. [Our translation]

[489] Isha Schwaller de Lubicz, *Her-Bak, Egyptian Initiate*, 65-6.

[490] Forman & Quirke, *Hieroglyphs and the Afterlife*, 13.

another hieroglyph to be read in the correct way, others are syllabic corresponding to more than one sound. Other ideograms express a particular thing or idea, and still others, at the end of a word, called determinatives, provide the context for the word, especially useful for homonyms or words pronounced and/or written alike but with different meanings. Each hieroglyph also had a certain color, which had to be considered when 'reading' an image or a text.[491]

For the ancient Egyptians, a word, written with the 'divine' hieroglyphs, had *power*. Naming something gave it existence, gave a thing or a person meaning. By inscribing the name of the deceased on the walls of his tomb was, for example, a way of giving him eternity in the afterlife.[492] To write with hieroglyphic symbols provided not only a means of pronunciation through phonetics like our alphabet, but the images themselves provided a certain magical power if used appropriately in a ritual setting where the hieroglyphic words were pronounced in liturgy and hymns.[493] That is to say, that the *sound* of the hieroglyphs contributed to their power, which is another reason why any translation of the hieroglyphs cannot reproduce the power of the words. As it is said in the *Corpus Hermeticum XVI*: "The very quality of the speech and the (sound) of Egyptian words have in themselves the energy of the objects they speak of."[494]

To go beyond the phonetic aspect of the hieroglyphs and try to understand the deeper meaning embodied in the symbols is to try to decipher a sacred language.[495] As Max Guilmot says:

> Each hieroglyph is a carrier of a meaning that allows us
> to enter into the way of transmutations. The symbolical

---

[491] Ibid., 110.

[492] Tom Hare, *ReMembering Osiris* (Stanford: Stanford University Press, 1999), 95.

[493] Jacq, *La mystère des hiéroglyphes*, 54, 61.

[494] Brian Copenhaver, *Hermetica*, 58.

[495] Ibid., 122.

and initiatory texts of ancient Egypt are the food of consciousness, the accomplished expressions of an eternal present which is that of the sacred.[496]

And Christian Jacq:

Everything has meaning for he who knows how to read and write the divine words. In reading them, he perceives the eternal laws of creation. In writing them, he continues the work of the Creator.[497]

The hieroglyphs can be read on two levels at once: one, phonetically, like with our alphabet; two, symbolically through the images, which add another meaning to the words. One had to understand not simply what the hieroglyphic symbol represented but the essential nature of the symbol as well. A hieroglyph of a hare, for example, not only has the phonetic sound of "oo," but at the same time represents the *idea* or *essence* of a hare. So, the word "oon" (*wn* or *wnn* in transliteration) is written with a hare above one or two zigzag lines that phonetically represent the letter "n" and symbolically the element "water." Now the word *wnn* means to be, to exist, to come into existence. A hare is an animal that is extremely alive, constantly twitching, on the *qui vive*, apart from the fact that it is extremely fecund. So we have a hare then, coming into existence from water, which thus refers the reader, if one is imbued with Egyptian mythology, to the First Time when the world arose from the watery abyss onto a primeval mound, and so 'came into existence.' Another example is the hieroglyphs used for the *neter* of the sun, Re: a mouth and an arm. Phonetically, *r* and *c* (in transliteration), thus giving the sound "Re" or "Ra." As the *neter* of creation, however, the symbolism of mouth and arm is clear: creation (arm) is the result of a command (mouth): sound is life arising from the silence of death

---

[496] Guilmot, *Message Spirituel*, 8. [Our translation]

[497] Jacq, *La mystère des hiéroglyphes*, 34. [Our translation]

but from gestation as well. James P. Allen, author of a highly regarded Ancient Egyptian dictionary, says:

> [H]ieroglyphs have a dual nature: they are images of things in the real world, but they are also representations of ideas. By using the term 'divine speech' to describe the created world, the author of the Memphite Theology implies that everything in creation is itself a kind of hieroglyph of the creator's original concept.... The physical world is thus an 'image' of the original raw material of Atum in the same way that a hieroglyph is an 'image' of a physical thing.[498]

The hieroglyphs remained for the most part unchanged from the beginning to the end of the Egyptian civilization, over 3000 years. They did invent other writing systems: the *hieratic*, which was the hieroglyphs written in a cursive script almost from the beginning, as well as *demotic*, a later type of writing used in the Greco-Roman era for day-to-day needs. The hieroglyphs were kept unchanged, it seems, so that not only would they would be readable over millenniums and thus be immortalized,[499] but also because they were 'divine,' that is, they encapsulated the original creation of things and beings, and so if changed they would disturb *maat*, the natural order of the cosmos. It was said that the hieroglyphs were "all that Ptah created and that Thoth wrote," which is to say that the things created (Ptah is a creator *neter*) and their notation in hieroglyphics (Thoth is the divine scribe) were in perfect correspondence. The hieroglyphics were thus 'divine' in that they were more than mere signs but had the power of providing the essence of the object in question not only through the image but also through sound.[500]

---

[498] James Allen, *Middle Egyptian: An Introduction to the Language and Culture of Hieroglyphs*, 2nd Ed. (Cambridge, UK: Cambridge University Press, 2010), 177.

[499] Assmann, *Images et rites*, 114.

[500] Ibid., 116.

For some Egyptologists all the funerary literature was a response to fear. Henri Frankfort wrote

> The Coffin Texts and the Book of the Dead, the Book of Gates and, in fact, the whole funerary literature of Egypt, is a literature of the fear of death.[501]

Other Egyptologists have a more positive view of Egyptian sacred literature. They saw the use of the hieroglyphs and their recitation during sacred rites by lector priests as being transformative as long as the rites conform to Tradition. For them, the ritual recitation of sacred texts was, in fact, a means by which the acts of the original creation of the First Time were made present. As Jan Assmann says:

> But transformation is effective not only in the words uttered as divine speech. It is the language that creates the relation between the human world where there are priest-readers, the liturgical objects, the offerings, and the divine world where it has to do with conquering death and resuscitating the god.[502]

> In its meaning and its essence, sacred recitation was thus divine speech, cached in the medium of writing and realized in the context of cultic role playing. The priest did not utter it as something of his own, and he did not approach a divine image as a man.[503]

When we read the hieroglyphic texts of liturgical literature, we should assume that the hieroglyphs were chosen for a reason, not only for phonetic reasons, but also for a deeper message that the hieroglyphs as symbols impart:

> The famous collection of texts called 'funerary,' such as the Pyramid Texts, the Coffin Texts, and the Books of the Dead, are not dogmatic compositions but a group of maxims and rites that transmit a practical teaching, that

---

[501] Henri Frankfort, *Ancient Egyptian Religion: An Interpretation.* (Mineola, NY: Dover Publications, 2000), 117.

[502] Assmann, *Images et rites*, 119. [Our translation]

[503] Assmann, *Death and Salvation*, 246.

is, what must be done on earth to correctly prepare oneself for meeting the divine world.[504]

Ancient Egyptian funerary (or mortuary) literature is not meant to be theological or philosophical statements, but practical means to assure an eternal life for the deceased. Assmann makes the distinction between what he calls "mortuary liturgies" and "mortuary literature," the former being texts recited during the mortuary ritual on behalf of the deceased in order to endow him with life, member by member (be "re-membered"), and the latter being texts placed in the tomb to enable him to progress in his journey through the netherworld to finally arrive as a transformed being in the world of light.[505]

Apart from liturgical literature, the ancient Egyptians also wrote other *genres*. Of course, all we know is what has come down to us from temple and tomb inscriptions and the few papyrus scrolls that have been preserved. At the beginning of the dynastic period in the Old Kingdom, the hieroglyphs were used to simply identify persons, places, events, or possessions. As time went on, offering lists of food, drink, fabrics and ointments were carved on the walls of private tombs to eventually become a standard *Prayer for Offerings* for people to offer items to the deceased so he would be provisioned in the afterlife. From the beginning, therefore, writing was in the service of liturgical rituals. Alongside this, the *Autobiography* developed, also written on the walls of the tomb. Its basic purpose was not so much to delineate the deceased's life, as to show his worth, be justified before the *neters* and so be admitted to the divine realm. Also created in the Old Kingdom was the genre of *Instructions in Wisdom*, always written in the name of a sage, widely known

---

[504] Jacq, *La Sagesse Égyptienne*, 158. [Our translation]

[505] Assmann, *Death and Salvation*, 238.

for his wisdom. Here was given advice on how to comport oneself to have a fruitful and happy life.[506]

During the First Intermediate Period, when the society of the Old Kingdom broke down, the stela developed and continued thereafter. This contained both the *Offering Prayer* and the *Autobiography* and was placed before the tomb of the deceased. In the Middle Kingdom another genre developed: the tale. These tales, such as the *Eloquent Peasant* and the *Story of Sinuhe* always had an allegorical message. They were written in a very direct style without extraneous description.[507]

Mortuary Texts[508]

We group together the *Pyramid Texts, Coffin Texts,* and *Book of the Dead* because they follow one another in time as documents accompanying the deceased in his tomb as he journeys through the netherworld. The *Book of the Dead*, or as the Egyptians called it, *Coming Forth by Day*, was a collection of spells and vignettes drawn on Papyrus and put in the deceased's coffin to enable him to leave the underworld and arrive in the light of day in the world above and return to the mummy at night. These *Books of the Dead* were the latest collection of these spells that had their origin in the *Pyramid Texts* of the Old Kingdom 5th and 6th Dynasties, where they were carved on the walls of the pyramid-tombs of the pharaohs in order to aid them in overcoming obstacles and arrive in the afterlife after the death of their physical body. In the middle kingdom similar spells were written in and on the coffins of those who could afford it, and illustrations, or vignettes, were added to the texts. In the

---

[506] Miriam Lichtheim, *Ancient Egyptian Literature: A Book of Readings*, Vols. I-III: The Old and Middle Kingdoms (Berkeley: University of California Press, 1975-1980), 3-5.

[507] Ibid., 9-11.

[508] For an overview of afterlife books, see Erik Hornung, *The Ancient Egyptian Books of the Afterlife* (Ithica: Cornell University Press, 1999).

New Kingdom, such spells were written on papyrus, again with vignettes, and placed in the coffin of the deceased. Their main purpose was to help the deceased "pass through the dangers of the netherworld and attain the afterlife in the Field of Reeds,"[509] an Egyptian symbolic spiritual locality in which a higher state can be attained. All these 'books' have to do with "transfiguration or being transformed into a blessed spirit of light."[510] While these 'books' are seemingly for the purpose of aiding the deceased in his road to illumination in the afterlife, it could very well be that these 'books' were essentially used in Initiation rituals where their esoteric meanings were discovered. Throughout these texts, the deceased is incited to get up, raise himself, awaken, in other words, to come out of his passive state of sleep, of unconsciousness, to become alive once again. Whether this refers to the dead as mortuary texts or to the living as initiation texts makes no difference, for it depends on the listener or the reader to understand this symbolism on the level on which he finds himself:

> Thus the purpose of initiatory texts is far less a logical one than it is to provoke shocks, emotional reactions, or to grate against the cerebral need for sequential logic. Paradox, improbable images, the juxtaposition of unconnected phrases are freely employed. The texts appeal to sensation, to a feeling of emotive sensitivity.[511]

Pyramid Texts

The *Pyramid Texts* are the oldest extant religious literature in the world and were first discovered in the pyramid of Unas in 1881 by Gaston Maspero. They are hieroglyphic texts engraved inside the pyramids at Saqqara, the necropolis of Memphis, the Old

---

[509] R.O. Faulkner (Tr.), *The Ancient Egyptian Book of the Dead* (New York: Macmillan, 1985), 11.

[510] Forman & Quirke, *Hieroglyphs and the Afterlife*, 156.

[511] R. A. Schwaller de Lubicz, *Esoterism and Symbol* (Rochester VT: Inner Traditions International, 1985), 58.

Kingdom capital. The pyramids are the tombs of 5th, 6th, and 8th dynasty Old Kingdom pharaohs (2520-2195 BC) as well as those of some of their queens. The carved *Pyramid Texts* began with the pharaoh Unas, the last pharaoh of the Fifth Dynasty (c. 2350 BC), but they are thought to have existed orally much before that time and some of the texts were still being used in

Late Period tombs and coffins (664-332 BC). See Figure 60.

Using various mythological texts, the purpose was to assure the resurrection of the deceased pharaoh or his queen and their uniting with the *neter* Re, all the while ascending to become one of the circumpolar stars as a *neter* themselves.

Figure 60 Burial chamber of the pyramid of Unas

As previously mentioned, the circumpolar stars are those that never go below the horizon and are always present in the sky, which is to say that the pharaoh or his queen would become immortal.

These texts and their successors the *Coffin Texts* and the *Book of the Dead* are not at all easily understood. Being totally symbolic, they make references to various divinities, creatures, and things whose meanings have been lost over time. We are therefore unable to translate much of the texts beyond their literal or phonetic meaning. Nevertheless, this warning should be kept in mind:

> To understand the religious texts, they must be experienced, their correct interpretation only being possible starting from a spiritual orientation of thought. It follows that the translation—grammatically—of a religious document will have no resonance if the mental communion is missing from the interpreter.[512]

Scholars do not agree on the sequence that the texts should be read in the pyramids, some saying the beginning is in the sarcophagus chamber and others in the antechamber, or the corridor.[513] Some call the different texts "spells" while others call them "utterances." I would prefer to simply call them "texts," which is the most neutral of terms, since the contents of the different texts have different purposes: some provide information for the deceased to navigate the netherworld and counter dangers on his way to immortality, others are specifically meant to prevent certain beings from obstructing the deceased's journey, while still others glorify the deceased's efforts to join the creator god Re or the ruler of the dead, that is, Osiris. It is obvious that some of the texts were taken from rituals, but given how they are placed in the pyramid, it is clear they do not represent one continuous ritual since different texts have different contents. An earlier observer sees six different contents: funerary rituals, magical charms, a very ancient worship ritual, ancient religious hymns, fragments of old myths, and prayers and petitions on behalf of the dead king.[514] James P. Allen divides up the texts into three categories: offering texts in the burial chamber recited upon the presentation of various offerings to the deceased, the resurrection ritual in the burial chamber intended to release the *ba* from the mummy, and other texts in the antechamber and corridor spoken by the deceased's *ba* as it traverses the *Dwat* at night toward its resurrection at

---

[512] Guilmot, *Message spirituel*, 21.

[513] Hornung, *Ancient Egyptian Books*, 4.

[514] Breasted, *Development of Religion and Thought*, 93.

dawn.[515] It is in the *Pyramid Texts* that is found the first real proof of the existence of Osiris in Egyptian civilization. Naydler proposes that these texts, while used in a funerary context, are also "mystical" texts used in spiritual transformative rituals for the living.[516]

There are 759 different texts in the compilation of Raymond O. Faulkner published in 1969 and which include all the pyramids where hieroglyphs were found at that time. The texts in the first pyramid where they are found, that of Unas, number 227 or 228. The exact number overall is difficult to say since duplicates are present here and there. The number associated with a text does not indicate a sequence but only identifies the text. Also, the numbering takes into account the texts from all the pyramids without any indication as to which pyramid it belongs. The pyramids in which the texts have been found are those of the pharaoh Unas of the 5th Dynasty, the pharaohs Titi, Pepi I, and Pepi II of the 6th Dynasty, the six queens of Pepi I and II, and the 8th Dynasty pharaoh Ibi.

Maspero published his translations in French in 1894 from previous articles beginning in 1882 of the texts that were then known. The Egyptologist Kurt Sethe gave the original numbers to the texts in his translation in German of 1910 and which have been kept since, with certain changes and additions. Since the translation of Sethe, translations in English have been made by Samuel Mercer (1952), Raymond O. Faulkner (1969), and James P. Allen (2005). French, translations were made by Louis Speleers (1923) and Claude Carrier (2009-2010). The pyramid of Unas alone has been translated in English by Alexandre Piankoff (1969) and in French by Raphaël Bertrand (2012).

---

[515] Allen, *Middle Egyptian*, 321-22.
[516] Naydler, *Shamanic Wisdom*, 8.

Because of advances in the knowledge of the grammar and vocabulary of ancient Egyptian hieroglyphic texts, the later versions are no doubt more accurate phonetically, but because the texts are not always clear grammatically, one must also take into account the translator's understanding of the meaning behind the hieroglyphs when reading their translations, since various interpretations are possible.

It seems clear that the texts were much older before they were inscribed in the pyramid of Unas, since the architecture of the chambers which the texts reflect came into use in the 4th Dynasty, at least a hundred years before Unas. Also, some of the texts refer to burial practices even much older than that.[517]

Ritual texts form a great part of the *Pyramid Texts* and were no doubt spoken by a lector priest during the funeral. To ensure their effectiveness over time they were inscribed on the interior pyramid walls. Different rituals can be discerned from the texts. There was the Offering Ritual recited over the presentation of the offerings of food and drink to the deceased and included Purification and Opening of the Mouth rituals. There was also the Insignia ritual in which items of dress and sacred paraphernalia were offered to a statue of the deceased and presented to the *neters*. The offerings in the Offering ritual are each called the "Eye of Horus," which refers to the battle between Osiris and his brother Seth in which the eye of Horus was torn out by Seth and later restored. "The Eye of Horus" thus refers to the restoration of the deceased to a complete life in the hereafter. The Resurrection ritual was another ritual whose texts were inscribed on the walls of the pyramids. Its purpose was to enable the deceased's *ba* to leave his body and rise to join the *neters* in the sky. Apart from these ritual texts, there exist texts that were meant to help the deceased on his journey by giving

---

[517] James Allen, *The Ancient Egyptian Pyramid Texts*, 2nd ed. (Atlanta: SBL Press, 2015), 4.

him necessary information on finding his way or by opposing anything that could harm him on his journey.[518]

In general, the main purpose of the *Pyramid Texts* was to make effective the transformation of the deceased into an illuminated immortal being, an *akh*. For this to take place the *ba*, that is, the individuality of the deceased had to reunite with his *ka*, or life force, which had left the body upon his physical death. This symbolically corresponds to the sun *neter* Re who is born each morning in the East and dies each evening in the West. During his night journey in the *Dwat* or netherworld, Re embraces Osiris who is the *neter* of rejuvenation. Through this symbolic embrace Re is given new life so as to reappear the next day in the east while Osiris is reborn in Re.[519] On a macrocosmic level, this symbolic act allows the cosmos to continue to function; Osiris becomes Re and Re becomes Osiris, which is equivalent to the *ba* and *ka* joining in a mystical embrace creating an *akh*. This is the most vital element of Egyptian symbolism, for this fusion of energies is what each person is capable of in his or her life and is the ultimate meaning of the teaching of Egyptian civilization. Compared to being an *akh*, an illuminated spirit, man is 'dead' while his body lives, for he is cut off from those universal energies that could infuse his mind and body if only his ego would relent and allow the fusion to take place.

Another embrace, this time of Osiris and Horus, parallels that of Re and Osiris on a lower level of existence but encompasses the same symbolism. The embrace of Re and Osiris entails the functioning of the cosmos, while the embrace of Osiris and Horus entails the functioning of Egypt. Osiris, the passive spirit of gestation in the *Dwat*, the land of the dead, needs the active force of Horus to awaken him from unconsciousness and produce life. Likewise, Horus without Osiris would be a pharaoh

---

[518] Ibid., 6-7.
[519] Ibid., 8.

in name only, for his commands would be without effect in a land that was sterile. In Egyptian mythology, pharaoh is assimilated to Horus, he who ruled Egypt at the beginning as Horus the Elder. During the coronation ceremony, and perhaps during the pharaoh's rejuvenation during the *Heb-Sed* Festival, there took place the ritual of the embrace of Osiris with the new Horus-pharaoh. During the ritual, the *qeni* garment was placed on the pharaoh symbolizing Osiris's embrace. This ritual is presented in the *Pyramid Texts*, text 368:

> O Osiris the King, this is Horus in your embrace, and he protects you; it is well with him again with you in your name of 'Horizon from which Re goes forth'.[520]

The fusion of Osiris and Horus, with Horus ostensibly protecting Osiris, allows the pharaoh to be rejuvenated in the "Horizon," or place of transformation, where the sun is reborn every day and which the rebirth of Osiris represents. Now the pharaoh, as True Man, symbolizes the spiritual possibility of every human being and this "embrace" is therefore possible for all.

The texts were not placed haphazardly on the walls of the pyramid but were associated with the different rooms in which they were carved. To understand the texts, therefore, it is necessary to also understand the layout of the rooms and what they symbolize. The layout of the rooms of all the pyramids of the pharaohs that contain texts is basically the same. However, the same texts in different pyramids are not always found in the same place.

Like the pyramids of Giza, the approach to the pyramids begins at the edge of a canal connected to the Nile and where it could be surmised that the first Purification and Embalming rituals of the deceased pharaoh took place. A covered causeway then led to the temple alongside the pyramid through which one had to

---

[520]Faulkner (Tr.), *Pyramid Texts*, 121.

go to enter the pyramid. The causeway was covered with reliefs of daily life on the walls and the ceiling with gold stars on a blue background. The causeway could thus represent the level of the Earth before the pharaoh was to be reborn as an *akh* in the temple rituals in front of the pyramid or in the pyramid itself. We really do not know what rituals might have been performed in the pyramid temple or in the pyramid itself, since there is no hard evidence and different scholars have proposed different theories. We do know that at least some of the reliefs in the temple had to do with the pharaoh's *Heb-Sed* Festival whose purpose was to rejuvenate the pharaoh. During this festival it seems that the pharaoh took part in various Initiation rituals and some of the *Pyramid Texts* might very well refer to these:

> The main point is that the Pyramid Texts should be read as referring primarily to rituals of the living king and the inner experiences undergone by him during these rituals.[521]

The entrance to the pyramid proper of Unas (or the exit of the transfigured pharaoh) led to a descending passage, then to a small room (the 'vestibule') and finally a horizontal corridor divided by portcullises which seal the pyramid from intruders. It is only after the portcullises that the texts begin. The corridor leads to what is called the 'antechamber.' To the left of the antechamber is the *serdab* ("cellar" in Arabic) having three large niches but without any texts. The purpose of this room is unknown though some have suggested that statues of *neters* were placed there, which seems quite plausible given the niches. James P. Allen proposes that the *serdab*, being at the easternmost point of the structure "represented the eastern limit of the *Akhet*, the point at which the Sun, and the deceased's spirit, left the womb of the *Dwat* to proceed into Nut's birth

---

[521]Naydler, *Shamanic Wisdom*, 122.

canal."[522] Nut, of course, is the *neter* of the sky. To the right of the antechamber is the burial chamber in which the sarcophagus of the pharaoh lies towards the far wall, the sarcophagus representing the place where the transition is made between the physical and spiritual worlds.

Nevertheless, there is no real consensus among Egyptologists as to what the rooms represent or the relation of the texts to the rooms in which the texts are found.[523] Some scholars assume that the texts follow a Mortuary ritual that took place either in the temple or in the pyramid itself, though there is no evidence that any Mortuary ritual actually took place in either. Given this assumption, the texts are thus to be read in the order of the ritual. Naydler, in his book *Shamanic Wisdom in the Pyramid Texts*, does a good job of debunking this theory. Others see the texts as showing the rebirth of the pharaoh and his journey in the afterlife to arrive as a transfigured being in the form of an immortal star. Here, according to Allen, the texts are to be read in a sequence corresponding to the meaning of the rooms, where the burial chamber is the *Dwat*, in which Re unites with Osiris to rise again in the *Akhet,* the Eastern horizon, corresponding to the antechamber.[524] Alexandre Piankoff supposes that the texts are to read in the opposite direction, that is, the texts begin in the corridor where the pharaoh arises from the *Nun*, the primeval waters, ascends to the sky in the antechamber, and is received by Atum-Re in the burial chamber as a divinized being.[525] For Nicolas Grimal, the entrance hall corresponds to the valley temple, the corridor to the causeway, the antechamber to the mortuary temple, and the burial chamber to the inner sanctum or naos. The *serdab* would contain statues of the pharaoh as being

---

[522] Allen, *Pyramid Texts*, 12.

[523] Naydler, *Shamanic Wisdom*, 171-185.

[524] Allen, *Pyramid Texts*, 10-11.

[525] Naydler, *Shamanic Wisdom*, 182-83.

both in the pyramid and the mortuary temple. For Grimal, therefore, the texts should be read in both directions: from the entrance to the burial chamber, going from life to death, and from the burial chamber to the entrance, resulting in his resurrection. For the latter, in leaving the burial chamber, he leaves the *Dwat*, the netherworld, for the antechamber, *Akhet*, the horizon, where he becomes assimilated to Atum, the creator *neter*. From there he climbs through the corridor and the portcullises, or gates of heaven, to find immortality as the sun or a circumpolar star.[526] Of course, none of this was meant to be taken literally, but as the symbolic journey of man to illumination.

Naydler refuses all of these theories and asks us to allow the texts to speak for themselves according to the "existential situations they describe."[527] For him, these texts can be read not only as descriptions of external events, but also as interior experiences of inner transformation. This interpretation thus suggests that each text is complete in itself and should be read as such. In general, the texts were of a type called *sakhu* in ancient Egyptian, which translates as "recitations for making an *akh*," that is, making a transfigured spirit. For Jan Assmann, the texts in the burial chamber are recitations made by the priest for the deceased, while those in the antechamber and the corridor are words of the deceased addressing the gods.[528]

It seems quite clear that nothing is done haphazardly in the creation of ancient Egyptian monuments. If the rooms of a temple or pyramid are laid out in a certain way, there is a symbolic signification to it, which is not to say that every temple or pyramid is an exact copy of every other. On the contrary, the

[526] Nicolas Grimal, *A History of Ancient Egypt* (Oxford, UK: Blackwell, 1992), 127-28.
[527] Ibid., 185.
[528] Assmann, *Death and Salvation*, 241.

Egyptians never slavishly followed rigid rules but allowed for fluidity and change within a general form. If the *Pyramid Texts* are not all placed in exactly the same position within each pyramid, this is how the living world acts as well: for any species of tree, you will never find all the branches in exactly the same place while the overall form of the species is readily identifiable.

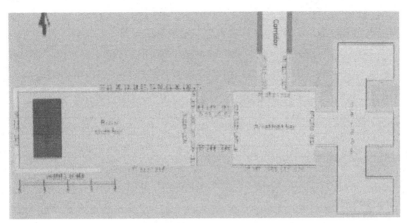

Figure 61 The floor plan of the pyramid of Unas

The two main rooms then, the antechamber and the burial chamber, must be looked at symbolically. See Figure 61.

The burial chamber, where the sarcophagus lies, can be assimilated to the *Dwat*, the realm of the dead and of Osiris. The antechamber can be assimilated to the *Akhet*, the Eastern horizon, the place of transformation from death to life, just as the sun, or Re, rises above the horizon in the East. If in fact this is the case, then the texts would be read from the burial chamber, through the antechamber, then to the corridor where the pharaoh begins his journey to the stars.

While this correspondence between the texts and the rooms is not always clear given the enigmatic nature of the texts, an argument can be made for it. If in fact the symbolism we have just proposed has meaning, we should then be able to see the same plan in tombs in later epochs. Since the symbolism refers to certain spiritual truths there would be no reason to change the layout of tombs throughout the Egyptian civilization. Now the reign of Unas was from 2375 B.C. to 2345 B.C., and if we look at the layout of the tomb of the queen Nefertari in the Valley of the Queens that was built in the 19th Dynasty (1289 B.C.-1189 B.C.) of the New Kingdom, we find the same essential two-room plan around a thousand years later: a descent into the tomb leading to a chamber and then, after another descent, into the burial chamber.[529] There are other niches and smaller rooms in the tomb of Nefertari, but the essential form is the same. Furthermore, if we look at the tombs in the Valley of the Kings, also in the New Kingdom, while more complex than that of Nefertari, the same basic plan unfolds. There may be other rooms, well shafts, etc., but there is always an antechamber and a burial chamber.

There are those that call ancient Egyptian civilization "conservative" because the *neters* and their temples did not fundamentally change over thousands of years. When people say this, it is an implied criticism, as if only change and what we would call "progress" is the natural and correct way for societies to evolve. However, the Egyptian vision had nothing to do with "progress"; their goal was to symbolize in stone what they saw as an unchanging truth based on the movements of the heavens, the flooding of the Nile, and other natural events, all symbolizing man's possibility of becoming an illuminated spirit, not only in the afterlife but also in his life on earth.

To summarize, after the deceased was laid in his sarcophagus in the realm of Osiris, he began his regeneration by entering each night the womb of Nut, the *neter* of the sky. His *ba*, his non-physical individuality, separated from the body and made its way as an Osiris from the burial chamber to his *ka*, or the life force that kept him living until his physical death. His individual

---

[529] François Tonic, *La Tombe de Néfertari* (Pointoise, France: Les éditions Nefer-IT, 2018), *passim*.

ka had joined that universal creator *ka* that reigned in the universe and could be assimilated to Re, who in his night journey met the Osiris of the deceased in the *Akhet* or antechamber. Here he embraced the Osiris of the deceased and imbued it with the illuminating light that made him an *akh* or transfigured spirit. As such, he could go into the corridor which led to the exit and, "coming forth by day," to follow his path to the stars. Meanwhile Re, rejuvenated by Osiris, could then rise again at the Eastern horizon taking part in the original creation of the First Time. We can see that this myth is a symbolic way of describing man's inner spiritual journey to enlightenment. The *ba*, in leaving the body is man's becoming detached from his mental, emotional, and bodily processes, from his ego. He then becomes free, to be open to the higher energies that pervade the universe, the universal *ka*, and thus able to join with them as does Osiris with Re. Every evening the *ba* must return to the tomb to be rejuvenated, symbolizing what every man does in his nightly sleep and the liberated man in his daily meditation.

Coffin Texts

The *Coffin Texts* are images and hieroglyphic texts drawn inside the coffins of nobles during mostly the Middle Kingdom (1987-1640 BC). These included mythological dramas, creation myths, theological assertions, and magical spells. They were often derived from and had the same purpose as the *Pyramid Texts*, to help the deceased on his path to salvation, but now were not reserved only for the pharaoh.

The emphasis was different than The *Pyramid Texts*, which were mostly concerned with the celestial realm of sun and stars to which the transfigured pharaoh was to attain. The *Coffin Texts*, on the other hand, dealt mostly with the obstacles and demons of the netherworld through which the deceased had to find his way in order to reach the ruler of the dead, Osiris. Some texts speak, for example, of not eating excrement or not walking upside down, of not rotting, of recovering power over the heart and head and all the limbs, of opening the ways to the netherworld and the sky. See Figure 62.

One of the passages in the *Coffin Texts* is *Book of Two Ways*, which describes in images a sort of 'map' of the netherworld with paths and waterways by which one could traverse the netherworld. For example, the "winding waterway" divided the sky into northern and southern parts where there were the Field of Offerings and the Field of Reeds, respectively.

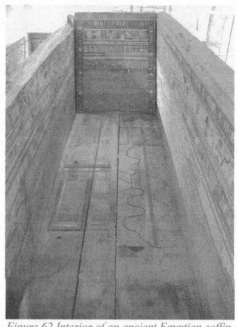

Figure 62 Interior of an ancient Egyptian coffin

There is, however, nothing sequential or clear about where the roads lead. Some texts speak of the realm of Osiris, others to the Eastern horizon of the rising sun, or still others to the place of *maat* or of paradise in the Field of Reeds. It would be useless to try and understand these 'places' in literal terms: the Egyptians always used different symbolic ways of explaining the same spiritual truths, truths whose symbolism has been lost over the millennia. Some texts in the *Book of Two Ways* are very telling, for example in Text 1108 we read "I know how to ferry He-Made-Himself across to the other side,"[530] intimating that to reach the shores of illumination one must work on oneself to this end. And Text 96 states "It is Re who creates me; it is I who create the soul of Re,"[531] thus showing how the individual in his

---

[530] Piankoff, *The Wandering of the Soul*, 30.
[531] Ibid., 37.

spiritual becoming returns the energy of his *ka* to its source in Re by fusioning with the universal *ka*. The Egyptologist Paul Barguet has this to say about this 'book':

> From a deep study of this book, a certainty emerges: it is truly an initiatory text; only he who has the right knowledge can overcome all obstacles and finally attain to a sort of seventh heaven, endowed with the radiance of the supreme god.[532]

Furthermore, he explains main episodes of the journey: one enters into the radiance of the sun at dawn in the East, takes the journey along the two ways, arrives at Rosetau (the necropolis), descends into the netherworld, travels across the domain of the night, crosses through doors, and arrives in the West where the blessed dead reign. He equates each of these steps to parts of the Egyptian temple, from the entryway to the Holy of Holies in the rear.[533]

Book of the Dead

Beginning in the New Kingdom and continuing into the Late Period, papyrus scrolls of images and hieroglyphic texts that modern Egyptologists called the *Book of the Dead* (according to the Egyptians, *Going Forth by Day*) were placed in the coffins of the deceased for anyone who could afford it.

"Going forth by day" because at night the *ba* of the deceased came back to the tomb in the netherworld, but in the day his *ba* would come out from the realm of the dead into the light, first and foremost to receive offerings. The papyrus texts were put in his tomb to help his *ba* make this transformative movement between the two worlds. These carried on the same purpose as the *Pyramid* and *Coffin Texts* such that some texts in the *Book*

---

[532] Paul Barguet, *Aspects de la pensée religieuse de l'Égypte ancienne* (Fuveau: Éditions La Maison de Vie, 2001), 21. [Our translation].

[533] Ibid., 23-24.

of the Dead and the *Pyramid Texts* were practically the same even though they were written two thousand years apart:

> In the Theban version [of the Book of the Dead] the main principles of the Egyptian religion which were held in the times when the pyramid texts were written are maintained, and the views concerning the eternal existence of the soul remain unaltered.[534]

Even before the *Pyramid Texts*, the texts in the *Book of the Dead* may, according to Budge, come even before the historical dynasties of ancient Egypt.[535] If there is a difference in emphasis between the *Pyramid Texts* and the *Book of the Dead*, it could be said that the *Book of the Dead* is more concerned with the journey to Paradise, the world of light, by overcoming the many obstacles on the way. These were, for example, having to answer questions by guardians of the gates, caverns, boats, etc., as to the names of what they are about to enter. Now to know the name of something for the ancient Egyptians was to understand its essential nature and to have power over it. It is only by knowing these names, then, that one has arrived at a certain stage of consciousness that allows the traveler to go further, to have the knowledge necessary for his *ba* to leave his body and travel to the celestial realms.[536] The *Pyramid Texts* are more focused on protecting the body of the deceased, restoring his functions after death, and showing the means for becoming a circumpolar star that never sets. The journey itself is not so much emphasized. Thus, one purpose of the *Book of the Dead* is to give the deceased the knowledge necessary for his *ba* to leave his body and travel to the celestial realms.

The two most important texts of the *Book of the Dead* are numbers 17 and 125. Text number 17 is quite long and begins

---

[534] Budge, *Book of the Dead*, xxxi.

[535] Ibid., xiii.

[536] Jacq, *La mystère des hiéroglyphes*, 82.

with a description of the act of creation, referring to the *neters* Atum and Re. It goes on reciting parts of the myth of Osiris and Horus, and brings in many other *neters*, all of which to bring benefit to the deceased. There are many asides such as "Who is he?," "What does this mean?," etc., whose answers are just as obscure as the text before it. In fact, there is no simple narrative to these texts, rather symbolic statements, one after another, that only one imbued with the meaning of the *neters* in the Egyptian pantheon could understand.

Text number 125 has to do with the judgement of the deceased before Osiris, where his heart is weighed against the feather of Maat or Truth. It contains the 42 sins that the deceased has not committed, which are pronounced before 42 *neters*, the witnesses. This text also contains the questions that the deceased must answer in order to approach Osiris, as well as the answers. For example:

> What is your name?
> I am the lower part of the papyrus-plant; "He who is on his moringa-tree" is my name.
> What did you find on it, the riverbank of Maat?
> It was a staff of flint called "Giver of Breath."

See Figure 63.

Figure 63 "The Weighing of the Heart" in the Book of the Dead

One can see that a profound knowledge of Egyptian symbolism would be necessary to understand the meaning that is being conveyed. No matter how much we study, however, we may never understand what is essentially a symbolic language that will forever remain indecipherable to us.

Other Books of the Afterlife

In the New Kingdom, various images and texts, or 'books,' were inscribed on the walls of the pharaohs' tombs in the Valley of the Kings in what was then Thebes but now called Luxor. They were composed of vivid symbolic images and hieroglyphs. They have been named the "books of the netherworld" or "books of the afterlife." Here is a list of the major ones:

- *The Amduat* or *That which is in the Netherworld* (The Egyptians called it *The Book of the Secret Chamber*)
- *The Book of Gates*
- *The Book of Caverns*
- *The Book of the Earth*
- *The Book of the Day*
- *The Book of the Night*
- *The Book of the Heavenly Cow*
- *The Litany of Re*

As to what these 'books' refer to, let us cite Alexandre Piankoff:

> No people of the ancient world glorified death to such an extent as the Egyptians. Life, as understood by them, was the glorious life after death. The coffin was the Lord of Life. The West, where the sun god disappeared in his descent below the horizon, was the Region of Life: the place of death to be passed through to achieve resurrection. Life and death, like day and night, were equally transitory, and as life ended in death, so death led to new life.[537]

---

[537] Alexandre Piankoff, *The Tomb of Ramesses VI. Egyptian Texts and Representations*, Bollingen Series XL, Vol. 1. (Princeton: Princeton University Press, 1954), 3.

Like most Egyptologists, Piankoff only interprets these books as to what the Egyptians surmised must take place after physical death. He does not consider them to be an esoteric guide for dying to a life based on the impulses of the ego, to be reborn on another plane of existence while still physically alive.

As for the book *That which is in the Netherworld,* it deals with the voyage of the divine boat through the central river in the netherworld during the twelve hours of the night. For each hour, there is a name, a guide, a guardian, and a gate, of which the traveler must know the names in order to continue his journey, that one must understand one's interior life in order to follow his Way to rebirth and illumination. See Figure 64.

Figure 64 The 12th hour of the Amduat in the tomb of Amenhotep II

The main figure in the boat is the sun *neter* Re, a ram-headed figure having horizontal horns surmounted by a sun disk, and whose name is 'flesh.' Why 'flesh'? Lucie Lamy proposes that "we are dealing here with the incarnation—the becoming flesh—of the divine principle of light."[538] For the first six descending hours he stands in a naos. In the first four ascending hours he stands within the coils of the serpent Mehen (see above) to be resurrected. In the eleventh hour the Mehen snake pulls the

---

[538] Lucie Lamy, *Egyptian Mysteries: New Light on Ancient Knowledge* (London: Thames & Hudson, 1981), 30.

boat to the Eastern gate of the sky; in the twelfth hour the *neter*, according to Lamy, enters into another huge serpent and becomes reincarnated as Khepri, represented as the scarab beetle, born each morning in the Eastern horizon:

> This god travels like this in this city along the backbone of this hidden image of the serpent, Life of the Gods. His gods tow him while he enters into its tail and comes out of its mouth, being born, in his forms of Khepri of the gods who are in his barge, when he rests above the image of Shu who separates the sky from the earth of complete darkness.[539]

Another quote from *That which is in the Netherworld* can be read on different levels. The "Great God" says:

> You are those who fight for my limbs, who protect me against Apopis. Life comes to you through my soul, you breathe through my body. May you remain in your holy places; it is decreed that you remain therein. I am here by day while those who follow me are in the Netherworld. I pass through the night and expel darkness.[540]

Likewise, from the *Book of Caverns* the "Great God" says:

> Behold, I light you, your faces are turned toward me, my face being turned towards you. I am he who protects his soul and who speaks to his body, a god great in the caverns of the Netherworld.[541]

And from the *Book of Gates* a netherworld *neter* says:

> Those who are stretched out on their sides, who repose in their place of rest, take up your flesh, collect your bones for yourselves, join your members for yourselves, put together your members for yourselves. (May) sweet winds be for your nostrils, looseness be for your swathings, removal for your kerchiefs! May light be for your divine eyes so that by them you may see the rays.

[539] Piankoff, *Tomb of Ramesses VI*, 314. [Translated by Piankoff]
[540] Ibid., 246. [Translated by Piankoff]
[541] Ibid., 57. [Translated by Piankoff]

From these quotes it seems evident that texts on the walls of tombs cannot be read literally as help for the dead pharaoh to pass into the next life. The "Great God," by using the plural, is not speaking only to the dead pharaoh; these texts thus need interpretation according to an understanding of spiritual things.

Most of the other books deal with the journey of the sun *neter* through the heavens or the netherworld, emphasizing the obstacles and rewards of the journey. *The Litany of Re,* on the other hand is a paean to the *neter* Re and pharaoh's union with him and other *neters*:

> One text comprises a Litany of Ra in which the sun-god is identified and worshipped as seventy-five forms, some with obscure names but others as familiar as Horus and even goddesses such as Isis.... Here we encounter the single thread underlying all religious thought In Egypt, a belief in a single creation unravelled through a myriad single features but present in all of them. The sun-god unfurls himself into every feature of creation, but remains its visible source of energy, of heat and light, distinct and aloof from the level of the rest of existence.[542]

Many of the books of the afterlife deal with passing through gates, mounds, or caverns. These are not meant to be actual physical places but represent obstacles that must be passed through to become an *akh*, an enlightened being. The deceased must also know the names of these places and their guardians, since to know the name of something is to have control over it. Nevertheless, the images and names are very difficult, if not impossible, to interpret, as they are made up of symbols of which we have lost the keys.

---

[542]Forman & Quirke, *Hieroglyphs and the Afterlife*, 117.

Chapter 13 Imagery and Sculpture

There is no such thing as "art" in ancient Egypt as we use the word in our time. Nothing was created to be beautiful, to be decorative, to enhance the reputation of the painter or sculptor. Images painted on temple walls or in tombs, statues of pharaohs or eminent men, were created to give a message, and not any message, but always of a symbolic nature representing one aspect or another of the eternal nature of the universe and man's possible transformation towards higher consciousness. As for us:

> By taking each visual form as a metaphor to decode, we may come closer to the aims of the composer.[543]

Moreover, the image or statue, due to the rituals by which it was dedicated, was infused with the spiritual energy of the objects or beings represented. An image of a food offering was no different than an actual food offering since both were infused with the spiritual energy to be given to the *neter* who was to receive the offering. True reality lies on the spiritual plane.[544]

> One principle reigned supreme: a depiction was not a depiction of a body, it was itself a body. This was true not only for statues of the dead in their tombs but also for those of gods in their temples.[545]

Images and statues were not created according to the executor's own predilections but followed hoary traditions of how things and beings are to be depicted according to a time-worn tradition. It was the priests who decided on the content of the image, not the executor of it. If an executor was judged good, it was not

---

[543] Stephen Quirke, *Exploring Religion in Ancient Egypt* (Chichester, UK: John Wiley & Sons, 2015), 32-3.

[544] Naydler, *Temple of the Cosmos*, 136-38.

[545] Assmann, *Death and Salvation*, 106.

because he was original, but because he came as close as possible to the traditional form using the best craftsmanship he could muster.[546] An image, therefore, should not be looked at separately as 'a work of art,' for this would leave out its connections to other images and thus distort its deeper meaning.

To achieve this form, the executor did not rely on perspective to copy what is seen with the eye, but on reproducing what was essential in the motif to be represented even if it was invisible. What was important was the message to be transmitted, not the exact replication of things. Both a front view and a top view of an object could be presented in the same image in order to provide as much meaning as possible. Size was also important: a person of higher rank was always depicted larger than his inferiors.

Statues of *neters*, pharaohs, and notables were made to ensure that the deceased would live eternally. Again, certain positions and norms were prescribed by tradition and often conformed to hieroglyphic figures. In order that the statue would become effective, the Opening of the Mouth ritual was performed on the statue to animate the five senses. In particular, the statues of the pharaoh in the temple allowed them to actively serve as an intermediary between man and the *neters* and thus maintain the divine order of *maat* through ritual ceremonies. This same ritual was performed on the mummy in the mortuary ritual so that the senses could be available in the afterlife. The position of the statue indicated a certain action and its appearance represented a particular message; so to understand the statue would mean for the observer to have a deep understanding of Egyptian civilization and the role of the pharaoh within it. In this way, the beauty of the statue, as in all Egyptian 'art,' does not rely only on its appearance but on the message it imparts. See Figure 65.

---

[546] Aldred, *Egyptian Art*, 15.

For example, if the pharaoh is wearing the *pshent* or double crown (the Osiris *hedjet* white crown of Upper Egypt and the Horus *deshret* red crown of Lower Egypt), this represents the king as the uniting principle of Upper and Lower Egypt, but, as with all Egyptian symbols, it can be interpreted on different levels up to the Original Cause. It can also symbolize the cosmic union of sky and earth through the pharaoh's intercession in the temple, and ultimately the union of man's spiritual energy with his psychic and physical bodies through his higher nature

Figure 65 Triad statue of the pharaoh Menkaura, 4th Dynasty

represented by the pharaoh. If one had lived within the Egyptian civilization and been privy to its teachings, all these different meanings are absorbed at once to produce a certain effect on the observer, but which can only leave us to use our discursive faculty to explain what we can:

> This consciousness of innate knowledge, of which the ordinary person is not yet cerebrally aware, is the supernatural force that is the signature of the work of art in the inspired moment of the artist, the present moment, without past or future.[547]

If Egyptian representations did not change or evolve over the millennia, it is because the wisdom which they symbolized was based on eternal spiritual and cosmological truths. To change a symbol, whether pictorial or sculptural, for only 'artistic' ends would simply not be part of their way of thinking. And the

---

[547] R.A. Schwaller de Lubicz, *The Temple of Man*, Vol. 1, 21.

reason for creating symbols was to provide a means to raise one's consciousness of the ineffable reality of the universe.

For this reason, books on Egyptian 'art' are beside the point. The details of how Egyptian painting sculpture were created lacks any importance relative to the symbolic meaning of the subject represented. In the case of ancient Egypt, the medium is not the message; it is only the symbolic content that matters.

Chapter 14 Monuments

The monuments of ancient Egypt, just as the imagery and sculpture, were never built for only functional purposes: the pyramid was not only a place to bury the pharaoh, a temple was not only a place to help the *neters* keep order in the universe, an obelisk was not only a representation of a sun's ray, a tomb was not only a place to bury the dead. The buildings themselves were symbols by which they were to have an effective action in the world.

Pyramids

One cannot speak of a pyramid without speaking of temples for the pyramid was a part of a temple complex and the symbolism of the pyramid is completely entwined within it. Apart from ensuring the transfer of the power of kingship during the Mortuary ritual to the next pharaoh, the pyramid complex was, first of all, the place where the pharaoh was transformed after his physical death into an *akh*, "a glorified being of light, effective in the Afterlife. The pyramid was an instrument that enabled this alchemy to take place…"[548]. But the pyramid was more than that: by having the pharaoh ascend to the circumpolar stars as an *akh*, the creation of the world continued and the sun rose every day. The shape of the pyramid reinforced this purpose: the pyramid, and perhaps even more the pyramidion that capped the pyramid, represented the primordial mound or the *benben* stone, the first appearance of creation at the First Time. In the same way, the pyramid rose beyond the cultivated valley of the Nile, out of the desert sands, a place of chaos that had to be kept at bay. Also, the pyramid was, as most

---

[548] Lehner, *The Complete Pyramids*, 20.

Egyptologists say, a symbol of the sun *neter* as creator with the shining pyramidion reflecting the sun's rays. See Figure 66.

Some Egyptologists propose that the pyramid was a 'ladder' by which the pharaoh's divine body rose to the stars. Other means of ascent were on the back of a bird, being carried up by burning incense or by clouds, or being taken in a boat. For the Egyptian mind, the means of ascent was not crucial, so there was no contradiction; it was only the *ascent* that was important. To the Egyptian mind, all these aspects were taken in together at once in a general belief in death and rebirth on all levels of existence, whether it be universal, cosmological, societal, or individual. There are various studies of the Great Pyramid showing that its measurements contain a great knowledge of the universe.[549] Whether this is in fact true and had an intentional purpose, or was simply the result of certain measurements arising

Figure 66 Pyramid of Kephren at Giza

from the pyramid's geometrical construction, we will no doubt never know.

The first pyramid constructed, as far as we know, was built at Saqqara in the Old Kingdom Third Dynasty of the pharaoh Djoser in Lower Egypt. It was not actually a pyramid with smooth sides, but a stepped pyramid having increasingly smaller thick slabs of stone (*mastabas*) rising on top of each other, the style of which continued into the early Fourth Dynasty. This could very well be a symbol of the primordial mound arising from the *Nun* at the beginning of time. It might also have been constructed as the site of the previously discussed *Heb-Sed* Festival jubilee of the pharaoh, as perhaps were pyramids built

---

[549]Enel, *Le Mystère de la Vie et de la Mort*, 116.

afterwards.[550] If this was in fact the case, the *Pyramid Texts* carved into the inner walls of Fifth and Sixth Dynasty pyramids, starting with Unas (now with smooth outer sides), could be construed as not being for the dead pharaoh in the afterlife, but "as relating to rituals and ritual experiences of the living rather than the dead king."[551]

The symbolism of the whole pyramid complex also reinforced the death and rebirth theme. The Mortuary ritual did not begin at the pyramid but at a valley temple on the edge of the Nile, where the pharaoh was first brought. Certain rituals took place there before the dead pharaoh was transported over a covered causeway to another temple on a side of the pyramid. Here other rituals took place before the pharaoh was placed in his tomb under or in the pyramid. Here again the symbolism of rebirth is clear: the pharaoh was brought forth out of the water of the Nile representing the original watery abyss, through the darkened corridor of the causeway, representing the *Dwat* or the netherworld, until he reached the pyramid representing the *benben* stone or original creation, which foretold his regeneration as an *akh*, a being of light taking his place among the circumpolar stars.

In the great pyramid of Kheops, the "king's chamber" had, according to many Egyptologists, two "air shafts" leading to the outside of the pyramid. The northern "air shaft," however, was, at the time the pyramid was built, centered on the celestial pole and the southern one on the constellation of Orion's belt. Now the *neter* Osiris was assimilated to the constellation of Orion. Could we assume then that the "king's chamber" was actually the chamber of Osiris? Some students of ancient Egypt thought the shafts had another purpose: the northern shaft was a passage to allow the *ka* of the pharaoh to reach the circumpolar stars and

---

[550]Naydler, *Shamanic Wisdom*, 91-95.
[551]Ibid., 122.

so become as eternal as these stars that never set, while the southern shaft pointing to Orion's belt rather allowed the *ka* to be continually reborn every year as is the sun every day.[552] [553] This directly corresponds respectively to the two forms of eternity found in the texts of ancient Egypt: *djet*, the eternal present outside of time, and *neheh*, cyclical time that constantly repeats, which also corresponds to two forms of spiritual generation: direct transformation and continuous spiritual growth. Two other shafts are found in the "queen's chamber": the northern one also pointing to the circumpolar stars and the southern one to the star Sirius next to the constellation Orion. Now Sirius is assimilated with the *neter* Isis, so the "queen's chamber" may in fact be the chamber of Isis. As mentioned previously, Sirius rises and sets once a year; it dips below the Western horizon and stays invisible for 70 days. When it arises in the East just after Orion, it announces the beginning of the Nile flood, which, by fertilizing the earth, is also associated with regeneration. It should be said here that the Embalming ritual also takes place over 70 days, the time it takes to be reborn in the *Dwat* or netherworld where Osiris holds sway. Another observation points to the fact that the three pyramids of Giza are aligned in the same way as the three stars of Orion's belt, with the third star being slightly offset and less bright than the other two, just as the third pyramid is offset and smaller than the two greater pyramids.[554]

In terms of symbolism, all the above shows how the heavens above, the sun and the stars, are intimately related to the buildings in stone erected by the ancient Egyptians. Pyramids and obelisks might, on one level, signify the power of the creator sun *neter* and his representative on earth, the pharaoh, but it

---

[552] Robert Bauval and Adrian Gilbert, *The Orion Mystery* (London: Mandarin, 1994), 100-108, 182.

[553] Lamy, *Egyptian Mysteries*, 28.

[554] Bauval and Gilbert, *The Orion Mystery*, 119-21.

shows too the intricate correlation among the heavenly bodies, mythology, theology, cosmology, monuments, and ritual. The periodic return of the stars of the ecliptic, for example, can be seen as another symbol of death and renewal. Yet one can never isolate a symbol in ancient Egypt. Every symbol is part of a vast network of a symbolic world that can be viewed at different levels of meaning, but that ultimately shows man's place in the universe and his possible transformation into a being of higher consciousness.

To maintain the presence of the pharaoh in the afterlife, a priesthood was established to carry out the various rituals necessary to this end. This was supposed to continue forever, since the circumpolar stars, where the pharaoh would reside, never set. The whole complex also had an economic use through its lands and workshops that produced food and artefacts that were distributed to the people. Nevertheless, through the vicissitudes of history, the complex eventually fell into disuse and died. Because of the cyclical nature of time that infused the Egyptian mind, they could assume that the complex would eventually die out. So, in the Fifth and Sixth Dynasties, starting with the pyramid of Unas, inscriptions were carved on the inner walls of the pyramids to insure the pharaoh's ascent to the sky. Given the ancient belief of the Egyptians in the power of the word, they no doubt felt that these inscriptions, now called the *Pyramid Texts*, would magically take the place of the abandoned rituals for eternity.

Temples

The word "temple" is used for both ancient Egyptian sacred buildings as well as contemporary buildings used as places of worship, but the purpose of each temple is completely different. The ancient Egyptians conceived of their temples as a microcosmos of the universe, and whose purpose was to keep the cosmos functioning through both the effective symbolism of their construction and the various rituals that took place within them, such as the Daily ritual discussed previously. There was no idea of the multitude entering into the edifice to placate a god, to receive favors, or to give thanks, for which our modern temples and churches were built. It is no doubt true that the cathedrals of the Middle Ages were also built on a symbolic basis and had a direct effect on one's being, but now the churches in our time are extremely far from that purpose:

> The Temple is something other than a church; it is the magic milieu that transports the human being beyond himself. In the Temple, what is human undergoes what normally it is incapable of understanding. It becomes conscious of a state of being that rational thought can no longer formulate.[555]

In fact, the Egyptian temple can never be understood in its entirety through scientific analysis; to understand the temple one would need to understand its symbolic nature, not through mental processes but through having lived a long spiritual discipline which included the temple rituals. See Figure 67.

Figure 67 Temple of Philae at Aswan

While the cathedrals were in the shape of the cross on which Christ was sacrificed, the shape of the ancient Egyptian temple

---

[555] R.A. Schwaller de Lubicz, *Le Miracle Égyptien*, 43.

symbolized the cosmos according to the myths handed down by Egyptian priests. The architecture took for inspiration ancient reed or tent shrines from early Egyptian history,[556] and every element of the temple had a specific symbolic purpose as an expression of cosmic principles and functions; absolutely nothing was added for simple decoration. Some even say that each temple was placed according to astronomical associations[557] under the notion that the land of Egypt reflected the heavenly sphere and that the Nile was the earthly equivalent of the Milky Way. In fact, temples were normally oriented towards the east, the land of the rising sun, of creation, and the foundation of a temple was always associated with a repetition of the original creation. Water was used to associate the temple with the watery *Nun* from which original creation arose and a mound with the primeval hill.[558] On a symbolic level, the temple was not only a microcosmos of the universe, it was also a microcosmos of all of Egypt—Egypt perhaps being a temple in itself with everything in society having a particular meaning relating to the regeneration of man and the cosmos. It should be emphasized that the form of the temple was not simply an abstract symbolism but had, for the Egyptians, an effective power to preserve the natural order. It might even be said that a temple was a power station providing energy for the functioning of the cosmos. To this end, each temple was dedicated to a *neter* (or *neters*) which had a specific function in the continuous creation and maintenance of the cosmos. In a way, the temple was the 'house' of the *neter(s)* to whom the temple was dedicated. The priests assured the functioning of the temple by following in perfect conformity the texts and rituals that guaranteed this functioning:

---

[556] Kemp, *Ancient Egypt*, 156.

[557] W. Marsham Adams, *Book of the Master of the Hidden Places* (London: The Search Publishing Co., 1933), 84. [A Kessinger Legacy Reprint]

[558] Hornung, *L'ésprit du temps*, 118.

Temples were conceived of as the seats of the *Neter*, each a dwelling place of the particular Principle to which each of them was dedicated. The temple inscriptions are quite explicit on this point: it constitutes the fundamental theme of esoteric teaching. And in reality the situation of a temple, its plan, its dedication, and its emblem make it the projection upon Earth of one aspect of the universal organism or 'macrocosm.'[559]

Another researcher put it this way:

It has been demonstrated that a number of the types of monuments which form part of the built landscape functioned as models of the cosmos. Within these microcosmoi, the ritual activities carried out would serve both to reflect and to guarantee the proper functioning of the cosmos. The cultic structure thus represented the entire process of cosmic maintenance: the structure existed within the Egyptian universe as a built element and at the same time acted to ensure its perpetual regeneration.[560]

It should be said that temple symbolism was never static, never meant to last forever. It was conceived as something living that grew and changed over time and carried within it a real knowledge which only the initiated could understand:[561]

The Temple becomes sacred when it is built from knowledge that includes all points of view: proportions and numbers, axes and orientations, choice of materials, harmony of figures, colors, lights, foundation deposits, and so on. It is this harmonious synthesis that creates the Temple, not a vulgar symbolization of the sky by the roof, of the earth by the floor, and other playthings of a childish symbolism.[562]

---

[559] Isha Schwaller de Lubicz, *Her-Bak, 'Chick-Pea,'* 446.

[560] Kamrin, *Khnumhotep II*), 14.

[561] Isha Schwaller de Lubicz, *Her-Bak, Egyptian Initiate*, 338-39.

[562] R.A. Schwaller de Lubicz, *The Temple of Man*, Vol. 1, 20.

According to R. A. Schwaller de Lubicz (see below), when a temple had lost the symbolic significance of its *neter* to which the temple was dedicated due to the changing movement of the heavens, such as the precession of the equinoxes, it was dismantled and a new temple was built dedicated to another *neter* that was in accord with the new cosmic reality. At one point in time, the *neter* Amon, represented by a ram, supplanted Mentu, represented by a bull, for "it was at this time that the position of the sun at the Spring Equinox moved from Taurus to Aries according to the precession of the equinoxes."[563] This happened according to an astrological plan carried down through the ages by the high priests and not the result of a decision by any particular pharaoh.[564] When building a new temple, the stones of the old temple were often reused in the new, thus using the old symbolisms to invigorate the latest evolution of the cosmos. The Egyptians never started over from scratch but allowed for older and different conceptions to be included in the latest symbolic manifestations of Egypt as a reflection of the cosmos.

The form of the Egyptian temple changed over time from the prehistoric era, through the Old, Middle, and New Kingdoms, though the main plan of the temple had basically the same form but with increasing complexity. For example, the Old Kingdom mortuary temples next to the pyramids of Giza had basically the same inner structure as New Kingdom temples such as that found in the Temple of Luxor or of Karnak.[565] Just as the *neters* could have different roles and actions depending on time and place, so the temples could change continuously as different

---

[563] Lamy, *Egyptian Mysteries*, 11.

[564] West, *Serpent in the Sky*, 116, 175.

[565] Richard H. Wilkinson, *The Complete Temples of Ancient Egypt* (London: Thames & Hudson, 2000), 16-29.

pharaohs could always add pylons, chambers, courtyards, etc. to the temple without interfering with the fundamental design.[566]

The sacred precinct of the temple was surrounded by a *temenos*, or an outer wall that was meant to keep *isfet*, or chaos, at bay, just as chaos surrounded Egypt in the form of the Nubians, Libyans, and Asiatics on the frontiers, always ready to invade the Egyptian world of *maat*. For this reason, the *temenos* wall was often in the form of a wave with alternate concave and convex sections to symbolize the watery abyss surrounding the temple precinct. In myth, this order also goes back to the time of creation itself when Atum created himself out of the watery abyss, and when the primordial mound or *benben* stone appeared, both symbolizing the creation of the world. This world, according to myth, was always surrounded by the chaotic waters that, if not repulsed by the temple rituals, would come crashing in and destroy all that had been created. This myth of world creation and maintenance was the basic symbolism of the Egyptian temple and is expressed in the temple architecture in an unbreakable unity:

> Just as everything in the Universe is bound by the same breath of life, within the architecture of the temple it would be a mistake to consider a part without relating it to the whole. Thus, we cannot dissociate one element of the construction from the others, since they are all used to express the same thought.[567]

The form of the temple proper in the New Kingdom carried the symbolism of creation further: an axis existed from the entranceway to the naos at the far end where the statue of the *neter*, to which the temple was dedicated, was placed. This axis was the symbolical path of the sun, but also the path of

---

[566] Hornung, *Conceptions of God*, 256.

[567] R.A. Schwaller de Lubicz, *The Temple of Man*, Vol. 1, 444.

transformation which a man may follow to become an *akh*, or a being of light.

The entrance to the temple proper is through a huge pylon gateway. The pylon was constructed in three parts: two large walls on either side of a lower portion containing the entrance to the temple. See Figure 68.

Figure 68 Pylon and obelisk at entrance to Temple of Luxor

The wall encircling the sacred precinct abutted onto the outer wall of the left and right portions of the pylon. In front of the pylon were often placed huge flagpoles representing the *neters* (the hieroglyph for divinity is a flag on a pole), as well as obelisks, and also colossal statues of the reigning pharaoh. An obelisk could be seen as a petrified sun ray with its gilded pyramidion on top reflecting the sun's rays in their act of cosmic maintenance. It could also be seen as a phallic symbol of creation, but there is no contradiction here as both symbolize the primordial act of creation, though on different levels of existence. The pylon as a whole no doubt represented a symbolic barrier to nefarious forces that would introduce chaos and disorder into the temple. This motive is often reinforced by huge reliefs on the front showing the pharaoh smiting the enemies of

Egypt. In terms of man, this could represent the necessary taming of his unbridled thoughts and emotions before he could enter and benefit from the spiritual transformation that the temple provided. It could also be said that the pylon signified creation itself, the two parts of the pylon and the middle lower entranceway representing, as in the horizon hieroglyph, the Eastern horizon with the sun appearing between two mountains. In other words, this represented the daily act of the rising sun maintaining the continuous creation of the world. When the doors of some temples were opened in the morning of each day, the sun's rays would traverse the temple's axis and fall on the divine statue of the *neter* in its shrine at the most sacred area in the rear, its reflection symbolizing the moment of creation.[568]

On the level of man, by entering the temple he began his own creation as a higher being through the activation of his interior vertical axis, just as the sun's light followed the axis of the temple. And just as Atum *created himself* out of the chaos of *Nun* at the "First Time," so a man creates himself by following temple rituals which rectify the chaos of his being. All the rituals, words, and gestures represented the acquisition of powers and knowledge that the deceased would need in the afterlife[569]—or the living person in this life. In ancient Egypt, symbolism was everywhere and could have multiple meanings without provoking any feelings of contradiction.

Upon passing through the pylon, one normally entered an outer peristyle courtyard open to the sky, a vast space with columns along the perimeter. This area could represent the cosmos as it was created in the beginning with the central area assimilated to a body of water (sometimes it was actually flooded during the Nile's inundation) and the surrounding columns the marsh plants around it. This courtyard might be called the "exoteric" area of

[568]Kamrin, *Khnumhotep II*, 18.
[569]Mayassis, *Mystères et Initiation*, 227.

the temple as it was sometimes open to certain groups of people for observing processions, giving offerings, or hearing of petitions. In this vein, it could represent man's earthly nature with all the roles he held within society and which he had to surpass in order to become a spiritual being through rituals that took place in the inner recesses of the temple.

Within the courtyard were placed royal statues and those of nobles as well. Now these statues were not simple memorials but also acted as simulacra of the deceased in whom his *ba* could reside and be animated by the temple rituals. They were often adorned with a stela with a "call for offerings" so that those who wished could recite the offering formula to provoke favor for the deceased from the *neters*.[570] See Figure 69.

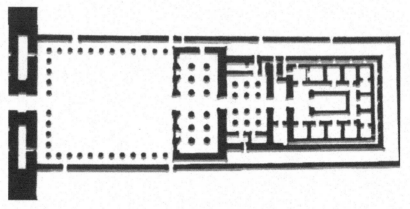

Figure 69 Basic ancient Egyptian temple floor plan

After the peristyle hall there usually followed a hypostyle hall filled with high columns having a ceiling made of giant slabs of stone often decorated with stars. On a cosmic scale, the floor could represent the level of the netherworld, the walls that of the earth, and the ceiling that of the heavens. The columns represented palm trees or marsh plants such as the papyrus and lotus, whose capitals and reliefs evoked the mythic watery world

---

[570] Wilkinson, *Temples*, 63.

from which creation began. These columns also referred to the Egyptian myth of the heavens being supported by four pillars. Capitals with closed buds were often in the outer areas of the temple and open plants towards the center, thus again emphasizing the "closed" or "hidden" nature of creation and its eventual "opening out" through ritual.[571]

Following the axis from the outer peristyle area, through the covered hypostyle court and onward to the sanctuary at the back containing the statue of the *neter* to which the temple was dedicated, the path rose and the space became increasingly darker. This evoked the mystery of creation out of the darkness of the watery abyss, and in this way the sacred shrine was assimilated to the primeval mound of original creation.[572] As such, this atmosphere provided the right environment for the sacred rituals to be effective. Likewise, doors were present to prevent or allow one to go further into the more sacred areas of the temple.

To go through a door, meant that one had opened to the divine, that is, arrived at a new level of being. The doors of a temple were thus given names that symbolically referred to gods or states of this new level.[573] The images on the walls of the temple were often drawn in rows or 'registers.' Often, the highest registers depicted notions of a metaphysical nature, the middle rows portrayed cosmological representations, and the lower row depicted images of the terrestrial world,[574] the lower rows being symbolic of the higher.

After the hypostyle hall, various rooms were available to house visiting statues and cultic paraphernalia such as that necessary

---

[571]Ibid., 66.

[572]Henri Frankfort, *Ancient Egyptian Religion*, 153.

[573]Wilkinson, *Temples*, 67-68.

[574]R A. Schwaller de Lubicz, *Symbol and the Symbolic*, 93.

for the Daily ritual. Rooms were also available for the priests to prepare themselves for processions and rituals. Further on there could be chapels with symbolic boats placed within, since the *neters* traversed the sky in boats sailing from East to West during the day and disappearing below the horizon into the netherworld during the night. Altars were also present where the priests would give offerings to the *neters* whose statues were present in the main sanctuary at the farthest end of the temple. The food and drink offerings were of utmost importance, for in the Egyptian worldview they sustained the *neters* in their tasks of maintaining the cosmos. Here, directly at the end of the axis starting from the pylon, was a room where the statue of the *neter* to whom the temple was dedicated was placed in an enclosed naos. This was the most sacred area of the temple and only the pharaoh and high priests, as his stand-in, had access to it. On either side there might be rooms with statues of other *neters* to whom the priests also made offerings. Some temples also had shrines on their roofs and crypts below the main level, which could have symbolized heaven and the netherworld, respectively.

Within the temple precinct there often existed a sacred lake which represented the watery abyss from which the forces of creation emerged. The priests bathed in the lake in order to be imbued with these forces and thereby purify themselves before entering the temple. Outside of the temple proper, but within the temple precinct, there may have been other structures such as warehouses, granaries, kitchens, and workshops, all dedicated to the life of the temple.

Connected to major temples there was also the *per ankh* or House of Life. This institution was a center of learning, but not in the same way as our modern schools and universities evolved as a means of accumulating *knowledge* for its own sake and its application to *outer* life, but as a place to achieve *sacred* understanding for its application to one's *inner* life. Here were found sacred texts that were written, copied, and stored for use by those priests or nobles found worthy to approach them. The subjects studied and written could be what we might call hieroglyphic writing, myths, theology, cosmology, astronomy, magic, ritual, crafts, and medicine,[575] as well as preparing Books of the Dead to be used for burials. Nevertheless, it should not be assumed that these subjects were kept apart in separate sections as are done in our schools, for all these subjects influence, and are influenced by, all the others. One could not study the stars, for example, without bringing in the cosmology of the heavens and the theology of the *neters*. 'Art' was never a subject to be 'studied,' for the 'artist' was a actually a craftsman who created content through texts and images that were provided by the priests and not from their own imagination. The creation of hieroglyphic characters, in fact, was based on a profound knowledge of the natural and material world, and it can be assumed that it was in the House of Life that the images and hieroglyphic texts found on temple walls and those of the tombs were elaborated according to a precise symbolic canon.[576]

Just as the pharaoh was the intermediary between the *neters* and man, so the temple was the intermediary between the heavens and the *Dwat* or netherworld. For this reason, the temple was sometimes referred to as the "horizon."[577] It was through the temple that order reigned between these two spheres of existence. Through the rituals taking place in the temple, the sun, descending in the evening into the *Dwat* in the West, would be assured of reappearing at dawn on the Eastern horizon, just as the deceased is reborn after the mortuary ritual. And man, in his spiritual journey that took him to his judgment before Osiris in the *Dwat*, would be assured of becoming an immortal *akh* as a

---

[575] Ibid., 74.

[576] Sauneron, *Priests*, 134.

[577] Hornung, *L'esprit du temps*, 115.

circumpolar star in the heavens. Now this spiritual journey of man symbolized in the temple is a symbolic way of showing the journey of man towards spiritual attainment.

One of the most intact temples of ancient Egypt is the New Kingdom temple of Seti I in Abydos. I can truly say from my own experience that walking through this temple in its half-light can change a receptive person's state, for the atmosphere is incredibly uplifting. The images and hieroglyphs on the walls are very well preserved and allow for a real study of what the temple represents. Most all the symbolism described above, such as the temple being a microcosm of the cosmos, can be found in this temple.

The images and writings on the walls have been described by the Egyptologist David O'Connor.[578] Some of the images and texts record the rituals that took place in the temple, some elaborate the role of kingship in Egyptian life and others put forth a paean to the *neter* to whom the temple is dedicated. For example, in the second hall the ritual scenes actually show the routes used for the appropriate *neter* that lead up to its boat chapel in which are found descriptions of the Daily ritual that is actually performed in it. The reason for these descriptions was to make the rituals effective through the power of the word written on the walls and thus allow the *neter*s to enter their statues in safety for eternity. Other texts offer praise to the *neters* celebrated in the temple as manifestations of the creator *neter*, Amon-Re, though the temple was actually dedicated to Osiris whose 'home' was in Abydos. In the Egyptian temple, it is always the pharaoh who presents offerings to the *neters*, for he is the only one who can have direct relations with them. In any description of a priest or noble presenting offerings to the *neters*, it is always done in the name of the pharaoh who has appointed him as his stand-in.

---

[578] David O'Connor, *Abydos: Egypt's First Pharaohs and the Cult of Osiris* (London: Thames & Hudson, 2009), 52-61.

The Temple of Luxor

R. A. Schwaller de Lubicz, originally a chemist with a mathematical mind and an interest in Hermetics and esoteric symbolism, spent 12 or maybe 15 years in Luxor, Egypt studying, for the most part, what is now called the Temple of Luxor. The ancient Greeks called the current city of Luxor Thebes; its ancient Egyptian name was Waset. The temple was built by the New Kingdom pharaoh Amenhotep III during the 1400's BC and added to by following pharaohs, including Ramses II. The temple was known in Ancient Egypt as *Ipet Resyt* (Sanctuary of the South) and was either dedicated to the Theban Triad Amon, Mut, and Khonsu or to the rejuvenation of the pharaoh during the annual Opet Festival, or perhaps both.

Through exact measurements of all the temple dimensions, proportions, orientations, and a complete reading of all the reliefs and texts on the walls, Schwaller de Lubicz came to the conclusion that the Temple of Luxor was a reproduction in stone of man, no doubt representing the symbolic pharaoh or the True Man, and which corresponded to certain stellar movements in the sky. Just as some have found universal knowledge in the measurements of the Great Pyramid, he also claimed to have found, through many mathematical and geometrical studies of the Temple, that it also contained such knowledge, which, as John Anthony West put it, "pertained to universal creative powers. This knowledge is not set down explicitly in books, but embodied in the building itself."[579] West says as well:

> The Temple tells, in stone, in its proportions and harmonies, its art and sculpture, the story of the creation of man; it signals his development, stage by stage, and it recreates in artistic form man's relationship to the universe."[580]

---

[579] West, *Serpent in the Sky*, 170.

[580] Ibid., 165

The proportions of the Temple are those of Adamic man, man before the fall, and of perfected man, man who has regained his cosmic consciousness through his own efforts. The Temple excludes the crown of the head, seat of the intellectual faculty. The cerebral cortex dualizes, permits distinctions, creates the illusion of separateness. Adamic man cannot distinguish, cannot

Figure 70 The Temple of Luxor

choose between good and evil, for this dichotomy did not exist at the First Time, and perfected man has reconciled Seth and Horus within himself. According to Schwaller de Lubicz, the walls, colonnades and sanctuaries all correspond to the place of various vital centers in man.[581] See Figure 70.

For Schwaller de Lubicz, an ancient Egyptian temple, seemingly dedicated to a 'god,' is in fact dedicated to the *neter* which the 'god' represents, that is, a universal principle that, while having its particular function, cannot be separated from the whole. He says too that all the temples of Egypt together were in fact a vast teaching where each temple was one aspect of the whole.[582]

---

[581] Ibid., 171-72.

[582] R.A. Schwaller de Lubicz, *The Temple of Man*, Vol. 2., 524, 538.

Some of the other aspects of the symbolism of the Temple of Luxor that Schwaller de Lubicz details are the following:

- Some stones used in the walls between rooms can only be completely understood by looking at the inscriptions or reliefs on both sides of the stone in each room.[583]
- A *neter* not born of woman, such as Atum arising out of the primordial *Nun*, does not have a navel.[584]
- The joints between stones were precisely placed to cut the figures to be carved on them in a way that emphasizes a certain principle.[585]
- Three different axes exist on the floor of the temple by which the temple was constructed.[586]

We could go on and on about the meaning of these elements and others that he describes, and which demonstrate a profound symbolism by which the Temple of Luxor was constructed as a teaching of the spiritual generation of man in accord with cosmic principles. According to Schwaller de Lubicz, this teaching was of an esoteric nature not destined for the mind, but to be understood in one's entire being, which is why it cannot be explained in mere words.

Now most Egyptologists are not convinced of his thesis and you will almost never see his work referenced in Egyptological studies. One would have to go oneself through his tome, *The Temple of Man*, to make an informed opinion.

---

[583] Ibid., 996.

[584] Ibid., 970.

[585] Ibid., 658.

[586] Ibid., 930.

Extended Bibliography

This bibliography contains works that were explicitly used to document the arguments made in this book as well as those works that influenced our ideas on the subjects discussed herein.

Cosmology and Science

Asimov, Isaac. *The Universe: From Flat Earth to Quasar.* Harmondsworth, England: Penguin Books, 1966.

Bak, Per. *How Nature Works: The Science of Self-Organized Criticality.* New York: Springer-Verlag, 1996.

Barnett, Lincoln. *Einstein et l'univers.* Translated from the English by Julien Nequaud (original title: *The Universe and Dr. Einstein*). Paris: Gallimard, 1951.

Bohm, David. *Unfolding Meaning: A Weekend of Dialogue with David Bohm.* London: Routledge & Kegan Paul (Ark Paperbacks),1985.

_____. *Wholeness and the Implicate Order.* London: Routledge & Kegan Paul, 1980.

Bronowski, J. *The Ascent of Man.* Boston: Little, Brown and Company, 1973.

Calder, Nigel. *Einstein's Universe.* Harmondsworth, England: Penguin Books, 1980. (First published in 1979 by The Viking Press, New York.)

Capra, Fritjof. *The Tao of Physics: An Exploration of the Parallels Between Modern Physics and Eastern Mysticism.* New York: Bantam Books, 1977. (First published in 1976 by Shambhala Publications, Boulder, Colorado.)

_____. *The Web of Life: A New Synthesis of Mind and Matter.* London: HarperCollins, 1996.

Collin, Rodney. *The Theory of Celestial Influence: Man, the Universe, and Cosmic Mystery.* New York: Samuel Weiser, 1973 (First published in 1954).

Croswell, Ken. *The Alchemy of the Heavens.* Oxford: Oxford University Press, 1996.

Damasio, Antonio. *Descartes' Error: Emotion, Reason, and the Human Brain.* New York: Quill imprint of HarperCollins Publishers, 2000. (First published in 1994 by G. P. Putnam's Sons.)

_____. *Looking for Spinoza: Joy, Sorrow, and the Feeling Brain*. New York: Harcourt, Inc., 2003.

_____. *The Feeling of What Happens: Body and Emotion in the Making of Consciousness*. New York: Harcourt, Inc., 1999.

Davies, Paul. *God and the New Physics*. London: Penguin Books, 1984. (First published in 1983 by J.M. Dent & Sons.)

Dawkins, Richard. *The Blind Watchmaker: Why the Evidence of Evolution Reveals a Universe Without Design*. New York: W.W. Norton & Company, 1996. (First published in 1986.)

Eddington, Sir Arthur. *The Nature of the Physical World*. (The Gifford Lectures, University of Edinburgh, Jan.-Mar. 1927). Ann Arbor, Mich.: University of Michigan Press, 1958.

Edelman, Gerald M. and Tononi, Giulio. *A Universe of Consciousness: How Matter Becomes Imagination*. New York: Basic Books, 2000.

Feynman, Richard P. *Six Easy Pieces: The Fundamentals of Physics Explained*. London: Penguin Books, 1998.

France-Culture. *Science et conscience: Les deux lectures de l'univers*. Papers submitted to the Cordoba International Conference, October 1-5, 1979. Paris: Éditions Stock, 1980.

Gamow, George. *One Two Three...Infinity: Facts and Speculations of Science*. New York: Bantam Books, 1961. (First published in 1947 by The Viking Press, New York.)

Gardner, Martin. *Relativity for the Million*. New York: Pocket Books, 1965. (First published in 1962 by The Macmillan Company, New York.)

Goodsell, David S. *The Machinery of Life*. New York: Springer-Verlag, 1998.

Hawking, Stephen W. *A Brief History of Time: From the Big Bang to Black Holes*. London: Bantam Press, 1988.

Hawking, Stephen W. and Penrose, Roger. *The Nature of Space and Time*. Princeton, N.J.: Princeton University Press, 1996.

Heisenberg, Werner. *Physics and Beyond: Encounters and Conversations*. Translated from the German by Arnold J. Pomerans. New York: Harper & Row, 1971.

_____. *Physics and Philosophy: The Revolution in Modern Science*. New York: Harper & Row, 1958.

Hofstadter, Douglas R. *Gödel, Escher, Bach: An Eternal Golden Braid*. New York: Vintage Books, 1989. (First published in 1979 by Basic Books, New York.)

Holland, John H. *Hidden Order: How Adaptation Builds Complexity.* Reading, Mass.: Perseus Books, 1995.

Kamshilov, M. M. *Evolution of the Biosphere.* Translated from the Russian by Minna Brodskaya. Moscow: Mir Publishers, 1976.

Kauffman, Stuart. *At Home in the Universe: The Search for the Laws of Self-Organization and Complexity.* New York: Oxford University Press, 1995.

Koestler, Arthur. *Janus: A Summing Up.* New York: Vintage Books, 1979.

Kuhn, Thomas S. *The Structure of Scientific Revolutions.* Chicago: University of Chicago Press, 1962.

Lachièze-Rey, Marc. "Le temps cosmique existe-t-il ?" *La Recherche.* Hors serie No. 5, April 2001. Paris: Société d'Editions Scientifiques.

Laszlo, Ervin. *The Systems View of the World: A Holistic Vision for Our Time.* Cresskill, NJ: Hampton Press, 1996.

Lovejoy, Arthur O. *The Great Chain of Being: A Study of the History of an Idea.* The William James Lectures delivered at Harvard University, 1933. Cambridge, Mass.: Harvard University Press, 1936.

Lovelock, J. E. *Gaia: A New Look at Life on Earth.* Oxford: Oxford University Press, 1987. (First published 1979 by Oxford University Press.)

Margolis, Lynn. *Microcosmos: Four Billion Years of Microbial Evolution.* Berkeley: University of California Press, 1997. (First published in 1986 by Summit Books, New York.)

Ouspensky, P.D. *A New Model of the Universe.* New York: Vintage Books, 1971.

_____. *In Search of the Miraculous: Fragments of an Unknown Teaching.* New York: Harcourt, Brace & World, 1949. (First published in 1931 by Alfred A. Knopf.)

_____. *Tertium Organum: A Key to the Enigmas of the World.* New York: Vintage Books, 1970 (First published in 1922 by Alfred A. Knopf.)

Padmanabhan, T. *After the First Three Minutes: The Story of Our Universe.* Cambridge: Cambridge University Press, 1998.

Pagels, Heinz R. *The Cosmic Code: Quantum Physics as the Language of Nature.* New York: Bantam Books, 1983. (First published in 1982 by Simon & Schuster, New York.)

Prigogine, Ilya. *The End of Certainty: Time, Chaos, and the New Laws of Nature.* New York: The Free Press, 1997.

Reeves, Hubert; de Rosnay, Joël; Coppens, Yves; Simonnet, Dominique. *La plus belle histoire du monde: Les Secrets de nos origines.* Paris: Éditions du Seuil, 1996.

Rensberger, Boyce. *Life Itself: Exploring the Realm of the Living Cell.* New York: Oxford University Press, 1996.

Russell, Bertrand. *The ABC of Relativity.* 3d ed. revised. New York: New American Library, 1959. (First edition published in 1925; First 3d edition published in 1958 by George Allen & Unwin, London.)

Schrodinger, Erwin. *What Is Life?: The Physical Aspect of the Living Cell.* With Mind and Matter and Autobiographical Sketches. Cambridge, UK: Cambridge University Press, 1992.

Scientific American Quarterly. Vol. 9, No. 1: "Magnificent Cosmos". New York: Scientific American, Spring 1998.

Smolin, Lee. *The Life of the Cosmos.* Oxford: Oxford University Press, 1997.

Talbot, Michael. *Mysticism and the New Physics.* New York: Bantam Books, 1981.

Thompson, d'Arcy Wentworth. *On Growth and Form.* Abridged edition edited by John Tyler Bonner. Cambridge, UK: Cambridge University Press, 1961. (Original edition first published in 1917.)

Thuan, Trinh Xuan. *The Secret Melody: And Man Created the Universe.* Translated from the French by Storm Dunlop (original title: *La Mélodie Secrète*). Oxford: Oxford University Press, 1995.

Vanin, Gabriele. *Astronomie: Images de l'univers.* French adaptation from the Italian by Hélène Raccah and Élisabeth de Lavigne. Paris: Librarie Gründ, 1995.

Waldrop, M. Mitchell. *Complexity: The Emerging Science at the Edge of Order and Chaos.* New York: Simon & Schuster, 1992.

Weinberg, Steven. *The First Three Minutes: A Modern View of the Origin of the Universe.* New York: Bantam Books, 1979 (First published in 1977 by Basic Books, New York.)

Wilber, Ken (ed.). *The Holographic Paradigm and Other Paradoxes: Exploring the Leading Edge of Science.* Boulder, Colorado: Shambhala Publications, 1982.

Wolf, Fred Alan. *Parallel Universes: The Search for Other Worlds.* New York: Simon & Schuster, 1990.

_____. *Taking the Quantum Leap: The New Physics for Nonscientists.* New York: Harper & Row, 1989.

Young, Arthur M. *The Reflexive Universe: Evolution of Consciousness.* Delacorte Press, 1976.

Zajonc, Arthur. *Catching the Light: The Entwined History of Light and Mind.* Oxford: Oxford University Press, 1993.

Zukav, Gary. *The Dancing Wu Li Masters: An Overview of the New Physics.* New York: William Morrow and Co., 1979.

Symbolism and Civilization

Alleau, René. *La science des symboles.* Paris: Payot, 1977.

Aulén, Gustave. *The Drama and the Symbols: A Book on Images of God and the Problems They Raise.* Translated from the Swedish by Sydney Linton. Philadelphia: Fortress Press, 1970. (First published in Sweden in 1965.)

Bevan, Edwyn. *Symbolism and Belief.* London: George Allen & Unwin, 1938.

Bronowski, Jacob. *The Origins of Knowledge and Imagination.* (The Silliman Foundation Lectures, 1967). New Haven: Yale University Press, 1978.

Burckhardt, Titus. *Principes et méthodes de l'art sacré.* Paris: Editions Dervy, 1995.

_____. *Science moderne et sagesse traditionnelle.* Translated from the German by Sylvie Girard. Milan: Arché, 1986.

_____. *Symboles: Recueil d'essais.* Milan: Arché, 1980.

Campbell, Joseph. *The Hero with a Thousand Faces.* Cleveland: World Publishing, 1956. (First published in 1949: New York, Bollingen Foundation).

Cirlot, Juan-Eduardo. *A Dictionary of Symbols.* Translated from the Spanish by Jack Sage. New York: Philosophical Library, 1962.

_____. *El Ojo en la Mitología su Simbolismo.* Barcelona: Laboratorios del Norte de España, 1954.

Coomaraswamy, Ananda K. *Christian and Oriental Philosophy of Art.* New York: Dover, 1956. (First published in 1943 by Luzac & Co. under the title *Why Exhibit Works of Art?*)

_____. *The Door in the Sky: Coomaraswamy on Myth and Meaning.* Ed. Rama P. Coomaraswamy. Princeton, N.J.: Princeton University Press, 1977.

_____. *Coomaraswamy Volume I, Selected Papers: Traditional Art and Symbolism.* Roger Lipsey (ed.). (Bollingen Series LXXXIX.) Princeton, N.J.: Princeton University Press, 1977.

_____. *Coomaraswamy Volume II, Selected Papers: Metaphysics.* Roger Lipsey (ed.). (Bollingen Series LXXXIX.) Princeton, N.J.: Princeton University Press, 1977.

_____. *The Transformation of Nature in Art.* New York: Dover Publications, 1956. (First Published in 1934.)

Dames, Michael. *The Avebury Cycle.* London: Thames & Hudson, 1977.

_____. *The Silbury Treasure: The Great Goddess rediscovered.* London: Thames & Hudson, 1976.

Copenhaver, Brian P. *Hermetica.* Cambridge UK: Cambridge University Press, 1995.

Dumézil, Georges. *Mythes et Dieux des Indo-Européens.* Paris: Flammarion, 1992.

Durkheim, Émile. *The Elementary Forms of Religious Life.* Abridged ed. Translated from the French by Carol Cosman. Oxford: Oxford University Press, 2001. (First published in French in 1912 by Alcan, Paris.)

Eliade, Mircea. *From Primitives to Zen: A Thematic Sourcebook of the History of Religions.* New York: Harper & Row, 1977.

_____. *Images and Symbols: Studies in Religious Symbolism.* Translated from the French by Philip Mairet. New York: Sheed and Ward, 1969 (First published in English in 1961 by Harville Press).

_____. *Myths, Rites, Symbols: A Mircea Eliade Reader.* 2 vols. Edited by Wendell C. Beane and William G. Doty. New York: Harper & Row, 1975.

_____. *Rites and Symbols of Initiation: The Mysteries of Birth and Rebirth.* Translated from the French by Willard R. Trask. New York: Harper & Row, 1975. (First published in English in 1958 by Harper & Brothers).

_____. *Shamanism: Archaic Techniques of Ecstasy.* Translated from the French by Willard R. Trask. Princeton, NJ: Princeton University Press, 1972. (First published in French in 1951 by Librairie Payot, Paris.)

_____. *The Sacred and the Profane: The Nature of Religion.* Translated from the French by Willard R. Trask. New York: Harcourt, Brace & World, 1959.

Frazer, Sir James George. *The Golden Bough: A Study in Magic and Religion.* Abridged ed. New York: The Macmillan Company, 1923.

Ginsburg, Herbert, and Opper, Sylvia. *Piaget's Theory of Intellectual Development: An Introduction.* Englewood Cliffs, NJ: Prentice-Hall, 1969.

Godwin, Joscelyn. *Mystery Religions in the Ancient World.* San Francisco: Harper & Row, 1981.

Gordon, Pierre. *The Original Revelation.* Translated from the French by Michael Allswang. Châteauneuf de Mazenc: Arma Artis, 2004. (First published in French by Editions Dervy in 1951 and reprinted by Arma Artis in 1980.)

_____. *Le sacerdoce à travers les âges.* Châteauneuf de Mazenc: Arma Artis, 1993.

_____. *L'image du monde dans l'antiquité.* Paris: Presses Universitaires de France, 1949.

_____. *L'origine de l'humanité d'après les traditions anciennes.* Châteauneuf de Mazenc: Arma Artis, 2001.

Govinda, Lama Anagarika. *Psycho-cosmic Symbolism of the Buddhist Stupa.* Emeryville, CA: Dharma Publishing, 1976.

Guénon, René. *Aperçus sur l'initiation.* 2d ed. Paris: Les Éditions Traditionnelles, 1953.

_____. *La Grande Triade.* Paris: Gallimard, 1957.

_____. *Le Roi du Monde.* Paris: Gallimard, 1958.

_____. *Le symbolisme de la croix.* Paris: Union Générale d'Éditions, 1957.

_____. *Symboles de la Science sacrée.* Paris: Gallimard, 1962.

Heschel, Abraham Joshua. *Man's Quest for God: Studies in Prayer and Symbolism.* New York: Charles Scribner's Sons, 1954.

Huxley, Aldous. *The Perennial Philosophy.* New York: Harper & Row, 1944.

Huxley, Francis. *L'Oeil: Mythes et métamorphoses.* Translated from the English by Pierre Janin. Paris: Éditions du Seuil, 1992.

_____. *The Way of the Sacred: The Rites and Symbols, Beliefs and Tabus, that Men Have Held in Awe and Wonder through the Ages.* New York: Dell Publishing Co., 1976.

Jung, Carl G. *Man and his Symbols.* Garden City, NY: Doubleday & Company, 1964.

Kirk, G. S. *Myth: Its Meaning and Functions in Ancient and Other Cultures.* London: Cambridge University Press, 1970.

Lévi-Strauss, Claude. *The Savage Mind.* Translated from the French. Chicago: University of Chicago Press, 1966.

_____. *Totemism.* Translated from the French by Rodney Needham. Harmondsworth, UK: Penguin Books, 1963.

Lévy-Bruhl, Lucien. *How Natives Think.* Translated from the French by Lilian A. Clarke. Salem, NH: Ayer, 1984. (First published in English in 1926 by G. Allen & Unwin, London.)

_____. *The Notebooks on Primitive Mentality.* Translated from the French by Peter Rivière. New York: Harper & Row, 1975. (First published in French in 1949 as *Carnets* by Presses Universitaires de France.)

Lings, Martin. *Symbol & Archetype: A Study of the Meaning of Existence.* Cambridge, U.K.: Quinta Essentia, 1991.

Meyer, Marvin W. (ed.). *The Ancient Mysteries—A Sourcebook: Sacred Texts of the Mystery Religions of the Ancient Mediterranean World.* San Francisco: Harper & Row, 1987.

Needleman, Jacob (ed.). *The Sword of Gnosis: Metaphysics, Cosmology, Tradition, Symbolism.* Baltimore: Penguin Books, 1974.

Neumann, Erich. *The Great Mother: An Analysis of the Archetype.* 2d ed. Translated from the German by Ralph Manheim. (Bollingen Series XLVII.) Princeton, NJ: Princeton University Press, 1963.

Nicoll, Maurice. *The Mark.* London: Vincent Stuart, 1954.

_____. *The New Man: An Interpretation of Some Parables and Miracles of Christ.* New York: Penguin Books, 1972. (First published in 1950: London, Stuart and Richards.)

Olivet, Fabre d'. *Hermeneutic Interpretation of the Origin of the Social State of Man and of the Destiny of the Adamic Race.* Translated by Nayán Louise Redfield. New York: G.P. Putnam's Sons, 1915.

Ouspensky, P. D. *In Search of the Miraculous: Fragments of an Unknown Teaching.* New York: Harcourt, Brace & World, 1949.

Panofsky, Erwin. *Meaning in the Visual Arts.* Ch. 2: "The History of the Theory of Human Proportions as a Reflection of the History of Styles (first published in German in 1921). Chicago: The University of Chicago Press, 1982 (First published in 1955 by Doubleday, Garden City, N.Y.)

Parisot, Roger. *L'initiation primordiale et l'origine des religions: Introduction à l'œuvre de Pierre Gordon.* Châteauneuf de Mazenc: Editions Arma Artis, 1993.

Perry, Mark. *On Awakening and Remembering: To Know Is To Be.* Louisville, KY: Fons Vitae, 2000.

Phaure, Jean. *Le Cycle de l'Humanité Adamique: Introduction à l'étude de la cyclologie traditionnelle et de la fin des temps.* Paris: Dervy Livres, 1983.

Piaget, Jean. *The Child's Conception of the World.* Translated from the French by Joan and Andrew Tomlinson. Savage, Maryland: Littlefield Adams, n.d. (First published in English in 1929 by Routledge and Kegan Paul, London.)

_____. *The Child and Reality: Problems of Genetic Psychology.* Translated from the French by Arnold Rosin. New York: Penguin Books, 1976. (First published in English in 1973 by Grossman Publishers.)

Piaget, Jean, and Inhelder, Bärbel. *The Psychology of the Child.* Translated from the French by Helen Weaver. Basic Books, 1969.

Quinn, William W., Jr. *The Only Tradition.* Albany, N.Y.: State University of New York Press, 1997.

Schwaller de Lubicz, R. A. *A Study of Numbers: A Guide to the Constant Creation of the Universe.* Translated from the French by Robert Lawlor. Rochester, Vermont: Inner Traditions International, 1986. Originally published as *Études sur les nombres* (Paris: Librairie de l'Art Indépendant, 1914).

_____. *La Doctrine: Trois conférences faites à Suhalia, Noël 1926.* Ile Rousse: Axis Mundi, 1988. Originally privately published in St. Moritz: Officina Montalia, 1927.

_____. *Nature Word.* Translated by Deborah Lawlor. West Stockbridge, Mass.: Lindisfarne Press, 1982. Originally published as *Verbe Nature* in *"Aor," R. A. Schwaller de Lubicz, Sa vie, son œuvre* by Isha Schwaller de Lubicz (Paris: La Colombe, 1963).

_____. *Propos sur ésotérisme et symbole.* 2nd ed. Paris: Dervy Livres, 1977. Originally published by La Colombe, Paris, 1960.

_____. *Symbol and the Symbolic: Egypt, Science and the Evolution of Consciousness.* Translated from the French by Robert and Deborah Lawlor. Brookline, Mass.: Autumn Press, 1978. Originally published as *Du symbol et de la symbolique* (Cairo: Schindler, 1950).

Santillana, Georgio de, and Dechend, Hertyha von. *Hamlet's Mill: An essay on myth and the frame of time.* Boston: David R. Godine, 1977.

Schuon, Frithjof. *Avoir un Centre.* Paris: Editions Maisonneuve & Larose, 1988.

_____. *Images de l'esprit: Shinto, Bouddhisme, Yoga.* Paris: Flammarion, 1961.

_____. *Light on the Ancient Worlds.* 2d ed. Translated from the French by Lord Northbourne. Bloomington: World Wisdom Books, 1984. (First published in 1967 in French by Editions Traditionnelles. First published in English in 1965 by Perennial Books.)

_____. *Stations of Wisdom.* Revised translation from the French. Bloomington: World Wisdom Books, 1995. (Published in French by Maisonneuve et Larose, Paris, 1992. Previously published in English by John Murray, London, 1961 and Perennial Books, London, 1980.)

_____. *The Transcendent Unity of Religions.* Revised edition. Translated from the French. Wheaton: The Theosophical Publishing House, 1993. (First published in 1957.)

Singleton, Charles S. *Journey to Beatrice.* Cambridge: Harvard University Press, 1958.

Smith, Huston. *Forgotten Truth: The Primordial Tradition.* New York: Harper & Row, 1977.

Spengler, Oswald, *The Decline of the West*, abridged ed. Oxford: Oxford University Press, 1961.

Thomas, Jacques. *Aperçus sur l'opération intellectuelle et la connaissance initiatique.* Milano: Archè, 1998.

Thompson, William Irwin. *The Time Falling Bodies Take To Light: Mythology, Sexuality & the Origins of Culture.* New York: St. Martin's Press, 1981.

Whitehead, Alfred North. *Process and Reality.* Corrected Edition. New York: The Free Press, 1978. (First published in 1929 by Macmillan Publishing Co., New York.)

_____. *Religion in the Making: Lowell Lectures, 1926.* New York: Fordham University Press, 1996. (First published in 1926 by The Macmillan Company, New York.)

_____. *Symbolism: Its Meaning and Effect: University of Virginia Barbour Page Lectures, 1927.* New York: Fordham University Press, 1927.

Ancient Greece

Aeschylus. *Aeschylus I: Oresteia (Agamemnon, The Libation Bearers, The Eumenides).* Translated from the Greek by Richmond Lattimore. Chicago: The University of Chicago Press, 1953.

Aeschylus. *Aeschylus II: The Suppliant Maidens, The Persians.* Translated from the Greek by Seth G. Benardete. *Seven against Thebes, Prometheus Bound.* Translated from the Greek by David Grene. Chicago: The University of Chicago Press, 1956.

Anonymous. *The Homeric Hymns: A Verse Translation.* Translated from the Greek by Thelma Sargent. New York: W.W. Norton & Co., 1973.

Aristotle. *On Man in the Universe.* Edited by Louise Ropes Loomis. Roslyn, NY: Walter J. Black, 1943.

Barnes, Jonathan. *Early Greek Philosophy.* London: Penguin Books, 1987.

Burkert, Walter. *Greek Religion.* Translated from the German by John Raffan. Cambridge, Mass.: Harvard University Press, 1985. (First published in German by Verlag W. Kohlhammer, Stuttgart in 1977.)

Burnet, John. *Early Greek Philosophy.* 3rd ed. London: Adam and Charles Black, 1920. Internet Release 1998.

Campbell, Joseph (ed.). *The Mysteries: Papers from the Eranos Yearbooks.* Bollingen Series XXX. Princeton, N.J.: Princeton University Press, 1978. (First published by Princeton University Press in 1955.)

Cornford, F. M. *Before and After Socrates.* Cambridge: Cambridge University Press, 1932.

_____. *From Religion to Philosophy: A Study in the Origins of Western Speculation.* Princeton, NJ: Princeton University Press, 1991. (First published in 1912 by E. Arnold, London.)

_____. *Principium Sapientiae: A Study of the Origins of Greek Philosophical Thought.* New York: Harper & Row, 1965. (First published in 1952 by Cambridge University Press.)

Drews, Robert. *The Coming of the Greeks: Indo-European Conquests in the Aegean and the Near East.* Princeton, NJ: Princeton University Press, 1988.

Fairbanks, Arthur (ed. & tr.). *The First Philosophers of Greece.* London: K. Paul, Trench, Trübner, 1898. Internet Release, 2001.

Fieser, James (ed.). *Presocratic Fragments and Testimonials.* Internet Release, 1996.

Graves, Robert. *The Greek Myths* (2 vols.). Rev. ed. Harmondsworth, G.B.: Penguin Books, 1960. (First published in 1955.)

Guthrie, Kenneth Sylvan (ed.). *The Pythagorean Sourcebook and Library: An Anthology of Ancient Writings Which Relate to Pythagoras and Pythagorean Philosophy.* Grand Rapids, Mich.: Phanes Press, 1987.

Guthrie, W.K.C. *Orpheus and Greek Religion: A Study of the Orphic Movement.* Rev. ed. New York: W.W. Norton & Co., 1952. (First published in 1935.)

Harrison, Jane Ellen. *Prolegomena to the Study of Greek Religion.* Princeton, NJ: Princeton University Press, 1991. (First published by Cambridge University Press in 1903).

Hawkes, Jacquetta. *Dawn of the Gods.* London: Book Club Associates, 1972. (First published by Chatto & Windus in 1968.)

Heidegger, Martin. *Early Greek Thinking: The Dawn of Western Philosophy.* San Francisco: HarperSanFrancisco, 1975.

_____. *The Question Concerning Technology and Other Essays.* Translated and with an Introduction by William Lovitt. New York: Harper & Row, 1977.

Heraclitus. *Fragments: A Text and Translation with a Commentary by T.M. Robinson.* Toronto: University of Toronto Press, 1987.

Hesiod. *The Works and Days, Theogony, The Shield of Herakles.* Translated from the Greek by Richmond Lattimore. Ann Arbor: University of Michigan Press, 1991.

Homer. *The Iliad.* Translated from the Greek by Richmond Lattimore. Chicago: The University of Chicago Press, 1951.

_____. *The Odyssey.* Translated from the Greek by E.V. Rieu. Baltimore: Penguin Books, 1946.

Hyland, Drew A. *The Origins of Philosophy: Its Rise in Myth and the Pre-Socratics.* Amherst, NY: Humanity Books, 1988.

James, George G. M. *Stolen Legacy: Greek Philosophy is Stolen Egyptian Philosophy.* Newport News, VA: United Brothers Communications Systems, 1989. (First published in 1954 by the Philosophical Library, New York.)

Kirk, G.S. *The Nature of Greek Myths.* London: Penguin, 1990. (First published in 1974 by Pelican Books.)

_____. Raven, J.E., and Schofield, M. *The Presocratic Philosophers.* 2nd ed. Cambridge, UK: Cambridge University Press, 1995. (First published in 1957 by Cambridge University Press, Cambridge.)

Lévêque, Pierre. *La Naissance de la Grèce: des Rois aux Cités.* Paris: Gallimard, 1990.

Martin, Thomas R. *Ancient Greece: From Prehistoric to Hellenistic Times.* New Haven: Yale University Press, 1996.

Mourelatos, Alexander P. D. (ed.). *The Pre-Socratics: A Collection of Critical Essays.* Rev. ed. Princeton, NJ: Princeton University Press, 1993. (First published in 1974 by Anchor Press.)

Murray, Gilbert. *Five Stages of Greek Religion.* Garden City, NY: Doubleday & Co., 1955.

Mylonas, George E. *Eleusis and the Eleusinian Mysteries.* Princeton, NJ: Princeton University Press, 1961).

Nietzsche, Friedrich. *The Birth of Tragedy and The Case of Wagner.* Translated by Walter Kaufmann. New York: Vintage Books, 1967.

_____. *Philosophy in the Tragic Age of the Greeks.* Chicago: Henry Regnery Company, 1962.

Olivet, Fabre d'. *The Golden Verses of Pythagoras.* Cutchogue, NY: Solar Press, 1995.

Plato. *The Works of Plato.* Translated by B. Jowett. New York: The Dial Press, n.d.

Vernant, Jean-Pierre. *Les origines de la pensée grecque.* 8th ed. Paris: Presses Universitaires de France, 2000. (First published by Presses Universitaires de France in 1962.)

West, M. L. *The Orphic Poems.* Oxford: Oxford University Press, 1998.

Consciousness and Spirituality

Bateson, Gregory. *Mind and Nature: A Necessary Unity.* New York: Bantam Books, 1979.

_____. *Steps to an Ecology of Mind.* New York: Ballantine Books, 1972.

Benoit, Hubert. *Lâcher Prise: Théorie et pratique du détachement selon le zen.* 4th ed. Paris: Le Courrier du Livre, 1985. (First published in 1954.)

_____. *La Doctrine Suprême selon la pensée zen.* 4th ed. Paris: Le Courrier du Livre, 1967.

_____. *De la réalisation intérieure.* Paris: Le Courrier du Livre, 1979.

Bentov, Itzhak. *Stalking the Wild Pendulum: On the Mechanics of Consciousness.* New York: Bantam Books, 1979.

Bergson, Henri. *Les Deux Sources de la Morale et de la Religion.* Paris: Presses Universitaires de France, 1942. (First published in 1932.)

Bucke, Richard Maurice, M.D. *Cosmic Consciousness: A Study in the Evolution of the Human Mind.* New York: E. P. Dutton, 1969.

Dennett, Daniel C. *Consciousness Explained.* Boston: Little, Brown and Company, 1991.

Dürckheim, Karlfried Graf. *Hara: Centre vital de l'homme.* 3rd ed. Translated from the German by Claude Vic. Paris: Le Courrier du Livre, 1974. (Originally published in 1967 as *die Erdmitte des Menschen* by Otto Wilhelm Barth Verlag; Bern, Munich, Vienna.)

_____. *La percée de l'Être ou les étapes de la maturité.* 2d ed. Translated from the German by P. and H. de Roguin in collaboration with R.M. de Pourtales. Paris: Le Courrier du Livre, 1971. (Originally published in 1954 as *Durchbruch zum Wesen, Vierte, unveränderte Auflage* by Verlag Hans Huber, Bern.)

Eccles, John C. *Evolution of the Brain: Creation of the Self.* London: Routledge, 1989.

Feldenkrais, Moshe. *Awareness through Movement.* New York: Harper & Row, 1977.

Globus, Gordon G., Maxwell, Grover, and Savodnik, Irwin (eds.). *Consciousness and the Brain: A Scientific and Philosophical Inquiry.* New York: Plenum Press, 1976.

Goleman, Daniel. *The Varieties of the Meditative Experience.* New York: E. P. Dutton, 1977.

Govinda, Lama Anagarika. *Creative Meditation and Multi-Dimensional Consciousness.* Wheaton, Illinois: The Theosophical Publishing House, 1976.

Grof, Stanislav. *Beyond the Brain: Birth, Death, and Transcendence in Psychotherapy.* Albany: State University of New York, 1985.

Guénon, René. *Introduction générale à l'étude des doctrines hindoues.* 4th ed. Paris: Les Editions Véga, 1952. (First published in 1921.)

_____. *Les États multiples de l'Etre.* 4th ed. Paris: Les Editions Véga, 1973. (First published in 1932.)

_____. *L'homme et son devenir selon le Vêdantâ.* 5th ed. Paris: Editions Traditionnelles, 1974. (First published in 1925.)

Humphrey, Nicholas. *A History of the Mind.* New York: Simon and Schuster, 1992.

Ibn'Arabi, Muhyiddin. *Voyage vers le maître de la puissance: Manuel soufi de méditation.* Monaco: Editions du Rocher, 1994.

James, William. *The Varieties of Religious Experience.* New York: Macmillan Publishing, 1961.

Julian Jaynes. *The Origin of Consciousness in the Breakdown of the Bicameral Mind.* Boston: Houghton Mifflin, 1982.

Koestler, Arthur. *The Ghost in the Machine.* London: Pan Books, 1970.

Laing, R. D. *The Divided Self: An Existential Study in Sanity and Madness.* London: Penguin Books, 1965. (First published in 1960 by Tavistock Publications, UK).

Lee, Philip R., *et al. Symposium on Consciousness.* Harmondsworth, UK: Penguin Books, 1977.

Lockhart, Robin Bruce. *Halfway to Heaven: The Hidden Life of the Carthusians.* London: Darton, Longman and Todd, 1999. (First published in 1985 by Methuen London).

Maslow, Abraham H. *Religion, Values, and Peak-experiences.* New York: Viking Press, 1970.

_____. *Toward a Psychology of Being.* 2d Ed. New York: D. Van Nostrand, 1968.

Maturana, Humberto R. and Varela, Francisco J. *The Tree of Knowledge: The Biological Roots of Human Understanding.* Revised ed. Translated from the Spanish by Robert Paolucci. Boston: Shambhala Publications, 1998.

Naranjo, Claudio, and Ornstein, Robert E. *On the Psychology of Meditation.* New York: The Viking Press, 1971.

Neumann, Erich. *The Origins and History of Consciousness.* Translated from the German by R. F. C. Hull. Bollingen Series XLII. Princeton: Princeton University Press, 1970. (Originally published in 1949 as *Ursprungsgeschichte des Bewusstseins.*)

Ornstein, Robert. *The Evolution of Consciousness: Of Darwin, Freud, and Cranial Fire: The Origins of the Way We Think.* New York: Simon & Schuster, 1991.

_____ (ed.). *The Nature of Human Consciousness: A Book of Readings.* San Francisco: W. H. Freeman, 1973.

_____. *The Psychology of Consciousness.* New York: Penguin Books, 1975.

Ornstein, Robert and Sobel, David. *The Healing Brain: Breakthrough Discoveries About How the Brain Keeps Us Healthy.* New York: Simon and Schuster, 1987.

Pelletier, Kenneth R. *Toward a Science of Consciousness.* New York: Dell Publishing, 1978.

Penfield, Wilder. *The Mystery of the Mind: A Critical Study of Consciousness and the Human Brain.* Princeton, NJ: Princeton University Press, 1975.

Rose, Steven. *The Conscious Brain.* Updated ed. New York: Vintage Books, 1976.

Sherrington, Sir Charles. *Man on his Nature.* 2d ed. (The Gifford Lectures, Edinburgh, 1937-38). Harmondsworth, UK: Penguin Books, 1951.

Sciences et Avenir No. 657, "Les miraculés du coma." Paris: Sciences et Avenir, Feb., 2002.

Siler, Todd. *Breaking the Mind Barrier: The Artscience of Neurocosmology.* New York: Simon & Schuster, 1990.

Tart, Charles T. (ed.). *Altered States of Consciousness.* Garden City, NY: Doubleday, 1969.

_____. *States of Consciousness.* New York: E. P. Dutton, 1975.

_____ (ed.). *Transpersonal Psychologies.* New York: Harper & Row, 1975.

Teyler, Timothy J. (ed.). *Altered States of Awareness: Readings from Scientific American.* San Francisco: W. H. Freeman, 1972.

Varela, Francisco J., Thompson, Evan, and Rosch Eleanor. *The Embodied Mind: Cognitive Science and Human Experience.* Cambridge, Mass.: The MIT Press, 1993.

Walker, Kenneth. *Diagnosis of Man.* Revised edition. Harmondsworth, U.K.: Penguin Books, 1962. (First published in 1942: Jonathan Cape).

Wilber, Ken. *The Atman Project: A Transpersonal View of Human Development.* Wheaton, Ill.: The Theosophical Publishing House, 1980.

_____. *The Spectrum of Consciousness.* Wheaton, Ill.: The Theosophical Publishing House, 1977.

_____. *Up From Eden: A Transpersonal View of Human Evolution.* Boulder: Shambhala, 1983.

Ancient Egypt

Adams, W. Marshall. *Book of the Master of the Hidden Places.* London: The Search Publishing Company, 1933. Kessinger Legacy Reprint.

Aldred, Cyril. *Egyptian Art in the Days of the Pharaohs 3100-320 BC.* London: Thames and Hudson, 1980. First published in Leipzeg, 1919.

Allen, James P. *Middle Egyptian: An Introduction to the Language and Culture of Hieroglyphs.* 2nd Ed., Revised. Cambridge, UK: Cambridge University Press, 2010. First edition published 2000.

Assmann, Jan. *Images et rites de la mort dans l'Égypte ancienne.* Paris: Cybele, 2000.

_____. *The Search for God in Ancient Egypt.* Ithaca: Cornell University Press, 2001. Translated from the German by David Lorton.

_____. *Death and Salvation in Ancient Egypt.* Ithaca: Cornell University Press, 2005. Translated from the German by David Lorton.

Aufrère, Sydney, *et al. L'Égypte Restituée.* 3 vols. Paris: Editions Errance, 1991-1997.

Baines, John, and Málek, Jaromír. *Atlas of Ancient Egypt.* New York: Facts on File, 1980.

Barguet, Paul. *Aspects de la pensée religieuse de l'Égypte ancienne.* Le Pin du Luquet, Fuveau, France: La Maison de Vie, 2001.

Bauval, Robert, and Hancock, Graham. *Keeper of Genesis: A Quest for the Hidden Legacy of Mankind.* London: William Heinemann, 1996.

_____. *The Egypt Code.* London: Century, 2006.

Behaeghel, Julien. *Osiris: le dieu ressuscité.* Paris: Berg International, 1995.

Breasted, James Henry. *Development of Religion and Thought in Ancient Egypt.* New York: Harper & Row, 1959. First published in 1912 by Charles Scribner's Sons.

Brunton, Paul. *A Search in Secret Egypt.* York Beach, Maine: Samuel Weiser, 1984. (First American edition published in 1936: New York, E. P. Dutton & Co.)

Budge, E. A. Wallis. *The Egyptian Book of the Dead: The Papyrus of Ani in the British Museum.* The Egyptian text with interlinear transliteration and translation, a running translation, introduction, etc. New York: Dover, 1967. Originally published by the Trustees of the British Museum, 1895.

_____. *Egyptian Language: Easy Lessons in Egyptian Hieroglyphics.* New York: Dover, 1983. Originally published by Kegan Paul, Trench, Trübner & Co., London, 1910.

_____. *Egyptian Religion: Egyptian Ideas of the Future Life.* London and New York: Routledge and Kegan Paul (Arkana), 1987. Originally published in 1899.

_____. *From Fetish to God in Ancient Egypt.* Reprint. New York: Dover Publications, 1988. Originally published by Oxford University Press, London, 1934.

_____. *Osiris and the Egyptian Resurrection.* 2 vols. Reprint. New York: Dover Publications, 1973. Originally published by The Medici Society, 1911.

Camacho, Jorge. *Le Mythe d'Isis et d'Osiris et sa relation avec le symbolisme hermétique.* Paris: La Table d'Emeraude, 1995.

Cauville, Sylvie. *Le Temple de Dendera : Guide archéologique.* 2nd ed. Cairo: Institut français d'archéologie orientale, 1995.

_____. *Dendera: Les chapelles osiriennes.* 3 vols. Cairo: Institut Français d'Archéologie Orientale, 1997.

_____. *Le Zodiaque d'Osiris.* Leuven, Belgium: Peeters, 1997.

_____. *L'Offrande aux dieux dans le temple égyptien.* Leuven: Peeters, 2011.

Champollion, Jean-François. *Lettre à M. Dacier relative à l'alphabet des hiéroglyphes phonétiques.* Fontfroide: Bibliothèque Artistique & Littéraire, 1989. Originally written in 1822.

Clark, R. T. Rundle. *Myth and Symbol in Ancient Egypt.* London: Thames and Hudson, 1978. First published in 1959.

Clayton, Peter A. *Chronicle of the Pharaohs: The Reign-by-Reign Record of the Rulers and Dynasties of Ancient Egypt.* London: Thames and Hudson, 1994.

Davies, W. V. *Egyptian Hieroglyphs.* London: British Museum Press, 1987.

Desroches-Noblecourt, Christiane. *Amours et fureurs de La Lointaine: Clés pour la compréhension de symboles égyptiens.* Paris: Stock-Pernoud, 1995.

_____, avec Elouard, Daniel. *Symboles de l'Égypte.* Paris: Desclée de Brouwer, 2004.

Dewachter, Michel. *Champollion: Un scribe pour l'Égypte.* Paris: Gallimard, 1990.

Dondelinger, Edmund. *Papyrus d'Ani: Le livre sacré de l'ancienne égypte.* Translated from the German by Marcelle Rognon. Paris: Philippe Lebaud, 1987.

Les Dossiers d'Archéologie 146-147, "Saqqara". (Dijon) March-April 1990.

_____ 149-150, "Thebes". (Dijon) May-June 1990.

Dunand, Françoise and Lichtenberg, Roger. *Les Momies: Un voyage dans l'éternité.* Paris: Gallimard, 1991.

Enel, *Le Message du Sphinx.* Paris: Arka, 1998. (First published in 1936.)

_____. *Les Origines de la Genèse et l'enseignement des temples de l'ancienne Egypte.* Vol I. Le Caire: Imprimerie de l'Institut Français d'archéologie orientale, 1935.

_____. *Le Mystère de la Vie et de la Mort : d'après l'enseignement des temples de l'ancienne Égypte.* Paris : Arka Éditions, 2002.

Erigène, Valentin. *Mystère & Pouvoir des Sons au temps des Pharaons: A la recherche d'une science perdue.* Paris: Guy Trédaniel, 1987.

Faulkner, R. O., trans. *The Ancient Egyptian Pyramid Texts.* London: Oxford University Press, 1969. Reprint. Warminster: Aris & Phillips, n.d.

_____, trans. *The Ancient Egyptian Coffin Texts.* 3 vols. Warminster, England: Aris & Phillips, 1973-1978.

_____, trans. *The Ancient Egyptian Book of the Dead.* Rev. ed. New York: Macmillan, 1985.

Forman, Werner and Quirke, Stephen. *Hieroglyphs and the Afterlife in Ancient Egypt.* Norman: University of Oklahoma Press, 1996.

Fowden, Garth. *The Egyptian Hermes: A Historical Approach to the Late Pagan Mind.* Princeton, NJ: Princeton University Press, 1993. First printed by Cambridge University Press in 1986.

Frankfort, H.A. and Frankfort, Henri. *The Intellectual Adventure of Ancient Man: An Essay on Speculative Thought in the Ancient Near East.* Chicago: The University of Chicago Press, 1977. Originally published in 1946 by The University of Chicago Press.

Frankfort, Henri. *Kingship and the Gods: A Study of Ancient Near Eastern Religion as the Integration of Society and Nature.* Phoenix edition. Chicago: University of Chicago Press, 1948, 1978.

_____. *Ancient Egyptian Religion: An Interpretation.* New York: Harper & Row, 1961. Originally published by Columbia University Press, New York, 1948.

Gadalla, Moustafa. *Egyptian Cosmology: The Absolute Harmony.* Erie, PA: Bastet Publishing, 1997.

Gardiner, Sir Alan. *Egyptian Grammar: Being an Introduction to the Study of Hieroglyphs.* 3rd ed. rev. Oxford: Griffith Institute, 1957. First published 1927.

Garnot, Jean Sainte-Fare. *La vie religieuse dans l'ancienne Égypte.* Paris: Presses Universitaires de France, 1948.

Grof, Stanislav. *Books of the Dead: Manuals for Living and Dying.* London: Thames and Hudson, 1994.

Guénon, René. "L'Œil qui voit tout." Chap. LXXII in *Symboles de la Science sacrée.* Paris: Gallimard, 1962.

Grimal, Nicolas. *A History of Ancient Egypt.* Oxford, UK: Blackwell, 1992. Translated from the French by Ian Shaw. First published in French by Fayard 1988.

Gros de Beler, Aude. *La mythologie égyptienne.* Paris: Le Scribe, 2005.

Guilhou, Nadine. "Myth of the Heavenly Cow". *UCLA Encyclopedia of Egyptology,* 12 Aug. 2010.

Guilmot, Max. *Les initiés et les rites initiatiques en Egypte ancienne*. Paris: Éditions Robert Laffont, 1977.

_____. *Message Spirituel de l'égypte ancienne*. Paris: Éditions du Rocher, 1988.

Hare, Tom. *ReMembering Osiris: Number, Gender, and the Word in Ancient Egyptian Representational Systems*. Stanford: Stanford University Press, 1999.

Hart, George. *A Dictionary of Egyptian Gods and Goddesses*. London and New York: Routledge and Kegan Paul, 1986.

_____. *Egyptian Myths*. London: British Museum Publications, 1990.

Hawass, Zahi. *Les tombes oubliées de Thèbes*. Paris: Thames & Hudson, 2010.

Héry, François-Xavier and Enel, Thierry. *La Bible de pierre: L'alphabet sacré de la grande pyramide*. Paris: Robert Laffont, 1990.

_____. *Le secret d'Abou Simbel: Le chef-d'œuvre de Ramses II décrypté*. Paris: Albin Michel, 1996.

Hobson, Christine. *Exploring the World of the Pharaohs: A Complete Guide to Ancient Egypt*. London: Thames and Hudson, 1987.

Hooke, S. H. *Middle Eastern Mythology*. Harmondsworth, England: Penguin Books, 1963.

Hornung, Erik. *The Ancient Egyptian Books of the Afterlife*. Ithaca: Cornell University Press, 1999. Translated from the German by David Lorton.

_____. *Conceptions of God in Ancient Egypt: The One and the Many*. London: Routledge & Kegan Paul, 1983. Translated from the German by John Baines. Originally published as Der Eine und die Vielen (Darmstadt: Wissenschaftliche Buchgesellschaft, 1971).

_____. *L'Égypte Ésotérique: Le savoir occulte des Égyptiens et son influence en Occident*. Paris: Éditions du Rocher, 2001. Translated from the German by Nathalie Baum. First published in German in 1999.

_____. *L'esprit du temps des pharaons*. Paris: Philippe Lebaud, 1996. Translated from the German by Michèle Hulin. First published in German in 1989.

Huxley, Francis. *L'Oeil: Mythes et métamorphoses*. Paris: Éditions du Seuil, 1992. Translated from the English by Pierre Janin.

Jacq, Christian. *La sagesse égyptienne*. Paris: Éditions du Rocher (Pocket), 1981.

_____. *La tradition primordiale de l'Egypte ancienne selon les Textes des Pyramides*. Paris: Bernard Grasset, 1998.

_____. *Le Monde magique de l'Egypte ancienne.* Monaco: Editions du Rocher, 1983.

_____. *Le mystère des hiéroglyphes : la clé de l'Égypte ancienne.* Lausanne : Éditions Favre, 2010.

Jean, Georges. *L'Écriture: Mémoire des hommes.* Paris: Gallimard, 1987.

Kamrin, Janice. *The Cosmos of Khnumhotep II at Beni Hasan.* London: Routledge, 2011. First published by Kegan Paul in 1999.

Katan, Norma Jean and Mintz, Barbara. *Hieroglyphs: The Writing of Ancient Egypt.* London: British Museum Press, 1985.

Kemp, Barry J. *Ancient Egypt: Anatomy of a Civilization.* 2nd Edition. London: Routledge, 2006. First edition published by Routledge in 1989.

Kingsley, Peter. *In the Dark Places of Wisdom.* Point Reyes, Calif.: The Golden Sufi Center, 1999.

Lambelet, Edouard. *Gods and Goddesses in Ancient Egypt.* 3rd ed. Cairo: Lehnert & Landrock, n.d.

Lamy, Lucie. *Egyptian Mysteries: New Light on Ancient Spiritual Knowledge.* Translated from the French by Deborah Lawlor. New York: Crossroad, 1981.

Lehner, Mark. *The Complete Pyramids.* London: Thames & Hudson, 1997.

Lichtheim, Miriam, ed. and trans. *Ancient Egyptian Literature: A Book of Readings.* Vols. 1-III. Berkeley and Los Angeles: University of California Press, 1973-1980.

Mayassis, S. *Mystères et Initiations de l'Égypte ancienne: Compléments à la religion égyptienne.* Milano: Archè, 1988.

_____. *Le livre des morts de l'Égypte ancienne est un livre d'initiation.* Milano : Archè, 2002.

Martin, Anaïs, *Le Corps en Égypte ancienne : Enquête lexicale et anthropologique.* Montpellier: Université Paul Valéry, Montpellier III, 2013. (See https://tel.archives-ouvertes.fr/tel-01089023)

Ministères de la Culture aux Musées Royaux d'Art et d'Histoire, Bruxelles. *Le Règne du Soleil Akhnaton et Nefertiti.* Catalog of the Exposition 17 January – 16 March 1975.

Moret, Alexandre. *Mystères Égyptiens* (nouvelle édition revue et corrigée). Modern reproduction of the book published in 1923 by Armand Colin, Paris. First edition published in 1913.

Naydler, Jeremy. *The Future of the Ancient World.* Oxford, UK: Abzu Press, 1994.

_____. *Temple of the Cosmos: The Ancient Egyptian Experience of the Sacred.* Rochester, Vermont: Inner Traditions, 1996.

_____. *Shamanic Wisdom in the Pyramid Texts: The Mystical Tradition of Ancient Egypt*. Rochester, Vermont: Inner Traditions, 2005.

O'Connor, David. *Abydos: Egypt's First Pharaohs and the Cult of Osiris*. London: Thames and Hudson, 2009.

Piankoff, Alexandre. *The Tomb of Ramesses VI*. Egyptian Religious Texts and Representations, Bollingen Series XL, Vol. 1. Edited by N. Rambova. Princeton, NJ: Princeton University Press, 1954.

_____. *The Shrines of Tut-Ankh-Amon*. Egyptian Religious Texts and Representations, Bollingen Series XL, Vol. 2. Edited by N. Rambova. Princeton, NJ: Princeton University Press, 1977. First published by Princeton University Press in 1955.

_____. *The Wandering of the Soul*. Egyptian Religious Texts and Representations, Bollingen Series XL, Vol. 6. Completed by Helen Jacquet-Gordon. Princeton, NJ: Princeton University Press, 1972.

Pizzarotti, Sabine. "Rituels et fêtes dans le temple : Les 'Mystères d'Osiris' du mois de Khoïak." *Égypte Afrique & Orient*. No. 67, Sep.-Nov. 2012, pp. 31-40. Avignon : Centre d'égyptologie.

Plutarch. *Moralia*. (Volume V, which includes "Isis and Osiris"). Translated with preface, introductions and notes by Frank Cole Babbitt. (Loeb Classical Library, No. 306.) Cambridge, Mass.: Harvard University Press, 1936.

Portal, F. *Les symboles des égyptiens*. Paris: Éditions de la Maisnie, 1979.

Question de No. 73, "Le Lieu du Temple: Géographie sacrée et initiation". Paris: Albin Michel, 1988.

Pritchard, James B. (ed.). *Ancient Near Eastern Texts Relating to the Old Testament*. 3d ed. with supplement. Princeton: Princeton University Press, 1969.

Quirke, Stephen. *The Cult of Ra: Sun-Worship in Ancient Egypt*. New York: Thames & Hudson, 2001.

_____. *Exploring Religion in Ancient Egypt*. Chichester UK: John Wiley & Sons, 2015.

Reed, Bika. *Rebel in the Soul: An Ancient Egyptian Dialogue between a Man and his Destiny*. Rochester VT: Inner Traditions International, 1997. Translated from the ancient Egyptian hieroglyphic text with commentary. First published by Thorsons in 1978.

_____. *The Field of Transformations: A Quest for the Immortal Essence of Human Awareness*. Rochester, Vermont: Inner Traditions International, 1987.

Reeves, Nicholas and Wilkinson, Richard H. *The Complete Valley of the Kings: Tombs and Treasures of Egypt's Greatest Pharaohs*. London: Thames and Hudson, 1996.

Réunion des Musées Nationaux (ed.). *L'art égyptien au temps des pyramides.* Paris: 1999. (Catalog of the exposition in Paris, New York, Toronto: 1999-2000.)

_____. *Naissance de l'écriture : cunéiformes et hiéroglyphes.* (Catalogue of the exhibition at Le Grand Palais, Paris, May 7 to August 9, 1982). Paris: Editions de la Réunion des musées nationaux, 1982.

Robinson, Andrew. *The Story of Writing.* London: Thames and Hudson, 1995.

Rosicrucian Digest. Vol. 85, No. 1, 2007. Various articles on ancient Egypt.

Rossini, Stéphane and Schumann-Antelme, Ruth. *Nétèr: Dieux d'Égypte.* Lavaur, France: Trismegiste, 1992.

_____. *Becoming Osiris: The Ancient Egyptian Death Experience.* Rochester, VT: Inner Traditions, 1998. Translated from the French by Jon Graham. First published in French by Editions Trismegiste in 1995.

Sauneron, Serge. *The Priests of Ancient Egypt.* Ithaca & London: Cornell University Press, 2000. Translated from the French by David Lorton. First published in French 1957.

_____. *Osiris: Rites d'immortalité de l'Égypte pharaonique.* Lavaur, France: Trismegiste, 1995.

Schäfer, Heinrich. *Principles of Egyptian Art.* Translated from the German by John Baines. Oxford: Griffith Institute, 2002. First published in Leipzeg 1919.

Schwaller de Lubicz, Isha. *"AOR", R.A. Schwaller de Lubicz: sa vie, son œuvre.* Paris: La Colombe, Editions du Vieux Colombier, 1963.

_____. *Her-Bak, "Chick-pea": The Living Face of Ancient Egypt.* Translated from the French by Edgar Sprague. Baltimore: Penguin Books, 1972. Originally published as *Her-Bak, "Pois-chiche": Visage vivant de l'ancienne égypte* by Flammarion, Paris, 1955.

_____. *Her-Bak: Egyptian Initiate.* Translated from the French by Ronald Fraser. New York: Inner Traditions International, 1978. Originally published as *Her-Bak "disciple" de la sagesse égyptienne* by Flammarion, Paris, 1956.

_____. *Journey into the Light: The Three Principles of Man's Awakening.* Translated from the French by Susan D. Resnick. Rochester, VT: Inner Traditions International, 1984. Originally published as *La lumière du chemin,* 1960.

_____. *The Opening of the Way: A Practical Guide to the Wisdom Teachings of Ancient Egypt.* Rochester, Vermont: Inner Traditions International, 1981. Translated from the French. Originally published as *L'ouverture du chemin* by Aryana, Paris, 1979.

Schwaller de Lubicz, R. A. *The Temple in Man: The Secrets of Ancient Egypt.* Brookline, Mass.: Autumn Press, 1977. Translated from the French by Robert and Deborah Lawlor. Originally published as *Le Temple de l'homme* (Cairo: Schindler, 1949).

_____. *The Temple of Man: Apet of the South at Luxor.* 2 Vols. Rochester VT: Inner Traditions International, 1998. Translated from the French by Robert and Deborah Lawlor. First published in French in 1957.

_____. *Le roi de la théocratie pharaonique.* Paris: Flammarion, 1961.

_____. *Le miracle égyptien.* Paris: Flammarion, 1963.

_____. *Le Temple de l'Homme: Apet du sud à Louqsor.* 3 vols. Paris: Dervy Livres, 1977-1985.

_____. *Symbol and the Symbolic: Egypt, Science and the Evolution of Consciousness.* Brookline, MA: Autumn Press, 1978. Translated from the French by Robert and Deborah Lawlor. First published in French in 1949.

_____. *Propos sur ésotérisme et symbole.* Paris: Dervy-Livres, 1977.

_____. *Esoterism and Symbol.* Rochester VT: Inner Traditions International, 1985. Translated from the French by André and Goldian VandenBroeck. First published in French in 1960 by La Colombe, Editions du Vieux Colombier.

_____. *Nature Word.* West Stockbridge, Mass.: The Lindisfarne Press, 1982. Translated from the French by Deborah Lawlor.

_____. *A Study of Numbers: A Guide to the Constant Creation of the Universe.* Rochester, VT: Inner Traditions International, 1986. Translated from the French by Robert Lawlor. First published in French in 1950 by Librairie de l'Art Indépendant.

_____. *La Doctrine : Trois conférences faites à Suhalia, Noël 1926.* Ile-Rousse, Corse : Editions Axis Mundi, 1988. Facsimilé de l'édition privée de St. Moritz : Officina Montalia, 1926.

Schwarz, Fernand. *Égypte: Les mystères du sacré.* Paris: Éditions du Félin, 1986.

_____. *Initiation aux Livres des morts égyptiens.* Paris: Albin Michel, 1988.

Scranton, Laird. *The Science of the Dogon: Decoding the African Mystery Tradition.* Rochester, VT: Inner Traditions, 2006. Originally published in 2002 by Xlibris as Hidden Meanings: A Study of the Founding Symbols of Civilization.

_____. *Sacred Symbols of the Dogon: The Key to Advanced Science in the Ancient Egyptian Hieroglyphs.* Rochester, VT: Inner Traditions, 2007.

_____. *The Cosmological Origins of Myth and Symbol.* Rochester, VT: Inner Traditions, 2010.

Seleem, Ramses. *Egyptian Book of the Dead: A New Translation with Commentary*. New York: Sterling Publishing Company, 2001.

Shafer, Byron E., ed. *Religion in Ancient Egypt: Gods, Myths, and Personal Practice*. London: Routledge, 1991.

Smith, Mark. *Four Lectures "Osiris and the Deceased in Ancient Egypt: Perspectives from Four Millennia"*. May 17-27, 2013 at EPHE, Paris, France.

Spence, Lewis. *The Mysteries of Egypt: Secret Rites and Traditions.* Mineola, NY: Dover Publications, 2005. First published in 1929 by Rider & Co., London.

Taylor, John H. (ed.). *Journey through the Afterlife: Ancient Egyptian Book of the Dead.* Cambridge, MA: Harvard University Press, 2010.

Tompkins, Peter. *Secrets of the Great Pyramid.* With an appendix by Livio Catullo Stecchini. New York: Harper & Row, 1971.

_____. *The Magic of Obelisks.* New York: Harper & Row, 1981

Vercoutter, Jean. *À la recherche de l'Égypte oubliée.* Paris: Gallimard, 1986.

Wente, Edward F. "Mysticism in Pharaonic Egypt?". *Journal of Near Eastern Studies,* Vol. 41 No. 3. Chicago: University of Chicago, 1982.

West, John Anthony. *Serpent in the Sky: The High Wisdom of Ancient Egypt*. New York: Harper & Row, 1979.

Wilkinson, Richard H. *Reading Egyptian Art: A Hieroglyphic Guide to Ancient Egyptian Painting and Sculpture*. London: Thames and Hudson, 1992.

_____. *Symbol and Magic in Egyptian Art.* London: Thames and Hudson, 1994.

_____. *The Complete Temples of Ancient Egypt.* London: Thames & Hudson, 2000.

_____. The Complete Gods and Goddesses of Ancient Egypt. London: Thames and Hudson, 2003.

Illustration Credits

Figure 1 This image is in the public domain.

Figure 2 Andrew Z. Colvin
(https://commons.wikimedia.org/wiki/File:Location_of_Earth_(1x9-English_Annot-small).png), https://creativecommons.org/licenses/by-sa/4.0/legalcode

Figure 3 Uploaded from Internet. Source given upon request.

Figure 4 This image is in the public domain.

Figure 5 Thomas T. from somewhere on Earth
(https://commons.wikimedia.org/wiki/File:Chauvet´s_cave_horses.jpg),
„Chauvet´s cave horses", https://creativecommons.org/licenses/by-sa/2.0/legalcode

Figure 6 This image is in the public domain.

Figure 7 Marek Kocjan
(https://commons.wikimedia.org/wiki/File:Great_Sphinx_of_Giza_2.jpg),
„Great Sphinx of Giza 2", https://creativecommons.org/licenses/by-sa/3.0/legalcode

Figure 8 L-BBE
(https://commons.wikimedia.org/wiki/File:Great_Pyramid_of_Giza_and_Egyptian_sky.jpg), „Great Pyramid of Giza and Egyptian sky",
https://creativecommons.org/licenses/by/3.0/legalcode

Figure 9 This image is in the public domain.

Figure 10 This image is in the public domain.

Figure 11 This image is in the public domain.

Figure 12 This image was created by the author of this document.

Figure 13 N.Manytchkine
(https://commons.wikimedia.org/wiki/File:Sri_Yantra_256bw.gif), „Sri Yantra 256bw", https://creativecommons.org/licenses/by-sa/3.0/legalcode

Figure 14 This image is in the public domain.

Figure 15A Atlant
(https://commons.wikimedia.org/wiki/File:Chartres_1.jpg), „Chartres 1",
https://creativecommons.org/licenses/by/2.5/legalcode

Figure 57 Cornell University Library
(https://commons.wikimedia.org/wiki/File:Temple_Complex_at_Karnak.jp
g), „Temple Complex at Karnak",
https://creativecommons.org/licenses/by/2.0/legalcode

Figure 58 This image is in the public domain.

Figure 59 This image is in the public domain.

Figure 60 Vincent Brown
(https://commons.wikimedia.org/wiki/File:Burial_chamber_in_Unas'_pyra
mid.jpg), „Burial chamber in Unas' pyramid",
https://creativecommons.org/licenses/by/2.0/legalcode

Figure 61 Mr rnddude
(https://commons.wikimedia.org/wiki/File:Unas'_Substructure.png),
Cropped, https://creativecommons.org/licenses/by-sa/4.0/legalcode

Figure 62 This image is in the public domain.

Figure 63 This image is in the public domain.

Figure 64 This image is in the public domain.

Figure 65 This image is in the public domain.

Figure 66 This image is in the public domain.

Figure 67 Marc Ryckaert (MJJR)
(https://commons.wikimedia.org/wiki/File:Philae_Temple_R03.jpg),
„Philae Temple R03",
https://creativecommons.org/licenses/by/3.0/legalcode

Figure 68 Glenn Ashton
(https://commons.wikimedia.org/wiki/File:Luxor_-
_obelisk_and_pylon.jpg), „Luxor - obelisk and pylon",
https://creativecommons.org/licenses/by-sa/3.0/legalcode

Figure 69 This image is in the public domain.

Figure 70 Francisco Anzola
(https://commons.wikimedia.org/wiki/File:Luxor_Temple_(2347092673).jp
g), „Luxor Temple (2347092673).

Index